MICHIGAN

A History of Explorers, Entrepreneurs, and Everyday People

ROGER L. ROSENTRETER

University of Michigan Press
Ann Arbor

*To all historians (both professional and amateur) who have
shared and preserved Michigan's remarkable past by telling stories.*

Copyright © by the University of Michigan 2014
All rights reserved
Published in the United States of America
The University of Michigan Press
Manufactured in the United States of America

♾ Printed on acid-free paper

978-0-472-07190-6 (cloth)
978-0-472-05190-8 (paper)
978-0-472-02887-0 (ebook)

2017   2016   2015   4   3   2

Library of Congress
Cataloging in Publication Program
101 Independence Avenue, S.E.
Washington, DC 20540-4283

The CIP Program is pleased to announce a new E-books Program. All current CIP
participants that simultaneously publish e-books and print books are eligible to
apply. Applications forms will be found on the publisher's main menu. Please go to
http://www.loc.gov/publish/cip/ebooks/index.html for more information.

Library of Congress Cataloging-in-Publication Data

Rosentreter, Roger L.
    Michigan : a history of explorers, entrepreneurs, and everyday people / Roger L.
Rosentreter.
        pages cm
    Includes bibliographical references and index.
    ISBN 978-0-472-07190-6 (cloth : alk. paper) — ISBN 978-0-472-05190-8 (pbk. : alk.
paper) — ISBN 978-0-472-02887-0 (e-book)
    1. Michigan–History. I. Title.
    F566.R67 2013
    977.4–dc23
                                2013020456

Preface

This manuscript is the product of my "lifetime" with Michigan history, which began unexpectedly, even somewhat accidentally. I had just finished the examination portion of my doctoral degree at Michigan State University when my good undergraduate friend Gail DeHudy (nee Kageff) told me about a state government job posting. At the time, I was starting my eighth year of continuous college. After earning a B.A. at Western Michigan University, I headed to MSU and pursued a master's degree intent on teaching American history at a community college. That plan was altered when earning a doctoral degree proved more attractive—even if my career plans became more uncertain as a result. By the fall of 1978, I had survived the doctoral exams, but the dissertation still lay before me—maybe two more years of schooling. My supportive parents must have wondered, "When will he be done?" (Less subtle family and friends probably queried, "What's a doctor of history?")

Without telling Professor Frederick D. Williams, my mentor and someone who expected me to finish my degree and enter academia, I pursued the state government job. During the interview I quickly discovered the position wasn't for me. However, in my naiveté, I did ask, "Do you have any other positions open?" Amazingly, they did not show me the door but mentioned an editorial vacancy with *Michigan History Magazine*. I had been an editor at the *WMU Herald* and the editor of my high school yearbook, so I expressed interest. (Introduced in 1917, *Michigan History Magazine* faced something of an uncertain future in the late 1970s as it transitioned from a traditional academic quarterly to a bi-monthly "popular" magazine.) When they offered the editorial job, I took it. Professor Williams probably felt a bit betrayed, although years later he admitted I had made the right choice. Nine years into the job, and after going back and finishing my doctoral degree, I found myself acting editor. Almost two years later, when my bosses realized I was either doing a good job or wasn't going to leave, the position became permanent. When my time at *Michigan History* ended in 2009, I marveled at thirty years in producing history publications—such an unforeseen and rewarding career.

Being an editor at *Michigan History* taught me much about my native state, while refining my writing and editing skills. I'm a firm believer that the strength of presenting history is telling stories. This manuscript focuses on those stories that are key to appreciating Michigan's rich past. It is not my intent to replace *Michigan: A History of the Wolverine State*, the durable Michigan "bible," first published by Willis Dunbar in 1965 and later revised by George May, or even Cleaver Bald's *Michigan in Four Centuries*, first published in 1954, albeit long out-of-print. Keeping in mind the maxim of a former well-published professor ("the challenge to writing history is deciding what to leave out"), my intent has been to be selective and avoid creating a publication that is too unwieldy.

As a cheerleader for Michigan's past, I particularly enjoy sharing stories that go beyond the state's boundaries, possessing national, even international, significance. Some of these stories are well known; others deserve revitalizing. Few American entrepreneurs enjoy more recognition than Henry Ford (his five-dollar workday proved revolutionary and the Model T carried "civilization into the wild places of the world"). But what about William Stout, whose inventiveness and orthodox style introduced Americans to commercial flying, or C. W. Post, who failed to find a cure at the world-famous Battle Creek San, but started a breakfast cereal revolution that W. K. Kellogg pursued with even greater success?

Students of Michigan history will recognize Senator Arthur Vandenberg, who led his reluctant political party to support programs that rebuilt war-torn Europe and pursued the elusive goal of worldwide peace, or G. Mennen Williams and William Milliken, distinctive leaders who overcame obstructionists—one to build a Michigan icon, the other to make Michigan an environmental leader. Less well-known is Frank Murphy, who espoused a sympathetic interpretation of government's role in protecting the average citizen—even one on the picket line, or Hazen Pingree, who laid the groundwork for Progressives by demanding a fairer playing field for those less fortunate.

Even casual students of Michigan history are familiar with Stevens T. Mason's determined efforts to make Michigan a state. But what about Milo Radulovich, an innocent family man who stood up to the ruthlessness of McCarthyism—an action that started the downfall of the architect of a reckless policy that ruined lives and careers? Courageous General George A. Custer enjoys a prominent place in Civil War lore, but what of the contributions of Alpheus S. Williams, Israel Richardson, Annie Etheridge and, for that matter, Libbie Custer?

Equally intriguing are the contributions of the *everyday people*: the voyageurs who paddled the canoes for La Salle and Cadillac; the pioneers who packed all their belongings into a wagon and settled the unbroken Michigan wilderness; the immigrants who spent long days working the dangerous Upper Peninsula mines; the men who knew nothing about soldiering but put on a blue coat, picked up a rifle, and confronted diseases and rebel bullets, or their wives who stayed home (in most cases), raised the families, and kept the homesteads running; the seemingly powerless workers who stood toe-to-toe with the world's most powerful corporation in 1937 and demanded changes; the young, unemployed boys of the 1930s who planted millions of trees on a badly scarred landscape; or the laborers who achieved President Roosevelt's goal of making America the Arsenal of Democracy. These anonymous Michiganians built the state, saved the Union, ended slavery, contributed to America's Industrial Revolution, secured much-deserved workers' rights; made "going north" more enjoyable for generations to come; and won World War II.

And this is only a partial list.

Another inventory includes those people who helped me learn and appreciate Michigan's past. They include former magazine editor Sandra S. Clark, who gave me ample opportunity to groom my editorial and writing skills, as well as assistant editors Sharon McHenry, who coordinated our four-year-long, World War II reader recollection series, and Paul Mehney, who helped me refine my personal passion with the Civil War. A treasured "unofficial" staffer is Ann Weller, an independent copy editor who has been reading Michigan manuscripts for years. As usual, I appreciate her reading this one.

The magazine's contributing editors—State Archaeologist Dr. John R. Halsey (now retired), former Walter P. Reuther Library director Mike Smith, Michigan Marker Program director Laura Rose Ashlee, and Tom Friggens ("our man in the U.P.")—willingly shared an opinion, reviewed a story, or authored one. At the top of this list stands Dr. Le Roy Barnett, Archives of Michigan reference archivist (retired). Lee and I met shortly after I started with *Michigan History*. He introduced me to my dissertation topic, and his ability to find another untold Michigan story is uncanny. Naturally, I asked Lee to read this manuscript, and I value his input.

A word of appreciation to magazine "regulars" (Sheryl James, Bill McGraw, Richard E. Shaul, and Chuck E. Harmon to name a few) who authored stories that heightened our understanding, often with topics that had been ignored or needed telling. Finally, thanks to the thousands of readers who inspired us to strive for variety and excellence.

A special thanks to MSU Department of History chairmen (most recently Walter Hawthorne) for permitting me to teach the Michigan history course during the past 20 years. Since leaving the magazine, I have enjoyed the opportunity to interact with other department historians. At the top of this list is recently retired Professor Sam Thomas, who read the entire manuscript and offered valued perspective.

I am indebted to the efforts of The University of Michigan Press: Executive Editor Kelly Sippell, whose editorial and managerial skills made this undertaking a reality; Associate Acquiring Editor Scott Ham, who patiently accepted my confident (and rarely met) promise to send manuscript pages "tomorrow"; and former Commissioning Editor Dedria Cruden, who started the ball rolling. I also want to acknowledge Mary Cary Crawford for her work on the index.

Finally, thanks to Louis, my four-legged assistant who eagerly offered to "take me" for a walk whenever I needed a writing break; my mother, who reminds me that my writing skills have no hereditary basis, but overlooks the role she and my father played in allowing me to pursue my passion for history; and Lisa, whose constant encouragement is only exceeded by her immeasurable thoughtfulness.

Roger L. Rosentreter
East Lansing
November, 2013

Contents

Introduction

Few U.S. states can boast a past as rich and varied as Michigan. Evidence of the earliest settlers (Native Americans, also called Indians) living in what we call Michigan occurred about 11,000 years ago; the last glacier retreated about 2,500 years ago. During the early 17th century, French explorers, fur traders, and missionaries arrived in the Great Lakes, and for the next 150 years, they founded Michigan's earliest settlements, trapped fur-bearing animals, and attempted to Christianize the Indians.

The French called the area *Michigan*, an Indian word meaning "great water." *Michi* means "great." The earliest written use of *Michigan* had many variations, such as *Machihiganing* and *Mitchiganons*, among others. By the mid-1700s, Michigan (spelled as we know it today) identified the lake between present-day Michigan and Wisconsin. In 1805, when the federal government created a political entity that encompassed the Lower Peninsula, it seemed logical to name it after Lake Michigan.

Following their victory in the French and Indian War, the British forced the French government to relinquish control of Michigan, and then adopted policies affecting the frontier (including Michigan) that angered Atlantic coast colonists and precipitated the American Revolution. At the end of the Revolution, the British agreed to leave Detroit and Mackinac, but it took them thirteen years. U.S. military prowess in August 1794, coupled with British concern over France and Napoleon I, led them to evacuate Michigan. American troops arrived in Detroit two years later.

The Great Lakes and the shared border with Canada greatly influenced Michigan's development. The lakes led explorers and settlers to Michigan and contributed to commercial and recreational usage that continues to this day. At the same time, the proximity to Canada affected Michigan's past, especially as escaped southern slaves "traveled" along the Underground Railroad to freedom in Canada (1840s and 1850s), while years later, Canadian booze flowed into this country during America's failed experiment with Prohibition (1920s).

The opening of New York's Erie Canal in 1825 brought settlers to Michigan by the thousands. As these pioneers tamed the wilderness, the path to statehood forced Michiganians to surrender the mouth of the Maumee River (present-day Toledo) for great, unknown stretches of the western Upper Peninsula that one Michiganian dejectedly noted would "remain forever a Wilderness." The area's extensive natural resource wealth soon replaced those frowns with smiles.

During the antebellum years, Michiganians planted seeds of education, successfully lobbied for a canal that still has national implications (the Soo Locks), and provided the birthplace for a new national political party (the Republicans). During the violent decade of the 1860s, the state overwhelmingly supported the Abraham Lincoln administration—sending 50 percent of its military-age male population (as well as a few women) to preserve the Union and end the tragedy of human slavery.

After the Civil War, manufacturing and natural resource exploitation ruled the state's burgeoning economy. Besides being a national leader producing lumber, copper, and iron ore, Michigan factories turned out everything from breakfast cereal to cigars. "Made in Michigan" meant Dowagiac stoves, Kellogg's corn flakes, Upjohn and Dow pharmaceuticals, and Grand Rapids furniture.

However, the automobile, which greatly changed how Americans lived, worked, and played, dominated the twentieth century. Michiganians were among the earliest American inventors of the horseless carriage. Twenty years after Charles King drove his "most unique machine" down Detroit's Woodward Avenue in March 1896, Michigan became the country's leading producer of automobiles. As the primary beneficiary of Michigan's new status as the "auto state," Detroit grew and its population peaked at 1.8 million people, making it America's fifth largest city in 1950. Automakers also played a key role in supplying materiel that made America the "Arsenal of Democracy" and contributed immeasurably to the Allied victory in World War II. Conversely, the state's dependence on the automobile led some to make this observation: "When America sneezes, Michigan gets pneumonia." This was painfully true during the Great Depression of the early 1930s, the Arab oil embargo of the mid-1970s, and even more recently as American automakers suffered a loss of market share to imports.

Michigan does have its share of disheartening stories, including Indian and worker exploitation, racial segregation and discord (especially in 1967), the wanton destruction of the state's natural resources, and the precipitous decline of its greatest city, which also became the nation's largest city to declare bankruptcy in July 2013. However, it is also true that during the half-century since the end of World War II, Michigan's labor unions expanded their influence, "Big Mac" linked the peninsulas at the Straits of Mackinac, and the creation of "Motown" advanced the Civil Rights movement.

Today, Michigan boasts a population of 10 million people. But Michigan's long-standing status as the nation's eighth most populous state will soon change as others grow more quickly. Michigan's geographical ranking as the 23rd largest state, however, grows to 11th in size when incorporating its Great Lakes waters. Finally, Michiganians still possess the distinctly unique way of answering the question, "Where are you from?" by simply holding up their right hand, palm out, and pointing. (This strategy also works for the Upper Peninsula by turning one's left hand horizontally, also palm out.)

On the whole, Michigan's story may be compared with the observations of an English immigrant who settled in Lenawee County during the early 1830s. John Fisher believed he was "in a Country where all is life and animation, . . . where everyone speaks of the past with triumph, the present with delight, [and] the future with growing confidence and anticipation."

Isle Royale

Calumet
Houghton

Ironwood

Marquette

Sault Ste.
Marie

Manistique

St. Ignace

Mackinaw City   Mackinac Island

Escanaba   Cheboygan

Beaver
Island   Petoskey

                                                            Alpena

                                    Grayling
Traverse City   Au Sable River

                                                            Tawas
                                                            City

Ludington

                    Mt. Pleasant

                                                Saginaw
Muskegon

        Grand   Flint   Port
        Rapids   Huron
                    Grand River

                                        Pontiac
                                ★ Lansing

        Battle
        Creek   Ann
Kalamazoo   Jackson   Arbor   Detroit

Niles

CHAPTER

1

First
Residents

Europeans found three primary tribes in Michigan: the Ojibwa, Odawa, and Potawatomi.

"A chief was not a man with power to command but a leader who demonstrated humility, generosity, and ability."

—Professor Charles E. Cleland,
MSU Department of Anthropology

Shortly after the last glacier retreated and created the familiar face of the future state of Michigan, the first inhabitants arrived. The earliest evidence of human life in Michigan occurred more than 11,000 years ago, although the archaeological evidence is "pitifully meager—a few broken stone tools, a spear point, an animal bone or two, the remains of a fire hearth."[1]

About 7,000 years ago, evidence exists of man-made copper objects. Working in shallow pits, prehistoric Indians used hammer stones that weighed between 10 and 36 pounds (sometimes attached to a handle) and chisels to break off pieces of copper from a larger rock. By hammering and reheating (called annealing), the Indians worked the copper into various shapes. According to former state archaeologist John R. Halsey, "Depending on what artifact was being produced or what finish was desired, additional steps of grinding, cutting, embossing, perforating and polishing were employed." Native Americans craftsmen created "tens of thousands of useful and artistic items, ranging from dozens of varieties of projectile points, knives, harpoons and awls to decorative gorgets, bracelets and beads." These items then were "widely traded" and have been found as far away as Florida and the Canadian prairies. The location of prehistoric Indian mining pits also aided miners in locating copper deposits during the Copper Boom of the 1840s.[2]

Artifacts found in burial mounds provided important information on the culture of the Hopewell Indians.

—— The Hopewell

Among the earliest Michigan settlers was a group of prehistoric people called the Hopewell who lived in the western and southern part of the Lower Peninsula. The Hopewell, named after an Ohio farmer who discovered burial mounds on his land, were part of a huge trading network that stretched across the central United States. Elaborate decorations and jewelry made from Michigan copper, North Carolina mica, and shells and pearls from the Gulf of Mexico were discovered in Hopewell burial mounds. Carved obsidian (a volcanic rock) from the Rocky Mountains and sharks' teeth from Virginia's Chesapeake Bay also have been found. The most ornate artifacts were in Ohio mounds. Michigan artifacts, such as pots and bowls, are simpler. Archaeologists believe the Hopewell also traded furs and food. In their eating habits, the Hopewell fit between hunter-gatherers and farmers; they may have grown some plants, but they were not a full-time farming people and they also hunted. Little evidence remains of Hopewell houses, which scientists believe had wooden pole frames covered with animal skins, grass or herb woven mats, or bark.[3]

Burial mounds were an important part of the Hopewell legacy. The Hopewell built their mounds in Michigan from 10 BCE until about 400 CE. No one knows why they stopped building mounds or where the Hopewell went after 400 CE. Today, seventeen Hopewell Mounds (called the Norton Mounds) still lie in a forest outside Grand Rapids. Another group of mounds, called the Converse Mounds, sat in downtown Grand Rapids, but in the mid-1850s, farmers, construction workers, and curious people dug them up.

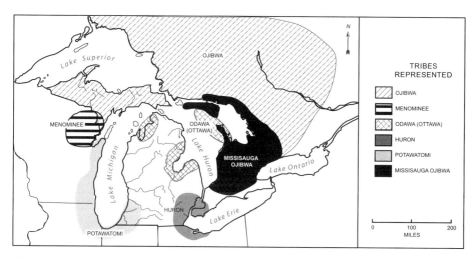

When the French arrived, these primary tribes lived in the region.

When the French arrived in the early to mid-seventeenth century, they found approximately 100,000 Native Americans, representing nine different tribes, living in the Great Lakes area.[4]

—— The Huron

The Hurons, the largest group, were among the first to greet the French as they explored the interior of North America. The French even gave this tribe their name. The word *Huron* comes from the Huron hairstyle that reminded the French of a wild boar (*hure* in French). The Huron called themselves the Wendat (pronounced Wyandot). This name may mean "islanders" or "peninsula dwellers" and comes from the peninsula between Georgian Bay and Lake Huron, near where the Huron once lived. The Huron were farmers, harvesting so much corn that they traded it to other tribes. An observer once noted that the Huron he was visiting had so many crops that "it was easier to get lost in the corn field" than in the surrounding forest. The Huron lived in large, palisaded villages consisting of long rectangular houses. Shaped much like the modern-day Quonset huts with a door at each end, these houses were covered with bark and stood up to 130 feet long and 30 feet wide. The house was divided into compartments where families lived and fireplaces stood along a central aisle. Families living in a long house were related. Among the Hurons, a child took the name of his mother's clan. (In the Algonquian system, it was just the opposite.) In a marriage, the new husband resided with the wife's family. The maternal uncle (mother's brother) educated the children (not the father), which meant "the father was in many ways a stranger in his own home."[5]

Although the French befriended the Huron, they also brought diseases that decimated them. More than 50 percent of all Huron died from diseases in the first twenty years after the French arrived. The Huron also suffered when their long-standing rival, the Iroquois, forced them to move to western Lake Superior. Eventually, the Huron moved back east, settling around the Straits of Mackinac. After the French founded Detroit in 1701, the Huron resettled there. After Michigan became a state, many Huron were forced west to Kansas and Oklahoma.

With the exception of the Huron, the tribes most easily associated with Michigan belonged to the Algonquians. Although the Huron and Algonquian tribes shared certain traits, like farming, the Huron spoke an Iroquoian language, described "as different from Algonquian as English is from Russian." Algonquian comes from the word *Algomequin,* meaning "people across the river." Michigan Indians moved here from the east. The Ojibwa (also called the Chippewa) were among the largest groups of American Indians. They along with the Odawa (more commonly called Ottawa) and Potawatomi formed the Three Fires Confederacy, also known as the Anishinabek. The Ojibwa were the "older brothers," the Odawa the middle brother, and the Potawatomi the youngest.[6]

—— The Ojibwa

The exact meaning of the word *Ojibwa* is unknown. One explanation is "to roast until puckered up," which describes the process of fire-curing the seams of moccasins worn by the Ojibwa. When the French arrived in the Great Lakes, an estimated 30,000 Ojibwa lived along the southern shore of Lake Superior and western Lake Huron. The Ojibwa were excellent hunters and fishermen. The French called the Ojibwa living along the rapids of the St. Mary's River (present-day Sault Ste. Marie) *Saulteurs* (People of the Rapids). During the warmer months, the Ojibwa settled in villages near the fishing grounds. Each village included a group of related families living in dome-shaped wigwams covered with birch bark. During the winter months, the Ojibwa abandoned the fishing areas and headed inland, surviving the cold months by hunting and eating dried fish and other storable foods like blueberries. In the spring they gathered maple sugar before heading back to their familiar fishing areas. Living in northern Michigan was difficult, especially during the winter. Tradition assigned the tasks. Men hunted and fished, women prepared the food and sewed the clothes, and children collected food and babysat their younger siblings. "All Ojibwa recognized bonds of kin and kindred." If a family suffered a food shortage, Ojibwa shared. "If anyone in a Ojibwa camp had food, everybody had food." According to Michigan State University anthropologist Charles Cleland:

> Among the Ojibwa there were a number of 'superfamilies,' called clans. Each child belonged to a clan of his father. The people belonging to a specific clan felt themselves to be closely related no matter where they lived. Although the exact number of Ojibwa clans is unknown, at least twenty are recorded among them the Loon, Raven, Beaver, Turtle, Crane, Pike, and Eagle clans. Members of one clan were required to marry another clan, resulting in a cross-cutting system of clan membership between villages. Marriage, therefore, tended to make family of strangers by uniting people of one village with people of another until the whole of the tribe was linked by a feeling of kinship.

Leadership among the Ojibwa, "as in other Michigan tribes," was achieved by respect because "no individual had the power to dictate to another." According to Cleland, "Leaders were revered for their generosity, wisdom, skill, and most of all, for their humility. Ambition, drive, and political calculation did not constitute a path to leadership."[7]

The Ojibwa allied themselves with the French during the French and Indian War and later with the British during the American Revolution and the War of 1812. Some Ojibwa were removed west of the Mississippi River (especially to Minnesota) during the antebellum years. Today, tens of thousands of Ojibwa live in nearly 150 different bands in the United States and Canada. In Michigan, about 3,000 members of the Saginaw Chippewa Indian Tribe of Michigan live on a Mt. Pleasant reservation.

—— The Odawa

As the "middle brother" of the Three Fires Confederacy, the Odawa were skilled traders. When the French arrived, approximately 3,000 Odawa lived east of the Straits of Mackinac in the area of northern Lake Huron. The Odawa traveled hundreds of miles exchanging goods with other tribes. Like the Ojibwa, they allied themselves with the French in the French and Indian War and with the British during the American Revolution and the War of 1812. Some Odawa were later sent west and their descendants live in Oklahoma today.[8]

Two notable and contrasting Odawa were Pontiac and Blackbird. The exact date and location of Pontiac's birth is uncertain, but most authorities agree his father was Odawa, although his mother may have been Ojibwa. Shortly after the British defeated the French in the early 1760s, Pontiac led a rebellion against the British who had enacted harsher trade policies. Although early historians gave Pontiac more credit than he deserved in this uprising, Pontiac's Rebellion was a formidable uprising that failed. Pontiac eventually left Michigan and was murdered by another Indian near St. Louis, Missouri, in 1769. Born in present-day Harbor Springs about 1815, Blackbird was an Odawa chief and the son of an Odawa chief. The family name, Mackadepenessy, means "black hawk," but was later mistranslated to mean "blackbird." After studying at Twinsburg Institution in Ohio and present-day Eastern Michigan University in Ypsilanti, Blackbird became an interpreter at the Protestant mission at L'Arbre Croche. During the late 1850s, he served the U.S. government as an Indian interpreter and as Harbor Springs postmaster. In 1887, Blackbird published his *History of the Ottawa and Chippewa Indians of Michigan*, which is free of the bias found in similar books about Native Americans written by white authors during the period.[9]

—— The Potawatomi

When the French arrived in the western Great Lakes an estimated 4,000 Potawatomi (the name has various spellings) lived in the southern Lower Peninsula. The Potawatomi were farmers in the summer and hunters in the fall. They also traveled west to the prairies to hunt buffalo in the spring. The Potawatomi were assigned the task of guarding the sacred fire of the Three Fires Confederacy. They were peacemakers who brought together rival tribes for feasts and to arbitrate disputes. The Potawatomi were among the most docile and affectionate Indians toward the French. As with the other tribes of the Three Fires, the Potawatomi sided with the French during the French and Indian War and the British during the American Revolution and War of 1812. With the 1833 Treaty of Chicago, many Potawatomi were forced to move west of the Mississippi River; other Potawatomi ended up in Oklahoma and Canada. The Potawatomi who followed tribal leader Leopold Pokagon escaped the horrors of the Trail of Tears by becoming taxpaying, land-owning Christians in Berrien and Cass Counties. Today, the Pokagon Band of the Potawatomi Indians is a federally recognized Indian Nation in a ten-county area in southern Michigan and northwestern Indiana with its tribal headquarters in Dowagiac, Michigan.[10]

Leopold Pokagon's son, Simon, was nicknamed the "Red Man's Longfellow" after writing several publications. In these works, Pokagon waxed nostalgically about the "vanishing" race of Native Americans. Speaking about the 1893 Columbian Exposition in Chicago, he declared, "On behalf of my people, the American Indians, I hereby declare to you, the pale-faced race that has usurped our lands and homes . . . . [While] your hearts in admiration rejoice over the beauty and grandeur of this young republic and you say, 'behold the wonders wrought by our children in this foreign land,' do not forget that this success has been at the sacrifice of our homes and a once happy race."[11]

—— Other Tribes

Several other tribes lived in parts of Michigan or its fringes when the French arrived.

An Algonquian tribe, the Menominee lived south of the Straits of Mackinac when first discovered by the earliest French explorers to the Upper Great Lakes. The name Menominee comes from an Ojibwa word meaning "wild rice people." Wild rice was an important staple for the Menominee, whose customs were similar to the Ojibwa. The Menominee numbered several thousand people when the French arrived. After selling their lands to the U.S. government in several pre–Civil War treaties, the Menominee were removed to a reservation in Wisconsin. By 1870, deadly diseases (smallpox, typhoid, influenza, and dysentery) had killed more than half of the tribe's 4,000 members. Today, the Menominee Indian Reservation, which is located in a Wisconsin county bordering Michigan, is about 354 square miles in size and is home to 3,000 people.[12]

Other tribes that lived in the Great Lakes area included the Fox, an unusually warlike Algonquian tribe, and the Sac (also Sauk), a Woodlands tribe associated with the Algonquians, who temporarily resided in the Saginaw Bay area before settling in present-day northern Illinois and southern Wisconsin. As Americans headed west after the American Revolution, the Fox and Sauk formed an alliance. Both suffered great losses caused by Euro-American disease before being relocated in Iowa and Oklahoma.[13]

—— Legends

Since Indians do not have a written language, legends play an important role in their culture. According to the legend of the Anishinabe, the all-powerful Creator, Kitche Manido first made the four basic elements—rock, fire, wind, and water. Then he fashioned the sun, the stars, and the Earth. Next, came the trees, plants, animals, and humans. From Kitche Manido, everything received a spirit and a purpose in the Circle of Life. The plants provided the food and medicines; the trees gave shelter; the animals sacrificed their lives to provide food and clothing for humans—the Anishinabe. The Anishinabe first lived along the Atlantic Ocean but made their way west, eventually settling in the Great Lakes. Once their journey ended, the Anishinabe separated into three groups (Ojibwa, Odawa, and Potawatomi) that settled in different part of the Great Lakes.[14]

Another well-known legend explained how the Great Manitou created the Sleeping Bear Dunes and the nearby islands of North and South Manitou. As the story was told, a mother bear and her two cubs lived peacefully on the western shore of Lake Michigan. One summer night there was a big thunderstorm and lighting set the forest on fire. The mother gathered her cubs and jumped into the lake to escape the flames. All through the night, they swam toward the distant shore and away from the fire. The cubs grew tired. First, the younger one sank beneath the waves, and then the older cub disappeared. The mother bear could not save them, but she made it to shore and fell into a deep sleep on the beach. As she slept, the Great Manitou whispered to her, "Because you always remembered me with thanks, I will take you to the Land of the Spirits. Your cubs are already there." The Great Manitou created two islands to honors the cubs—they are North and South Manitou. The Great Manitou then covered the mother bear with a blanket of white sand. Today, she rests under the Sleeping Bear Dunes National Lakeshore.[15]

According to anthropologist Charles Cleland, the Indians of the Upper Great Lakes shared three central cultural principles. First, "no man had the right to determine another man's fate." Group actions were "grounded on the idea of consensus." A chief was chosen to follow because he "had demonstrated humility, generosity, and ability." Second, Indians believed in sharing "all things, including goods, labor, and food." A person earned greater prestige and status by sharing, especially with those in need. "Generosity was expected." Finally, the principle that guided man on Earth was that "no creature was superior to any other, and all were unalterably linked in the great web of life." Exploiting the Earth's resources was forbidden because "these were not objects but living things."[16]

—— European Contact and Beyond

There is no doubt the arrival of the Europeans to the Great Lakes in the seventeenth century proved detrimental for the Indians. The French viewed them as un-Christian but treated them with more respect, even allowing inter-marrying. The British held Indians in contempt and used them as cannon fodder in the wars against the Americans. Although the Michigan Indians became reliant on European trade goods (guns, metal knives, and beads), it was not a completely one-way relationship. The Indians introduced the Euro-peans to the birch-bark canoe—essential to the fur trade and the primary means of travel in the Great Lakes area (excluding walking) for nearly two centuries after the first French arrived. One mid–eighteenth century observer may have been exaggerating, but he claimed the French voyageurs would not have traded the birch-bark canoe for "several barrels of gold." More than introducing Europeans to lightweight, easily reparable canoe, these tribes trapped animals whose furs ended up as hats that sat on the heads of Euro-pean men.

For Native Americans living in Michigan, the arrival of settlers in the 1820s introduced more dramatic changes. Michigan settlers wanted the Indi-ans' land and then wanted them to go away. In 1806, the Indians "owned" almost all of Michigan's future 57,900 square miles of land. Fifty years later, they owned 32 square miles. The treaties used by the U.S. government to acquire the land marked "one of the more disgraceful chapters in Michigan's history." Forced to sign these agreements, the Native Americans received cash, unrestricted fishing and hunting rights, annuity payments, and the ser-vices of teachers, agricultural experts, and blacksmiths. Sometimes the treaty conditions were fulfilled, but "many other" times they were ignored or later struck out of the agreement without telling the Indians. Annuity payments, "often timed for political advantage, drew a crowd of white merchants and whiskey sellers, so these monies soon returned to white hands." Indians were defrauded out of their land allotments guaranteed by the treaties. In 1889, the Burt Lake Ojibwa lost their claim to 890 acres of Cheboygan County, deeded to them "forever," after a wealthy lumber baron who wanted their land convinced the county sheriff to burn the Indians' homes for nonpayment of taxes. It was one "of many such cases." After treaties transferred ownership of the land, the government adopted a re-settlement policy. Some Michigan Indians, especially the Potawatomi and Wyandot who lived in the southern Lower Peninsula, suffered the infamous "Trail of Tears." Other Michigan Indians were more fortunate, especially those living in the then-sparsely settled northern part of the state or others who accepted a British offer to relocate in Canada.[17]

Today, about 140,000 Michiganians claim Indian descent, ranking Michigan tenth among the states. Of Michigan's eleven reservations, the largest are in Isabella and Baraga counties. Too often today, any awareness of Michigan's rich Indian heritage consists of casinos (Michigan has about two dozen) or the places carrying an Indian name. (But beware, Henry Schoolcraft mixed Indian, European, Latin, even Arabic syllables to create pseudo-Indian names.) Fortunately, efforts to understand and keep Indian culture alive are being undertaken by the Native American Institute at Michigan State University. Founded in 1981 by Professor George Cornell, the institute assists North American Indian organizations and tribal governments while promoting and enhancing the general public's awareness of Michigan Indian communities, history, and culture. The institute also seeks to achieve a better understanding of the Indian past through its American Indian Studies series published by the Michigan State University Press.[18]

CHAPTER
2

The French
Presence

The travels of Father Jacques Marquette and Louis Jolliet took them to the Mississippi River.

". . . I am eager to go, for a woman who totally loves her husband has no stronger attachment than this company; wherever he may be."

—Madame Cadillac's response
when asked to join her husband at Detroit

The French arrived in the Great Lakes during the early seventeenth century looking for the elusive Northwest Passage—a shortcut to China. Instead, they found furbearing animals and Indians to Christianize. Until the eve of the American Revolution, the French explored and occupied the western Great Lakes. In the process, they trapped the area's animals, disrupted the lives of native peoples, founded Michigan's earliest settlements, and fought wars with their colonial rival Great Britain. Even in the twenty-first century, the French legacy is evident in Michigan in the names of towns, streets, and geographical features.

Samuel de Champlain led the earliest French explorations to the Great Lakes. In 1608, Champlain, the "Father of New France," established a trading post at the narrows of the St. Lawrence River that became the city of Quebec. A few years later, Champlain, intrigued by waterways that flowed from the west, traveled the Ottawa River and explored the Georgian Bay area of eastern Lake Huron. He spent the winter of 1615 among the Huron, learning about the area beyond the lake. Soon, Champlain directed other young Frenchmen to explore the west.[1]

—— Earliest Explorers

One of Champlain's earliest students was Etienne Brulé. Born in France in 1592, Brulé arrived in New France (later called Canada) in 1608. Two years later, at Champlain's urging, the young Frenchman moved into the wilderness, living among the Algonquian Indians and learning their language. Brulé accompanied Champlain to visit the Huron and, although captured and tortured by the Iroquois, lived with the Huron. In 1622, Brulé became the first white man to see Michigan when he arrived at present-day Sault Ste. Marie on the St. Mary's River. Notwithstanding several "remarkable exploits" to his credit, Brulé had a dark side. According to Champlain, the young Frenchman "was recognized as being very vicious in character, and much addicted to women." Brulé's decision to sell his services to the English led to his downfall, and around 1633 Hurons loyal to the French killed him. Because of Brulé's treason, Champlain chose not to avenge his former student's death. However, a sympathetic biographer later concluded that Brulé was "endowed with a great spirit of independence, with initiative and indisputable courage [and] a striking example of the fascination that the free life of the Indians held for young Frenchmen in the first century of the colony's history."[2]

The next Frenchman to reach the western Great Lakes was Jean Nicollet de Belleborne. Born in France in 1598, Nicollet possessed the qualities that Champlain sought—"persistence, steadfastness, love of the wilderness, and a talent for adventuring." Twenty years old when he arrived in New France, Nicollet spent the next two years living among the Huron. He then served as an official interpreter for the French colony before becoming, according to one later-day observer, "more Indian than European." In 1634, Nicollet—at Champlain's urging—headed west and became the first European to pass through the Straits of Mackinac. Nicollet soon reached Green Bay where he saw smoke from a village. Hoping to have found the Northwest Passage, and possibly expecting to greet Chinese royalty, Nicollet put on a beautiful robe "all strewn with flowers and birds of many colors." Instead of finding a short-cut to China, the young Frenchman had discovered the Winnebagoes, who "feasted him and admired him and thought him descended from the gods." The Indians also spoke of a great river that lay farther west, claiming it was only three days' journey. Nicollet returned to Quebec and the following year accidentally drowned in the St. Lawrence River. His earliest biographer claimed he was "equally and singularly loved" by both the French and the Indians.[3]

—— Furs and More Furs

As the French continued their explorations, they discovered the Great Lakes offered an untapped reservoir of furs. By the early seventeenth century, the European demand for pelts had outrun supply, and trappers soon sent all types of pelts (bear, deer, fox, mink, beaver among others) to France—Europe's fashion center. Hats of every description were made from the furs, and the most desirable fur came from the beaver. For more than two centuries, beaver hats were in vogue in Europe.[4]

The fur trade was a barter system with Indians doing the trapping and curing the skins and exchanging them with traders for manufactured goods—knives, blankets, hatchets, cooking pots. *Made Beaver* (the equivalent of a single beaver pelt) was the term fur traders used to describe both the quantity and quality of all pelts. For example, it took "a number of lowly muskrat skins to equal one Made Beaver." Pelts became a kind of currency, and European trade goods were measured in terms of Made Beavers. A musket might be priced at fourteen Made Beaver, a blanket at seven Made Beaver, and a hatchet at one Made Beaver. But "the value of goods relative to Made Beaver could fluctuate a good deal."[5]

Initially, the Indians took the pelts to Quebec and Montreal. However, the industry soon changed. Trappers headed inland as beaver—neither a migratory nor a prolific animal—were exterminated from an area. As the Frenchmen moved farther west into the North American interior, the Indians became increasingly dependent on the trade, especially for European goods (knives and blankets) and liquor. At the time, most colonial Frenchmen were addicted to furs, while their English rivals along the Atlantic coast were more interested in populating and growing their colonies. Despite these differences, the North American fur trade led to a series of wars between the French and British.[6]

The workhorses of the fur trade were the *voyageurs*, a French word meaning "travelers." Voyageurs paddled the canoes that carried trade goods exchanged with the Indians for furs. Standing no taller than five feet, six inches, voyageurs were the period's most colorful and hardworking men. Known for their exceptional physical strength, these men paddled their birchbark canoes (up to sixty strokes per minute) for fourteen hours a day. On the Great Lakes, the fur trade used Montreal canoes that measured 36 feet long and carried a crew of up to twelve men and three tons of cargo. Smaller canoes were used inland and on rivers. Every hour the paddling stopped so the men could enjoy a few puffs on their clay pipes. When forced to portage, the voyageurs carried the cargo and the canoe. Bundles of furs weighed on average ninety pounds each, and a voyageur was expected to carry at least two bundles at one time; some carried more. Four men carried the canoe on their shoulders. According to one contemporary, voyageurs moved along the portages "at a pace which made unburdened travelers pant for breath in their endeavor not to be left behind." Another observer noted that his voyageurs took their canoes out of the water, mended breaches in them, reloaded, cooked breakfast, shaved, washed, ate, and re-embarked in less than an hour. Comparing them to a pony, he concluded that voyageurs "are short, thick set, and active, and never tire." Voyageurs dressed colorfully. A short shirt, a red woolen cap, a pair of deerskin leggings (that reached from the ankles to a little above the knees and were held up by a string secured to a belt at the waist), a breechcloth, a pair of deerskin moccasins, a gaudy sash, and a pipe completed the voyageur's outfit. To counter the work and the boredom, voyageurs often raced their canoes, told exaggerated stories (called "pulling the long bow"), and sang lively songs. Among the most favorite were *A la Claire Fontaine* ("By the Clear Running Fountain") and *Alouette* ("Lark").[7]

Because of their Herculean labors, the voyageurs also had legendary appetites. During the latter stages of the fur trade, one entrepreneur recorded the *daily* ration for each man was twelve pounds of venison or four or five big whitefish. Despite this gargantuan amount, one voyageur demanded more, leading the businessman to conclude that "it would have taken twenty pounds of animal food to satisfy him." Voyageur cuisine was "hearty and robust, calculated to stick to the ribs. . . . Whatever it lacked by way of seasoning, one ingredient was prerequisite—grease, and plenty of it." After eating a fried venison steak, one observer complained, "The roof of my mouth would become so thickly cased over with tallow as to necessitate the use of my knife to remove it." As they traveled, the voyageurs augmented their fare with whatever "they happened to get their hands on." One favorite dish was rubbaboo—a sort of pemmican stew. An observer recorded that "pemmican is supposed by the benighted world outside to consist only of pounded meat and grease; an egregious error; for, from experience on the subject, I am authorized to state that hair, sticks, spruce leaves, stones, sand, etc. enter into its composition, often quite largely."[8]

Because of their vast knowledge of the waterways of the Great Lakes, voyageurs accompanied the French explorers who traveled the interior of the North American continent. These hearty men, who took great pride in their profession, boldly boasted they could "live hard, lie hard, sleep hard [and] eat dogs."[9]

—— Pageant of the Saint

Beginning in the 1660s, the French strengthened their hold on the Great Lakes by establishing outposts at strategic places like Sault Ste. Marie and the Straits of Mackinac. This was partly in response to the arrival of an English challenge pushing south from the Hudson Bay. In late 1670, Jean Talon, the *intendant* (royal administrative official) of New France, responded to the English threat by sending Simon-François Daumont de Saint-Lusson, a young French nobleman who had arrived in Canada in 1663, west "to extend God's glory and to promote the king of France" by taking possession of the central region of North America. (Saint-Lusson's mission also included confirming rumors of copper deposits along the Lake Superior shore.)[10]

On June 14, 1671, hundreds of Indians representing fourteen different nations gathered at Sault Ste. Marie for the equivalent of a modern-day pep rally. Father Claude Allouez "delivered a harangue" extolling the powers of the French king designed to ensure the Indians' loyalty. A Jesuit who had arrived at Quebec in 1658, Allouez studied the Huron and Algonquian languages and earned the Indians' respect. In 24 years of missionary work, Allouez personally baptized some 10,000 Indians. On this June day, the veteran Jesuit told the Indians, "Your canoes hold only four or five men. . . . [while] our ships in France hold four or five hundred, and even as many as a thousand." When the French king attacked with his armies, it would be "more terrible than the thunder; the earth trembles, the air and the sea are set on fire by the discharge of his cannon." While the Indians might count the scalps they took in battle, the French king would set "rivers of blood" flowing. Conveniently overlooking the British, Allouez concluded, "No one now dares make war upon him, all nations beyond the sea having submissively sued for peace." In an equally dramatic gesture, Saint-Lusson declared that the following lands—and all the people living there—belonged to France:

"Lakes Huron and Superior, the island of Manitoulin, and all other countries, rivers, lakes as well discovered as to be discovered, which are bounded on one side by the Northern & Western Seas and on the other side by the South Sea including all its lengths and breadth." Cheers for King Louis XIV, the erection of a giant cross, and a great bonfire concluded what became known as the Pageant of the Sault. Presumably the Indians got the point, not so the British.[11]

—— Black Robes Arrive

In the years immediately following the pageant, another group of Frenchmen played an active role in exploring the Great Lakes. Nicknamed "Black Robes," the Jesuits were members of the Society of Jesus founded by St. Ignatius Loyola in 1540. Jesuits sought to convert Indians to Christianity. They also spent much time exploring the North American wilderness. As early as 1641, Fathers Charles Raymbaut and Isaac Jogues had joined the Odawa at Sault Ste. Marie where they held the first mass in Michigan. Years later, the observations of Fathers Claude Dablon and Claude Allouez resulted in an exceptional map of Lake Superior. The French upper class developed empathy for the Jesuits through the *Jesuit Relations*, annual reports published from 1632 through 1673 that detailed Jesuit activities and assisted their fund-raising efforts.[12]

The best-known Jesuit missionary was Jacques Marquette. He spent only nine years in North America, yet his accomplishments and legends during this brief time have given him a legendary reputation. Born in France in 1637 into a prosperous family, Marquette began his theological studies at the age of seventeen. Desiring to be a missionary from a young age, he arrived in Quebec in September 1666. After a one-year apprenticeship and well on his way to mastering six different Native American languages, Marquette served at the Jesuit mission at Sault Ste. Marie. A year later, he transferred to the mission at Chequamegon Bay (present-day Ashland, Wisconsin). There, Marquette heard about the Illini Indians. When the Huron at Chequamegon fled back to the east, Marquette followed, founding a mission on the northern shores of the Straits of Mackinac that he called St. Ignace.[13]

On December 8, 1672, Marquette saw a lone paddler approaching St. Ignace in a canoe. It was Louis Jolliet, whom Marquette had met earlier in Quebec. Born in Canada in 1645, Jolliet had trained for the priesthood before turning his interests to fur trading and exploring. He had been selected to

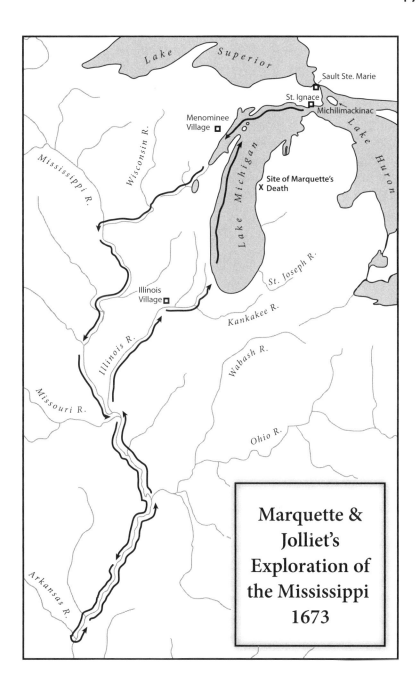

Marquette &
Jolliet's
Exploration of
the Mississippi
1673

lead an expedition westward to explore the Mississippi River. Although the French had known of a great river to the west that rivaled the St. Lawrence River, no Frenchman had seen it. Since the river's mouth remained "a disquieting and undiscovered secret," Jolliet had been chosen to find out if the river emptied into Spanish-held Gulf of Mexico or possibly flowed westward, providing the elusive Northwest Passage. Marquette received his orders to accompany Jolliet with great enthusiasm, recording his eagerness to seek out "new nations that are unknown to us, to teach them to know our God."[14]

On May 17, 1673, after months of preparation, Marquette and Jolliet, along with five other men (described as "sturdy, blocky men, thick in the shoulders, narrow-waisted, short of limbs, tireless, enured to hardship and steady in the face of danger") set out in two canoes from St. Ignace. They traveled along the northern shore of Lake Michigan and paddled about thirty miles a day. Marquette wrote in his journal, "Our joy at being chosen for this expedition roused our courage and sweetened the labor of rowing." In two weeks, they reached present-day Menominee, Michigan, where the Menominee warned the Frenchmen if they went any farther west they would meet Indians "who never show mercy to Strangers, but Break their Heads without any cause." The Indians also told Marquette and Jolliet that the great river "was full of horrible monsters, which devoured men and Canoes together." Marquette thanked them for the advice but explained that the saving of souls required they proceed. Undeterred, the Frenchmen pushed on, crossing Wisconsin. On June 17, 1673, after 500 miles of paddling, they entered the Mississippi River. Marquette recorded that they felt "a joy" that he could not express.[15]

The Frenchmen followed the Mississippi River, meeting Indians and discovering new plants, birds, and animals, including herds of buffalo and a fish described as "a monster with the head of a tiger, a pointed snout like a wildcat's, a beard and ears erect, a grayish head and neck all black." After a month on the Mississippi, the explorers realized it flowed south, not west toward the Pacific. Near present-day Arkansas, they turned around, fearing hostile Indians or capture by the Spanish. Despite the difficulty of paddling against the Mississippi's mighty current, the Frenchmen reached Lake Michigan, then paddled up the west shore to present-day Green Bay, Wisconsin. Marquette wintered at a Jesuit mission near Green Bay, while Jolliet headed east to draw maps and share the news about their explorations.[16]

The two men never saw each other again. The following year, Marquette returned south to work among the Illini. During the spring of 1675, suffering from failing health, Marquette headed back to St. Ignace. On the journey, he and his two companions became the first white men to travel up the eastern shore of Lake Michigan. But Marquette never saw St. Ignace, dying on May 18, 1675. The exact location remains uncertain, although it may have been at the mouth of the Marquette River near present-day Ludington. As for Jolliet, a boating accident and a fire destroyed all his notes and maps made during the Mississippi River expedition. He recovered and resumed his commercial activity, becoming a "merchant of consequence." Future explorations took him to the Hudson Bay (where he warned the king about the English threat to Canada) and to Labrador, which he mapped.[17]

Although unfamiliar to most Americans, Louis Jolliet is hailed in Canada as "one of the most genuine and most impressive examples of the heroes produced

This statue of Father Marquette stands near Fort Mackinac on Mackinac Island.

by New France." Conversely, Father Marquette is remembered in the United States in statues (in the U.S. Capitol and on Mackinac Island, among others), as well as by a university, a popular Michigan river, the largest city in the Upper Peninsula, and numerous streets. Yet, his legacy is not without controversy. Was he "a robust, optimistic, gentle, and truly zealous missionary who exercised an intense personal influence over the Indians" or was he a "synthetic hero" who "merely followed in the footsteps of others," including those of Louis Jolliet? Both positions have their advocates.[18]

—— Walking with La Salle

Shortly after Marquette's death, Rene-Robert Cavelier, de La Salle, arrived in the Great Lakes. Born in France in 1643 to a wealthy upper bourgeoisie family, Cavelier studied to become a Jesuit before being overtaken by "a perpetual need to change his occupation and environment." Nicknamed *inquietus* because of his "lack of steadiness," Cavelier left France in 1667 to follow an older brother and an uncle who lived in Canada. Cavelier acquired several thousand acres of land near Montreal and considered farming. However, he soon sold most of his lands, hoping to use the monies he earned to "gratify the demon of adventure lodged within him." Cavelier's obsession was to find the Northwest Passage. At the same time, Cavelier elevated himself to the nobility by calling himself "de la Salle," a name he had taken from his family's estate in France.[19]

Intent upon exploring the Ohio River, La Salle first headed to Lake Ontario in July 1669. His party then separated, with Fathers Dollier de Casson and Brehant de Galinee heading west and eventually passing through the straits at the future site of present-day Detroit before paddling up the western shore of Lake Huron to the Jesuit mission at Sault Ste. Marie. La Salle never reached the Ohio but returned to Quebec where he established a close relationship with Governor Louis Baude de Frontenac, "his powerful protector." According to one later-day observer, "The two individuals had seemingly every reason to get on well together; their personalities were equally strong, but complementary, their respective interests could be of mutual advantage, and they shared an antipathy towards the Jesuits."[20]

La Salle's relationship with the governor benefited the explorer in several ways. First, La Salle was awarded a grant of a French fort on Lake Ontario that he renamed Frontenac (present-day Kingston). He then received royal permission to establish forts (at his own expense) on Lakes Erie and Michigan. Although some detractors considered him a fool "fit and ready for the madhouse," La Salle also received the authority in the

This print captures the voyage of the *Griffon*, the first sailing vessel on the Great Lakes.

spring of 1678 to explore the North American interior. These efforts began during the winter of 1678–79, when craftsmen, under the direction of La Salle's trusted lieutenant Chevalier Henri de Tonty, built a 45-ton sailing vessel on the Niagara River (near present-day Buffalo). La Salle named the boat the *Griffon* after the mythical winged beast (half lion and half eagle) on Governor Frontenac's coat of arms.[21]

In August 1679, La Salle and a crew of about thirty men set sail, reaching St. Ignace after twenty days of "extremely dangerous sailing." La Salle sailed the *Griffon* into Lake Michigan, entering Green Bay where he had earlier arranged to take on a load of pelts. He directed the boat's crew, reduced to only six men, to return to Niagara, unload the pelts, and return to Lake Michigan. In the meantime, La Salle and fourteen men paddled south intent upon rendezvousing with the *Griffon* at the mouth of the St. Joseph River (then called the Riviere des Miamis after the Indian tribe living in the area). La Salle arrived at the river's mouth on November 1. Recognizing the area's advantages, he built Fort Miami, a stockade of 40 by 30 feet (present-day St. Joseph) that became the first European settlement in the Lower Peninsula. An impatient La Salle left Fort Miami and headed south, arriving at the Indian village at present-day Peoria, Illinois, in early January 1681. "At a prudent distance" from the Indian camp, the Frenchman built a fort called Crevecoeur ("broken hearted"). In late February, La Salle made the arduous journey back to Fort Miami hoping to hear about the *Griffon*. The Frenchman later learned the *Griffon* had disappeared on its return trip with no known survivors. The first sailing vessel on the Great Lakes also became the first ship to sink on the lakes.[22]

Desperate to find out what happened to his boat and its cargo of furs, the explorer returned to Niagara. On March 25, La Salle and five companions, four *coureurs de bois* ("runners of the woods" or independent adventurers who possessed many skills) and a Mohegan named Saget left Fort Miami. The men used a magnetic compass to determine direction and an astrolabe to determine latitude but were unable to determine longitude, so they did not know how many miles it was across the peninsula. There were no roads to follow and the men avoided trails to prevent being noticed by the Indians. Two days after leaving Fort Miami, La Salle recorded, "We continued our march through the woods, which was so interlaced with thorns and brambles that . . . our clothes were all torn and our faces so covered with blood that we hardly knew each other." On one occasion, Indians followed the Frenchmen for three days through "mud or water up to our waists." La Salle chronicled, "We made no fire at night, contenting ourselves with taking off our clothes, which were wet, and wrapping ourselves in our blankets on some dry knoll, where we passed the night." Near the present-day village of Dexter, La Salle's men cut down an elm tree and painstakingly built a dugout canoe. After five frustrating days of paddling on the Huron River, La Salle complained, "For as the river was almost everywhere encumbered by heaps of wood, which the swollen waters carry down or cast into its bed, we got weary of carrying our baggage every moment when the masses of wood prevented the canoe from passing; moreover, the river made enormous bends, and we observed after five days of rowing we had made less progress than we usually made in one day's march." Near present-day Belleville (where a statue of the explorer stands today), they abandoned their canoes and continued on foot. When they reached the Detroit River, south of Grosse Ile at a spot where the river was three miles wide, two men built a canoe and headed north to Michilimackinac, while La Salle and the others rafted the river and continued cross-country. Near Point Pelee in Ontario, the Frenchmen built another canoe and paddled along the Lake Erie shore, reaching Niagara one month after leaving Fort Miami. In the process, they became the first Europeans to walk across the Lower Peninsula.[23]

During the next several years, La Salle returned to the Great Lakes, stopping at St. Ignace and Fort Miami on a number of occasions. In the spring of 1681, La Salle and an entourage that filled more than a dozen canoes left Fort Miami on a journey that led them to the Mississippi River. But this wandering Frenchman, who was "in a greater hurry all the time," saw his career come to a disastrous end in the Gulf of Mexico. After spending months wandering around the future states of Texas and Louisiana futilely looking for the mouth of the Mississippi River, La Salle's frustrated men mutinied and murdered him on March 19, 1687. They left his body for the wolves. While biographers admired La Salle's "almost superhuman strength, tenacity, and courage," he led a hard life, "devoid of comforts, rife with hardship, denial, and betrayal; unredeemed by riches, glory, or even love." His followers often questioned his leadership, because, as one of his friends concluded, La Salle "never took any one's advice."[24]

—— A Town at "the Straits"

The late seventeenth and early eighteenth centuries formed a period of transition for New France. First, the French strengthened their presence in the Great Lakes by building forts at strategic locations: St. Joseph (1686), at present-day Port Huron; de Buade (1690), at St. Ignace; and a second St. Joseph

(1691), at present-day Niles. Then, King Louis XIV ordered the western forts abandoned. The king wanted to make peace with the Indians, especially the Iroquois, while allowing the Jesuits to attempt to Christianize the Indians without outside interference. The royal policy proved unpopular in Canada and was ignored by trappers and government officials. The strategy changed again when the French and the Iroquois signed a peace treaty in 1701. As those treaty negotiations were being held in Montreal, one Frenchman was crossing the Atlantic Ocean preparing to lead an expedition that would have an enormous impact on Michigan.[25]

Born in 1658 to a middle-class French family and well educated, Antoine de la Mothe Cadillac arrived in New France in 1683. After marrying Marie Therese Guyon, Cadillac settled in Quebec where he gained the trust of Governor Frontenac, who appointed him a captain in the army and gave him command of Fort de Baude at St. Ignace. Cadillac's tenure (1694 through 1697) at "the most important military and trading station" in New France's backcountry proved controversial. In a short time, Cadillac enjoyed great personal wealth by manipulating the fur trade. But in the process, he angered the Jesuits by liberally dispensing brandy to the Indians and fleecing the trappers, who refused to complain because of Cadillac's close relationship with Frontenac. One government official who summed up Cadillac's role noted, "Never has a man amassed so much wealth in so short a time and caused so much talk by the wrongs suffered by his trading partners."[26]

Cadillac disagreed with the decision to abandon the western forts, traveled to France, met with King Louis XIV, and proposed a new outpost—a self-sustaining village where farmers could produce crops. Cadillac envisioned a settlement that controlled the routes of the fur trade and kept the British and their Indian allies out of the western Great Lakes. Since Mackinac was too far north and its climate too hostile for farming, Cadillac suggested placing the new fort along the straits (*Le Detroit*) that connected Lakes Erie and Huron. The king agreed.[27]

In early July 1701, Cadillac, with about one hundred men and his nine-year-old son Antoine, left Montreal, traveling the safer 600-mile northern route along the Ottawa River, then into Lakes Huron and St. Clair. They paddled into the Detroit River, stopping at Grosse Ile where Cadillac considered building his fort. Instead, he moved back up the river and chose a spot on the north bank where the river was the narrowest. The location was easily defensible and offered a good view both up and down the river.[28]

On July 24, Cadillac marked the location of his town and his men used axes to begin the arduous process of felling logs that were at least 20 feet long.

They embedded the logs four feet into the ground, creating a crude fort. A bastion was built at each corner and a moat surrounded the stockade, which occupied about one city block. "Some sort of structure for mass" was built that later became Ste. Anne's Church. (Today, Ste. Anne's is the nation's second oldest continuously operated Catholic parish, although Ste. Anne's Church on Mackinac Island, which moved from St. Ignace in 1780, takes exception to that claim.) The stockade had two gates and one street, and the houses (on 25 foot square lots) were constructed by placing logs vertically—a poor decision that was later reversed (by placing them horizontally). Houses were "only tall enough to just permit standing inside," floors were hard-packed earth, doors were propped up because there were no hinges, and since there was no glass, square open holes covered in thinly scraped skins served as windows. "All of this is no easy task," Cadillac wrote, "as everything has to be carried on the shoulders, for we have no oxen or horses yet to draw loads, nor to plough, and to accomplish it, it is necessary to be very active." Cadillac named the settlement Pontchartrain du Détroit, after Count Pontchartrain, the French minister of colonies.[29]

A proud Cadillac expressed joy with his new settlement: "The banks [of the river] are so many vast meadows where the freshness of those beautiful streams keep the grass always green. These same meadows are fringed with long and broad avenues of fruit trees which have never felt the careful hand of the watchful gardener." Besides an ample variety of game ("wood rats as big as rabbits") and a "bountiful supply" of fish, the area's trees were "as straight as arrows [and] of enormous size and height." Cadillac concluded a few months after arriving at Detroit, "Can it be thought that a land in which nature has distributed everything in so complete a manner could refuse to the hand of a careful husbandman who breaks into its fertile depths, the return which is expected of it?" The following year he added, "This country, so temperate, so fertile, and so beautiful that it may be called the earthly paradise of North America, deserves all the care of the King to keep it up and to attract habitants to it, so that a solid settlement may be formed there which shall not be liable to the usual vicissitudes of the other posts in which only a mere garrison is placed."[30]

To convince Native Americans and other Frenchmen that Detroit was permanent—not just another fur-trading settlement—Cadillac asked his wife to join him. Marie Therese Cadillac left Montreal in a canoe, ignoring the advice from friends that she not enter the Michigan wilderness. The 31-year-old mother of seven children responded, "Do not waste your pity on me. . . . I know the hardships of the journey, the isolation of the life to which I am going; yet I am eager to go for a woman who totally loves her husband has no stronger attachment than his company; wherever he may be." Madame Cadillac arrived at the fort in October with her thirteen-year-old son and Marie-Anne Picote de Bellestre, the wife of Cadillac's second in command. When Madame Cadillac stepped ashore at Detroit, Indian women expressed surprise. According to her husband, the Indians kissed the women's hands and "wept for joy, saying that French women had never been seen coming willingly to their country." During the years that Madame Cadillac lived at Detroit, she gave birth to six more children.[31]

Detroit quickly became an important fur-trading center as Huron, Odawa, Potawatomi, and Miami built camps near the fort. To attract French settlers to Detroit, Cadillac issued land grants to the *habitants,* as the French settlers were known. These "ribbon farms" (so-called because they were only several hundred feet wide) extended inland from the river up to three miles each, giving all landowners river frontage. The *habitants* also paid Cadillac an annual fee and worked on his farm.[32]

Despite being an effective administrator, Cadillac suffered growing attacks on his character and leadership. Government officials criticized him for showing "too much greed" with his fur-trading activities. Comte de Pontchartrain, chancellor of France and Cadillac's longtime supporter, questioned if he was making profits "using just and legal means." Besides angering the Jesuits by giving the Indians brandy for furs, Cadillac further upset the missionaries by encouraging marriages between the *habitants* and Native Americans. (He argued it was "absolutely necessary" to allow Frenchmen to marry the Indian women because "marriages of this kind will strengthen the friendship of these tribes.") One 1707 report called Cadillac a tyrant, his colony "very burdensome to the colony of Canada," and his fort "so small and of such extraordinary shape as to be irrecognizable." Even a disillusioned Governor Frontenac added, Cadillac "is so much in the habit of stating what is untrue that it is almost impossible for him to write otherwise."[33]

Some of Cadillac's problems stemmed in part from falsehoods of his own creation. His claim of noble birth was deceptive. He was a commoner, and his father had been a "lowly local judge." His coat of arms was phony; even his name was part of his "aristocratic charade." His real name was Antoine Laumet. Later-day historians contended that Cadillac was "one of the worst scoundrels ever to set foot in New France" and "an impudent liar" and "a cunning adventurer in search of personal enrichment." One critic explained that Cadillac's image, what he called the "Cadillac myth," can be explained because Detroiters chose to see their city's founder as a great man. He added that Cadillac's voluminous correspondence "can create the impression that he was a visionary who was forced to struggle against less-gifted men." Cadillac did have defenders. Detroit historian Clarence Burton asserted that the founder of Detroit was a great man and that "men of positive natures invariably make enemies." Canadian historian Agnes C. Laut claimed Cadillac "retired with a clean record after having seen every one of his plans 'frustrated by knaves, fools, incompetents.'" However, as the negative reports mounted—and Detroit did not grow (its French population stood at a paltry 62 Frenchmen in 1708)—Cadillac had to go. In 1710, Pontchartrain reappointed Cadillac governor of the Louisiana Territory and transferred him to present-day Mobile, Alabama.[34]

As the eighteenth century unfolded, the French returned to the Straits of Mackinac, building Fort Michilimackinac (1715), and to the St. Joseph River by reoccupying Fort St. Joseph (1719–20). In 1750, the French reestablished a post at Sault Ste. Marie. However, during the French period, the total French population of all of these settlements, including Detroit, never exceeded 1,500 people. This peaceful existence changed when the colonial struggles between France and Great Britain heated up. By the late 1740s, British colonists began moving into Ohio, which led to war. No battles were fought in Michigan; however, Michigan Indians and Frenchmen played an important role in a conflict that determined the area's future.[35]

—— A Decisive War

The French and Indian War began informally in June 1752 when a force of Odawa and Ojibwa, led by Charles-Michel Mouet de Langlade, destroyed a pro-British Indian settlement at Pickawillany in western Ohio. The child of the marriage of a Frenchman and an Odawa woman, Langlade was born at Mackinac in 1729. He was educated in Montreal, possessed military talents, and inspired the Indians. Langlade's decision to attack "the richest British trading post west of the Appalachians" drove some British traders back east and allowed him to return to Detroit with "a vast quantity of booty." However, his success only temporarily delayed the coming war.[36]

Full-scale warfare began two years later over disputed land claims in the Ohio River Valley. On May 28, 1754, an ambitious 22-year-old Virginian officer ordered his men to fire on a smaller force of French soldiers in the wilderness of western Pennsylvania. The larger American force, led by Lt. Colonel George Washington, had arrived in the vicinity of the Allegheny and Monongahela rivers to protest French efforts to build Fort Duquesne (present-day Pittsburgh, Pennsylvania), which was designed to stop American colonists from moving west. The commandant of the French force, Ensign Joseph Coulon de Villiers de Jumonville, who had grown up at Fort St. Joseph, was murdered in cold blood after surrendering. Captain Louis Coulon de Villiers, who was at Fort Duquesne, avenged his brother's death by attacking Washington's men. After an all-day battle, the Virginians surrendered. Washington and his men returned home, but only after he signed a surrender document admitting they had wrongly invaded French territory and "assassinated" Joseph Villiers. (Washington later claimed being misled by the interpreter, who translated the surrender document that was written in French.)[37]

Elsewhere, Langlade continued to distinguish himself on the field of battle, suggesting the tactics used to humiliate British General Edward Braddock's force in 1755, defeating Major Robert Rogers at Lake Champlain in 1757, and assisting in the capture of Fort William Henry in New York. Langlade also was at the Battle of Quebec in 1775, where two of his brothers died. But the surrender of the French stronghold in September 1759—the first in a series of setbacks—marked a turning point in the war that signaled an end to French rule in the Great Lakes.[38]

CHAPTER

3

The British Take Control

The British, who arrived in Detroit during the fall of 1760, remained in Michigan for 35 years.

"Drive off your lands those dogs clothed in red, who will do you nothing but harm."

—*Odawa leader Pontiac to his followers*

As the French and Indian War ended in North America, the British moved quickly to consolidate their gains in Canada. During the late summer of 1760, Major Robert Rogers received orders to take possession of Detroit. In the recent war, the 29-year-old New Hampshire native, who commanded a battalion of Americans known as Rogers' Rangers, had "outwitted and out-fought the Indians at every engagement and struck respectful fear in the hearts of French regulars and militia."[1]

Rogers and 200 Rangers left Montreal in mid-September, joining up with Captain Donald Campbell and a company of Royal Americans at Fort Pitt. Accompanying Rogers was Indian agent George Croghan, who sent Indian messengers ahead to inform the Indians that the British were coming. Earlier that year, Croghan had convinced Detroit-area Indians that the British would provide rivers of rum and cheap trade goods to undermine their traditional alliance with the French. Harsh weather slowed the Rangers' progress, but on November 29, Rogers and about 275 troops landed at Fort Pontchartrain. Enlarged three times during the 1750s, the fort, which had a circumference of 1,200 yards, was in good condition. Captain Campbell described it as "very large," with wooden pickets that stood twelve to fifteen feet tall and enclosing 80 houses and shops, a barracks, and Ste. Anne's Catholic Church. Unfortunately, the fort tilted down toward the river, which allowed a person standing on the opposite side of the river to see into the fort, compromising its security.[2]

Following an exchange of courtesies with the fort's French commander, Rogers took Detroit's surrender. The Royal Americans, dressed in their distinctive red coats and blue pants (quite a contrast with the Rangers' green buckskins and green Scotch caps), marched into the fort with drums beating. As the French Fleur-de-lis was lowered and the British Union flag was raised, several hundred Indians outside the fort yelled expressions of approval, while the more subdued local residents took an oath of allegiance to the British crown en masse. Under guard, the French garrison went to Fort Pitt (present-day Pittsburgh) where they were exchanged. Major Rogers headed to Fort Michilimackinac to take command of that French fort but was turned back

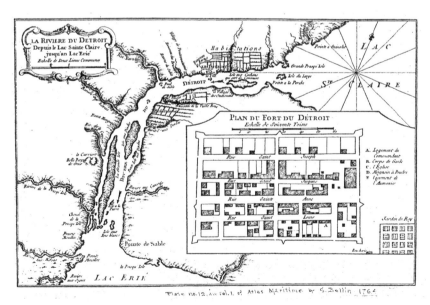

This French survey from the 1750s shows the French settlements on the Detroit River before the British assumed control of Michigan.

by ice in Lake Huron. He returned to Fort Pitt, leaving Captain Campbell in command of Fort Detroit.[3]

More than 150 years of French rule in Michigan had ended.

In a short time, the British soldiers and Detroit's French population developed a cordial relationship. A French-speaking Scotsman who had come to America with the British army in 1756, Campbell socialized with the *habitants*. Despite being described by one fellow officer as "fat and unwieldy," Campbell "was an alert and competent commander." He spoke French, a distinct advantage, and he earned the friendship of the local citizens, including the Indians. He held weekly Sunday night card games with members of both sexes, which led him to conclude that, "the women surpass our expectations." However, Campbell was concerned with the Indians' demands.[4]

During the French and Indian War, the British provided the Indians with abundant gifts, unlimited quantities of rum, and grandiose promises. With the war over, British policy changed dramatically. According to General Jeffrey Amherst, the British commandant in North America, offering gifts to the Indians was bribery. As a result, the British stopped giving the Indians gunpowder, lead, and rum. Furthermore, British efforts to regulate the fur trade led to chaos and fraud as the British forced the Indians to exchange pelts at the forts—a major change from French practices. Finally, dishonest British traders distributed shoddy goods to the Indians at high prices. At a time that called for the utmost tact and diplomacy, Amherst "insisted on economy and discipline."[5]

Indian frustration and distrust with the British turned to disgust, then hatred. During the summer of 1761, representatives from the New York–based Seneca arrived in Detroit intent on promoting a war against the British. However, the Great Lakes Indians remained unconvinced. When Captain Campbell discovered the Seneca's intentions, he threatened, "If they proceed in their Designs against the English it will terminate in their utter Ruin and Destruction." The Seneca plot, which fell apart, caused little concern for General Jeffrey Amherst, who claimed he "never" feared an uprising. Back in New York, the 44-year-old battle-hardened Amherst believed the Indians lacked the ability to undertake "anything serious." More important, he expressed confidence that he had the power "not only to frustrate them, but to punish the Delinquents with Entire Destruction."[6]

Not all British leaders shared Amherst's confidence. In September 1761, Sir William Johnson, Britain's most respected Indian agent, traveled to Detroit to discuss matters with the natives. After a week of socializing, Johnson gathered with representatives from an assortment of nations (Odawa, Huron,

Potawatomi, Ojibwa, Miami, Shawnee, and Delaware). Complimenting the Indians on their friendly behavior toward the British, Johnson claimed they were now subjects of the British king, who cared for them and their welfare. He reassured them their land was safe and that the British would only take land "to which they have lawful claim." At the same time, Johnson received a communiqué from General Amherst reminding him "to avoid all presents in the future." That included ammunition, since "nothing can be so impolitic as to furnish them the means of accomplishing evil which is so much dreaded." Johnson did not share Amherst's new policy with the Indians, which may explain their response to Johnson's comments. One Odawa leader noted his people had begun to see the British as friends. Certainly, Johnson was pleased, reassuring Amherst that the Indians were "extremely well Disposed towards the English [and] unless greatly Irritated thereto they will never break the Peace Established."[7]

During the fall of 1761, British troops occupied the abandoned French forts at Michilimackinac, La Baye (present-day Green Bay and renamed Edward Augustus), and St. Joseph (present-day Niles). The winter was peaceful, but Captain Campbell expressed an uneasiness: "Every thing is now quiet, tho I am certain if the Indians knew General Amherst's sentiments about keeping them short of powder it would be impossible to keep them in temper."[8]

—— Relations Deteriorate

Campbell's fears were realized as the Indians came to understand Amherst's policy. As they returned from a winter of hunting, they found no rum to celebrate the hunt and no ammunition to shoot game to feed their families. This had never happened under French rule. Equally as important, Spain's decision to enter the ongoing war on the French side led to rumors that the French might return to the Great Lakes. By July, Campbell worried that the Indians "only want a good opportunity to fall upon us if they had the encouragement from an enemy." A few months later, Indian agent George Croghan confirmed those suspicions when he told Sir Johnson the western tribes believed the British were making plans to annihilate them: "They had great expectations of being very generally supplied by us, and from their poverty and mercenary disposition they can't bear such a disappointment." Croghan hoped Amherst's restrictive policies "may have its desired effect." But he added, the Indians "are a rash, inconsistent people and inclined to mischief and will never consider the consequences, though it may end in their ruin." Despite these forewarnings, Amherst remained unconcerned. He concluded in late October 1762, "I cannot think the Indians are so blind to their own Interest as to attempt any mischief." At the same time, he ordered Major Henry Gladwin to return to Detroit and take command. A skilled and competent officer who had seen action (including Braddock's disaster), Gladwin became Detroit's "greatest resource . . . a block of granite." Amherst also sent new commanders to Michilimackinac and Sault Ste. Marie.[9]

By the spring of 1763, the situation worsened for the Indians. Besides denying them gunpowder and rum, the British charged the Indians high prices and showed their contempt toward the natives, who were unwelcome at the forts. As this list of grievances grew, a Delaware Indian in the Ohio Valley urged Indians to free themselves of vices caused by their relationship with Europeans. The Prophet, as this evangelist was called, "decried the baneful influence of all white men because it had brought the Indians to their present unhappy plight." One Indian leader who listened carefully to the Prophet's teachings was Pontiac. Although no image of him exists, contemporaries described the Odawa chief in his early forties as "a man of medium stature, very well formed and strong," possessing a personality that was "commanding and imperious," "absolute and peremptory" and "proud, vindictive, war-like and easily offended."[10]

In the meantime, Gladwin received word that hostilities between France and Great Britain had ended. Indians expressed disappointment when they received the news, but Gladwin believed if he gave the Indian chiefs a few medals as rewards for their help in defeating the French "they would be satisfied." In late April, Gladwin informed Amherst, the Indians "say We mean to make Slaves of them, by Taking so many Posts in their country, and that they had better Attempt Something now to Recover their Liberty, than Wait till We are better Established."[11]

Several days after Gladwin penned that letter, Pontiac called a war council at the mouth of the Ecorse River, about ten miles south of the fort. A *habitant* who attended the council, and later recounted the event, claimed the forceful Odawa leader "spoke with so much eloquence that his narrative had just the effect upon them that he desired." Pontiac reviewed the Prophet's message on the negative influence of white men, wisely exempting the French from this argument. Pontiac told his followers to "drive off your lands those dogs clothed in red, who will do you nothing but harm." Several hundred Indians who listened enthusiastically "were all ready to do what he demanded of them."[12]

A few days after the meeting, Pontiac and about fifty warriors appeared before the fort's gates. After being allowed into the stockade, most of the Indians performed a ceremonial dance. As the dancers distracted the British soldiers, other Indians made careful observations of the fort's inner defenses. When the dancing ended, Pontiac and his followers left, promising to return a few days later "in greater numbers." The next day, Pontiac sent runners to the nearby Potawatomi and Huron villages, urging them to attend another war council. On the appointed day, the Indians gathered at the Potawatomi camp about two miles south of the fort. Pontiac implored his listeners to "exterminate from our lands this nation which seeks only to destroy us." Listing all the well-known grievances against the British, he urged, "We must all swear their destruction and wait no longer. Nothing prevents us; they are few in numbers, and we can accomplish it." Reminding his listeners that Indians all across the frontier would attack other British posts, he predicted that, once defeated, the English "may never come again upon our lands." Pontiac explained he would request a meeting with Major Gladwin. Once the Indians were inside the fort, the signal to attack the unsuspecting Redcoats would come when Pontiac turned over a wampum belt (a beaded belt that was green on one side and white on the other). At the same time, the Huron and Potawatomi would attack Englishmen outside the fort. The real question was, could the plan be kept a secret?[13]

—— Pontiac's Rebellion

At about 10:00 AM on May 7, 1763, Pontiac and some fifty warriors appeared before the fort's gates. Trailing behind this vanguard were another 250 Ojibwa, each carrying a concealed weapon. The Indians entered the fort without incident. Much to Pontiac's surprise, Gladwin's men stood armed and ready. The fort's guard had been doubled and soldiers not on guard duty were drawn up under arms. It was no understatement when Pontiac told Gladwin, "We are greatly surprised, brother, at this unusual step thou hast taken, to have all the soldiers under arms." Gladwin dismissed Pontiac's concern by claiming that other Indians were visiting that day and he wanted "to have the garrison under arms when they came. Fearing that these strangers might be affronted by such a reception, he had resolved to begin the custom with his greatest friends, the Ottawa." Pontiac recognized the ruse, but could say nothing—nor could he turn over the belt and spring his trap. Instead, the Indians left the fort. Younger warriors criticized Pontiac for failing to give the signal to attack, but the Indian leader vowed he was not yet defeated. How had Gladwin learned of Pontiac's plan? Theories abound, and according to one writer, historians have maintained "a cottage industry" to determine how Gladwin learned of Pontiac's plan. In one case, the existence of a Christian Indian or a sympathetic *habitant* whose British lover lived in the fort may explain how Gladwin learned of the plan.[14]

The next day, Pontiac returned to the fort, presented Gladwin with a calumet and proposed smoking this "peace" pipe. Gladwin agreed. But when Pontiac and 65 canoes of his followers arrived the next day, Gladwin only allowed small groups of Indians into the fort. An enraged Pontiac returned his followers to their camp and ordered his men to attack Englishmen living outside the fort. After a week of death and destruction that left fifteen English dead and an equal number prisoner, Pontiac proposed a ceasefire. Gladwin agreed, sending Captain Campbell and another British officer to accompany a small delegation of *habitants* to a nearby home to discuss Pontiac's terms. Suddenly, the Indian leader changed his mind and the two officers became hostages. Gladwin refused to meet with Pontiac until his officers were released.[15]

The Indian uprising that began in Detroit soon spread across the frontier. The attack on Michilimackinac was spectacular. On June 2, 1763, Captain George Etherington and about forty soldiers watched as the Indians distracted the Redcoats by engaging in a game of lacrosse in front of the fort. Etherington ignored advice from a trader that he should be wary of the Indians. The fort's gates were left open and the unsuspecting soldiers watched the game unfold. Several times the ball flew over the fort's walls and each time it was retrieved. But on one occasion, the Indians grabbed tomahawks, knives, and clubs that had been concealed by the women watching the game. In a matter of minutes, the fort fell. A British trader who hid as the events unfolded wrote many years later, "I beheld, in shapes the foulest and most horrible, the ferocious triumphs of barbarian conquerors. The dead were scalped and mangled, the dying were writhing and shrieking under the unsatiated knife and tomahawk; and from the bodies of some, ripped open, their butchers were drinking the blood, scooped in the hollow of joined hands and quaffed amid shouts of rage and victory." Etherington and 13 of his men survived the attack, but another 21 men died. A few days later, Fort St. Joseph fell just as quickly, when 100 Potawatomi overwhelmed the fort's much smaller garrison. Most of the garrison was killed, although its commandant was taken prisoner. By early summer, only forts at Detroit, Niagara, and Pitt remained in British hands.[16]

Back in Detroit, Gladwin continued to frustrate Pontiac—at one point boldly suggesting the Indians quit shooting at the fort and save their gunpowder for hunting. But the British had many problems. Gladwin commanded fewer than 140 men; Pontiac's followers totaled as many as 1,000 warriors. Despite never losing complete control of the waterways and periodically receiving supplies from the east, the British suffered from a constant shortage of supplies. Gladwin also worried about flaming arrows being fired into his wooden stockade.[17]

On the foggy morning of July 28, 1763, a 250-men British force led by Captain James Dalyell rowed their 22 canoes up to the fort's dock. The young officer, one of General Amherst's aides, rested his men for two days, then proposed a surprise attack on Pontiac's camp. The experienced Gladwin argued against the attack, but the overconfident and rash Dalyell ignored the suggestion. He shared "Amherst's contempt for indians as intelligent fighters" and predicted that Pontiac—once he heard about the arrival of reinforcements— "would abandon the siege and slink away into the forest before the young officer had an opportunity to win glory by drubbing him in battle." At 2:30 AM on July 31, Dalyell's force quietly moved out of the fort. Pontiac ambushed Dalyell's command about two miles from the fort. In a matter of minutes, Dalyell and nineteen Redcoats were killed; their blood ran into the nearby creek that became known as "Bloody Run."[18]

Throughout the rest of the summer, the Indians harassed the fort but made no direct assaults. By autumn, the siege began falling apart as Pontiac's followers deserted him to gather provisions for the upcoming winter. The Indians also learned that the French and Indian War had ended and that the French were not coming back to Michigan. In late October, Pontiac made one last appeal to his followers, but to no avail. A dejected Pontiac dictated a note to Gladwin that when translated read, "All my young men have buried their hatchets. I think you will forget the bad times which have taken place for some times past. Likewise I shall forget what you may have done to me, in order to think of nothing but good." The translation ended with Pontiac wishing Gladwin "a good day."[19]

Pontiac's Rebellion, "the most formidable Indian uprising in American history," ended with a whimper. Having lost credibility with his own people, Pontiac left Detroit for Illinois. Six years later, an Indian assassin murdered the aging Odawa leader. His remains were buried in St. Louis, although the exact location is unknown. As Pontiac headed west for his self-imposed exile, Major Gladwin was equally ready to leave Detroit. Tired of the wilderness, the battle-hardened veteran declared shortly after the siege ended, "I hope I shall be relieved soon, if not, I intend to quit the service for I would not choose to be any longer exposed to villany and treachery of the settlement & Indians." Gladwin got his wish. When reinforcements arrived in August 1764, he returned to England, left the army, and led the life of a country gentleman.[20]

—— The American Revolution

After Pontiac's Rebellion, the British continued to struggle to govern the western territories. They did not re-garrison the posts at Sault Ste. Marie and St. Joseph but returned to Michilimackinac. More important, the British wanted to keep the Indians at peace and cut costs after years of expensive warfare. To accomplish these goals, the British issued the Proclamation of 1763, requiring colonists to remain east of the Appalachian Mountains. The Ohio River Valley also was placed under British military control, which called into question colonial land claims. The Proclamation obligated Americans to pay taxes to maintain the troops in the west but denied them the right to move west. Americans were angered when the British issued the Quebec Act of 1774, which extended Canada's southern boundary to the Ohio River and eliminated colonial land claims in the west. This act, which also granted religious freedom to Canada's French Catholics, so irritated Americans they cited it in the Declaration of Independence as proof of King George's tyranny.[21]

Michigan saw no fighting during the American Revolution. However, Detroit, a settlement then of about 1,500 people, was the center of British power on the frontier. Besides the all-important fur trade that passed through Detroit and Michilimackinac, it served as the headquarters of the British Indian Department, the supply base for outposts further west, and the site where the British distributed presents and gunpowder to the Indians. Detroit "was the great war emporium of the West" where the British organized raids that inflicted death and destruction on Americans living along the Ohio River.[22]

The architect of the British effort was Henry Hamilton. A native of Ireland, Hamilton had served with distinction in the British army during the French and Indian War. On November 9, 1775, the 41-year-old Hamilton arrived in Detroit after a hazardous journey by canoe from Montreal. During part of the trip, the new lieutenant governor disguised himself as a Canadian peasant to avoid capture. Hamilton quickly got to work. "With presents, threats, and flattery," [he] "stirred up the Indians to let loose their fury upon the unprotected [American] settlements of the frontier."[23]

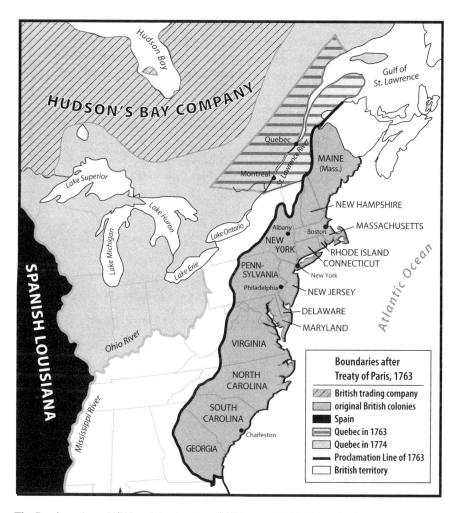

The Proclamation of 1763 and Quebec Act of 1774 outraged British colonists.

The Ojibwa, Odawa, Wyandot, Shawnee, and Delaware hated the Americans, but keeping thousands of Indians loyal to the British crown proved challenging. Hamilton often met with them, explaining how the British understood their concerns. In mid-June 1777, he held a two-day council with chiefs from several tribes, even joining the Indians in a war dance and singing war songs. Most important, Hamilton distributed presents, including rum, to maintain the Indians' loyalty. In mid-1777, he reported that fifteen war parties, totaling more than 300 Indians and British rangers, had left

Detroit to wreak havoc on American settlements. Throughout the Revolution, the Indians brought plenty of prisoners and scalps to Detroit. Hamilton, who ordered hundreds of scalping knives for the Indians, boasted about doing everything in his power to crush the rebellion. In the process, he earned the nickname "hair buyer" because he supposedly paid for scalps. Hamilton was not alone paying for scalps, and 1777 was known simply as the "bloody sevens."[24]

Detroit also served as a British prisoner camp. In March 1779, the British incarcerated 500 Americans there. Late in the Revolution, the British returned

From his base in Detroit, Henry Hamilton orchestrated British attacks on Americans.

to Detroit with 350 Kentucky prisoners. The fame of one American prisoner preceded his arrival. Already a legend for exploring and settling the American frontier, Daniel Boone helped cut a trail through the wilderness to Kentucky. Along the Wilderness Road, he founded Boonesborough, a favorite resting place for travelers. Admiration for Boone led the Indians to bring him to Detroit shortly after his capture in early 1778. Like his Indian allies, Governor Hamilton was impressed with Boone and even tried to buy the frontiersman. The Indians refused, but Hamilton gave Boone a horse, a saddle, blankets, clothing, and silver trinkets to trade with the Indians. After spending ten days in Detroit, Boone and his captors journeyed to Ohio where he later escaped.[25]

—— Hamilton vs. Clark

The Americans were aware of Hamilton's activities, and on several occasions the Continental Congress discussed a campaign to capture Detroit. These efforts came to naught, usually because of a lack of funding. But the growing stories about the "hair buyer" led one American to act. George Rogers Clark, a Virginia surveyor who moved to Kentucky during the early 1770s, possessed a natural talent to command men. During the summer of 1778, Clark led a small army that captured several British frontier forts, most notably Fort Sackville at Vincennes (in present-day Indiana). Clark's success shocked the British, prompting Hamilton, who feared Detroit would become an American objective, to lead a force of regulars, Detroit militia, and Indians to Vincennes. Since Clark had left the area, Hamilton easily recaptured Fort Sackville. While at Vincennes, Hamilton planned the conquest of Kaskaskia (in Illinois) and ordered forces from Michilimackinac (to be led by Charles Langlade) and St. Joseph to join him. In the meantime, Hamilton sent most of his militia back to Detroit, while his Indian allies returned to their villages.[26]

When Clark learned Hamilton was at Fort Sackville, he vowed to recapture it. As he later wrote, "The enemy could not suppose that we would be so mad" to march 180 miles through "a drowned country in the depth of winter." Leaving St. Louis, Clark's small army traveled through the midwinter's snows and rain—sometimes wading through icy water up to their shoulders. Eighteen days later, the Americans reached Vincennes. Provided with dry clothes and food by local residents, Clark duped Hamilton into thinking he was badly outnumbered and forced the British commander to surrender Fort Sackville on February 25, 1779. Hamilton languished in a Virginia prison for two years before being released. He never returned to Detroit, but continued serving the British empire until his death in 1796. As for Hamilton's men, Clark gave them an oath of neutrality, provided them with boats, arms, and provisions, and sent them back to Detroit: "This act of magnanimity was calculated to aid the American cause, and it did." In the following months, Clark claimed he had spies in Detroit who "answered every purpose that [he] could have wished for by prejudicing their friends in favor of America."[27]

Clark's victory at Vincennes led many Indians to declare their neutrality. In June 1779, the British held an Indian council at Detroit, but to no avail, as the Odawa, Ojibwa, and Potawatomi indicated their intent to make peace with the Americans. Clark's success also led the British to strengthen their forts at the Straits of Mackinac and Detroit. In 1779, Major Patrick Sinclair, commandant at Michilimackinac, worried that his fort at the northern tip of the Lower Peninsula could not withstand an American attack. Sinclair chose nearby Mackinac Island to build a new fort, believing the island's high limestone bluffs and deep harbor to be a perfect location. After buying the island from the Ojibwa for a dozen canoes loaded with goods and merchandise, Sinclair and his men dismantled the mainland fort and shipped it to the island. They then burned what remained of Michilimackinac in mid-1781.[28]

George Rogers Clark captured Fort Sackville in present-day Indiana.

Back at Detroit, Captain Richard Berringer Lernoult, a long-time veteran of the British army, replaced Hamilton and realized the settlement needed a new fort. The old French fort was in disrepair, while the nearby higher ground compromised its defensive position. Completed in the spring of 1779, Fort Lernoult was designed to survive an attack "by a properly equipped army." The fort's earthen ramparts were 26 feet thick at their base and narrowed to twelve feet wide at the top. They stood eleven feet high with sharpened stakes (called pickets) placed along the exterior walls. Outside the ramparts ran a wide deep ditch, while the land surrounding the fort was cleared to provide a good field of fire. Inside the fort, a deep well for fresh water was dug and plenty of cannon were mounted. After learning about the fort, George Rogers Clark sent Lernoult a sarcastic note thanking him for building the fort "as it saves the Americans some expences (*sic*) in building" one. Although rumors spread across the frontier about Clark leading a well-armed American army northward, these reports were unfounded and the Americans never attacked Detroit. Clark later complained he "lost Detroit for want of a few men!" The British garrison on Mackinac Island also waited in vain since the Americans never attempted to attack the island fort.[29]

Although many Indians had taken themselves out of the fight, some still aided the British cause. The last significant battle of the American Revolution, fought at Blue Licks, Kentucky, was a decisive British victory. On August 19, 1782, a force of Great Lakes Indians led by Captain William Caldwell, who operated out of Detroit, won a lopsided, fifteen-minute battle that left more than 70 Kentuckians dead. The British lost seven men. Although the battle played no role in the on-going negotiations to settle the Revolution, the victorious British commander settled in the Detroit area after the Revolution. Caldwell engaged in commercial activities in Detroit and periodically resumed his military career. He saw limited service at the Battle of Fallen Timbers in August 1794 and at the Battle of the Thames in October 1813. Following the War of 1812, Caldwell returned to his Detroit River home near Amherstburg, Ontario.[30]

—— Four Flags over Niles

One of the Revolution's more intriguing events occurred eighteen months earlier in February 1781, when a small Spanish raiding party captured Fort St. Joseph at present-day Niles. Responding to ongoing fears of a British attack on Spanish-held St. Louis, a Spanish/Indian force marched 400 miles from St. Louis, suffering from winter's cold and hunger. The Spaniards, now allied with the Americans, easily captured the virtually undefended outpost. The attackers spent one day there before returning west. Their presence provided future settlers an opportunity to boast Niles was "the city of four flags" (French, British, Spanish, and American). More important, the Spanish later offered this action as proof that the Ohio River Valley might be annexed to someone other than the Americans.[31]

Borders were central to the discussions settling the American Revolution. American commissioners were adamant that the nation's western boundary be the Mississippi River. The French and Spanish disagreed, both hoping (for different reasons) to keep the Americans between the Atlantic Ocean and the Alleghenies. The British sided with the Americans, preferring to have the United States control the land between the Mississippi River and the Appalachians rather than a rival European power. Another key issue was the boundary between the United States and Canada. Two options were discussed: one, to extend the 45th parallel from the St. Lawrence River, placing Michigan's northern Lower Peninsula and the Upper Peninsula in Canada, while southern Ontario would be included in the United States. A second option divided the border along the Great Lakes. The Americans preferred the latter and the British "raised few, if any, real objections," since they were more concerned about "the subject of the loyalists, the payment of debts, and the fisheries." This proposal also allowed both countries to use the Great Lakes. Both decisions proved fortuitous for Michigan's future. One last element that often intrigues is why the newly established international boundary placed Isle Royale, which lies closer to Ontario than the United States in western Lake Superior, in the United States. In the 1780s, it was believed that Isle Royale was more centrally located in Lake Superior and would have naturally fallen into American waters.[32]

The Treaty of Paris that formally ended the American Revolution on September 3, 1783, called for the British to evacuate the western posts "with all convenient speed." It took them thirteen years. The British delayed their departure because they were protecting the fur trade and its important centers of Detroit and Mackinac. The British also encouraged the Indians to resist American efforts to settle the Ohio Valley. During those years, the U.S. government protested the British presence, but to little effect. Besides keeping troops at Detroit and Mackinac, the British developed the local government, even sending Detroiters to the polls in 1792 where they elected three delegates to the Upper Canada (present-day Ontario) provisional assembly.[33]

—— Governing in Absentia

Despite the British presence on American soil, the U.S. government adopted two policies that had a major impact on the future development of Michigan and the United States. After convincing several of the original thirteen states to abandon their western land claims, the Congress passed the Land Ordinance of 1785, establishing a system to survey all of the lands, setting up townships six miles square, and introducing a uniform numbering system. Land sold for one dollar an acre and buyers had to purchase at least 640 acres (later reduced to 80 acres). Considered one of the most important laws in American history, the ordinance guaranteed an orderly distribution of land. The Northwest Ordinance of 1787 established the Northwest Territory and divided it into future states (no fewer than three and no more than five). The ordinance introduced a governing system that expanded as more people moved into the territory. A territory began with a governor, secretary, and three justices—all appointed by the president. As its population increased, it added a legislative body, and when it had 60,000 people, it could apply to

Congress for statehood. The Northwest Ordinance guaranteed future states would enter the Union as equals with the original thirteen states. Eventually, five states were formed in the Northwest Territory: Ohio (1803), Indiana (1816), Illinois (1819), Michigan (1837), and Wisconsin (1846). The ordinance also prohibited the practice of human slavery in the territory at a time when slavery was practiced throughout most of the United States. But before any new states were created in the Northwest Territory, the Americans had to force the British to cross the border into Canada.[34]

Besides encouraging the Indians to resist the ever-growing flood of white settlers heading into the Ohio River Valley, the British grew bolder by proposing an independent Indian nation between the Ohio River and the Great Lakes. At the same time, they saw the Indians as a "trifling, expendable commodity." All this resulted in a bloody, undeclared war in Ohio between whites and natives. As the frontier grew increasingly unstable and bloody, a desperate American government looked to its army. It was not a reassuring sight. The U.S. Army, which in 1789 mustered only a few hundred soldiers, suffered from poor discipline, low morale, drunkenness, and inferior equipment. Despite these handicaps, President George Washington ordered the army to subdue the Indians and get the British off American soil.[35]

The first effort, an October 1790 campaign in western Ohio, was a disaster as the Americans fled after encountering the Indians. Washington then turned to Arthur St. Clair, the 55-year-old governor of the Northwest Territory. The president cautioned St. Clair, a veteran of the American Revolution, to "beware of surprises." In September 1791, the former major general boasted of the "utter destruction" of his foes, as he led an untrained force of regulars and militia north from Cincinnati. Despite inadequate

Five states were carved out of the Northwest Territory.

supplies and worsening weather—compounded by his refusal to take proper defensive measures or conduct adequate reconnaissance—St. Clair declared his army seemed "to be in perfectly good disposition for battle." Rarely has an American commander been more wrong. On November 4, 1791, the Indians attacked and in a matter of moments, the Americans were left "a frightened rabble." St. Clair's command of 1,400 men suffered massive casualties—including more than 600 dead—in one of the worst defeats the U.S. Army ever suffered at the hands of the Indians.[36]

—— Wayne to the Rescue

A frustrated President Washington, who described St. Clair "as worse than a murderer," appointed Anthony Wayne commander of the U.S. Army. A Revolution veteran who had earned the nickname "mad" because of his battlefield impetuosity, the 47-year-old Wayne impressed the British ambassador to the United States, who believed he was "unquestionably the most active, vigilant, and enterprizing [sic] Officer in the American Service." More recently, a sympathetic biographer concluded that Wayne would "win by finesse or by brute force, by deception or by direct assault, but eventually he would find a way to persevere until the object was at hand." Yet Wayne had his detractors, including Washington. Despite his brilliance during the Revolution, Wayne had earned a postwar reputation of being a drunkard and fiscally irresponsible. Wayne was not the president's first choice to replace St. Clair, but he turned out to be a fortunate one.[37]

Wayne reorganized the army near Pittsburgh and introduced demanding training and discipline into what he called the Legion of the United States. He also improved conditions among the soldiers, which instilled *esprit de corps*. In May 1793, when the Legion shifted its operations to Cincinnati, Wayne was confident that his men possessed the ability to accomplish its mission. In late spring of 1794, the Legion marched north, and Wayne carried orders authorizing him to "dislodge" the British who had occupied an abandoned French fort near present-day Maumee, Ohio. American intelligence reported that the British garrison stood at 400 Redcoats and 2,000 Indians at Fort Miami, with an additional 1,500 militiamen at nearby Detroit. Although those numbers were highly inflated, Wayne faced a formidable challenge.[38]

On several occasions, Wayne held out an olive branch to the Indians, which they rejected as the British supplied arms, ammunition, and words of encouragement. Despite suffering a setback on June 30 when the Indians attacked the American camp leaving 100 soldiers dead, Wayne continued advancing eastward along the north bank of the Maumee River. Reinforced by Kentucky volunteers, the 2,000-man Legion positioned itself between the Indians and the British at Fort Miami. From this position the Americans boasted they could challenge "the English, Indians, and all the devils in hell." Wayne again offered to negotiate. This time, some Indians argued they should avoid a fight; others disagreed. But it was too late. At about 9:00 AM on August 20, Wayne's men confronted a force of 1,000 Indians near present-day Maumee, Ohio. The Battle of Fallen Timbers (fought in an area where a recent tornado had knocked down many trees, which gave it the name) lasted only an hour, and Wayne performed superbly, directing his troops where the fighting was the heaviest. According to one Indian, "We were driven by the sharp ends of the guns of the Long Knives." Wayne's losses were 33 dead and 100 wounded. The soldiers counted 44 Indian dead but believed that the Indians carried away some of their dead and wounded. The victor boasted the Indians had been "taught to dread [and] our soldiery to believe in the Bayonet." The defeated Indians fled to Fort Miami, but the British kept the gates closed, forcing the Indians to keep running from the victorious Americans.[39]

In the several days after the battle, tensions were high as the Americans camped around the British fort. Wayne's men rode within pistol shot of the Redcoats, as their general considered his next move, even provoking the British to make the first move. As one story goes, Wayne urged a sergeant to go to the river near the fort and retrieve a pail of water. The man replied, "Why, General, were I do so, they would shoot me from the Fort." Wayne responded, "That's the very thing I want them to do, John, let them shoot you, and we'll massacre every soul of 'em." The American and the British commanders exchanged communiques filled with bluster and demands. Major William Campbell, the fort's commandant, grew increasingly frustrated and in a terse letter asked Wayne, "In what light am I to view your making approaches to this garrison?" If the Americans continued in their "threatening manner," Campbell asserted it was his "indispensable Duty to my King and Country" to resort "to those measures which the thousands of either nation may hereafter have cause to regret." In his reply, Wayne agreed he knew of no existing war between the United States and Great Britain. However, the British had caused "an Act of the highest aggression" by building a fort "far within the well known and acknowledged limits of the United States." Wayne ordered Campbell to remove his command from American soil. Despite his bold talk, Wayne lacked adequate artillery and supplies for a siege and, more important, he had no intention of bringing on an international incident. At the same time, Campbell refused to abandon the fort. At one point, his patience nearly worn out, Campbell prepared to open fire on American dragoons riding near the fort. Another war between the two countries seemed imminent. Instead, the Americans remained near the fort for about a week, chasing Indians and destroying their villages and all their gardens, cornfields, and grass. After honoring their fallen comrades, the Americans fell back, establishing a post at present-day Fort Wayne, Indiana.[40]

The Battle of Fallen Timbers ended the frontier Indian Wars—at least temporarily. At the same time, the Indians had lost their homes, their crops, and "most important of all, they had lost much of their faith in their British allies." As one Indian veteran of the battle recalled years later, "The British dealt treacherously with us." Three months after the battle, the United States and Great Britain signed the Jay Treaty, designed to improve strained relations between the two countries. Although the treaty's commercial provisions (most notably those dealing with the fur trade) favored the British, Great Britain also agreed to evacuate all American territory by June 1, 1796. During the summer of 1795, General Wayne gathered hundreds of Indians at present-day Greenville, Ohio. The Indians pledged to quit making war on Americans and ceded all of Ohio and parts of Indiana, as well as a strip of land six miles wide from the River Raisin to Lake St. Clair, Mackinac Island, and the Straits of Mackinac. In exchange, the Indians received $20,000 in goods and a promise to receive $9,500 in goods "every year forever."[41]

On July 11, 1796, a contingent of American soldiers commanded by Captain Moses Porter, a Revolution veteran who had served from Bunker Hill to Yorktown, arrived at Detroit aboard the schooners *Weazall* and *Swan*. Around noon, the British flag was lowered and the Stars and Stripes raised. According to one of General Wayne's aides who witnessed the ceremony, "The exchange was effected with propriety and harmony by both parties." Wayne added that the British had surrendered Detroit and other forts on American soil "in the most polite, friendly and accommodating manner." On September 1, Americans occupied Fort Mackinac.[42]

Michigan was finally part of the United States.

CHAPTER

4

Michigan Becomes American

"Perry's Victory on Lake Erie" captures the pivotal 1813 battle.

"That from and after the thirtieth day of June next, all that part of the Indiana territory, which lies north of a line drawn from the southerly bend or extreme of Lake Michigan, until it shall intersect Lake Erie, and east of a line drawn from the said southerly bend through the middle of said lake to its northern extremity, and thence due north to the northern boundary of the United States, shall, for the purpose of temporary government, constitute a separate territory, and be called Michigan."

—Public act signed by President Thomas Jefferson on January 11, 1805

On July 13, 1796, Lt. Colonel John Hamtramck arrived in Detroit with more American troops, increasing the U.S. presence to 400 soldiers. Born in Canada to Luxembourgian parents, Hamtramck joined the American army during the Revolution where he earned accolades from Generals George Washington and Anthony Wayne. In many ways, Hamtramck surprised Detroiters. He spoke fluent French and was a Roman Catholic—distinct advantages in the Detroit of the 1790s. He also stood five feet, five inches tall—quite a contrast with his British predecessor Lt. Colonel Richard England, who was six feet, six inches. Also unlike England, whose family lived in Detroit, Hamtramck's wife had died two months earlier and his two young daughters did not accompany their father. Despite a "peppery temper and a stern manner," Hamtramck moved quickly to introduce an American presence by issuing a proclamation to "Friends and fellow citizens" that controlled the sale of alcohol (especially to soldiers and Indians). Despite having to borrow 30 barrels of meat from the British across the river, Hamtramck also established a steady food supply for Detroiters.[1]

—— Wayne Reaches Detroit

A month after Hamtramck's arrival, Detroit hosted General Wayne. Accompanied by Winthrop Sargent, acting governor of the Northwest Territory, Wayne received a rousing reception that included a cannon salute, a review of his troops, and a special welcome from the Indians who enthusiastically greeted him. Nicknamed by the Indians "Chief-who-never sleeps," "Blacksnake" ("because of his deceptive advance"), and "Tornado" ("remembering the impetuosity of his charge at Fallen Timbers"), Wayne was pleased they also called him "Father." The American general was feasted and feted as "each of the leading merchants tried to outdo the others." The French also welcomed the Americans. Announcing his desire to make his parishioners "loyal Americans," a Ste. Anne's priest extended a personal invitation to General Wayne and his officers to attend a special Mass praising God for bringing the Americans to Detroit. As Wayne prepared to leave Detroit in mid-November, the *habitants* assured him of their loyalty to the United States and of "their joy in becoming united to Citizens Free and Generous." Wayne promised to share his experiences with President Washington and thanked the citizens for the honor of naming Michigan's first county after him.[2]

Wayne found Detroit "beautifully" situated on the riverbank, bustling with waterborne commerce despite being in "the Center of a Wilderness." Fort Lernoult (soon renamed Fort Detroit) was in need of repair, but the general found the houses "well finished & furnished, & inhabited by people from almost all nations, among whom are a number of wealthy & well informed Merchants & Gentlemen & fashionable well bred Ladies."[3]

Detroit's population was now about 500 people. Despite its size, Detroit was cosmopolitan since war and commerce had attracted "all sorts of people" to the settlement. One American who visited Detroit shortly before Wayne's arrival noted, "The inhabitants of the town are as great a mixture . . . as ever I knew in one place." Among Detroit's heterogeneous white population, the British were the most influential, the French the most numerous, and the Americans the fewest. Distressed with the arrival of the Americans, some Brits moved across the river into Ontario. Others adjusted, agreeing with Irishman John Askin that the American arrival had not "given any Cause of dislike." Even William Macomb, a Canadian assemblyman and Detroit's wealthiest resident, teamed up with another British businessman, George McDongall, to guarantee a smooth transition to American control. According to historian Cleaver Bald, Detroit's French population was "volatile, generous, hospital, and sociable to a fault . . . men and women [who] enjoyed life to the full." Some French families traced their roots to the settlement's founding a century earlier while for families like the de Beaubien, St. Aubin, Campau, and Navarre, their major contributions lay in the city's future. Only a few Americans lived in Detroit at this time because the British disliked them and required they take a loyalty oath to the king.[4]

There were plenty of Indians in Detroit, especially the Potawatomi, Odawa, and Huron. Trade representatives from other nations also visited the village, especially during the early spring when the Indians brought their pelts to Detroit and outnumbered the whites. Indians interacted well with the *habitants*, which contrasted noticeably with the British, who provided the Indians with presents. Land-hungry Americans "viewed the Indians with even less regard [and were] very impatient and even brutal on their insistence that the natives should be dispossessed." Detroit was also home to a small slave population (divided among Indians and African Americans) and a few free blacks.[5]

Detroit's cosmopolitan nature contributed to the problems of establishing an American governmental presence. Besides a lack of qualified Americans, many of the French were illiterate "and on the whole, there was little enthusiasm among them for self-government." The inability to find capable and willing men to fill various governmental positions led to multiple appointments. One of Detroit's few Americans, 70-year-old Peter Audrain, who spoke English and French, held four positions. A few other appointees had held offices during the British reign.[6]

The interaction of Detroit's three primary nationalities also contributed to animosity, uncertainty, and instability. The Americans considered the British "Tories," while the British dubbed the Americans "Yankee foreigners."

The predominant French language, customs, and religion provided barriers, leading one intolerant American to view the *habitants* as "exceedingly ignorant and lazy."[7]

Solomon Sibley was one of the earliest American arrivals. A graduate of Rhode Island College (present-day Brown University), Sibley left his native Massachusetts to practice law in Marietta, Ohio. Seeking greater opportunities, he arrived in Detroit in July 1798. Initially disappointed with a village that lacked "taste or elegance," Sibley became "perfectly contented," despite complaining that "we have no ladies here that I care a fig for. . . . [I] take no pleasure in listening to their French nonsense—They speak no English & I speak no french (sic)." Sibley overcame the town's social limitations and soon after beginning his law practice, he accepted an appointment as Wayne County's deputy county prosecutor—a first step in an admirable record of public service.[8]

A late 1798 census led to Detroit's first American election to fill Wayne County's seat in the territorial legislature. Eligible candidates had to be three-year U.S. residents and own 200 acres of land in the county. British citizens were denied the right to run for office. Voters (only males) had to be two-year U.S. residents and own at least 50 acres in the county. This requirement was liberally interpreted so that homeownership also qualified as owning 50 acres. Curiously, James May, who did not satisfy the residence requirement, earned the support of the former British subjects, while the *habitants* and the Americans supported Solomon Sibley. The three-day election was held in mid-December, and since voting was *viva voce*, "pressure could be exerted" on voters. According to May—the loser—Sibley provided free liquor to voters, threatened his supporters with bodily harm, and received "many illegal votes." May protested the election results, but an investigation proved inconclusive. Following his victory, Sibley asked voters to share with him their concerns before he set out for the Northwest Territory capital of Cincinnati.[9]

American democracy had come to Michigan.

—— Michigan Territory Is Created

More governmental changes followed quickly. In 1803, Ohio entered the Union as a state and the federal government placed the balance of the Northwest Territory into the newly created Indiana Territory. This decision—done without consulting Michiganians—placed the new territorial capital (Vincennes) twice as far from Detroit as Cincinnati. The new territory also lacked a legislature. Angry Detroit citizens protested the development, sending petitions to Congress urging the creation of a Michigan Territory. In the fall of 1803 the Senate agreed, but the House of Representatives rejected the proposal by a single vote. A year later, the issue was reconsidered, and with the backing of President Thomas Jefferson, the Michigan Territory became a reality. On January 11, 1805, Jefferson signed the bill establishing the new territory, effective July 1. Detroit, which had adopted a city charter in 1802, was declared the territorial capital. The Michigan Territory included all of the Lower Peninsula and a sliver of the eastern Upper Peninsula.[10]

One of the first issues Detroit leaders addressed was fire. The town's houses, barns, warehouses, taverns, and shops were crowded together, and as General Wayne had observed, "The streets were so narrow as scarcely to admit two carriages to pass each other." Since the wooden structures were all tinder dry, "a spark was more dangerous than a hostile Indian." The city's comprehensive ordinances required houses to have a filled barrel of water, burning coals to be carried in closed containers, and residents to participate in bucket brigades. These ordinances proved of little value on June 11, 1805. The day dawned clear and warm with light winds but ended disastrously. Early that morning a fire started in John Harvey's stable—possibly when an ember from a pipe was carelessly discarded. In a matter of minutes, fire engulfed the barn, quickly spreading to the adjoining buildings. The bucket brigade was overwhelmed, and the hose on the fire engine jammed. Residents gathered whatever possessions they could carry and saved their household goods by throwing them into the river. After three hours, all that remained were smoldering ruins and stone chimneys. Only one of Detroit's 200 buildings within the stockade survived the flames. The fort, which lay outside the city, also had been spared. Amazingly, no one was seriously hurt. One witness recorded, "In the course of three hours, . . . nothing was to be seen of the city except a mass of burning coals, and chimney-tops stretching like pyramids into the air." The lack of any wind "allowed the flames and smoke to ascend to a prodigious height, giving the city the appearance of an immense funeral pile."[11]

In the days immediately following the fire, gloom and doubt threatened to overwhelm Detroiters. A rumor claimed the fire had been started by "persons in the lumber trade." Displaced residents sought sanctuary with friends along the river or lived in tents or crude lean-tos made from tree branches. Financial assistance arrived from collections taken at Michilimackinac and Montreal. On a lighter note, baker Jacques A. Girardin remembered placing loaves of bread in his oven before the fire forced him to flee. "To his astonishment," the bread was well baked and he shared it with his desperate neighbors. Father Gabriel Richard also actively organized relief efforts. In 1798 the 41-year-old priest, who had fled revolutionary France, arrived in Detroit and assumed his duties as assistant pastor at Ste. Anne's cathedral. Although Father Richard "had the appearance of an ascetic, . . . he was interested also in the physical and mental needs of the people, and his active mind was always busy with ideas for their betterment." After surveying the city's devastation, he was heard to say, *Speramus Meliora; Resurget Cineribus,* ("We hope for better things; it will arise from the ashes"), which later became Detroit's motto.[12]

—— William Hull: First Governor

Three weeks after the fire, William Hull reached Detroit to assume his responsibilities as governor of the newly organized Michigan Territory. Connecticut-born, a Yale University graduate, and a lawyer of considerable ability, the 52-year-old Hull had governmental experience working as a federal treasury agent and a Massachusetts justice of the peace and a state senator. His military record was equally impressive. In 1775, at the age of 21, Hull raised and commanded a company of volunteers. Service during the Revolution included Boston, White Plains (where he was wounded), Trenton, Valley Forge, and Stony Point, as well as a promotion for bravery from General Washington and recognition of conspicuous gallantry by General Wayne. Hull left the army in 1786 as a lieutenant colonel. His Jeffersonian political sympathies may explain Hull's appointment as territorial governor. But Hull had little knowledge of the frontier and no experience in dealing with the French—disadvantages in Detroit. Hull took his oath of allegiance in Albany, New York, from Vice President George Clinton as he headed west, traveling with his wife, five of their eight children, and Stanley Griswold, newly appointed secretary of the Michigan Territory.[13]

Hull arrived in Detroit on July 1, 1805. After recovering from the initial shock of his ravaged capital, he started governing by administering the oath of office to Judge Augustus Elias Brevoort Woodward, who had arrived a day earlier, and Judge Frederick Bates, who had been in Detroit for several years and served as postmaster and land commissioner, and "was somewhat acquainted with the people." Hull understood Detroit was hardly a typical American city and that establishing a new government posed great challenges. He prepared a lengthy, optimistic introduction—which was translated into French—explaining everything from the freedoms found in the Bill of Rights to future plans to erect "a City on the desolated ground, the Sight of which is so afflicting at the present moment." To reassure Detroiters, he addressed responsibilities (those of the government, the residents, even the British neighbors) and the mission ahead to lay a foundation "which will be of immense consequence not only to the People who now inhabit the territory, but to those who shall Succeed them." It was a lofty goal.[14]

The governor's most immediate problem (after finding a place to house his family, which took a week) was rebuilding Detroit. He persuaded the federal government to donate 10,000 acres of land so the new capital could expand as it was rebuilt. The grant provided each citizen over the age of seventeen with a lot not less than 5,000 feet square. Leftover land was sold, and the proceeds used to build public buildings. Hull turned to Judge Woodward to design a new city. A native New Yorker, but raised in Virginia, the 31-year-old Woodward was fluent in Latin, Greek, French, and Spanish. He also idolized Thomas Jefferson, whom he counted among his friends. Although cultured and talented, Woodward was also unconventional and controversial. According to his biographer, Woodward took "a puckish delight" in his eccentricities. Despite his many idiosyncrasies that "alternately delighted and dismayed" Michiganians (including a reputation for infrequent bathing), Woodward proved to be a skilled judge and an urban planner ahead of his time.[15]

A committee of one, Woodward proposed an elaborate plan based on the work of Pierre Charles L'Enfant, the French architect who designed Washington, DC. Enthusiastically, he told Detroiters the fire had been "a blessing . . . [and] your new metropolis . . . is destined to have no common name" among North American cities. The Woodward Plan called for a series of circular parks called "circuses." Streets—some 200 feet wide—radiated from the circuses like spokes of a wheel. As Detroit grew, this pattern could be repeated. A later-day observer credited Woodward with "the first example of mass production in a city which has made a science of mass production." Many Detroiters lacked an understanding of Woodward's vision. Opposition, criticism, and apathy generated a growing controversy, worsened by the fact the plan took months to complete. Critics wondered why a frontier town of several hundred people needed such wide streets. They also accused Woodward of "erecting a monument to himself" when the main north-south street was named Woodward. (The justice claimed the name came from the fact the road ran "toward the woods.") Woodward's plan initiated Detroit's rebirth, yet it survived only eleven years before being "legislated out of existence partly in favor of a more traditional grid pattern, because of greed, partly because of public pressure, and partly because a hundred years is too long to wait for a dream to come true." A defiant Woodward charged, "You have withered my beautiful plan of Detroit, and have spoiled the beauty and symmetry of the city of Detroit for all time." Today, the city's Grand Circus Park, Campus Martius, and the streets radiating from these circuses survive as part of Woodward's plan.[16]

Hull and Woodward both worked to rebuild Detroit, but the two men struggled working with each other. Everything from organizing a local militia to determining laws to govern the territory proved divisive. The governor found Woodward "insidious, and doing all in his power to injure me," while the justice criticized Hull for a "lack of tact, energy and firmness." Despite an unwillingness to compromise that hindered territorial growth, there were occasional bright spots. In an 1807 decision, Woodward ruled that slaves who escaped from Canada could not be forcibly returned to their masters since slavery did not exist in Michigan (except for those masters who owned slaves when the Americans arrived in 1796). Furthermore, as he pointed out, there was no reciprocity agreement between the United States and Great Britain on the matter. Woodward's decision solidified Michigan public opinion against slavery and, according to one later-day Michigan legal scholar, marked the "beginning of the end of American slavery." In the same year of Woodward's ruling on slavery, Governor Hull negotiated the Treaty of Brownstown with the Odawa, Ojibwa, Wyandot, and Potawatomi. The Indians sold five million acres in the southeastern quarter of the Lower Peninsula for one penny an acre, while retaining hunting and fishing rights. Hull believed Michigan Indians could be won over to the American side, but the governor faced a U.S. government unwilling to provide the necessary resources for the job, while British agents outspent the Americans

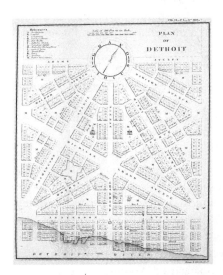

Judge Woodward's vision for Detroit included streets that radiated from circular parks called "circuses."

by a ten-to-one margin. Despite pleading with the federal government that it was "better to feed them than fight them," Hull struggled in achieving his goal.[17]

—— Tecumseh, the Prophet, and Tippecanoe

Hull's efforts to befriend (or at least neutralize) the Indians came at the same time that two Shawnee brothers sought to drive whites out of the Ohio River Valley. The brothers had grown up in Ohio and had witnessed the bloody fighting of the early 1790s—a war that claimed their father and a brother. For Tecumseh, who had fought the Americans at Fallen Timbers, the Treaty of Greenville was a turning point. His brother, known as the Prophet or Tenskwatawa, had a spiritual experience when the Master of Life told him Indians must reject the white man's ways, including the selling of their land. Viewing himself as "the voice of an oppressed people," the Prophet argued the Indians "were losing almost everything—their lands, security, livelihoods, culture, dignity and self-respect even their very identities." Only by strictly observing the ways of their fathers could the natives hope to regain their greatness. The Prophet's teachings reinforced Tecumseh's dream of a Pan-Indian movement, and the two brothers moved their center of operations to a site on the Wabash River, near the Tippecanoe Creek (present-day Lafayette, Indiana). As Prophetstown (as it was called) flourished, Indiana territorial governor William Henry Harrison grew apprehensive—despite the brothers' reassurances that their intentions were peaceful. Harrison characterized the revival as "an engine set to work by the British for some bad purpose." Harrison's 1809 Treaty of Fort Wayne (where "carefully selected compliant" Indian leaders sold three million acres in Indiana) pushed Tecumseh over the edge. At a meeting with Tecumseh in September 1810, Harrison declared, the Shawnee leader is "a bold, active, sensible man, daring in the extreme, and capable of any undertaking." Harrison's apprehensions about Prophetstown prompted him to attack the Indian settlement on November 7, 1811, when Tecumseh was away. Both sides suffered about the same number of casualties, but Harrison declared victory.[18]

More important, Harrison's victory disrupted Tecumseh's plans. Dealing with an Indian "problem," openly aggravated by the British, was only one of several issues pushing Americans toward war with Great Britain. For years, the British had violated American rights on the high seas by stopping

U.S. ships and seizing sailors—some of whom were Americans. "War Hawks," mainly western Americans, looked to war as an easy opportunity to conquer Canada, which had a vastly smaller population than the United States. On June 18, 1812, Congress declared war on Great Britain.

—— Another War with Great Britain

As war neared, Governor Hull, who had been away from Detroit since the previous fall, assumed command of the newly created North Western Army. The aging governor eagerly sought the military appointment, despite later claiming he accepted it "with great reluctance." In early summer 1812, Hull assembled an army of 2,000 regulars and militia at Dayton, Ohio. His orders, issued before the declaration of war, called for him to march to Detroit, cross the river, and invade western Ontario. As the confident Americans headed toward Detroit, they placed signs on their caps that read "conquer or die."[19]

Despite this naïve optimism, the Americans along the western frontier suffered from several major disadvantages. British Fort Malden at Amherstburg commanded the deepest channel on the Detroit River, while Fort Detroit was located away from the river. To control the river, American cannon had to fire over the town. The naval forces also offered another major difference. The Great Lakes provided the "only highway for the rapid movement of men and supplies" and the British Navy controlled the lakes.[20]

From the Maumee River in northwestern Ohio, Hull sent the schooner *Cuyahoga* to Detroit carrying his baggage, papers, and supplies. Hull had not been informed of Congress's declaration, but the well-informed British seized the *Cuyahoga* as it passed Fort Malden. Papers aboard the vessel detailed Hull's plans and the size of his army. Despite this setback, Hull's arrival at Detroit on July 5 relieved the town's residents. A week later, the North Western Army crossed the Detroit River and placed Fort Malden under siege. Prospects looked bright, especially since Hull commanded a force twice as large as the British force. As American raiding parties wreaked havoc on the countryside, Hull issued a bombastic proclamation urging Canadians to accept his offer of "Peace, Liberty and Security." Boasting that his army "will look down all opposition," Hull proclaimed that the United States offered Canadians an opportunity to be "emancipated from tyranny and oppression, and restored to the dignified status of freemen." Apparently his words worked, since Canadian militiamen and Indians went home or deserted.[21]

As the siege continued, the war shifted northward to Mackinac Island where nothing went right for the Americans. Preoccupied with his own concerns, Governor Hull failed to inform Lt. Porter Hanks, the American commandant at Fort Mackinac, that war had been declared. A seven-year army veteran, Hanks commanded 61 men at Fort Mackinac. His British opponent, Captain Charles Roberts, was a twenty-year veteran of the British army and led a mixture of regulars, militia, and Indians from Fort St. Joseph, about 50 miles from Mackinac Island. Besides being badly outnumbered, Hanks had other problems: Most of the inhabitants on Mackinac Island were British sympathizers, the nearest American posts (Detroit and Chicago) were hundreds of miles away, and the British controlled the Great Lakes.[22]

Shortly after being informed that war had broken out, Roberts acted. On July 16, his colorful collection of Redcoats, *voyaguers*, and Indians paddled toward Mackinac Island, which they reached without being detected. At 3:00 AM the next day, Roberts's men landed at a cove on the northwest shore of the island. Fort Mackinac was about two miles south of this point. Roberts moved his men, along with two cannon, to the high ground overlooking the fort. As the British got into position, Michael Dousman, a former Michigan militia captain who lived on the island, alerted the island's civilian population that the British had landed. Dousman had been captured the previous night and agreed to tell the village of the impending battle in exchange for his freedom. Dousman also promised not to say anything to Lt. Hanks. Around mid-morning, Roberts sent a flag of truce to the American commander demanding his surrender "in order to save the effusion of blood." Hanks' position was hopeless. With the water supply outside the fort's walls, outnumbered ten to one, and fearing an Indian massacre if he did not surrender, Hanks capitulated. The American soldiers were sent to Detroit, while most of the civilians took an oath of allegiance to the British crown.[23]

The fall of Fort Mackinac disheartened Hull, who feared its loss "opened the northern hive of Indians." When Hanks arrived at Detroit he discovered the American position unraveling quickly. On August 4, Ohio militiamen suffered a lopsided battlefield defeat at the hands of Tecumseh's men, south of Detroit near present-day Brownstown. Hull also learned that American efforts to invade Canada at Niagara and Lake Champlain had stalled, which allowed the British to focus their attention on Detroit, where they sent their most able commander—General Isaac Brock.[24]

—— Detroit Surrenders

On August 8, Hull broke off his siege of Fort Malden and returned his army to Detroit—a "fatal and unaccountable step [that] dispirited the troops," according to one American officer. A few days later, Brock arrived at Fort Malden with reinforcements, positioned his artillery opposite Detroit, and demanded the town's surrender. A seemingly confident Hull replied, "I am ready to meet any force which may be at your disposal." The American general had good reason to send his defiant response. Fort Detroit mounted 26 pieces of artillery and plenty of ammunition and ample provisions. The city of Detroit was pallisaded on three sides, and the fourth side was in common with the fort. Despite the American advantages, Brock, whose command possessed fewer cannon, opened fire. British guns produced "great confusion" as Detroiters dodged shells, packed up their valuables, and "kept a vigilant eye upon the movements of the enemy." At dawn on August 16, Brock's force of 330 Redcoats, 400 militia, and 600 Indians crossed the Detroit River.[25]

Hull did not contest the British landing—despite possessing a force equal in size to Brock's. An American artillery officer later boasted that he "had his fuse ready, and by one discharge could have blown Brock's close column to pieces." Instead, Hull ordered him not to fire. As Brock's men landed on Michigan soil, a constant fire from Brock's guns led to Americans casualties, including one cannon ball that killed Lt. Hanks, the unfortunate commander of Fort Mackinac. Playing on Hull's fears of Indian atrocities, Brock fabricated a document that purposefully fell into American hands, detailing a large body of Indians headed to Detroit. The British commander followed with a surrender demand that read, "It is far from my inclination to join in a war of extermination, but you must be aware, that the numerous body

Governor Hull's surrender to British General Isaac Brock in August 1812.

of Indians who have attached themselves to my troops, will be beyond control the moment the contest commences." Concern for the town's many civilians, including his own family, Hull suddenly raised a white flag, claiming, "I have done what my conscience directed. I have saved Detroit and the Territory from the horrors of an Indian massacre." Since Hull had not consulted with his officers before surrendering, many Americans were stunned and outraged. One disgruntled U.S. officer later recorded, "Even the women were indignant at so shameful a degradation of the American character." At noon, Brock led his victorious forces into Fort Detroit. The Stars and Stripes was lowered and, as a British band played "God Save the King," the Redcoats hoisted the British flag. Detroit was once again under British rule.[26]

—— Traitor or Scapegoat?

Hull's regulars were imprisoned in Canada and the militia sent home. The loss of Detroit—the only time in U.S. history that an American city has surrendered to a foreign enemy—shocked Americans. Comparing Hull to Benedict Arnold, the *National Intelligencer* demanded an investigation since "a tale remains to be told, which will make the blood of every American boil with indignation." From Detroit, Judge Woodward noted, "As a military operation, this enterprise was conducted on the part of the British general, with a degree of genius, judgment, energy and courage, reflecting the highest lustre on his personal character; and presenting, in every point of view, a contrast the most complete to that of the American general."[26]

While Hull languished in a Canadian prison, Colonel Lewis Cass (paroled after the city's surrender) headed to Washington, DC, to explain what had happened. Detroit's surrender had been "a mortifying experience" for Cass who had anticipated military glory. On the way to the capital, he authored a bitter, incriminating letter to Secretary of War William Eustis, attacking Hull for abandoning the capture of Fort Malden against the wishes of the army and "without the shadow of an enemy to injure us." Cass commanded a regiment of Ohio militia in Hull's army but did not witness Detroit's surrender being on patrol south of the city at the time. Yet, he claimed gathering his information "thro' a medium, which admitted of no doubt." Cass maintained that the Americans had ample supplies and troops—and that "not many [Indians] were visible" in Brock's force: "To surrender without firing a gun, tamely submit without raising a bayonet, disgracefully to pass in review before an enemy as inferior in the quality as in the number of his forces were circumstances, which excited feelings of indignation more easily felt than described." Cass concluded that if Hull's courage "had been equal to the spirit and zeal of the troops, the event would have been as brilliant & successful as it now is disastrous and dishonour-able" [sic]. Absent from the carefully crafted and one-sided report was any mention of a failed mutiny Cass and other officers had contemplated.[28]

Officials in President Madison's cabinet saw the value of Cass's exposé, especially in a war with so many early and unexpected American setbacks. Charged with treason, cowardice, neglect of duty, and conduct unbecoming an officer, Hull went on trial in Albany, New York, on January 3, 1814. The presiding judge was General Henry Dearborn, hardly impartial since his dismal failure on the Niagara front had given General Brock time to move to Fort Malden and more easily effect Detroit's surrender. Equally significant, all the prosecution's witnesses (officers who served under Hull) were promoted *before* the trial. After a three-month hearing, the court found Hull guilty of cowardliness and neglect of duty but acquitted him of treason. The judge sentenced the disgraced governor to death but recommended mercy because of his "advanced age" and earlier service during the American Revolution. Hull retired to Massachusetts where he spent his remaining years trying to exonerate himself. He never returned to Michigan.[29]

Too cautious to command in a situation that required decisiveness and imagination, William Hull was the wrong man to lead an army in wartime. He also served as a scapegoat for the Madison administration, which had plunged an unprepared nation into war. Had the government listened to the governor's pre-war suggestion to bolster the U.S. naval force on the Great Lakes, the disaster at Detroit might have been avoided. As for preventing an Indian massacre had he continued the fight and lost, one British witness conceded, "It would have been impossible to restrain the Indians."[30]

—— "Remember the River Raisin"

The American government responded to the loss of Detroit by organizing a new and larger northwestern American army and placing it under the command of General William Henry Harrison. His orders included protecting the western frontier, retaking Detroit, and capturing Fort Malden. In January 1813, Harrison ordered one of his subordinate commanders, General James Winchester, to move his 1,300-man command to the rapids of the Maumee River (in Ohio). A few days after arriving at the rapids, Winchester—against direct orders from Harrison—moved most of his men to Frenchtown (present-day Monroe). Winchester made the risky move in response to reports that the British planned to burn Frenchtown. When the Americans reached the settlement, they defeated a smaller British force and captured a large quantity of flour and beef. For the first time in months, the Americans ate well. However, Winchester failed to take adequate defensive precautions, while ignoring reports the British were headed to Frenchtown. At dawn on January 22, Colonel Henry Proctor's force of 1,300 men (500 Redcoats and militia and 800 Indians) surprised the unprepared Americans. Shortly after the fighting started, Winchester was captured and faced threats of an Indian massacre if he did not surrender the rest of this army. Although many Americans continued offering a stubborn resistance, Winchester ordered them to lay down their guns after receiving Proctor's reassurances that the wounded Americans would receive proper care. American casualties at the Battle of the River Raisin—the largest battle ever fought on Michigan soil—totaled 220 killed, 80 wounded, and more than 500 taken prisoner. Only a few Americans escaped capture. The British reported 24 killed and 161 wounded.[31]

Fearing the arrival of American reinforcements, Proctor moved his army and all the captured Americans who could walk to Fort Malden. He left behind a few men to guard approximately 80 seriously wounded Americans, with promises that sleds would bring them to Fort Malden. Following a sleepless, anxiety-filled night worsened by a British comment that "the Indians are excellent doctors," the Americans discovered their British guards had disappeared. About mid-morning, 200 Indians entered Frenchtown and began plundering the buildings. They murdered the more seriously wounded Americans and forced those who could walk to carry out the plunder. The wounded soldiers who could not keep up were, according to one survivor, "inhumanely massacred; the road was, for miles, strewed with the mangled bodies." The massacre of approximately sixty wounded U.S. soldiers outraged the American public. The editor of one national newspaper described the killings as one of the worst acts of "cold blooded butchery ever committed . . . by civilized man." Some survivors returned home, many were never heard from again, and a few remained in captivity until well after the war ended. The River Raisin massacre even upset some of the victors, with one British officer admitting it was "a sad affair, and caused intense feeling in our camp." Serving with the British at the River Raisin, Dr. Robert Richardson predicted, "Be assured we have not heard the last of this shameful transaction. I wish to God it could be contradicted." Colonel Proctor was promoted to general for his battlefield success at Frenchtown, but he won the undying enmity of Americans as "Remember the River Raisin" became an American battle cry.[32]

The August 1812 surrender left Detroit an occupied city. When General Brock returned east, he announced that American laws remained in effect. Colonel Proctor appointed Justice Woodward—the only member of the American territorial official not associated with the military—secretary of the occupied territory. The decision placed Woodward in a quandary. Accepting service from an enemy during wartime smacked of treason. Proctor acceded to Woodward's suggestion to query the Madison administration for instructions. In the meantime, Woodward (who never received a reply from the president about this delicate matter) lost no time making himself useful. "In a hundred ways," including working to ransom American prisoners held by the Indians, Woodward "acted as a buffer" between Michiganians and the Redcoats. In the process, he endured criticism, including one outraged southern congressman who denounced him as a traitor and proposed dissolving the Michigan Territory. The tense relationship between Woodward and Proctor worsened following the Battle of the River Raisin as the judge worked to publicize British battlefield actions. Fearing Woodward's actions might lead to his "being held accountable" for the massacre, Proctor banished key Americans from the territory. The chosen men, with Woodward acting as their spokesman, refused to leave and issued a list of their own demands. Proctor withdrew his order but denounced Woodward as "an Artful, designing, & Ambitious Man." The American justice accused the British general of ignoring international law and violating the terms of the city's surrender agreement. A frustrated Proctor finally agreed to the judge's request to leave Detroit. By mid-March 1813, Woodward headed east, providing good "high propaganda value" for the Madison government. The justice only returned to Detroit after the Americans reoccupied the city.[33]

—— "We Have Met the Enemy"

The war resumed in earnest during the spring and summer of 1813, especially in northwest Ohio. However, the situation changed drastically with U.S. Commodore Oliver Perry's impressive September defeat of the British fleet near present-day Sandusky, Ohio. In a day-long fight, the two equally weighted fleets battled until favorable winds and dogged determination forced the British to surrender, allowing a victorious Perry to send the dramatic communiqué, "We have met the enemy and he is ours." The British struggled to explain this unprecedented naval disaster, while the Americans hailed it as "the most complete of any in naval annals." The Battle of Lake Erie, coupled with a large American army marching north, left the British position untenable. Proctor abandoned Detroit and Fort Malden and retreated northeastward up the Thames River toward Chatham as Commodore Perry ferried General Harrison's enthusiastic army across the Detroit River. On September 29, Colonel Richard Johnson's mounted Kentucky riflemen wearing "their blue hunting shirts, red belts, and blue pantaloons fringed with red" received "a hearty welcome" as they liberated Detroit. (Before reaching the Michigan capital, the Kentuckians stopped in Frenchtown and buried the remains of Kentuckians killed at the River Raisin.) The Stars and Stripes, hidden since the city had surrendered, was hoisted up the Mansion House flagpole. Once again, Detroit was part of the United States.[34]

On October 4, Proctor turned his tired and dispirited army and faced the hard-charging Americans west of Moravian Town. Heavily outnumbered, the British force "silently awaited, each determined to do his duty, but few with any doubt as to the result," a British officer recalled. The next morning, the Americans took advantage of the poorly positioned Redcoats, and Colonel Johnson led his Kentucky cavalrymen in "an impetuous charge." According to General Harrison, Johnson's men, who were yelling, "Remember the River Raisin," "broke through the enemy with irresistible force. In one minute the contest was over." As Proctor abandoned his shattered army (he was later court-martialed), Johnson led another brigade of Kentuckians who engaged Tecumseh's 800 Indians. After the Indian leader was killed early in the fighting, the battle raged for about thirty minutes before some Kentuckians got behind the Indian position, which quickly collapsed. The Indians fled into the swamps, followed by the Kentuckians who sought to avenge River Raisin. Tecumseh's body was never identified, but years later, Colonel Johnson's role in the death of the famed Indian leader helped his election to the U.S. vice presidency in 1844. Thirty-three Indians were found dead on the field, "and others must have been killed in the retreat." British casualties were 45 killed, 36 wounded, and 600 captured, while American losses were 7 killed and 22 wounded.[35]

Two days later, Harrison withdrew his army, but not before plundering and burning Moraviantown in revenge for River Raisin and to prevent the British from using it as a base that winter. Although the outcome of the war was yet to be decided, serious fighting in southeastern Michigan had ended. However, over the course of the next year, American and British forces tangled along the Thames River, which "became a sort of no-man's land" and the site of numerous raids and counter-raids."[36]

This mural chronicles the death of Indian leader Tecumseh at the Battle of the Thames.

—— Setback at Mackinac

Despite losing Detroit, the British still occupied Fort Mackinac, and given the lateness of the season, any American effort to retake this strategic waterway had to wait until the next year. In the spring of 1814, Lt. Colonel Robert McDouall arrived at Mackinac with a relief force of two companies of veteran Redcoats (120 men) and considerable supplies and ammunition. "An extremely capable officer," McDouall had been chosen to reinforce (and then assume command) of Mackinac because the British understood the "great Importance of this Post." Among the defensive changes, the British built a stockaded blockhouse on the high ground behind the fort (the site where the British had placed a cannon and forced the American surrender two years earlier). McDouall boasted that "no force that the enemy can bring will be able to reduce" the stronghold dubbed Fort George.[37]

The long-anticipated American army/navy force arrived off Mackinac Island on July 26, 1814, and the British were ready to receive them. Aboard the American fleet of five warships, Lt. Colonel George Croghan commanded a force of about 750 men (five companies of regulars, about 250 Ohio volunteers, and a detachment of U.S. artillerymen and U.S. Marines). The ships had plenty of firepower but could not elevate their guns to bombard the fort. A few days later, the Americans sailed around the north side of the island where their naval guns swept the beach with "a tremendous fire." Colonel George Croghan landed his 850-man force, including several six-pounders, and planned to establish a defensive presence on the island that he hoped the British would attack. According to Mackinac Island historian Brian Dunnigan, the American plan reflected "timidity and indecision . . . in a situation where boldness and imagination were called for." McDouall placed his outnumbered Redcoats in a natural defensive position, while concealing his Indian allies in the woods on his left. As the fight started in a large clearing on the northern end of the island, the Americans attempted to flank the British position, but were caught in a severe firefight from the Indians hidden in the trees. Both sides utilized artillery, but the American gunners proved ineffective, firing over the heads of the British position. Croghan's flanking force, led by second-in-command Major Andrew Hunter Hamilton, took fire from the concealed Indians that left Hamilton dead and threw the Americans into confusion. The flanking effort having failed, the Americans retreated to the beach after "an exhausting and humiliating day." Americans casualties totaled 66 men, mostly regulars; British losses were "negligible." Fort Mackinac could not be retaken and most of the American force returned to Detroit. Sinclair left the *Tigress* and *Scorpion* to watch the fort and prevent the British from receiving additional supplies. Their crews were told to keep shifting their boats to avoid possible enemy capture. The Americans ignored the advice, and one night in early September, a small British force approached the *Tigress,* boarded, and captured her. A few days later, the *Tigress*—with a British crew and still flying the American flag—approached the unsuspecting crew of the *Scorpion* and captured her. These two actions cost the British eight men, but secured their hold on the northern Great Lakes.[38]

The fiasco at Mackinac ended fighting in the western Great Lakes. Two years of intense and unrelenting warfare had left the United States and Great Britain eager for peace. In December 1814, the War of 1812 formally ended with the signing of a treaty at Ghent, Belgium. In February 1815, when word reached Detroit that Congress had ratified the treaty, Detroiters gathered for an all-night party. To demonstrate there were no hard feelings, they invited prominent Canadians, including British officers, to a Grand Pacification Ball, which was hailed as "a great success." Later that year, Forts Malden and Mackinac were exchanged.[39]

—— Bright Spot among the Gloom

Despite the war's many setbacks, the United States' power and prestige was enhanced by surviving another war with the world's leading power. In 1817, the United States and Great Britain signed the Rush-Bagot Treaty—the first serious effort to disarm the Great Lakes. Michigan, however, suffered greatly as months of enemy occupation devastated the territory's few settlements. On March 5, 1815, Justice Woodward painted a dismal picture of life in Michigan: "The desolation of this territory is beyond all conception." Residents living along the River Raisin had so little food they ate boiled hay. Most of the farm fencing had been "entirely destroyed," and the windows in houses were left without glass. Even their clothes had been "plundered" from the settlers. According to another observer, everywhere one looked there was "hunger-& ruin-& famine-& desolation." The Indians also suffered and "came to be regarded as a people whose well-being was of no great concern to those who were now in firm control."[40]

One bright spot from the war was Lewis Cass. Promoted to brigadier general before the Hull trial, Cass served as an unofficial aide-de-camp to General Harrison at the Battle of the Thames. Despite exaggerated assertions of later-day political biographies, Cass saw no action. However, after the victory, Harrison appointed Cass military governor of Michigan; a few days later, President Madison elevated the Ohioan to civilian governor. During the next eighteen years, Cass overcame numerous obstacles to promote Michigan's development and prepare it for statehood. At the same time, he earned a reputation as a skilled politician and shrewd businessman, which benefited him and Michigan.[41]

CHAPTER
5

Settling the "Land of Ills"

This painting of a busy Detroit harbor shows Michigan's rapid growth in the 1830s.

"The chief business of the pioneer was to live."

—Early Michigan pioneer

In July 1836, John M. Gordon, a Baltimore banker, arrived in Michigan. On the verge of becoming the nation's 26th state, the Michigan Territory was at the height of a land rush that witnessed the sale of more than four million acres of public land in that year alone. As he toured the southern Lower Peninsula buying land, Gordon kept a diary as "a convenient mode" of informing his friends "should any of them wish to invest" in Michigan. A native Virginian and a Yale University graduate, Gordon noted bad roads, good soil, and throngs of travelers flocking west. A Dearborn innkeeper claimed that 40 wagons, averaging 100 settlers, stopped at his inn daily. At Ann Arbor, land that sold for $10 an acre four years earlier was now priced at $2,000 an acre—thanks to efforts to harness the power of the Huron River. Farther west, the Kalamazoo prairies "seized" Gordon's imagination "more than any other place." On another occasion, Gordon visited a recently arrived pioneer family. As the mother and her younger children gathered flowers, the father and "his sturdy sons" cut trees to construct a log cabin. Gordon confided in his diary, "There is something wild and pleasing at thus finding oneself on the frontier of settlement."[1]

Gordon was clearly impressed with the hustle and bustle of what he saw in Michigan. However, such activity had been only a few years in the making. Twenty years earlier, as Michigan climbed out of several years of wartime devastation, things looked bleak. Everything from food to fence rails was in short supply, the economy was stagnant, most of Michigan belonged to the Indians, and primitive transportation links to the east prevented settlers from easily reaching Michigan. In 1818, one New Yorker headed to Detroit saw "hundreds removing to the west, and not one in fifty with an intention to settle in [the] Michigan Territory."[2]

Economically, fur trapping still dominated the region's economy—as it had for decades. After the War of 1812, the federal officials, who blamed British trappers for inciting the Indians, only allowed Americans to engage in the fur trade on American soil. The decision greatly benefited John Jacob Astor, a German immigrant, who set up the American Fur Company in 1808. Headquartered on Mackinac Island, Astor's company resembled a modern-day corporation as it smashed all competition and acquired great political influence. Astor exploited "the natural resource that interested him, furs . . . as quickly as possible." At its peak, the American Fur Company employed up to 3,000 boatsmen and trappers and 400 clerks on Mackinac Island. Michigan furs helped him become America's first millionaire, but in the process "he destroyed the wild animals that were the mainstay of the Indians' way of life," forcing them to turn to their only remaining alternative—selling their land to whites. In 1834, Astor sold the American Fur Company, which soon shifted its operations westward to St. Louis.[3]

—— Rugged Life of Surveying

When federal surveyors arrived in Michigan immediately after the War of 1812—part of a plan to provide land grants to veterans—an American general serving in Detroit told them, "The territory appears to be not worth defending and merely a den for Indians and traitors. The banks of the Detroit River are handsome, but nine-tenths of the land in the territory is unfit for cultivation." The surveyors started their work in the summer of 1815 confronted with threatening Indians who questioned the legitimacy of earlier treaties.

Once this problem was resolved, the surveyors endured an unusually wet season that left them "completely worn out." In December, Edward Tiffin, surveyor general of the United States, received word his surveyors had "suffered almost ever[y] difficulty that could be expected for mortals to endure." Tiffin suspended the surveying of the Michigan Territory, declaring in his official report that "the country is, with some exceptions, low, wet land, with a very heavy growth of underbrush, intermixed with very bad marshes [and] not more than one acre in a hundred, if there were one out of a thousand" could be farmed. President James Madison informed Congress in February 1816 that Michigan was "unfit for cultivation" and veterans' bounty lands were transferred to Illinois and Missouri.[4]

Despite a tradition that grew around Tiffin's observations, it is doubtful that his negative report led settlers to go elsewhere. However, extensive wetlands where mosquitoes bred did affect Michigan's reputation. A few years after the War of 1812, the War Department built a fort near present-day Saginaw. In less than a year, the entire garrison—with the exception of one lucky enlisted man—was sick with malaria. The fort's commander sourly noted that only "Indians, muskrats and bullfrogs" could live on the Saginaw River. The post was abandoned, while a popular rhyme went, "Don't go to Michigan, that land of ills. The word means ague [malaria], fever and chills." More than mosquitoes posed a problem. Just getting to the territory was challenging. Pioneers traveling overland from the east encountered the Black Swamp in northwestern Ohio, which was as bad as the name implied and often left southeastern Michigan flooded. If the wetness was not discouraging enough, there was no easy or inexpensive way to transport farm produce back east. Nearly a decade after the war, one Detroiter glumly noted, "Our country is too far inland to admit of our growing grain with a view to exportation."[5]

Governor Lewis Cass understood how desperate the situation looked, but he contended that Tiffin's surveyors had "grossly misrepresented" the quality of Michigan land. At the same time that the surveyors quit, the federal government told Cass to stop distributing provisions to destitute Michiganians. The governor lashed out at the Secretary of War, charging that the loss of the bounty lands, combined with a general "ignorance of the most common acts of domestic life" by the *habitants,* promised a dark future. "By opening the land offices," Cass predicted, "we should have a population from the United States which would gradually teach the Canadiens [i.e., Detroiters] our acts and industry," especially farming. These efforts would raise revenues and improve conditions. Furthermore, Washington failed to understand just how devastating the war had been. "Resources of the country were perfectly

Portrait of Lewis Cass in the Michigan State
Capitol.

exhausted," he explained, and the number of persons killed, especially those "murdered by the indians . . . is much greater than has generally been believed." Michiganians, Cass continued, possessed "unshaken fidelity" to the United States. Despite experiencing their "darkest period," they had "rejected the threats and promises of the British and withstood the attacks and plundering of the Indians." Suffering from doubling prices and a poor harvest, he despaired, "a lamentable prospect is before us." A few months after Cass's emotionally charged letter, residents in Detroit and Frenchtown (present-day Monroe) sent heart-rending petitions to Congress seeking financial aid.[6]

Congress paid a few of the claims, but, more important, the surveyors returned. Tiffin sent his men back in mid-1816 and, within in a short time, he predicted, "There will be a good deal of excellent land that I expect will readily sell." Land sales officially began during the summer of 1818. Two years later, the government lowered the minimum price to $1.25 and the minimum purchase to eighty acres. Once a purchase was finalized, a record of the transaction was sent to the General Land Office and the new owner received a patent signed by the president. (Beginning in 1833 a secretary signed the president's name.) Within a few years, 2.5 million acres of Michigan land had been sold.[7]

Surveying was a challenging profession and the surveyor general concluded only men as "hard as a Savage" made good surveyors. In Michigan, surveyors began by marking two lines—a north-south meridian line and an east-west base line. (Today, the two lines intersect at the border of Ingham and Jackson counties, east of present-day highway U.S. 127.) All the land surveyed in Michigan started from these lines of reference, with the townships numbered east or west and north and south of there. Townships were six miles square, and the sections within each township were numbered 1 to 36.

Each section contained 640 acres (later divided into smaller parcels). According to historian Alan S. Brown, "The beauty of the system was obvious; when township, section and subdivision lines were accurately surveyed the settler or eventual owner had a unique designation for his property." A surveyor, working with a compass, ran a straight line measured off in one-mile increments. Chainmen and axemen assisted in clearing the brush and placing a hardwood stake at the section corners. William Austin Burt, who migrated from Massachusetts in 1824, was among Michigan's best surveyors. Possessing "a precise, scientific mind," Burt earned a reputation "as an ingenious inventor, a knowledgeable woodsman and a determined surveyor with an obsession for accuracy." Inaccurate surveys often resulted from a government policy that paid surveyors by the mile surveyed. Despite losing money, Burt refused to be rushed, which earned him accolades for his work. Burt (and his five sons who also were surveyors) worked for the government for many years, inventing in the process a solar compass he used to explore Michigan's iron fields. By early 1825 the southern third of the Lower Peninsula had been surveyed; the Lower Peninsula was completed by 1840 and the Upper Peninsula by 1851.[8]

With the surveyors at work, Cass used a presidential visit to point out the territory's considerable advantages. In August 1817, President James Monroe traveled to the Midwest, giving Michiganians an opportunity to express their needs (especially for roads), while impressing the chief executive with their loyalty and erasing memories of the embarrassing surrender of Detroit a few years earlier. During his five-day stay in Detroit, Monroe assured the Michiganians that "any inconvenience of which you may complain . . . cannot be of a long duration." He predicted, "At a period and on conditions just and reasonable, you will become a member of the Union, with all the rights of the original states." Monroe later recommended more Indian land in Michigan be purchased, while his "favorable impressions" provided the territory with good publicity in the eastern press. Reports in several eastern newspapers praised Michigan's "incalculably great advantages," especially its "luxuriant" soil. After visiting western New York, one Detroiter reported that "many of the people to the east begin to feel an itching for Detroit."[9]

—— Change in Ownership

Before lands could be surveyed they needed to be acquired from the Indians, and Cass, serving a dual role as U.S. superintendent of Indian Affairs and governor, negotiated several treaties. In the Treaty of Saginaw (1819), the

Odawa and Ojibwa sold some six million acres of the northeastern Lower Peninsula for $3,000, annual payments of $1,000, farm implements, and the services of a blacksmith and teachers to instruct them in the ways of agriculture. Cass's most dramatic treaty negotiations occurred during the summer of 1820 when he and his entourage reached Sault Ste. Marie. The governor explained to the Ojibwa that the Treaty of Greenville had given the United States title to the nearby old French fort. The Indians claimed the land was a sacred burial ground and could not be sold. The Anglophobic Cass saw his fears of British influence confirmed when Sassaba, an Ojibwa leader whose brother had died with Tecumseh at the Battle of the Thames, met the governor wearing the coat of a British general. Sassaba kicked aside Cass's gifts and "thrust a war lance into the ground at the Cass's feet before stalking back to his lodge where he defiantly hoisted the British flag." Without hesitation, Cass marched to Sassaba's lodge and tore down the offensive flag. The governor returned to his camp as his men prepared for a fight. Instead, Cass's bold action so stunned the Ojibwa they acceded to Cass's requests.[10]

To counter any possible British threat from across the river, the U.S. Army opened Fort Brady at Sault Ste. Marie (the Soo) in 1822. A year later, Henry Schoolcraft arrived. Born in New York, he had developed an interest in mineralogy, impressing Secretary of War John C. Calhoun, who hired him to join Cass's 1820 expedition to Lake Superior. These explorations and Schoolcraft's published journals about the copper deposits of the Keweenaw Peninsula led to his appointment as a U.S. Indian agent. At the Soo, Schoolcraft met and married Jane Johnston, whose mother was Ojibwa. With the assistance of his gifted wife and her family, Schoolcraft acquired an extensive knowledge of Indian lore that he published in numerous books. His six-volume masterpiece on Indian tribes of the United States (published in the 1850s) "contains valuable and indispensable material on the Indians and is a monument to a great American explorer and ethnologist." Schoolcraft's writings also inspired poet Henry Wadsworth Longfellow to write his epic, *Hiawatha*. Promoted to U.S. superintendent of Indian Affairs, Schoolcraft moved to Mackinac Island in 1833 and remained in government service until 1841.[11]

In 1842 the Indians signed their last Michigan land treaty with the U.S. government. By then, the Indians had experienced considerable changes. During the late 1820s, the federal government proposed moving all Indians west of the Mississippi River. Viewed as a leading authority on the tribes, Cass opposed the plan, arguing the loss of their ancestral homes would impose great hardship on them. However, when the proposal earned President

Andrew Jackson's blessing, Cass became a convert, arguing that "a barbarous people . . . cannot live in contact with a civilized community." Michigan Indians affected by the "Trail of Tears" included the Huron or Wyandot who lost their tribal identity after being shipped west, as well as most Potawatomi, who had experienced several western relocations. Many Ojibwa and Odawa moved to Canada to elude the U.S. government, while others avoided deportation by settling on several small reservations in northern Michigan. As a result, more Indians remained in Michigan than were sent west. Several hundred Potawatomi, led by Leopold Pokagon, employed a unique strategy to avoid relo-

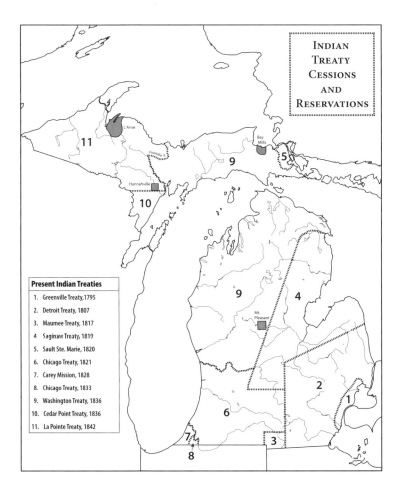

INDIAN TREATY CESSIONS AND RESERVATIONS

Present Indian Treaties

1. Greenville Treaty, 1795
2. Detroit Treaty, 1807
3. Maumee Treaty, 1817
4. Saginaw Treaty, 1819
5. Sault Ste. Marie, 1820
6. Chicago Treaty, 1821
7. Carey Mission, 1828
8. Chicago Treaty, 1833
9. Washington Treaty, 1836
10. Cedar Point Treaty, 1836
11. La Pointe Treaty, 1842

cation by converting to Catholicism and using treaty monies to "buy back" 840 acres of land near Dowagiac in Cass County. Pokagon "sought to transform his people in minimal ways that allowed them to remain in Michigan." Despite challenges, including one that required the Pokagon Potawatomi (as they were called) to seek—and receive—a favorable ruling by the Michigan Supreme Court to prevent their relocation at a later date, Pokagon "wedded ancient Potawatomi tradition to a setting of ceaseless change." Pokagon's son, Simon, continued his father's work and in the process became a recognized author dubbed the "Red Man's Longfellow." Today, the Pokagon Band of Potawatomi is a federally recognized nation with approximately 5,000 members over a ten-county area in southwestern Michigan and northern Indiana.[12]

—— Addressing Transportation Needs

Cass also addressed transportation needs by encouraging the federal government to build roads. In May 1816, the Secretary of War authorized the building of a road from Detroit south to Fort Meigs (present-day Perrysburg, Ohio). Completed three years later, the Military Road (as it was called) ran 78 miles, bridged all rivers, and became Michigan's first graded and drained road. (The soldiers who labored on the project received an additional fifteen cents a day and an extra ration of rum.) Other military roads funded by the federal government were soon under construction from Detroit to outlying settlements (Pontiac, Fort Gratiot, Saginaw, and Chicago). By the early 1830s, stagecoaches crossed the southern Lower Peninsula on roads that still needed years to complete. In some places, the road was simply a cleared strip through the woods where the stumps had been cut as short as possible. During the wet season ruts developed into mud holes. One pioneer traveling north out of Detroit on the Saginaw Road cynically recalled that "it was a matter to determine where the mud was deepest, on the pike or in the ditches." Along swampy ground, logs were laid side-by-side forming "corduroy roads," leading one European traveler to record, "such hopping and jumping; such slipping and sliding; . . . such shifting of logs." Broken wheels and axles were a common occurrence.[13]

While the experience of these early roads left one pioneer "jolted to jelly," travelers could look forward to a night's stay at a tavern or inn that sprang up along the bi-ways. At first, these might only be a settler's cabin, with simple meals, shared beds and minimal privacy. One exception was the Mansion House in Yankee Springs, which opened in the late 1830s on the road between Kalamazoo and Grand Rapids. Run by William Lewis, a New

York immigrant who arrived in Barry County in August 1836, the inn enjoyed a widespread reputation for excellence. Lewis's success also earned him the nickname "prince of the innkeepers" for an enterprise that grew to nine buildings and accommodations for up to 100 people a night. "Possessing a fine sense of humor, a keen intellect and . . . a reputation of never forgetting a face or name," Lewis also enjoyed a reputation as an exceptional storyteller, whose accomplishments were set to verse in 1844:

> If you're hungry and wish for a dinner,
> Breakfast, supper, and lodging to boot,
> If you're a Turk, a Christian, or sinner,
> Yankee Springs is the place that will suit.
>
> The landlord's a prince of his order—
> Yankee Lewis, whose fame and renown,
> Far and near throughout Michigan's border,
> Is noised about country and town.[14]

Travel to Michigan by water improved considerably when the *Walk-in-the-Water* became the first steamboat on the Great Lakes. Named for an Indian chief, the 330-ton boat had a top speed of ten miles per hour with fares ranging from seven to eighteen dollars, including meals. Enthusiastic Detroiters who turned out on the morning of August 27, 1818, were both excited with the vessel's arrival and a bit shocked to see Judge Woodward astraddle the boat's bowsprit waving a bottle. Most important, as a local newspaper boasted, "passage between this place and Buffalo is now, not merely tolerable, but truly pleasant."[15]

Rewards for taming the territory also earned Michiganians more self-government. In 1819, Congress allowed residents to elect a nonvoting delegate to Congress, and territorial secretary William Woodbridge won the distinction of being Michigan's first congressman. A few years later, a legislative council was approved—a process where voters nominated eighteen men, nine of whom were selected by the president. In 1827, when voters chose these men directly, Michigan entered the second stage of territorial government. During these years the Michigan Territory grew considerably larger. When Illinois became a state in 1818, the rest of the original Northwest Territory (mostly Wisconsin) was added to the Michigan Territory. In 1834, lands that later became Iowa and Minnesota, as well as parts of North and South Dakota, were added as the Michigan Territory expanded westward to the Missouri River.[16]

—— Erie Canal Opens the West

In the fall of 1825, the single most important event in Michigan's early development occurred. The brainchild of New York governor DeWitt Clinton, the Erie Canal was built by a combination of "Yankee ingenuity and Irish sweat." Traversing northern New York State from Albany to Buffalo, the 363-mile waterway provided an easy transportation link to the Midwest, while dramatically reducing shipping costs. At Albany, the canal dumped into the Hudson River—connecting Michigan to New York City by water. Passengers traveled along the 42-foot-wide canal in boats that varied in size from 60 to 80 feet in length; the larger ones carried as many as 100 passengers. Horses walked along a towpath pulling the boats. During the day, passengers remained on deck, singing or talking with the other passengers, ever mindful to duck when passing under a bridge. At night, travelers retired inside the hot, stuffy cabin to dirty and smelly bunks where closed windows kept out most of the mosquitoes, but not the stench of the canal. Boats traveled at between two and four miles per hour (depending on the number of horses pulling or if traveling through the night) and passengers paid between one and four cents per mile. When a canal boat reached Buffalo, passengers boarded steamboats for the three-day journey across Lake Erie to Detroit.[17]

During canal construction, Michiganians anticipated its impact as a "conveyance of a great influx of population" that opened up eastern markets to Michigan exports. Remembering it had taken up to two months to reach New York before the War of 1812, the *Detroit Gazette* boasted, "We can now go from Detroit to New York in five and a half days." New Yorkers were equally excited. An 1825 observer recorded:

> The preparation to welcome boats from Detroit and Buffalo, on their reaching this city, is extensive and grand beyond precedent. . . . Neither the Declaration of Independence, the evacuation of New York City by our old [British] taskmasters, nor the late arrival of Lafayette has been more enthusiastically celebrated than the completion of the canal for while independence conferred liberty, the canal was necessary to secure it.

By the mid-1840s, Michigan farmers shipped 485,000 bushels of wheat and more than 500,000 barrels of flour east, confirming the canal's value to the state's economy.[18]

—— Michigan Fever

As the Erie Canal carried easterners west, a flood of reports back east confirmed Michigan held great promise. New Yorker Samuel W. Dexter, living in a Washtenaw County town he named, enthusiastically observed, "The interior of Michigan is delightful—a mixture of prairies, oak openings, and woodland. Abounding in clear streams, fine lakes, and cold springs, it is a rolling country well adapted to good roads and admirably situated for conveying its produce to market." After exploring the Kalamazoo prairies in 1829, a 30-year-old Vermonter wrote home he had just experienced the "Fairy or Enchanted Land." A Buffalo newspaper noted, "It seems as though the whole eastern country was pouring out its millions for Ohio and Michigan," and boats leaving Buffalo daily were "literally packed down and overrun with passengers, good chattels, wares and merchandise; so much so, that in some instances passengers have been literally pushed ashore, to prevent the boat from being overladen." "Michigan Fever" (as the phenomenon was called) even had its own song that appeared in 1831:

> Come all ye Yankee Farmers,
> Who'd like to change your lot,
> Who've spunk enough to travel
> Beyond your native spot,
> And leave behind the village
> Where Pa' and Ma' do stay,
> Come follow me and settle
> In Michi-gan-i-a.
>
> Then come ye Yankee Farmers,
> Who've mettle hearts like me,
> And elbow-grease in plenty,
> To bow the forest tree;
> Come take a "Quarter Section,"
> And I'll be bound you'll say,
> This country takes the rag off,
> This Michi-gan-i-a.[19]

The 1830 census recorded 27,278 people were living in Michigan. A decade later, the population stood at 212,000 people—the greatest increase of any state or territory in the United States during the 1830s. Population increases also were reflected in land sales. In 1830 public land sales stood at 147,000 acres, increasing in 1834 to 498,000 acres and peaking in 1836 at 4.2 million acres (one-ninth of Michigan's total land area). Sales in that year netted $5.2 million dollars—more than one-fifth of the total receipts for land sales across the entire country.[20]

By late 1836, more registered ships operated out of Detroit than any city on Lake Erie, including Buffalo, which was twice as large. Though these numerous ships brought merchandise and goods from the east, they mainly carried passengers. During May 1836, 90 steamboats docked in Detroit, "each boat loaded with passengers." In 1837 an average of three steamboats arrived daily with two or three hundred passengers each. On one day in May, 2,400 persons arrived in Detroit, and during a single week in June, 55 ships entered Detroit harbor. During a ten-day stay in the city, one visitor saw "emigrants constantly pouring through this little city," while the compiler of the 1837 city directory estimated 1,000 passengers arrived daily. In June 1836, "a man given to counting things, reported that one wagon left Detroit for the interior every five minutes, dawn to dusk, from early spring to late autumn."[21]

Approximately two-thirds of the settlers coming to Michigan during the pioneer period had roots in western New York or New England. They came "in droves" with more money and material possessions than many of the pioneers who settled the other Midwestern states. One later-day Detroiter concluded, "It seemed as though all New England" was headed to Michigan. A New York writer found Michiganians "the most intelligent population of the middle class (the bone and sinew of the community)" he had ever known. He added, "Every one seems so contented, may even be delighted, with his adopted home, that I am catching a little of the spirit of those around me."[22]

Detroit was an early benefactor of the migration. In the 1830s, the city's population increased almost fivefold to more than 9,000 people, and residents talked about improving the city's architecture, even discussing the need for shade trees. Detroit was no longer a French town tied to the fur trade. One 1838 observer explained, "Detroit is, in all its peculiar characteristics, an eastern city, and the habits of the east prevail above those of the west. It is a growing place, and destined to become one of the largest western cities."[23]

Soon other settlements sprang up across southern Michigan "like beads on a string." By the mid-1830s towns along the Territorial Road included Ann Arbor, Jacksonburg (later Jackson), Marshall, Battle Creek, Bronson (later Kalamazoo), St. Joseph, and New Buffalo. Towns along the Chicago Road included Ypsilanti, Coldwater, Constantine, White Pigeon, and Niles. Towns were followed by the creation of counties. Michigan's second county was

COPYRIGHT 1881, BY SILAS FARMER.

Before moving the capital to Lansing, state legislators met in this Detroit building.

established following President Monroe's visit and appropriately named after him. For other counties, the legislature determined a county's boundaries, named it, formally organized it (after an adequate number of settlers lived there), and determined a county seat. When Michigan entered the Union as a state in 1837, it had 28 organized counties (on the way to 83; the last county being Dickinson, organized in 1891). County names varied from geographical features (Oakland and Lake) to President Andrew Jackson's "cabinet member" counties (Jackson, Eaton, Calhoun, Barry, Berrien, Cass, Van Buren, and Ingham). Many counties have Indian or Indian-sounding names—largely thanks to Henry Schoolcraft. Determining the governmental center of a county often was easy, but sometimes it generated controversy as communities competed for this lucrative prize. The influence of New York and New England also is reflected in how the newcomers merged their experiences into a new governmental system. "Towns" (or townships) were most popular in New England, while New Yorkers preferred "counties." In towns, annual meetings elected officers, voted on taxes, and passed ordinances. In counties, elected officers levied taxes and passed laws. The combined system adopted in Michigan saw the supervisor represent his township with other supervisors at the county level. At both the township and county levels, there were a number of elected positions.[24]

Michigan in the 1830s enjoyed "an abundant amount of descriptive material." Its relatively late settlement, "the greater articulateness" of its settlers, and an assortment of travelers' accounts explain this phenomenon. Detailed travelers' accounts include *A Winter in the West* (Charles Fenno Hoffman), *Society in America* (Harriet Martineau), and *A Fortnight in the Wilderness* (Alexis de Tocqueville). Beginning in the mid-1870s, the state Pioneer and Historical Society began publishing pioneer reminiscences. Although these stories are revealing and often charming, they must be considered with some caution since they were written well after the pioneer period.[25]

—— The Pioneer Experience

After landing in Detroit, pioneer families experienced constant hardship and struggle as they battled to conquer the wilderness and overcome its privations and diseases. The pioneer experience usually started with a prospective settler stopping at a federal land office located in Detroit, Monroe, White Pigeon, Kalamazoo, Ionia, or Flint. Maps indicated lands available to purchase, while surveyor's notes served as a guide to the land's quality.[26]

Getting a family to the newly purchased land provided the first challenge. Rains quickly turned roads or trails into quagmires that required loading and unloading the wagon to continue the journey. One frequently told story about the misery of travel concerned a pioneer coming across a beaver hat floating in a mud hole. As the man waded into the water to retrieve it he discovered a man beneath the hat who protested, "Leave me alone, stranger, I have a good horse under me, and have just found bottom." Settlers who lived near a mud hole might offer to help stranded travelers, but at a price. On one occasion, an enterprising tavern keeper even included his "particularly profitable mud hole" when selling his business. The absence of any bridges meant crossing even the smallest creek or stream might prove risky. In 1836 the *Detroit Daily Advertiser* reported that the road out of Detroit "looks at certain times as if it had been the route of a retreating army, so great is the number of different kinds of wrecks which it exhibits."[27]

After surviving the trip, a pioneer family would build a lean-to as a temporary shelter until a log cabin could be constructed. Building a cabin required chopping down 50 to 60 trees of uniform size. After dragging them to the area where the cabin was to be "raised," the logs were stacked into a rectangular structure with ends notched so they fit together. The gaps between the logs were filled with small strips of wood and mud called "chinking." Dirt floors were common, but some pioneers split logs and fashioned "puncheon" floors. The roof (which did not effectively keep out the rain or snow) was made of shingles (called "shakes") that were sliced from logs and held down by saplings because nails were unavailable on the frontier. A doorway and a window were cut; a blanket might serve as a door, although sometimes a door was crafted from split logs and hung on wooden or leather strap hinges. A wooden catch with latch was added. To lift the latch from the outside a string went through a hole above the latch. To "lock" the cabin, the latchstring was pulled inside the cabin. One pioneer recalled that "the latch-string was usually left outside at all times, as tramps and thieves were almost unknown." With glass unavailable, greased paper acted as a window. Cabins varied in size, but a good-sized structure measured 18 by 24 feet. A chimney was added at one end of the cabin, and wet clay served as the mortar that held the chimney together and fireproofed it.[28]

The cabin's fireplace served many needs: sole source of heat, a meeting and entertaining place, and the kitchen stove. An iron crane swung back and forth over the fire, supporting the kettles and pots of iron and copper. One pioneer recalled that daily fare was "necessarily frugal." Besides the challenge of cooking over an open fire ("no easy or pleasant task," one remembered), settlers struggled with a shortage of food, especially during their first year in the wilderness. Potatoes, bread, and meat (when available) constituted the usual meal. Tea, coffee, sugar, and butter were rarely seen, leading one settler to acknowledge many years later that "we were hungry all the time." The absence of matches required keeping a fire burning all the time. If the fire went out, it could be restarted using flint or steel or borrowing an ember from a distant neighbor. As one pioneer eloquently recalled, "Scarcely did the vestal virgins of Rome, or the priests of ancient Judah, guard the sacred fires of their altars with greater care than did our pioneers guard the fires of their hearthstones." There were no walls dividing the cabin, so blankets set off a bedroom, with children sleeping in the loft. The family had a few cherished pieces of furniture brought from the east, and a bed with springs made from crisscrossed rope and a mattress constructed from a tick filled with dry grass, hay, or straw.[29]

When the cabin was finished, the land had to be cleared. In heavily wooded areas, trees were "girdled" (stripped of their bark around their trunk), so they died more quickly. Using an axe, the men felled the trees and burned them to clear a field. Incredibly, Michigan pioneers burned more timber than sawmills devoured in later years. Corn was planted first because it needed no plowing. Wheat followed after the ground was plowed, usually using a team of oxen. Once the grain was harvested, it was hauled to a gristmill, sometimes miles away. Settlers also brought along cows, sheep, and pigs, which foraged in the forest. Tapping maple trees and boiling the sap in open fires to make sugar proved popular. "It was not usually very clean," one early Michiganian noted, "but it was highly prized by people who could not afford to buy sugar from the market." Hunting supplemented the family diet, and as one pioneer recalled, "Nearly every farmer knew enough to butcher pigs and cattle." A spinning wheel was an essential tool, and one mother "spun, wove, colored and made up the wearing apparel for her whole family" while a small stick replaced a lost button. Clothing was simple and basic. One settler remembered, "If a person had good clothes he was most fortunate." Buckskin was commonly used in the clothing and pioneers often went barefoot—even to church. Women made soap and candles, while a skilled man could split "100 rails in a day." Survival required self-sufficiency.[30]

The wilderness was alive with wild animals, especially during the early years of settlement, and some of the most memorable confrontations occurred with bears. Many early settlers were awakened by their hogs screeching as a bear carried the poor victim off. One time when a husband was away, his wife had finished feeding the hogs only to discover a huge bear marching "with his eyes fixed on the pigs." Attempts to distract the bear failed, so the woman grabbed a log chain. With the bear only ten feet away, she "swung the chain towards him, nearly reaching him at every swing, and screaming as she did." As the bear retreated, the woman armed herself with an axe, found her children who were playing, and escorted them home safely. Other animals proved nuisances. The whole country seemed to be a "paradise of wolves," while rattlesnakes made an unwelcome appearance. Besides preying on sheep, wolves made the night "hideous" by their howling. On one occasion, a young pioneer confronted a wolf on the path to school. "I raised my dinner basket, and, shaking it, screamed with all my might," he recalled. "At this the wolf turned, leaped over the fence and ran off." Poaching raccoons, deer, and blackbirds also posed problems, especially during harvest season. Blackbirds flocked to a family's cornfield by the "million," forcing one Saginaw settler to spend much of his day running amid the stalks.[31]

—— Land of Ills

The worst pest was the omnipresent mosquito. One settler wrote: "Our mosquitoes are as large as those of York State and about as saucy. They are cannibals in every sense of the word." Fires and smoky smudge pots around the cabin might ward off mosquitoes, but, as one settler noted "it seemed they could stand as much smoke as we could." Mosquitoes brought the ague. Rarely fatal, the ague or malarial fever was so common that many refused to regard it as a disease but, like hard work, "a concomitant of the frontier." The ague started with chills and was followed by fever, aches, and profuse sweating. The attacks often occurred at certain times of the day so work schedules were arranged to accommodate a person's "shakes." The "fevers kept us all in a shaking condition, or else in a state of burning, day and day, for months," one pioneer recalled. A common adage went, "He ain't sick, he's just got the ager." Quinine (called Peruvian bark) offered relief, but as one disgusted early Michiganian recalled, "The contest with fever and ague was fearful, and [the] ague usually had the best of it."[32]

Pioneers faced other diseases (dysentery, biliousness, piles, typhoid, and tuberculosis), but none more deadly than cholera. On July 4, 1832, the steamer *Henry Clay* stopped in Detroit carrying troops to Illinois for the Black Hawk Indian uprising. As the vessel lay at the wharf, two infected soldiers were removed to the fort. The next day, Detroiters woke up to discover a dozen solders had died during the night. A week earlier, city leaders had adopted health measures in response to fears that the highly infectious disease—which had arrived on U.S. shores weeks earlier from Europe—might head west. Their efforts had little impact as panic set in. The vessel moved to Hog Island (present-day Belle Isle), before stopping at Port Huron. By then, the *Henry Clay* had become "a floating charnel-house." The vessel's captain later reported circumstances had become "violent and alarming" as discipline broke down and soldiers scrambled ashore, many later dying "unwept and alone." Fewer than 200 of the 800 men aboard the *Henry Clay* and three other vessels reached Chicago. As this tragedy unfolded, Detroiters turned the territorial capitol into a hospital. An effort to ward off the deadly disease by burning pitch in the streets left smoke hanging "like a pall over the stricken town." As the death toll rose, the city discontinued ringing the "passing bell." Outlying towns "caught the infection of terror" as they stopped travelers heading west. At Ypsilanti, the militia manning a roadblock fired on a stagecoach whose driver ignored demands to turn back, while a Washtenaw County deputy sheriff arrested Territorial Secretary Stevens T. Mason for traveling west. By late July, the worst had passed, but people kept dying. Eight died in Marshall—a town of 70 people. In Detroit, Father Gabriel Richard, who labored tirelessly among the sick and dying, was among the dead. Cholera returned to Michigan on several more occasions. In 1834, there was less panic, but more deaths when seven percent of Detroit's population perished in one month, including Territorial Governor George Porter. Father Martin Kundig orchestrated the city's response with the mayor complimenting the Catholic priest for being "fearless and serene."[33]

According to R. Carlyle Buley, one of the leading authorities of the Old Northwest, "Nothing was more vital to the conquest of the wilderness than health, but over none of the factors involved did the settlers seemingly have less control." The effects of exposure, decaying vegetation, swamps, poor food habits, lack of sanitation and hygiene, coupled with a lack of knowledge on prevention and cure, left pioneers unhealthy. Given all the illnesses, it is of little surprise that one pioneer recalled, "The pale, sallow bloated faces of that period were the rule; there were no healthy faces except of persons just arrived." A doctor was a jack-of-all-trades who often practiced medicine by riding the circuit. He possessed limited knowledge and simple equipment, relying upon his eyes, ears, and nose to diagnosis a patient. He served as his own pharmacist and often relied upon bleeding—performed with his lancet or jackknife. Bleeding recommendations suggested taking up to a cup or more of blood each time, which explains how the "arms of patients were often so scarred from repeated bleeding that locating a vein for another bleeding became a difficult task." As one pioneer recalled, the doctor "came every day, he purged, he bled, he blistered, he puked, he salivated his patient, he never cured him." Early Michiganians experimented with a multitude of "root" cures. Sweating and snakeroot with a purge of white walnut bark peeled upward might break a fever or a poultice of peppermint and tansy leaves might cure dysentery. Superstitious cures also abounded, with one suggesting wearing a spider around the neck or drinking one's urine to cure the ague. Despite a general feeling among pioneers that doctors "killed quick, but cured slow," Mackinac Island was the site of one medical breakthrough. In 1822, Alexis St. Martin, an American Fur Company employee, suffered a non-fatal gunshot wound to his abdomen. Dr. William Beaumont, a U.S. army surgeon at Fort Mackinac, treated St. Martin, whose wound never completely healed. Instead, it provided a "window" to the stomach, allowing Dr. Beaumont to observe the human digestive process. His 1833 treatise on the subject was "the first important study" in this field.[34]

—— Churches and Schools

Pioneers left their churches behind, but they remained God-fearing Christians. Catholics coming to Michigan, especially to the Detroit area, had ample religious opportunities, but initially Protestants were less fortunate. "For a long time," circuit riders preached "wherever they found an audience." In 1818, Michigan's first Protestant church (Methodist) opened in Dearborn. However, most early settlers relied upon itinerant preachers who not only brought God's word, but news from the outside world. The size of the congregation mattered little. One pioneer recalled a preacher who offered a two-hour sermon to four people: "It was delivered with as much enthusiasm as if he had had an audience of a thousand people." As more settlers arrived, churches were among the earliest institutions added to a town.[35]

Despite the many demands that had to be met to conquer a wilderness, the early settlers introduced schools to the frontier to educate their children. In 1827, the Michigan Territorial Council adopted a law requiring townships to employ a schoolmaster "of good morals" once fifty people lived in the township. The curriculum consisted of reading, writing, English, French, arithmetic, spelling, and "decent behavior." (Latin was later added for older pupils.) Schools were open six months, some running only three months in the spring and three months in the fall. The schooling was not free and parents were issued "rate bills" based on a student's attendance. Students matriculated with few amenities and whatever school books they could bring from home. Teachers used a penknife to create or repair new quills for the pupils and a ruler to draw lines on slate boards or paper (a rarity) for writing practice. Young children "sometimes drew out the letters of the alphabet in a tray filled with moist sand." Recitation was an important part of the daily lesson. Students failing to answer a question correctly went to the back of the class. A teacher's ruler also served to crack knuckles of a difficult student, while a birch rod meted out harsher punishment. Teachers (mostly males) also boarded with families, receiving part of their salary in meals and lodging. Once Michigan became a state, improving educational opportunities became a first priority.[36]

Settlers also came into contact with Michigan's original inhabitants. Although pioneers arrived with some fears of confronting Indians, there were no hostile Indians in Michigan. (However, the 1831 Black Hawk uprising in Illinois resulted in the Michigan militia being called out and left some settlers in the southwestern Lower Peninsula apprehensive.) Not all pioneers would have agreed with one early settler who found the Indians "a kind-hearted set of fellows, full of life and fond of fun." Yet, early Michiganians recalled being generally tolerant, sympathetic, and even appreciative of the natives. The Indians introduced the newcomers to survival techniques, especially remedies for ailments. It was not uncommon to find Indians spending a cold winter night sleeping before a settler's fireplace. However, they could be "troublesome" especially when intoxicated—a condition blamed on the fur trader. The manner in which Indians approached a cabin also annoyed the settlers. Instead of announcing his presence, the Indian peeked in the cabin window until noticed by the settlers. One pioneer woman, alone with her sister and two young boys, recalled being startled when she saw an Indian peering through her window. She eventually allowed his family to spend the night. The next morning the Indian mysteriously disappeared, but soon returned with a venison steak as payment for the evening's comfort.[37]

The impact of the pioneer experience on women is under-appreciated. There is no doubt early Michigan women were "rugged and accustomed to hard physical labor." They had to be if they hoped to survive. Early marriages and large families were the norm, and children came "in almost annual crops." Yet, the hardships of frontier life, especially frequent childbearing, took its toll, leaving many wives worn out in their thirties and dying at too young an age. The pioneer family, according to one Michigan survivor, "consisted of a succession of wives for one man, each with several children."[38]

—— Not All Hardships

Finally, a pioneer life included numerous occasions for socializing. Even work was considered a good reason to have fun. Cabin raisings, spinning bees, quilting bees, as well as games of wrestling, running, horseshoes, and tug-of-war, helped break the isolation and hard work of living in the wilderness. At a husking bee, ears of corn were piled in the middle of the floor and two teams raced to husk it. If a girl found a red ear of corn, she gave it to a favorite boy. If the boy found a red ear, he got a kiss from the girl of his choosing. Afterward a dance was held and refreshments served. As one pioneer recalled fondly, the "grand feast . . . to which they all did ample justice [while] never taking offense at the simplicity of the meal." Another interesting, albeit cruel, contest was the gander pull. An old goose was plucked, greased and tied by his feet to the limb of a tree. Riding a horse bareback, a man attempted to pull the gander's head off. In something of an understatement, as one settler exclaimed, occasions like these "were the pleasantest part of the pioneer's life."[39]

Despite the troubles and challenges they faced, many early Michiganians agreed with John Fisher, who settled near Tecumseh in 1831. Comparing his native England with his new home, Fisher believed he was "in a Country where all is life and animation, . . . where everyone speaks of the past with triumph, the present with delight, the future with growing confidence and anticipation." Proud to attach "his destiny and ambition" to America, Fisher asked himself, "How long do I plan to remain in Michigan?" His answer, "As long as I live."[40]

The pioneer period in Michigan did not last long. By the 1850s the settlers had conquered the Michigan wilderness—at least in the southern Lower Peninsula. With the introduction of sawmills, houses replaced log cabins. Crude frontier towns became cities, while better roads and a new mode of transportation (railroads) made travel less adventurous. In September 1831, President Andrew Jackson invited Lewis Cass to join his administration as Secretary of War. Before Michigan's governor left Detroit for Washington, he was honored with a public dinner. One of the toasts declared that Michiganians would remember Cass for his "zealous and successful exertions to promote their welfare." Another observer added that Cass found the territory "weak from the devastations of war, and left it strong. . . . It can be affirmed safely that the present prosperity of Michigan is now more indebted to Governor Cass than to any other man, living or dead." As Cass prepared for national service, Michigan prepared to become a state. It would be a difficult but exciting journey.[41]

CHAPTER

6

Quest for Statehood

Stevens T. Mason navigated Michigan into the Union as the 26th state and served as its first governor.

"I am in favor of getting it while we can, for at best, if we are cut down in the south, as we certainly shall be, our State will be quite poor and small enough."

—Senator Lucius Lyon, regarding accepting the
congressional compromise of the
western Upper Peninsula to replace
the loss of the Toledo Strip

On January 12, 1835, acting Territorial Governor Stevens T. Mason told the legislative council that Michigan faced a crisis. He explained that Michigan's request to Congress to call a convention to write a state constitution had been denied. Mason declared that the Michigan Territory had a "right" to be admitted to the Union as a state; so he asked the council to call a convention. The council agreed; delegates would be elected in April and gather in Detroit in early May.[1]

Born in Virginia in 1811 and raised in Kentucky, Stevens T. Mason came to Michigan when his father was appointed territorial secretary in 1830.

Mason's descendants had arrived in America from England during the late seventeenth century, and later-day Mason family members included George Mason, a member of "that galaxy of great Virginians" whose many accomplishments included writing the U.S. Constitution. Stevens T. Mason's family moved to Lexington, Kentucky, when he was a young child. Financial reverses and the election of Andrew Jackson as president in 1828 led Mason's father to seek an appointment as secretary of the Michigan Territory. The appointment was made in May 1830, and John Mason and his son arrived in Detroit in mid-July. The family soon followed and the Masons were "a welcome addition" to Detroit's official and social life.[2]

During the family's first Michigan winter, Secretary Mason served as acting governor when Governor Lewis Cass was away. Cass's absence also gave the younger Mason an opportunity to gain "a considerable familiarity" with his father's routine. But Cass's appointment as President Andrew Jackson's Secretary of War, coupled with John Mason's decision to leave Michigan for Texas, had an enormous impact on the younger Mason. On July 12, 1831, President Jackson appointed Stevens to succeed his father. Why Jackson chose the nineteen-year-old Mason—who could not legally vote—remains unclear. Mason's biographer, Lawton Hemans, concluded it was either a long-standing friendship between the elder Mason and Jackson, the president's desire to have American allies in Mexican-owned Texas (which he hoped to someday acquire) or "the spirited but frank [and] engaging manner" of the younger Mason that impressed the president. Regardless of the reason, Jackson's action proved controversial and quickly became "the topic of general comment" in Detroit in mid-1831. Public meetings were held and a petition was signed and sent to the president claiming that Mason's appointment was "derogatory" and violated "the genius and spirit" of the U.S. Constitution. Much of the opposition came from the business community and members of the Whig party, but efforts to circulate similar petitions outside of Detroit fell on deaf ears.[3]

Mason was not idle as his critics mobilized against him. He immediately sent a letter to the president explaining the situation, noting, "I desire not to convey the idea that I am in trouble or difficulty. I see my way clear and feel a confidence in maintaining myself against all opposition, if sustained by you, of which I feel a perfect assurance." The politically suave Mason predicted, "This difficulty will soon be removed by the appointment of a Governor." Mason also published a letter in the *Detroit Free Press* tracing his family's Michigan experiences in "simple language [that was] temperate and free from arrogance." As for his critics' concern about his possible role as acting governor, Mason reassured them should this occasion arise, he would consult "wiser and older men." The letter earned Mason some compliments from his critics. Mason also had his uncle William T. Barry (Jackson's postmaster general) and Richard M. Johnson (a family friend from Kentucky and a soon-to-be U.S. vice president) review letters he sent to those U.S. senators whose support he needed when the Senate took up his nomination.[4]

On August 6, 1831, George B. Porter of Pennsylvania was appointed Michigan's territorial governor. Twenty years older than Mason and from a distinguished family (Porter's father had served on the General George Washington's staff during the Revolution), Porter "did much to relieve" the pressure on Mason. However, in his three years as governor, Porter was often away, leaving Mason as acting governor and occasionally stirring Mason's critics. One Whig newspaper referred to the acting governor as "the stripling." Conversely, Mason grew popular and was more commonly known as "Tom."[5]

Mason's life changed dramatically following Governor Porter's sudden death in July 1834. Although three years had removed most of the hostility caused by his appointment, Mason faced a series of major issues. Shortly after Porter's passing, cholera swept through Michigan—the second epidemic in three years. At the same time, Congress increased the Michigan Territory to include the present-day states of Wisconsin, Minnesota, Iowa, and the eastern portions of the Dakotas. Finally, there was the ongoing struggle over statehood.[6]

Mason's January 1835 decision to ask the legislative council to call a constitutional convention followed several years of frustration. In October 1832, Michigan voters supported a call for statehood. The following year, Congress received a formal petition from Michigan requesting admission into the Union. Normally, a territory asked Congress for an enabling act before it wrote a state constitution; after a constitution was written, it was submitted for congressional approval. While Congress consented to the admission of new states, there had been exceptions. In 1796, Tennessee wrote a state constitution without an enabling act, then demanded—and received—admission into the Union. Furthermore, since the Northwest Ordinance of 1787 guaranteed statehood for parts of the Northwest Territory (including Michigan), Michiganians viewed this as a sacred agreement that even Congress could not alter. More specifically, Congress could not delay Michigan's admission. The Ordinance guaranteed statehood when a territory's population exceeded 60,000 people. When Congress denied Michigan's request for an enabling act—despite a late 1834 census that showed that more than 85,000 people lived in the Lower Peninsula alone—Mason and many Michiganians were outraged. As Mason declared, "With such a population, Michigan will assume her station as a member of the Union with a character, which must entitle her to importance and respect."[7]

—— A Bloodless War Begins

Michigan's early 1835 decision to call a constitutional convention also precipitated the Toledo War, a conflict with Ohio over the community of Toledo, which was located at the mouth of the Maumee River. Disagreement over who owned the area around Toledo, which was called the Toledo Strip, began in the early nineteenth century. According to the Northwest Ordinance, the boundary between the future northern and southern states in the Northwest Territory would be an east-west line that intersected the southern tip of Lake Michigan. Because of the uncertainty of the exact location of the lake's southernmost point, Ohio included a provision in its 1803 state constitution that it owned the mouth of the Maumee River regardless of where any future survey might place it. For the next thirty years, both the Michigan Territory and the state of Ohio claimed ownership. One survey, known as the Harris Line, put the land in Ohio. Two later surveys, including one in 1834 by U.S. Army engineers, put the disputed land in Michigan. The mouth of the Maumee River was important to Ohioans who planned to build a canal connecting the Great Lakes with the Ohio River, via the Maumee and Wabash rivers. The controversy intensified as canals like the Erie or the Baltimore & Ohio promoted settlement and commercial growth. Some Ohioans even contended that the proposed canal/river system connecting Toledo to New Orleans would make the Lake Erie town (Toledo) a second New York City.[8]

Michigan's decision to call a constitutional convention—an act of defiance to federal authority—left Ohioans uneasy. Ohio governor Robert Lucas realized that if the boundary issue was not resolved before Michigan joined the Union, Ohio might lose advantages it enjoyed as a state. For example, once Michigan became a state, it could submit the border dispute to the U.S. Supreme Court, something it could not do as a territory.

Ohio responded to Michigan's call for a constitutional convention by reaffirming its claim to the disputed territory. Describing Ohio's actions as "unjustifiable" and "high-handed," a confident Governor Mason declared, "We are the weaker party, it is true, but we are on the side of justice; and, with the guidance of Him who never forsakes the weak . . . we cannot fail

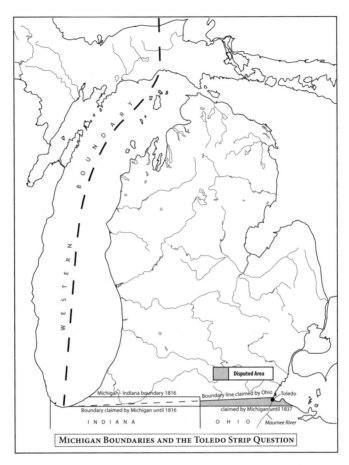

MICHIGAN BOUNDARIES AND THE TOLEDO STRIP QUESTION

Michigan expanded west after the "Toledo Strip" was awarded to Ohio.

to maintain our rights against the encroachments of a powerful neighboring state." Michigan retaliated in February 1835 with the Pains and Penalties Act, which made it illegal for Ohioans to carry out any official governmental activities in the Toledo Strip upon "pain" of a $1,000 fine and five years imprisonment.[9]

The situation along the border soon intensified. In early March, Detroiters expressed their displeasure with Ohio in a petition to President Jackson. At the same time, the legislative council declared that Michigan would resist "by all measures in our power" any Ohio effort to control the Toledo Strip.[10]

U.S. Secretary of State John Forsyth worsened the situation when he informed Governor Mason that if the Pains and Penalties Act remained in effect, Congress might force a compromise with Ohio. A dismayed Mason offered to resign if the president could not support him. President Jackson did not ask for Mason's resignation. Instead, he turned to his attorney general for a ruling. Though neutral to the merits of the conflicting claims, Jackson was anxious to maintain the support of Ohio's powerful congressional delegation.[11]

To Jackson's consternation, U.S. Attorney General Benjamin Butler sustained Michigan's position and concluded that Ohio had no right to assume control of the Toledo Strip without Congress's approval. Butler argued the Pains and Penalties Act was a legitimate measure for Michigan to use to resist incursions into the Toledo Strip. The attorney general also noted that since the president had jurisdiction over territorial officials, he could remove them; the same was not true for elected state officials, like Ohio's Governor Lucas. When Mason received a copy of Butler's opinion, he sent a letter to Lucas explaining that Michigan would not surrender any portion of the Toledo Strip.[12]

President Jackson next turned to two presidential commissioners to resolve the growing border dispute. Benjamin C. Howard of Maryland and Richard Rush of Pennsylvania arrived in Toledo in time to witness the first hostilities of the Toledo War. On April 1, Michigan partisans held elections in the disputed territory; five days later, Ohio partisans—who represented a majority of Toledo's citizenry—also went to the polls. On April 8, Monroe County Sheriff Nathan Hubble and a small posse arrived in Toledo to arrest several prominent Toledoans for violating Pains and Penalties, including the holding of elections. At the home of Benjamin Stickney, one of the most outspoken Ohioans, the sheriff was threatened with bodily harm. Hubble broke down the door of the Stickney house and arrested another Ohioan after wrestling a gun out of the Ohioan's hands. In the meantime, Stickney's wife alerted other Ohioans of what was occurring. According to Hubble, Toledo came alive with gunfire and blowing horns. The sheriff and his posse fled Toledo with their prisoners as several dozen armed Ohioans chased behind.[13]

Governor Lucas also ordered the border be resurveyed. In light of Sheriff Hubble's arrests of the Toledoans, the Ohioans chosen to survey the border were understandably apprehensive. Lucas urged the surveying crew to move quickly, and if confronted by a "superior force," to retreat immediately until forces "sufficient to protect them" could be collected. As a final word of encouragement, he warned them to "be cautious, keep a sharp look out,

[and] do not suffer yourself to be surprised." The Ohioans apparently failed to heed his advice. At noon on April 26, fourteen miles south of Adrian, Michigan, a posse of approximately thirty Michiganians, commanded by Lenawee County Undersheriff William McNair, surprised the Ohio surveyors while they were encamped in a field owned by a "Mr. Phillips." Gunshots were exchanged; no one was injured, although one Ohioan claimed a bullet passed through his clothing at what became known as the Battle of Phillips Corners. Nine Ohioans were taken into custody and imprisoned in Tecumseh, Michigan. Two were released for lack of evidence, while six others posted bail that ranged between $400 and $800 each. One prisoner refused bail and remained a prisoner, under orders, he claimed, from the Ohio governor. Three surveyors who eluded the Michiganians reported they confronted "an armed force of several hundred men," and deemed it "prudent" to halt their efforts until "some efficient preparatory measures" could be taken.[14]

As Michigan continued to enforce the Pains and Penalties Act, President Jackson's commissioners met separately with Mason and Lucas. After talking with Lucas, Commissioner Howard observed that the Ohio leader was "very firm in his character and though doing what nine tenths of the nation will hereafter pronounce wrong, [he] will listen to no argument upon the point." The commissioners found Mason equally determined. The young governor agreed not to take "any step that will lead to a broil" as long as Ohioans stayed out of the Toledo Strip. Fearing war "was imminent," the commissioners suggested a compromise: Michigan should suspend the Pains and Penalties Act and stop prosecuting the Ohioans who violated it, while Ohio re-ran the Harris Line. Finally, Ohio and Michigan would establish joint ownership of the disputed territory until Congress resolved the matter. Mason labeled the proposal "dishonorable and disreputable," while Lucas, not surprisingly, responded favorably to it.[15]

—— Writing a Constitution

As Ohioans and Michiganians struggled on the border, Michigan delegates met in Detroit and drafted a state constitution. The constitutional process had begun in late January when the state's Democrats held a convention where they paid tribute to the right of forming a state government. However, the Whigs, the territory's other political party, criticized the Democrats, who represented a majority of the delegates assembling at the territorial capitol in Detroit on May 11. Despite the Democratic majority, a Whig (John Biddle) was elected president, and Charles Whipple and Marshall J. Bacon were chosen as secretaries.[16]

The delegates to Michigan's first constitutional convention selected various committees and went to work. The most controversial provision focused on the age of voters. Many of the newly arrived settlers had voted for constitutional convention delegates. Mason was credited with suggesting that voting rights be given to every white male citizen above the age of 21 years old who had lived in Michigan for six months, and to every white male who lived in Michigan at the time of the signing of the constitution. The constitution also offered a 176-page document, entitled, "The Appeal of the Convention of Michigan to the people of the United States," which detailed Michigan's position on the contentious boundary issue with Ohio.[17]

After 38 days of debate and decision, Detroiters greeted the new document with booming cannon and a fireworks display. Yet, not everyone was pleased. A disgusted local Whig newspaper predicted, "If such a Constitution so repugnant to the safety of the Union" should be endorsed by Congress, then the country's days were "numbered." Conversely, another Whig conceded that "on the whole [it was] a very tolerable production." Mason's biographer later concluded that "overwhelming sentiment for statehood compelled support" for the constitution. On a less partisan note, as the delegates met, Lewis Cass, home from the nation's capital, presented Michigan with an image that was adopted as the state seal. An inscription read, *Si Quaeris Peninsulam Amoenam Circumspice* ("If you seek a pleasant peninsula, look around you"). Cass crafted the future state motto from an inscription found on St. Paul's Cathedral in London ("Reader, if thou seekest his monument, look around you").[18]

—— Border Tensions Worsen

As Michigan finished its constitution, the Ohio legislature met in a special session to "adopt prompt measures" to protect Ohio's rights in the Toledo Strip. The Ohio lawmakers listened to Governor Lucas as he described Michigan's actions as "reckless vengeance, scarcely paralleled in the history of the civilized nations." The Ohioans passed a law that declared that the forcible arrest of an Ohio citizen in the Toledo Strip was punishable by up to seven years in prison. They set aside $300,000 to "maintain the supremacy" of Ohio laws in the Toledo Strip, and—to prove that Ohio owned the disputed land— ordered a court session be held in Toledo in early September.[19]

In midsummer, tensions along the border worsened. In July a Michigan posse, led by Monroe County Deputy Sheriff Joseph Wood, arrived in Toledo to arrest Two Stickney, one of Benjamin Stickney's sons. (Curiously, Major Stickney named his sons after numbers and his daughters after states.) At the Davis Inn, Stickney resisted, and in the ensuing struggle Wood was stabbed with a penknife. Wood was taken to a nearby inn where a local physician pronounced the wound mortal. After the attack, Stickney and his followers warned the Michiganians to "keep away" because they had "their knives sharpened and rifles loaded." The Ohioans threatened to resist any future arrest efforts as long as they had "a drop of blood left" in their bodies. Wood survived his attack (later described as a scratch) and earned the distinction of being the only casualty of the Toledo War. The day after Wood was wounded, the Monroe County district attorney observed that "all law and authority emanating from Michigan is openly trampled upon and set at defiance by a large portion of the citizens of Toledo." In retaliation for wounding the deputy sheriff, Mason ordered a 250-man posse to return to Toledo and arrest Stickney. When the Michiganians reached Toledo, they discovered Stickney had fled. Mason requested his extradition, but Lucas understandably refused.[20]

As the Michiganians searched for Stickney, the Michigan legislative council rejected the compromise proposed by President Jackson's commissioners. Mason sent the council's decision to the president with a note predicting, "The General Government may expect a serious collision. . . . The consequences attending such a state of things are deeply to be regretted, but they must rest with those who might prevent their occurrence." On August 29, citing Mason's overzealous defense of Michigan's rights, President Jackson fired Mason to preserve "the public peace." Unaware of the president's actions, Mason led another posse into Toledo to stop the Ohioans from holding their planned court session.[21]

The several hundred Michiganians marching to Toledo were enthusiastic. Twenty-one-year-old J. Wilkie Moore recalled that the Michigan men "had a vast amount of fun." Farmers along the way welcomed Mason's men "enthusiastically because [they] were 'fighting for Michigan.'" Despite the gaiety, Moore and his fellow Michiganians "were all very much in earnest." On the evening of September 6, the Michiganians (some estimates place the number at more than 1,000 men) camped eight miles from Toledo. According to Moore, they expected "bloodshed" the next day.[22]

Late on the morning of September 7, Mason's "army" entered Toledo but found no Ohio governmental officials. The Michiganians remained in Toledo for a few days and entertained themselves by eating the vegetables and fruit from Benjamin Stickney's garden and orchard. Following a public review of "his troops," Mason led them back to Monroe. In a final act, Mason dramatically threw his hat to the ground, praised the men for "their soldierly bearing," and declared he would defend Michigan's boundary rights "the last drop of blood in his veins."[23]

Mason was confident he had prevented the Ohioans from trespassing in the Toledo Strip, but his confidence was unwarranted. During the early morning darkness of September 7, the Ohioans had gathered in a Toledo schoolhouse. They hastily opened and adjourned their court session before fleeing back across the border. According to one legend, the proceedings were recorded on bits of paper and placed in the clerk's bell-crowned hat. The court then adjourned to a nearby tavern to celebrate. The festivities were rudely disrupted when word arrived that Mason and his men were nearby. In their haste to escape, the Ohioans lost the clerk's hat. It was retrieved, and the judicial party made its escape without further incident. When Mason returned to Detroit, he learned that not only had he failed to prevent the Ohio court session, but he had been fired. Mason's firing also ended the Toledo War, while Michigan's quest to become a state entered a new stage.[24]

—— A "Non-State" Holds "State" Elections

On October 5, 1835, Michigan voters went to the polls, electing a state governor (Mason) and a state legislature. They also elected a congressman (Isaac Crary) and approved the state constitution. However, Michigan was not a state—at least in the eyes of the federal government. In his inaugural address on November 1, Mason urged all Michiganians "to await with patience" congressional action. To minimize any conflict, the state legislature chose the state's first U.S. senators (Lucius Lyon and John Norvell) before adjourning; the legislature planned to reconvene in February 1836, confident Michigan would be a state by then.[25]

In his inaugural address, Mason promised to work with territorial officials. He soon got his chance when a new territorial secretary, John S. Horner, a Virginia lawyer, arrived in Detroit. Boasting he would discharge his duties "under all circumstances," Horner soon ran into more trouble than he ever imagined. Rallies denounced him and critics described him as "immensely fat" and "sour-faced." Two thousand people in Monroe gathered to censure him, while Detroiters resolved that Horner should "relinquish the duties of his office and return to the land of his nativity." Horner jeopardized any chance of success when he pardoned Ohioans who had violated the Pains and Penalties Act. Horner recognized that the pardons would be "unsavory to some extent," but he failed to realize the extent of their unpopularity. From Monroe he noted:

> I placed the pardons . . . amidst a wild and dangerous population, without any aid, a friend, servant or bed to sleep in, in the midst of a mob excited by . . . bad men. I could not enlist a friend, or an officer of the Territory. . . . The district attorney had the effrontery and timidity to say, 'that, if he acted, the mob would throw him and myself in the river.' Threats were made, and communications in writing, insulting and menacing in the extreme, were received.

Horner concluded, "There never was a government in Christendom with such officers." As a final indignity, the governor stopped in Ypsilanti where a mob barraged his room with stones and horse dung. Horner remained in Detroit until May 1836, but he was generally ignored. He then moved to Wisconsin, where President Jackson appointed him secretary of the newly organized Wisconsin Territory.[26]

—— Congress Debates Admission

During the winter of 1835–36, Michigan's efforts to join the Union were focused on the nation's capital. Ohio re-marked the boundary line according to its interpretation and without further incident. In December 1835, as Congress convened, Michigan's congressional delegation—Representative Crary and Senators Norvell and Lyon—prepared to take their seats. They would have a long wait as Congress spent the next months debating Michigan's admission.

The most vocal opponents included the Whigs (who disliked Michigan's strong ties with the Democratic party), Ohio's congressional delegation (who feared the loss of Toledo), and Indiana and Illinois legislators (who worried their states might lose their port cities on Lake Michigan if state boundary lines were redrawn). Some critics suggested that Michigan begin the process of applying for admission all over again. Whig Senator John Davis of Massachusetts noted, "I do not like the mode in which Michigan has conducted this business. . . . She has assumed rights that all agree are not well founded, and the consequence is, that she stands in an embarrassing posture. She claimed to be a State before she could be one." Others expressed different concerns. According to one New York legislator, Michigan's plan to give voting rights to 21-year-olds proved that illegal aliens, especially the Irish, were trying to take over the United States and make it a "Catholic Country."[27]

Michigan had its defenders. Congressman John Quincy Adams of Massachusetts believed Michigan deserved the Toledo Strip "by every law, human and divine." The former president concluded that "never in the course of [his] life" had he known of a controversy in which "all the right was so clear on one side and all the power so overwhelmingly on the other." Another Michigan supporter was Senator John M. Niles of Connecticut. Opposed to any suggestion that Michigan retrace its steps, Niles declared:

> There is a point beyond which a free people cannot be driven. . . . Why are the people of Michigan to be vexed and harassed in this way? They feel that they are treated harshly; that great injustice is done them. They have been opposed and resisted in every course they have pursued to obtain admission into the Union; and you have now divided their territory. . . . Do you wish to drive that people to desperation; to force them into acts of violence?

Niles concluded, if there was anything "wrong or unusual" with Michigan's quest for statehood, it was because of the "neglect of Congress."[28]

In June 1836, the House passed the Northern Ohio Boundary bill by a vote of 143 to 50. (The Senate had passed the bill earlier by a vote of 24 to 17.) The bill awarded the Toledo Strip to Ohio and offered Michigan the western Upper Peninsula and immediate statehood. The measure also required Michigan to hold a convention to "assent," or approve, the compromise.[29]

The Northern Ohio Boundary Act asserted Congress's claim that no measure, including the Northwest Ordinance, could prevent it from altering the boundaries of a territory. The Congress also contended that it was "expedient" to give Ohio the mouth of the Maumee River to guarantee the completion of the canal connecting Lake Erie with the Ohio River. As important, 1836 was a presidential election and the states of Ohio, Illinois, and Indiana together had 35 electoral votes; the "state" of Michigan would have three electoral votes. Although President Jackson was not seeking reelection, he hoped his handpicked successor, Vice President Martin Van Buren, would win in the fall election. Realistically, Jackson did not want to upset voters in Ohio, Illinois, and Indiana by siding with Michigan over the Toledo Strip.

——Just Say No

Michiganians were appalled with the Northern Ohio Boundary Bill. They expressed their discontent by holding meetings and passing resolutions. The *Detroit Free Press* labeled the bill "unlawful, tyrannical and unjust," while Monroe citizens described Congress's actions as "oppressive, unconstitutional and dangerous to the permanency of our Republican Institutions." Elsewhere, 1,000 Detroiters signed a petition claiming that the Upper Peninsula was a "sterile region on the shores of Lake Superior, destined by soil and climate to remain forever a Wilderness."[30]

Some Michiganians offered a different opinion. Lucius Lyon acknowledged that Michigan had been unfairly treated and that the western Upper Peninsula (U.P.) was a place "where we can . . . supply ourselves now and then with a little bear meat." But the western U.P., he predicted, "may at some future time be esteemed very valuable." He noted:

> A considerable tract of country between Lake Michigan and Lake Superior is known to be fertile and this with the fisheries on Lake Superior and the copper mines supposed to exist there may hereafter be worth to us millions of dollars. At any rate, it can do us no harm and I am in favor of getting it while we can, for at best, if we are cut down in the south, as we certainly shall be, our State will be quite poor and small enough.

More important than what the western U.P. might offer, Lyon concluded, "We are wholly without the means of redress."[31]

Governor Mason appeared equally resigned to Michigan's fate. Declaring that Congress's decision violated "every principle of justice," Mason observed that Michigan's alternatives were "resistance or unqualified submission." The governor acknowledged his "first impulse" was to resist Congress's demands, but that course of action offered "so little hope of gain but the certainty of permanent loss and lasting injury to ourselves and the nation."[32]

On July 25, 1836, after "a great diversity of opinion," the Michigan legislature agreed to hold a convention of assent. On the second Monday of September, 50 delegates from across the states would be chosen on the basis of the distribution of the population. Two weeks later, these delegates would gather at the Washtenaw County Courthouse in Ann Arbor.[33]

The election of delegates to the convention of assent was heated. The *Detroit Free Press,* the state's largest newspaper, argued that continuing the struggle for Toledo would involve Michigan "in heavy expense, in loss of character, [and] in dangers and sufferings not to be calculated until they have happened." The *Constantine Republican* added, "The boundary line is . . . fixed and established, irrevocably. . . . The assent required by Congress . . . is nothing more than assenting to be a state in the Union, with certain privileges as a condition, or refusing assent, deprived of those privileges." On the west side of the state, the *St. Joseph Peninsular* argued that the ongoing controversy over the Toledo Strip was not important "to the interests and prosperity of the state." On the other hand, Monroe Democrats believed that the Toledo Strip was more valuable than "the whole of Wisconsin." Comparing Congress's request for assent to a robber who "forces the traveler . . . to give up his purse," the *Monroe Sentinel* suggested that "Michigan ought not to attend to her own affairs; to go on with her state government, unless stopped by the general government; and if stopped, relinquish no rights, but to submit to superior power." Elsewhere, Cass County Democrats resolved that Michigan should "never sign the bond of our disgrace, whereby we are to be compelled to surrender our honor, as well as our rights."[34]

On September 28, 49 delegates (no delegate from Michilimackinac County attended) gathered in Ann Arbor. After much heated debate, the convention rejected the compromise by a vote of 28 to 21. The victors argued Congress had no power "to dispose of the territory . . . upon the mere grounds of expediency."[35]

—— Cooler Heads Prevail

As the impact of the convention's decision became evident, some Michiganians expressed concern for the future. They worried about a plan to distribute surplus revenue in the federal treasury among the states. As important, many people had moved to Michigan and purchased public land in 1836. A percentage of those land sales would be returned to the states. In both cases, only states, not territories, would receive these monies. Others believed that Michigan should enter the Union as quickly as possible and then try to get the Toledo Strip back by appealing to the U.S. Supreme Court. Finally, some advocates wanted Michigan in the Union to restore the balance between free and slave states represented in the U.S. Senate. Arkansas, a slave state, had been admitted when the Northern Ohio Boundary Bill passed, creating a temporary imbalance in the senate.[36]

In late October, Governor Mason received "numerously signed petitions" asking him to call another convention for the "immediate acquiescence in the preferred terms of admission." In mid-November, Mason acknowledged the importance of assent but said it was too late to convene the legislature to call for another election. Instead, he suggested that if the September proceedings stemmed from the "distorted representations of designing men," then the people had "an inherent and indefeasible right . . . to reverse acts of their agents they found prejudicial to their interests." Mason recommended those Michiganians favoring assent "take the measure with their own hands" and form a new convention.[37]

The day after the governor's pronouncement, a committee of Wayne County Democrats issued a circular that declared that since the people represented the state's highest authority, voters would hold an election on December 5–6. Each county would elect twice as many delegates as it had state representatives. These delegates would meet in Ann Arbor on December 14 to reassess the congressional compromise.[38]

The call for another convention proved controversial, but the election was held in most counties. Opponents to the election, especially the Whigs, refused to participate. On December 14, 82 delegates gathered in Ann Arbor. Because of the unusually cold temperatures, critics labeled the gathering, the "Frostbitten Convention." After a short debate, the delegates approved the congressional compromise. However, there were still obstacles.[39]

On December 27, 1836, President Andrew Jackson sent the results of both conventions to Congress. Showing signs of favoritism, the president noted the results of the latter convention fulfilled the assent requirement and that Michigan should be admitted into the Union. Throughout January, Congress again immersed itself into debate over Michigan's admission to the Union. The primary concern was the extralegal nature of the December convention. Because that gathering had not received the sanction of the state legislature, the results—especially the forfeiture of the Toledo Strip—might not withstand legal scrutiny at a later date. Several congressmen suggested Michigan begin the process of admission all over again. The most outspoken critic was Senator John C. Calhoun of South Carolina. The former vice president labeled the December convention "irregular," "revolutionary," and a "lawless assemblage." Calhoun viewed the proposed Michigan admission measure as "more unconstitutional and dangerous" than any previous bill he had seen in 22 years in the Congress. Describing "every" aspect of Michigan's admission process as "irregular" and "monstrous," the nation's leading advocate of states rights feared "the noble principle of self-government" forever changed if the bill passed. Michigan had its defenders, most notably, Senator Judah Dana of Maine who explained the Frost-Bitten Convention was as an understandable reaction to the loss of Toledo. He concluded:

> When passion had subsided and opportunity had been given for reflecting upon the situation of a State, out of the Union, they discovered that they were depriving themselves of great and inestimable advantages, that their present state was one of weakness and exposure, and strength and protection could only be found in the Union. Was it, then, wonderful that a change of sentiments should have taken place?

Senator James Buchanan of Pennsylvania attributed Calhoun's concerns to his "ardent imagination and creative genius." The future president added, "I feel none of these terrors. . . . Since I came into public life, I have known the country to be ruined at least twenty times; . . . Yet it would seem that the more we are thus ruined, the more we flourish. Experience has taught me to pay little attention to this doleful predictions."[40]

—— Statehood Is Achieved

On January 5, 1837, the Senate voted 25 to 10 to recognize the December election results. Twenty days later, the House of Representatives concurred by a margin of 132 to 43. On January 26, 1837, without any apparent ceremony, President Jackson signed the bill making Michigan the nation's 26th state. Two weeks later, Detroiters celebrated their new state. In the evening, residents placed candles in the windows of their homes, while bonfires on Jefferson Avenue presented a "brilliant spectacle." Throughout the day, Governor Mason—the person most responsible for helping Michigan become a state—was honored. In a speech, he noted it was time to forget the past and time to unite and advance Michigan's prosperity. The evening ended with an unidentified speaker who declared: "Nature has done her work, may her sons put the polish on; that education and internal improvements be our motto; let no sister state outdo us—if they undertake it, may they find themselves barking up the wrong tree."[41]

Michigan had achieved its quest for statehood.

CHAPTER
7

Building a State

The Soo Locks (circa 1855) opened up Lake Superior to unrestricted boat travel.

"Let free schools be established and maintained in perpetuity, and there can be no such thing as a permanent aristocracy in our land; for the monopoly of wealth is powerless, when mind is allowed freely to come in contact with mind."

—Benjamin Pierce, Michigan's
first superintendent of Public Instruction

With the trials of statehood behind them, Michiganians eagerly prepared to conquer the wilderness and build a state. The nation buzzed over changes—everything from new forms of transportation to reform movements to improve American society—and Michiganians vowed not to be left behind.

In the same month that Michigan joined the Union, a legislative committee addressed the state's infrastructure needs. The committee concluded a failure to move quickly would not only miss opportunities, but "swell the power and abundance of [our] wiser neighbors." Convinced the proposed internal improvement system would pay for itself, even yield a profit in twenty years, the legislature adopted the Internal Improvements Act in March 1837. Unwilling to say no to any settled part of the state, the program called for three statewide railroads and three canals: in the first tier of counties, the Michigan Southern Railroad (Monroe to New Buffalo); in the second tier of counties, the Michigan Central Railroad (Detroit to St. Joseph); in the third tier, the Clinton & Kalamazoo Canal (connecting those two rivers); and, finally, in the fourth tier, the Michigan Northern Railroad (St. Clair to Grand Haven), while a canal would connect the Saginaw River with the Grand River. A third canal was proposed to circumvent the rapids of the St. Mary's River at Sault Ste. Marie. With the exception of the canal at the St. Mary's River, the proposed program offered something to everyone in the southern Lower Peninsula. The ambitious program would be primarily funded by a $5 million loan negotiated by the state.[1]

Even before statehood, Michigan had experimented with railroads. In November 1836, the Erie and Kalamazoo—the first railroad west of the Allegheny Mountains—offered service between Toledo and Adrian. Under state government direction, the prospects for greater gains seemed realistic and early results confirmed that enthusiasm. In early 1838, hundreds of citizens witnessed the groundbreaking ceremonies in Mount Clemens for the Clinton and Kalamazoo Canal. Further to the south, excited residents turned out all along the tracks from Detroit to Ypsilanti to watch the Michigan Central's first train, although having to pull the locomotive back to Detroit by horses portended an uncertain future. In his January 1839 state-of-the-state report, Governor Mason enthusiastically reported construction progress, but financial problems soon slowed, and even stopped, construction. A dismal return on the loan (mishandled by Mason, according to his critics), coupled with the impact of nationwide depression, posed difficulties. Only a massive federal land grant and the sale of the unfinished, but marketable, Michigan Central and Michigan Southern railways saved the state from further financial obligations and embarrassment. Under private ownership, both lines reached Chicago in the early 1850s, much later than the original timetable. The Michigan Northern and the canals were abandoned. A final legacy of the internal improvements craze was a constitutional prohibition on state government involvement in such future projects. The fiasco also had political fallout as Governor Stevens T. Mason did not seek re-election in 1839 and soon left the state. Despite the many struggles, historian George May concluded, "There can be no doubt that railroad development in Michigan progressed more rapidly as a result of the state's action than if it would have done without."[2]

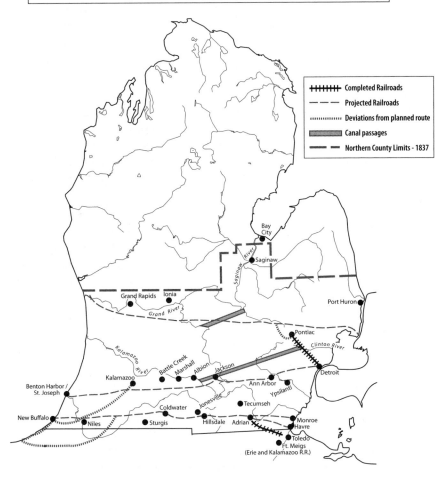

RAILROADS AND CANALS PROPOSED AT THE TIME OF STATEHOOD

+++++++ Completed Railroads

– – – Projected Railroads

.... Deviations from planned route

▨▨▨ Canal passages

━ ━ Northern County Limits - 1837

Bay City

Saginaw

Saginaw River

Grand Rapids   Ionia

Grand River

Port Huron

Pontiac

Clinton River

Kalamazoo River

Battle Creek   Marshall   Albion   Jackson

Kalamazoo

Ann Arbor

Detroit

Benton Harbor / St. Joseph

Ypsilanti

Coldwater   Jonesville   Tecumseh

New Buffalo

Niles   Sturgis   Hillsdale   Adrian

Monroe
Havre
Toledo
Ft. Meigs
(Erie and Kalamazoo R.R.)

In 1837, Michigan's legislature adopted this ambitious "internal improvement" plan.

— Building the Soo Locks

At the same time the legislature moved aggressively forward on the internal improvements in the southern Lower Peninsula, they singled out the rapids of the St. Mary's River at Sault Ste. Marie—the point where Lake Superior drops about twenty feet into Lake Huron—for special attention. First, they appropriated $25,000 to hire an engineer to produce a feasibility study. The December 1837 report called for a 75-foot wide canal with three locks (each with a six-foot lift) to negotiate the twenty-foot drop from Lake Superior to Lake Huron. The legislature asked Congress for a land grant to fund the proposed $112,000 cost, but moved forward without a response from Washington—appropriating another $25,000 and signing a construction contract. Workers for the company who won the contract arrived in early May 1839 ready to start digging. However, the planned canal passed through the grounds of Fort Brady and destroyed the fort's mill race (water channel). Ignoring the commandant's request to move the canal to a different location, the workers started digging until troops drove them from the area. The secretary of war later pointed out that if the contractor had not trespassed, but had "sought a friendly conference" demonstrating that the work "would not be injurious to the interests of the government," they could have continued digging. Instead, the contractor abandoned the job and the worsening economy placed the project on a backburner.[3]

Michigan's congressional delegation continued lobbying for federal assistance, especially as the western Upper Peninsula mineral boom of the 1840s magnified the navigational bottleneck at the Soo. (For example, in 1845, it took seven weeks to drag the 150-foot-long *Independence* around the rapids on greased rails.) Henry Clay was among the most distinguished critics of building a canal. The Kentucky senator alleged that putting a canal at Sault Ste. Marie would be "a work quite beyond the remotest settlement of the United States, if not the moon." Michigan senator John Norvell rebutted:

> The senator from Kentucky ought to have known the country better. Gentlemen, have . . . made a sorry exhibition of their geographical and statistical attainments. . . . It is a pity that we cannot once in awhile peep out of our narrow shells and look abroad upon that broad and magnificent fabric of nature comprised within the boundary of the Great Lakes states.

Finally, in 1852, Congress (fueled with support from President Millard Fillmore) granted Michigan a right of way through Fort Brady and 750,000 acres of public land to build a canal at the Soo. In that same year, 23-year-old Charles T. Harvey, the western sales agent for a Vermont-based manufacturer of mining scales, was in Sault Ste. Marie recovering from a bout with typhoid. Harvey saw an opportunity and convinced his employer to form the St. Mary's Falls Ship Canal Company and bid on the canal project. Having been to the western Upper Peninsula, Harvey understood the potential mineral wealth being held back by the difficulty to negotiate the rapids. "A stellar salesman" and the company's newly appointed general agent, Harvey lobbied state authorities and won the contract for his company. (Their bid was not the lowest, but the state commission favored Harvey's company "based upon their reputation and the likelihood that the job would be completed to specification.") Governor Robert McClelland signed the contract on June 19, 1853, giving Harvey's company two years to complete the project. If it missed the deadline, the state and the company would lose the land grant.

Digging began almost immediately. Despite adverse weather (especially heavy snows and harsh winter temperatures), debilitating diseases (most notably cholera that killed dozens of workers), food and supply shortages, as well as several strikes that disrupted progress, hundreds of workers labored year-round. The laborers, many hired from the east, survived eleven and a half hour days, earning twenty dollars a month; room and board was provided. The men used hand drills, sledgehammers, and crowbars, carting away the debris using wheelbarrows. Black powder blasted huge boulders into little pieces, while limestone, shipped from the quarries near Detroit, was used to line the locks' interior walls. One year into the project, John W. Brooks of Detroit, "a gifted civil engineer" and company vice president, assumed control of the project and navigated it to completion. But one major hurdle remained and Harvey came to the rescue. In late 1854, the project appeared doomed when what appeared to be an easily removed sand bar proved to be solid ledge of rock beyond the ability of the company's existing dredge. Harvey had a local blacksmith devise a two-foot-long, cone-shaped iron punch that he attached to a 30-foot oak shaft. Using a steam engine, the punch, which had a striking force of several tons per square inch, crushed the ledge. Harvey boasted, "Not a piece of rock came up as large as a man's hand." Managers marveled at Harvey's success since it cost far less than they had anticipated.

Within the two-year deadline, Harvey, Brooks, and hundreds of laborers completed two 350-foot locks (arranged in tandem) and a one-mile canal—at about the anticipated cost of one million dollars. On June 22, 1855, hundreds of spectators watched the steamship *Illinois* pass through the "Soo Locks." The state operated the locks until 1881 when the U.S. Army Corps of Engineers assumed control. Great Lakes shipping soon outgrew Harvey's locks and others were added. When the original locks were replaced in 1896, General Orlando Poe, one of the army's most admired engineers, praised the original work, claiming, "they were long in advance of their day, and if commerce had not outgrown their dimensions they would have done good service for a century." The newest lock, the Poe 2, opened in 1968. Today, the Soo Locks remain the world's busiest shipping canal.

—— Addressing the Needs for Schools

As Michiganians struggled with internal improvements, they enjoyed considerable success carrying out the mandate set forth in the Northwest Ordinance that "schools and the means of education shall forever be encouraged." Shortly after the War of 1812, territorial leaders introduced "the Catholepistemiad, or University, of Michigania." This ambitious plan with an unwieldy title (and varying pronunciations) "was a centralized system of education" with a governing board "empowered to establish all grades of schools and to select the teachers of these schools." The proposal met with plenty of criticism, especially in the sparsely populated Michigan Territory, and never developed as its founders had hoped. However, it established the principles that public education should be tax supported and under public (not religious) auspices. During the 1820s, the territorial legislature required a township to hire a teacher when its population reached fifty families and to build a schoolhouse when it reached 200 families. The flood of eastern pioneers who appreciated education and wanted their children educated explains the growing demand for schools. In 1831, Oakland County had a paltry population of 5,000 people but averaged three schools per township and boasted that "every child" would have an opportunity "of regularly attending a good school" by the following year. Yet government mandates went unenforced and unfunded, so the territorial period was a time of extravagant dreams and meager realities. But as Michigan neared statehood, two men believed "Michigan could achieve true greatness by making state-supported schools a reality."[4]

Isaac Crary and John D. Pierce, the fathers of Michigan education, shared much in common. Both were from the east, well educated, settled in Marshall during the early 1830s, and possessed a "common interest in the fields of government and education." According to legend, during the summer of 1834 the two men sat on a log under a tree discussing the English translation of a French report on the Prussian educational system and how it might be applied to Michigan. The Prussians used a separate state educational system—devoid of religious influence—that "united the primary, secondary, and higher schools in a system at public expense and under state control." Ironically, the two men "borrowed educational ideas from an autocratic government to help maintain a free, democratic society." As chairman of the education committee at the 1835 state constitutional convention, Crary guided proposals that created a public school system and introduced the office of superintendent of public instruction—the first state constitution to do so. The article also pioneered an innovative proposal for the sale of school lands (section 16) by creating a perpetual, state-controlled fund for the support of schools. Crary was motivated by the sale of school lands in neighboring states, which had been "inefficient, wasteful, and unfair to the public generally." As Michigan's lone congressman during the admission process, Crary managed this departure "from custom and tradition" through the congressional debate on Michigan's admission. His successful efforts "meant there would be money to build the primary school fund."[5]

—— Creating a School System

While Congressman Crary lobbied in Washington, Governor Mason appointed Benjamin Pierce the state superintendent of public instruction— the nation's first. Pierce prepared a lengthy report he delivered to the legislature in January 1837. As he later recalled, "It was a day when all was astir with activity and life—the watchword was progress and improvement [and most pioneers] were anxious for schools." A Brown College graduate with teaching and administrative experience, Pierce contended a statewide system of public education was the greatest possible improvement. "Without education," he reasoned, "no people can secure themselves against the encroachments of power." The common school was "the foundation of our whole system of public instruction, as they are indeed the chief support of all our free institutions." American government "proceeds from the people—is supported by the people—and depends upon the people," Pierce contended, so "children of every name and age must be taught the qualifications and duties of American citizens." Pierce stressed these schools should be free because with free schools "there can be no such thing as a permanent aristocracy in our land; for the monopoly of wealth is powerless, when mind is allowed freely to come in contact with mind." Pierce expected the wealthy would create schools, albeit private ones, so if the state did not create schools for the poor, this would "widen the distinction that already existed between rich and poor by creating 'an aristocracy' of learning as well as of wealth." Pierce also placed great emphasis on teachers who needed to be trained and well-paid (although women could be paid less than men). Hiring "incompetent teachers is a waste of money, a waste of time, and a waste of intellect," he surmised. Pierce's multi-faceted plan called for primary schools, founding and funding libraries, construction of schoolhouses, establishment of county academies or branches for the university, organization and support for the university, and the disposal of both school and university funds.[6]

In March 1837, the legislature approved much of Pierce's bold course of action by establishing a primary school district in each township and obligating districts to file annual reports with the state superintendent. Districts paid taxes for the support of schools, while state funding ("in proportion to the number of pupils between the age of five and seventeen") came from Crary's Primary School Fund. Advances soon appeared. School lands (totaling more than one million acres statewide) started selling and at high prices. More students attended schools, with total enrollments exceeding 44,000 students by 1839—a six-fold increase over two years earlier. Yet, problems developed, many tied to the impact of the Depression of 1837. The sale of school lands slowed, a shortage of quality teachers developed (primarily because of low wages), and many districts submitted incomplete annual reports or none at all. But as Pierce accurately predicted in 1841 when he stepped down as superintendent, "though difficulties may have arisen, and may impede, the march will be onward."[7]

The two other education bills adopted in 1837 focused on the University of Michigan. The laws established a governing board (called the Board of Regents) and took advantage of an offer of 40 free acres of land by placing the school in Ann Arbor. Students, who paid no tuition and could be fourteen years old, started attending classes on September 25, 1841. A student's day began at 5:30 AM and included two sessions of religious studies and classes in Greek, Latin, mathematics, logic, and philosophy. The school's first class had six students, and enrollment grew slowly; by the late 1840s it totaled 89 students. Plagued by faculty dissension, dropping enrollment, and financial problems, the school's future looked bleak until the arrival of Henry Philip Tappan in 1852. A man of "considerable note," especially in the field of philosophy, Tappan remade the University of Michigan during his presidency. He broadened the course of study (adding civil engineering and law) and hired outstanding faculty without regard to their religious affiliation. According to historian Willis Dunbar, "In less than a decade, the university had been transformed from a struggling, poorly attended school to one of the leading educational institutions of the nation."[8]

A unique provision of the education legislation was the establishment of branch campuses. In reality, these were secondary schools designed to train teachers and prepare men to attend the university. Branch campuses also offered a female department (a concession since girls were not allowed to attend the university). Seventeen towns applied for branch campuses, and eight were approved (Pontiac, Monroe, Kalamazoo, Detroit, Niles, White Pigeon, Tecumseh, and Romeo). Although there was "considerable protest" when the state withdrew funding from these schools in the mid-1840s, the total enrollment peaked at 315 students.[9]

Two other notable educational accomplishments included the establishment of schools to train teachers and educate future farmers. Approved in 1849 and formally opened in early 1853 in Ypsilanti, the Michigan State Normal School (present-day Eastern Michigan University) trained teachers for common schools. At the time, only three other states sponsored such schools—none west of the Alleghenies. Normal enrolled both men and women in degree programs for one year (common schools) or four years (high schools). The school also soon added a "model school," giving students a chance "for actual experiences under the supervision of trained teachers."[10]

As the Normal School opened its doors, farmers began complaining the curriculum at existing colleges offered little for their children whose future lay in farming. They also criticized both the University of Michigan and the Normal School for ignoring the obligation to offer farming classes. The issue reached a critical point at the 1850 Constitutional Convention when the *Kalamazoo Gazette* circulated powerful editorials that detailed the advantages of an agricultural education. In 1855, John C. Holmes, secretary of the State Agricultural Society, persuaded the legislature to establish a separate agricultural school—despite efforts by the University of Michigan and Normal School to block an independent school. As a compromise because "a number of towns" wanted the new school, the Michigan Agricultural College (MAC) campus was located in a wilderness area about ten miles east of Lansing. MAC (present-day Michigan State University) opened its doors in 1857. School enrollment never posed a problem, but it was not smooth sailing. Finances neared a crisis until Congress adopted the 1862 Morrill Land Grant Act, which provided state agricultural schools with land grants. Since MAC was the nation's first agricultural school, it earned the title as the "Pioneer Land Grant School." At the same time, MAC benefited from new leadership, most notably Trustee Hezekiah G. Wells and President Theophilus Abbot. A "highly successful" administrator, Abbot hired new faculty that included Robert C. Kedzie, who demonstrated how neglected muck land could become "a source of 'wealth and abundance,'" and William J. Beal, whose work "led to the modern miracle of hybrid corn." When Abbot left the presidency in 1885, MAC "was firmly established as a state institution."[11]

—— A New State Capital

As Michiganians focused on transportation improvements and educational advances, they also relocated their state capital. In 1847 state legislators prepared to choose a permanent state capital—an issue that proved contentious.

During the 1835 constitutional deliberations, Detroiters successfully lobbied to postpone this issue until ten years after Michigan entered the Union. It was a victory that backfired since 60 percent of the state's population lived outstate by the late 1840s. As the legislature undertook this debate, towns boasted their virtues, while disparaging their rivals. A port city with a 150-year history, Detroit "looked" like a capital with its many fine residences, as well as the current capitol. Detroiters also claimed relocating the capital would cost $200,000. (It actually cost one-tenth that amount.) Recalling Detroit's surrender during the War of 1812, critics countered the capital should be centrally located as in neighboring states. Ann Arbor and Jackson fell from consideration because they already enjoyed state patronage (the university and prison, respectfully), while Marshall lay too far south. A deadlocked legislative committee offered three proposals: (1) stay in Detroit, (2) move to Marshall (the home of a committee member), or (3) find a central wilderness location in the third tier of counties.[12]

Weeks of debate led to votes on numerous locations, including one day when the senate voted 51 times, which may explain why one exasperated legislator suggested the capital be moved to Copper Harbor—the isolated settlement at the tip of the Keweenaw Peninsula more than 500 miles from Detroit! Possibly the most influential man in the debate was not a legislator. James Seymour, a Genesee County developer who owned a sawmill along the Grand River in what became North Lansing, offered free land in Ingham County and a capitol built at his own expense. Demonstrating great marketing skills, Seymour provided each legislator with a map with bold red arrows showing how his proposed site was equidistant from the state's population centers. With each frustrating day Seymour's offer looked better. Finally, both houses concurred. The new state capital would be placed in Ingham County's Lansing Township and named "Michigan." Michigan, Michigan, never worked and the new capital was renamed for John Lansing Jr., an American Revolution veteran and New York delegate to the Constitutional Convention. A few days after agreeing on a site, the exhausted legislators gathered at a public dinner where "much hilarity and good feeling" soothed any hurt feelings.

—— An Island King

Two unrelated "royal" distractions of the antebellum period included dealing with a self-proclaimed king, while provoking a real monarch that might have led to a third war with Great Britain.

James Jesse Strang dreamed of becoming the next Caesar or Napoleon. Arriving in Wisconsin in 1843, the 30-year-old New Yorker seized an opportunity to reach his lofty goals. Despite claiming to be "the perfect atheist," he converted to Mormonism. When Mormon leader Joseph Smith was murdered in Illinois in March 1844, Strang claimed to be Smith's successor. Not all Mormons agreed, most notably Brigham Young, who excommunicated Strang before leading most Mormons west to Utah. However, a handful of Mormons followed Strang and settled on an uninhabited island in northern Lake Michigan. Beaver Island had everything Strang and his followers needed: virgin timber, tillable land, a deep and sheltered bay, and exceptional offshore fishing. It also was 25 miles from the mainland, a perfect place to protect this fledgling community from troubling outside pressures. By the mid-1850s, the Mormon colony boasted 2,500 followers and rivaled Mackinac Island as a refueling stop for Great Lakes steamers. But Strang's kingdom proved controversial, especially with non-Mormons, called Gentiles, who resented the Mormons for an assortment of reasons, most notably their practice of polygamy. At one point, U.S. federal marshals—at the bequest of President Millard Fillmore—arrested Strang on an assortment of charges and brought him to Detroit for trial. The Mormon leader defended himself, earned an acquittal on all charges, and then ran for the state legislature. With a district encompassing much of northern part of the state and his followers most of its constituency, Strang won easily.[13]

Following his election, Beaver Island witnessed an elaborate ceremony where Strang crowned himself king. However, Strang ruled his kingdom as an autocrat, which led to his downfall. Describing women's clothes as impractical and unhealthy, the king decreed female subjects dress in loose, knee-length smocks worn over modest pantaloons. Most Mormons accepted the change. But when two women refused, Strang had their husbands whipped. The two men vowed revenge and on June 16, 1856, they ambushed the Mormon leader, beating and shooting him. As Strang lay dying, his murderers fled to Mackinac Island where a local judge fined them $1.25 before releasing them. With Strang gone, the Gentiles attacked Beaver Island and drove the Mormons away. After burning the island tabernacle, the attackers took control of the Mormon printing office and printed a manifesto declaring, "The dominion of King Strang is at an end." Years earlier, Strang had predicted "all the works of man are destined to decay." But the future "monarch" concluded, "Fame alone of all the productions of man's folly may survive." The Beaver Island monarch had achieved his goal.[14]

—— Aiding Rebellious Canadians

In the same year Michigan joined the Union, a rebellion in Canada led to the little-known Patriot War. The short-lived uprising against the British government posed a problem for officials on both sides of the Michigan border as a mixture of expatriate Canadians and idealistic Americans (called "Patriots") sought to overturn what they viewed as the "yoke of British oppression." Public meetings passed supporting resolutions, raised funds, and accepted volunteers for the quasi-military raids (called "filibusters") that left London and Washington, DC, angry, confused, and frustrated. The Patriots violated American neutrality laws and jeopardized peaceful relations between the United States and Great Britain.[15]

The Patriot War in Michigan culminated in the fall of 1838 as the Patriots undertook some of their boldest moves. Invasions into Ontario from Michigan left dozens of casualties among both the Patriot invaders and the Canadian defenders. The new aggression forced governments on both sides of the border to strengthen their defenses and moved the United States and Great Britain closer to conflict. Throughout October and November reports and rumors filled the newspapers and official government correspondence. Although the Patriots' exact plans remained a mystery to both U.S. and Canadian authorities, their renewed activity jeopardized the fragile peace along the border. The previous winter British and Canadian authorities had tolerated the inability of the U.S. government to stop the Patriots, but in late 1838 the governor general of Ontario urged U.S. General Hugh Brady in Detroit "to think no pains too onerous" to prevent a reoccurrence of the Patriot invasions across the border. The governor claimed he had faith in Brady but he was prepared "for the worst."

Washington ordered its officials on the border to be increasingly vigilant. General Brady was told to disarm any armed body he found in Michigan and arrest them. Although more U.S. troops had been sent to the border, Brady only had 100 regulars to defend a 140-mile border that included the U.S. arsenal in Dearborn and the fort in Detroit. U.S. Marshall Conrad Ten Eyck added deputies to assist Brady, but reports indicated that Patriots were gathering in Michigan towns intent on some future action. Arrests were made and groups were disarmed, but even in the face of these setbacks, the Patriots acted. On the evening of December 3, "General" Lucius V. Bierce, an Ohio lawyer, led a ragtag force of 150 Patriots across the river and landed about four miles north of the small community of Windsor. The Patriots routed a small band of Canadian militia, but by daybreak the Canadians had recovered and the timely arrival of British regulars with a field piece and Indian allies left the invaders outnumbered and fleeing, including General Bierce who was described by a subordinate as "wanting in courage." As the "battle of Windsor" unfolded, Detroiters "anxiously" watched, according to one observer, "the melancholy spectacle of burning buildings, a steamboat wrapped in flames, and the flashes of the guns of contending parties on the opposite shore." When it was over, 21 Patriots had been killed in action, five others summarily executed after being captured, and 44 captured. The prisoners were later tried; six were hanged (including Hiram B. Lynn of Ann Arbor), and 18 (including two Michiganians) were sent to Van Dieman's Island (present-day Tasmania). General Brady's troops arrested many of Patriots who successfully eluded the Redcoats and escaped back to Michigan. Four loyal Canadians died in the fighting.

The days immediately following the battle were filled with foreboding for citizens and authorities on both sides of the Michigan-Canadian border. An angry mob met U.S. troops landing captured Patriots at the city wharf. General Brady faced threats of assassination, while sentiment among some Detroiters, especially in the press, led one citizen to write, "You would think that instead of sustaining any loss [the Patriots] had conquered Canada."

But the Patriot War had ended, at least along the Michigan frontier. In the fall of 1839, one Patriot leader claimed, "The smoldering embers will soon again be lighted." Yet, a few months later he confessed that the Patriot liberators had reached an agreement with the Canadians: "We have come to the conclusion not to go until we are wanted; and the [Canadians] say when they want us, they will send."

CHAPTER

8

The Fight against Slavery

Slaves traveled north along the Underground Railroad to escape slavery.

"We were working for humanity."

—Erastus Hussey (Battle Creek)
on the purpose of the Underground Railroad

By the time the Patriot War faded from the news, Michigan was home to a growing and determined anti-slavery movement that left the state "a beacon of liberty in the Great Lakes." Anti-slavery sentiment began as early as 1807 when Justice Augustus Woodward's "sharp indictment against slavery . . . helped to solidify public opinion in Michigan against the institution of slavery." During the early pioneer period, itinerant preachers—men like Elijah Pilcher, a 22-year-old Methodist Episcopal, or Luther Humphrey, a Presbyterian who so opposed slavery that "he would neither eat nor wear anything made by slave labor"—condemned slavery as they traveled the Michigan wilderness. One preacher who left a more extensive record of his activities was Guy Beckley, a Vermont Methodist Episcopal minister who arrived in Ann Arbor in 1839. Within a few years, Beckley preached in 30 different towns in eleven counties and founded an anti-slavery newspaper. First issued in

117

April 1841, the *Signal of Liberty* offered stories about escaped slaves refreshing themselves "on their journey to a 'land of freedom.'"[1]

The anti-slavery message also resonated with early settlers. Ann Arbor founder John Allen, a Virginian from a slave-owning family, praised his departure from "a land of oppression and Tyrany [sic], and placing us in a land of liberty and peace, where the sweat, the groans, and blood of the Afflicted Sons and Daughters of Afffrica [sic], shall never rise in Judgment to condemn us." At the same time, Quaker settlers, who were among the most outspoken opponents of slavery, willingly aided escaped slaves. Michigan not only developed hostility to slavery, but citizens welcomed blacks living in Michigan. An 1827 territorial law gave free blacks some protections against kidnapping and required that escaped fugitives receive due process before being returned to slavery. Although the law also required blacks living in the territory to register with the county courts and post a $500 bond "guaranteeing good behavior," the measure went unenforced, and according to one jury, "no such law ought to exist or be enforced in a free republican country."[2]

Michigan's first anti-slavery society (Elizabeth M. Chandler's Logan Anti-Slavery Society) dates to October 1832, and soon other communities followed. Four years later, abolitionists gathered in Ann Arbor and founded the Michigan State Anti-Slavery Society. The 75 delegates who gathered in Ann Arbor adopted fourteen resolutions that denounced slavery as "a practical denial" of the Declaration of Independence, criticized slavery advocates who used the Bible to defend the institution, and demanded Congress abolition slavery.[3]

M. Chandler, who co-founded Michigan's first anti-slavery society, created this abolitionist image, which appeared in an 1837 book entitled *Slavery Illustrated in Its Effects upon Women.*

—— Dealing with Slavecatchers

Michigan's shared border with Canada—where slavery ended in 1833—led to several highly visible incidents in efforts to return escaped slaves south. In July 1831, Lucie and Thornton Blackburn ran away from Kentucky slavery, settling in Detroit where Thornton took a job as a mason. Two years later, their master tracked them and had them arrested. As word spread, the city's small black community mobilized. Two free black women visited Lucie in jail and spent the day with her. One of the women (Mrs. Deacon G. French) secretly exchanged clothes with Lucie, who walked out of the jail with the other woman. By the time the ruse was discovered the next day, Lucie had already crossed into Canada and freedom. As the sheriff took Thornton from the jail, the city's black residents attacked him. In the confusion, Thornton crossed the Detroit River and joined his wife. The Blackburns remained in Sandwich (present-day Windsor) for several weeks before Canadian officials, who rejected Michigan extradition requests, released them. The Blackburns settled in Toronto and never returned to Michigan. The "Negro Riot of 1833," as it was dubbed, led local whites to take up arms and indiscriminately arrest and imprison many blacks. Those found guilty of assisting in the Blackburns' escape were assigned to city work details. Some blacks fled Detroit, even abandoning their homes and property. A company of troops also arrived from Fort Gratiot, and for several weeks Detroit "was an unhealthy place" for its black citizens.[4]

Two of the most pivotal conflicts with slave catchers occurred in 1847. In January, slave catchers shattered the mid-winter quiet when they rode into Marshall intent on returning the Adam Crosswhite family to Kentucky. As word spread, both black and white residents rallied, threatening the slave catchers with tar and feathers. During the confusion, the Crosswhites fled to Canada. Describing the Michiganians as "barbarians," the outraged Kentuckians returned home where a sympathetic state legislature demanded the Crosswhites be repatriated. Eventually, a federal court ruled against the Michiganians and fined them $2,000—the estimated value of the Crosswhites if they had been sold. Zachariah Chandler, a prominent Detroit businessman (and later a U.S. senator) paid the fine. The Crosswhites returned to Marshall. Later that same year, two dozen heavily armed Kentuckians arrived in Cass County and kidnapped 50 escaped slaves before outraged and armed residents intervened. The Michiganians forced the slave catchers to justify their actions before a local judge, who happened to be outspoken opponent of slavery. The judge released the fugitives, who were quickly skirted off to the safety of Canada.[5]

——Abolitionists on the National Stage

As the episodes thwarting the slave catchers made headlines, the work of several Michigan abolitionists received national recognition.

In 1825, eighteen-year-old Elizabeth Chandler authored an emotional poem entitled, "The Slave Ship," which earned her a job writing for a national anti-slavery periodical. Born in Delaware and raised a Quaker, Chandler became "one of the most powerful women writers of her time." Urging women to work for the immediate emancipation of slaves, she created one of the most enduring abolitionist images—a kneeling female slave with the slogan, "Am I not a Woman and a Sister." Settling near Tecumseh in 1830, Chandler wrote for William Lloyd Garrison's abolitionist newspaper the *Liberator*. With her good friend, Laura Smith Haviland, she also founded Michigan's first anti-slavery society. Chandler died prematurely young in 1834, but her writings continued to influence the abolitionist movement.[6]

As a young girl, Laura Smith devoured many books, including one that captured the horrors of the Middle Passage bringing Africans to the new world. Although raised a Quaker in eastern Ontario, she converted to Methodism because it took a more active stance against slavery. Smith married

Laura Smith Haviland, posing with some of the devices southerners used to restrain or punish slaves, earned a national reputation as an outspoken abolitionist and Underground Railroad agent.

Charles Haviland, and by the late 1820s the couple and her parents had migrated to Lenawee County. Eventually a mother of eight children, Haviland merged her intense religious enthusiasm with a hatred of slavery. Besides organizing Michigan's first anti-slavery society, the Havilands also opened the Raisin Institute, Michigan's first integrated, coeducational school. After surviving a devastating illness that took the lives of her husband, parents, and one child, Haviland redoubled her efforts to aid escaped slaves. In 1846 in Toledo, Ohio, slave catchers overtook Haviland's train as she escorted several escaping slaves. When threatened at gunpoint, she boldly responded, "I fear neither your weapons nor your threats; they are powerless. You are not in Tennessee." This audacity led slave owners to place a $3,000 reward on her head. During the Civil War, Haviland worked as a nurse in Washington DC, then later at the Freedmen's Bureau. In an often-told story, she boarded a segregated streetcar in the nation's capital with former slave Sojourner Truth. The conductor ordered Truth off the bus but Haviland interceded, prompting the man to ask, "Does she belong to you?" Haviland defiantly responded, "No, she belongs to humanity."[7]

In 1843, a former slave changed her name to Sojourner Truth because, as she said, "The spirit calls me, and I must go." Born in 1797 to slave parents in New York, Isabella (her only name) experienced all the horrors of slavery, including being sold three times and surviving a cruel master who repeatedly beat and molested her. One year before New York finally ended slavery in 1827, Isabella ran away, taking her infant daughter, but leaving her other children behind. Isabella met abolitionists William Lloyd Garrison and Frederick Douglass, changed her name, and began a new career as an outspoken abolitionist and women's rights advocate. Despite being illiterate, she published her autobiography, *The Narrative of Sojourner Truth: A North-*

Sojourner Truth denounced slavery and advocated women's rights.

ern Slave in 1850. The following year, she gained national notoriety with her "Ain't I a Woman" speech. Truth settled in Battle Creek before the Civil War, but later visited Washington, met President Lincoln, and worked for the Freedmen's Bureau. After the war, she continued advocating for women's rights, even trying to vote (unsuccessfully) for President Ulysses S. Grant in 1872. Truth's passing in 1883 led to one of Battle Creek's largest funerals. Today, a 12-foot-tall Sojourner Truth statue in downtown Battle Creek stands as a dramatic tribute to a remarkable woman.[8]

On January 1, 1851, Henry Bibb, an escaped Kentucky slave who spent a decade living in Michigan, urged all blacks living in the United States to move to Canada "where laws make no distinction among men, based on complexion." Born in 1815, Bibb never knew his slave master father and was separated from his slave mother at a young age. He had several masters, including one who abused Bibb's wife and sold the family "down the river." Bibb escaped, arriving in Detroit alone in January 1842. His life changed measurably after meeting abolitionists in Adrian. Bibb lectured widely against slavery and even went south searching (unsuccessfully) for his family. Like Sojourner Truth and other escaped slaves, he detailed slavery's cruelties in his autobiography. The more stringent 1850 Fugitive Slave Law, which implemented draconian measures to return escaped slaves to their masters, led Bibb and his new wife to re-settle in Chatham, Ontario. They fought slavery by publishing a newspaper (*Voice of the Fugitive*), founding a school for runaway slaves, and organizing a program that distributed land to escaped slaves so they could "make it on their own." The land venture was designed to undermine southern claims that blacks needed slavery to survive. Dying prematurely young at the age of 39, Bibb is often forgotten among antebellum black leaders, yet he "offered vision, hope and most important, a voice to the thousands of fugitives in search of a new life."[9]

—— The Underground Railroad

Critics of slavery like Haviland and Bibb also "worked" on the Underground Railroad, which was neither underground nor a railroad, but earned its name from a frustrated slaveowner who claimed he lost his slaves along "an underground road." (The antebellum popularity of railroads led to the name change.) The Underground Railroad violated federal laws on returning escaped slaves, which explains the efforts at secrecy. Railroad jargon (agents, stations, and depots) identified sympathetic people and stops along the route. In Michigan, several routes were established, which one leader explained was a "zigzag" of safe places that ended at the Detroit River where fugitives crossed to the safety of Canada. One operator boasted that the size of the network made it "almost an impossibility" for slave hunters to trace their fugitives "without finding themselves on the wrong trail. . . . Hardly any two [fugitives] went over the same road and very little was known about the way lest the pursuers might follow." Besides using all possible modes of transportation, the escaped slaves usually traveled at night and hid in barns, cellars, outbuildings, woods, and swamps during the day. Fugitives used disguises; girls dressed as boys, and boys dressed as girls, and Quaker bonnets worked nicely to conceal the faces of escaping slaves.[10]

Among the Underground Railroad's most passionate leaders was Erastus Hussey. Born in western New York in 1800, Hussey arrived in Michigan in 1824, first settling in Plymouth, before moving to Battle Creek and opening a dry goods store. Recruited to the Underground Railroad in the early 1840s, the Husseys (Erastus, his wife Sarah, and their daughter Sally) became legendary. They received fugitives who had passed through Cassopolis, Ramptown (a black settlement), and Schoolcraft. After feeding them, the Husseys drove the fugitives to the next stop in Marshall, about ten miles away. The Husseys also edited an abolitionist newspaper and sometimes hand-delivered it when a recalcitrant postmaster refused. Erastus Hussey also took an active role in thwarting the efforts of slave catchers. On one occasion, a rumor that 30 armed slave catchers were headed to Battle Creek led him to circulate handbills telling the slave catchers to "Stay away from Battle Creek." The effort worked as the slave catchers turned back. Another equally bold Underground Railroad agent was John Lowry. A native New Yorker who settled in southern Washtenaw County, Lowry placed a large sign on poles "that could be seen from a distance" that declared, "Welcome to the Fugitive Captive." The sign had two figures, a white woman and a black man, holding a scroll. The woman held the scales of justice and a broken chain, while the man's chains were broken. The face of the slave, according to Lowry's daughter, was "all aglow with triumph." The words, "Liberty to the Fugitive captive and the oppressed over all the Earth, both male and female of all colors" appeared below the images. The sign proved to be something of a tourist stop, but according to a neighbor, Lowry was in earnest and "was of a sort not safe to tamper with."[11]

Two African Americans who played prominent roles in the Underground Railroad included William Lambert and George DeBaptiste. Lambert was a free black from New Jersey who arrived in Detroit in 1838 and quickly became an Underground Railroad agent—even claiming that he never lost a runaway to a slave catcher. George DeBaptiste, a free black, chose to leave southern Indiana for Detroit after helping more than 100 Kentucky slaves to freedom. A successful businessman after coming to Michigan, DeBaptiste owned a freight-hauling steamboat. However, it was suspected that his real business was transporting slaves across the river. Lambert and DeBaptiste also worked together on the Detroit Vigilance Committee to assist runaways and protect the interests of the city's black residents. They lobbied to enfranchise blacks and established a school for black children who had been denied admission to public schools. Detroit's Second Baptist Church, founded in 1836, also served as a key Underground Railroad stop.[12]

How many escaped slaves traveled through Michigan along the Underground Railroad? Records were not kept, so no one is certain. The Husseys helped 1,000 fugitives, while Dr. Nathan Thomas in Schoolcraft assisted 1,500 persons. William Lambert claimed helping "thousands" of slaves to freedom, and Detroit's Vigilance Committee assisted 1,043 fugitives across the border during an eight-month period in the 1850s. Exact numbers mattered less than the fact the Underground Railroad provided a constant reminder of how northerners willingly undermined the South's peculiar institution.[13]

Michigan was a safer haven for escaped slaves than elsewhere in the Midwest, but it was not a utopia for black settlers. Abolitionists had their critics, with one opponent suggesting lynching was the "only way" to handle abolitionists. Erastus Hussey, who admitted he expected to be arrested every day, saw his anti-slavery newspaper office burned to the ground by opponents. At the 1835 constitutional convention, delegates overwhelmingly rejected the suggestion of giving blacks the vote, fearing it might encourage them to move to Michigan. The state also adopted laws preventing blacks from serving in the militia, outlawing interracial marriage (although a few such marriages existed), and promoting de facto segregation in public places. Yet, Hussey and the others would not be deterred. Years later, he explained that he knowingly violated fugitive slave laws "out of sympathy for colored people and for principle." More simply, he concluded, "We were working for humanity."[14]

The abolitionist movement in Michigan gathered steam and then went political. In 1840, New York abolitionists formed the Liberty Party, and its only presidential nominee had Michigan connections. Born in Kentucky in 1792, James Birney spent years struggling with the issue of slavery. Family members were divided over slavery—Birney's father gave him slaves as a wedding gift, while an aunt who raised him rejected slavery. A graduate of present-day Princeton University, Birney served in elected positions (both in his native Kentucky and later in Alabama) and practiced law successfully. His conversion to abolitionism included working for the American Colonization Society and publishing an abolitionist newspaper in Cincinnati. After his 1840 defeat (the party earned a paltry 6,700 votes nationwide), Birney settled in Michigan. From his home in Bay City, he used his legal expertise to defend fugitive slaves, and then ran again for president in 1844—an election that saw his party receive a considerable increase in votes. However, a horse-riding accident ended Birney's public career, and he left Michigan in 1855. Shortly before his death in 1857, he predicted only war would bring an end to slavery.[15]

—— War with Mexico

During the decade following Michigan's admission to the Union, the annexation of Texas brought the slavery question into state politics. On more than one occasion, the Michigan legislature petitioned its congressional delegation to oppose annexation, which the Whigs claimed would lead to war with Mexico and perpetuate the institution of slavery. Even Democrats opposed annexation, most notably Congressman Robert McClelland (D-Monroe)—further evidence of a growing split within the Michigan Democratic party. Following a decade-long controversy, Texas joined the Union in early 1845. Within a year, the United States and Mexico were at war.

Michigan's congressional delegation supported President James Polk's May 1846 declaration of war against Mexico, but the conflict generated much controversy. Michiganians generally favored the annexation of Texas (formerly part of Mexico), which precipitated the conflict. On June 3, Detroiters gathered at city hall in "unprecedented" numbers and resolved that Mexican "insults and injuries" had left the United States no recourse but to "resort to arms." Michigan quickly filled several companies of regular infantry and a company of dragoons that saw combat. During the battle for the Mexican capital, Lt. Colonel Joshua Howard, a regular army veteran from Detroit, led the 15th U.S. Infantry as it stormed the Castle of Chapultepec. When the Americans, which included three companies of Michiganians, placed the Stars and Stripes over the key position, General Antonio Lopez de Santa Anna, the Mexican leader, declared, "I believe if we were to plant our batteries in Hell the damned Yankees would take them from us." In late 1847, the federal government allowed Michigan to raise a regiment of volunteers. By the time the First Michigan Volunteers arrived in Mexico, not only had the

war ended but the U.S. Senate had ratified the peace treaty. The Michiganians escorted supply trains, dealt with Mexican guerrillas, and struggled with
the boredom of garrison life. They also suffered from disease. By the time
the Michiganians headed home in mid-1848, sickness had so debilitated the
men that more one-third of the regiment rode in wagons. The First Michigan
Volunteers suffered no battlefield fatalities but lost more than 200 men to disease. Approximately 1,500 Michiganians served in the Mexican War—more
men than many other more populous states.[16]

Opposition to war, especially by the Whig party, continued throughout
the conflict. Senator William Woodbridge (W-Detroit) opposed the war but
voted for it, later explaining, "The whole matter is most unhappy & every way
to be regretted—but we could not help it." Michigan petitioners demanded
peace, while newspaper editorials denounced a war whose apparent goal was
the expansion of slavery. The *Marshall Statesman* condemned the war as an
"injustice," adding, "We may be traitors, but if so, it is because we desire to
preserve inviolate the honor of the Republic, to extricate her from the difficulties into which unprincipled men have plunged her." The Michigan State
Anti-Slavery Society called the war "unjust, unchristian, uncalled for," while
Michigan Liberty Party characterized war supporters as "traitors to the best
interests of the nation." The settlement of the war, most notably the territorial
acquisition called the Mexican Cession, generated continued debate on the
extension of slavery that led to the formation of the Republican Party a few
years later.[17]

As war raged in Mexico, Pennsylvania congressman David Wilmot introduced an amendment banning slavery from any territory acquired from
Mexico. The Wilmot Proviso passed in the House of Representatives along
sectional lines but failed in the Senate. Michigan Senator Lewis Cass, who
rejected state legislative overtures to support the Wilmot Proviso, proposed
a solution to the intensifying slavery debate. He maintained Congress lacked
the constitutional authority to interfere in governing the territories. The
federal government could authorize self-government in the territories, he
asserted, but those powers were limited. Cass's "Doctrine of Popular Sovereignty," which earned the support of many Democrats, also had many critics,
including abolitionists and some slaveholding southerners who feared any
measure that might restrict slavery's growth. Popular sovereignty overlooked
earlier decisions like the Northwest Ordinance, while some critics charged
Cass with refusing to take a firm position on a controversial matter. Cass
rejected this criticism, claiming popular sovereignty was "simply the doctrine
of our revolutionary fathers [who believed Americans were] capable of regu-

lating our internal policy in all and every respect whatsoever and we have the sole and exclusive and inherent right of governing ourselves as in our wisdom we think proper." Supporters of popular sovereignty also hoped Cass's treatise would end the worsening sectional acrimony over slavery in the territories.[18]

—— Lewis Cass for President

Some Michigan Democrats, most notably Congressman Kinsley Bingham of Livingston County who supported the Wilmot Proviso, criticized popular sovereignty. However, most Michigan Democrats put aside their differences as favorite son Lewis Cass won the 1848 Democratic presidential nomination. The party's national convention also adopted popular sovereignty as the party's position on territorial slavery and selected General William O. Butler, a War of 1812 veteran, as Cass's running mate. The Kentucky slaveholder balanced the ticket but contributed little to the Democrat team. As Michigan's first major political party presidential nominee (and last until Gerald Ford in 1976), Cass resigned his Senate seat and made a triumphant tour back to Detroit. As was the norm at the time, the candidate did not actively campaign but spent the months prior to the election at home corresponding with supporters.[19]

Cass's Whig opponent was General Zachary Taylor, whose 40-year military career made him a popular hero following impressive victories in Mexico. Despite comparisons to George Washington and Andrew Jackson, Taylor had no political ambitions, claiming, "Such an idea never entered my head, nor is it likely to enter the head of any sane person." Respecting their candidate—who admitted he had never voted or declared a party allegiance—the Whig party did not adopt a party platform in 1848. A Louisiana slaveholder, Taylor disappointed some northern Whigs, while elating Democrats who dreamed of victory. President James Polk reassured fellow Democrat Cass, "I think I may safely congratulate you upon the almost certain prospect of your election." But challenges lay ahead. Southerners feared popular sovereignty would prevent slavery's establishment in the western territories, while northerners viewed Cass as too sympathetic to southern principles. At the same time, anti-slavery advocates, especially in New York, formed the Free Soil Party. Boasting "Free Soil, Free Labor and Free Men," they chose former Democratic president Martin Van Buren as their presidential nominee.[20]

During the campaign, the Whigs attacked Cass in a variety of ways. An article in the *Detroit Advertiser* charged he was "the most plethoric man in the Senate, and decidedly a heavy speaker. His eye is dull, his voice wheezy, his actions awkward, and his style is forever running after a climax that it does not reach." More bluntly, the *New York Tribune* contended, "The country does not deserve a visitation of that pot-bellied, mutton-headed cucumber Cass." Trying to offset Taylor's legitimate war record, Cass's handlers exaggerated his War of 1812 record, prompting an obscure Whig congressman from Illinois to address notions that the Michiganian was a war hero. On the floor of the House of Representatives, Abraham Lincoln cynically questioned if Cass ever "saw any live, fighting Indians?" Elsewhere, Cass and his supporters tried to avoid discussing the divisive issue of territorial slavery—even distributing two different campaign biographies for northern and southern voters. In reality, Cass "was most certainly a politician—a cautious, middle-of-the-road politician who took a measured stance on every substantive issue except those involving national honor and territorial expansion. . . . [he] was simply a partisan Democrat who placed the Constitution above personal morality."[21]

Cass won Michigan and the states of the Old Northwest, but he lost the election 163 electoral votes to 127. Taylor won 1.3 million votes to Cass's 1.2 million. Free Soiler Van Buren won about 10 percent of the popular vote, but no electoral votes. (In Michigan, the Free Soil vote stood at 16 percent—more than double what James Birney had received in 1844.) According to historian Willard Carl Klunder, Cass "lost the election because of the same characteristics that had gained him the nomination. He was a venerable, moderate politician who served his party faithfully but without flair, thereby making few political enemies, and attracting even fewer passionate supporters." Outgoing President James Polk consoled Cass: "You cannot regret more deeply than I do the unfortunate result." Polk urged Cass to return to the Senate, which he did. (At that time, state legislatures elected U.S. senators.)[22]

In Michigan, the temporary cease-fire between the warring factions of the Democratic party ended with Cass's defeat. Within months the more stringent Fugitive Slave Law (part of the Compromise of 1850 designed to resolve the divisive territorial issues) left the intraparty differences "impassable." Senators Cass and Alpheus Felch avoided the vote on the Fugitive Slave Law, but Congressman A. W. Buel, a Detroit Democrat, voted for the bill, which earned him attacks for supporting a "cruel, unjust and infamous" law and a reelection defeat. Michiganians denounced the law, and many agreed with enraged Olivet residents who vowed to continue helping escaped slaves, claiming that any official who enforced the law had "too little soul to appreciate the blessings of freedom." At about the same time, the Michigan Free Soil Party adopted a resolution rejoicing in the "frequent escape of slaves" and deemed it "a duty incumbent . . . for every man . . . to aid and comfort them on their way to freedom."[23]

—— Birth of a Political Party

The fervor over the territorial question intensified in 1854 with the passage of the Kansas-Nebraska Act, which repealed the Missouri Compromise of 1820 and opened up free territory to slavery. Anti-slavery forces responded aggressively. Outraged northerners agreed with one Michigan Free Soil newspaper that asked, "Will the North quietly submit to be tricked and wheedled out of this free territory?" Detroiters at a public meeting viewed the Missouri Compromise with "all the solemnity of a national compact, second only to the constitution," while Pontiac residents charged Kansas-Nebraska Act supporters as "traitors to freedom." The need for action led to calls for the "friends of freedom" to unify "irrespective of party . . . to forget party ties and preconceived political feelings, and unit together in a solemn covenant to act and suffer all things to destroy American slavery."[24]

Achieving this goal was not without some difficulties. But on July 6, 1854, Whigs, Democrats, and Free Soilers gathered in Jackson. Since no building could accommodate a crowd estimated at 1,500 persons, it met outside in an oak grove. Jacob Howard of Detroit, a former Whig congressman and Underground Railroad conductor, chaired the platform committee. The Jackson meeting adopted Howard's recommendations demanding the repeal of the Kansas-Nebraska Act and the Fugitive Slave Law and nominated a slate of candidates, including Democrat Kinsley Bingham for governor. Those who "gathered under the oaks" called themselves Republicans—the first use of the name nationally—and argued they were "battling for the first principles of republican government, and against the schemes of aristocracy, the most revolting and oppressive with which the earth was ever cursed, or man debased."[25]

In November, Michigan Republicans swept into office. In an early demonstration of their power, they placed obstacles in the way of enforcing the Fugitive Slave Law. In January 1855, newly elected Senator Erastus Hussey introduced the Personal Freedoms Act, which easily passed the legislature (18 to 9 in the Senate and 40 to 28 in the House). The law "extended habeas corpus, trial by jury and legal appeal rights to blacks" and ordered county prosecuting attorneys to defend arrested slaves "at no cost." Furthermore, the law forbade state and local officials from cooperating with federal officials in recovering escaped slaves. Jailers who imprisoned a fugitive slave could be fined, while fines and imprisonment awaited anyone who falsely accused a person of being an escaped slave.[26]

In 1856, Michigan Republicans looked eagerly to their first presidential election. During the campaign a former Illinois congressman—brought out of political retirement by the Kansas-Nebraska Act—made his only Michigan visit. Abraham Lincoln arrived in Kalamazoo on the afternoon of August 27, 1856, to stump for Republican presidential nominee John Fremont. A large and enthusiastic crowd (some estimates claimed 30,000 people) met the former congressman in a city decked out for the occasion with banners, bands, and plenty of free refreshments. Lincoln offered two main themes in his 30-minute speech: the question of slavery ("not only the greatest question, but the sole question," he concluded) and the future of the Union. Lincoln's comments were greeted, according to one sympathetic newspaper, with "great cheering."[27]

The Republicans enjoyed a complete victory on election day in 1856. As an estimated 85 percent of Michigan's eligible voters cast a ballot, the Republicans won the state's six electoral votes. Traditional Democratic voters deserted their party, forcing one party leader to concede the electorate no longer trusted the Democrats, especially on the slavery issue. Reflecting on slaveholding demands, the Democratic *Kalamazoo Gazette* concluded, "Southerners must stop outraging Northerners." Despite their electoral success, the Republicans did have problems. There were too many office seekers for the eligible offices, which led to disappointment and dissatisfaction within the party. After a grueling intraparty debate, the Republican majority in the legislature chose Zachariah Chandler to replace Lewis Cass to become the state's first Republican U.S. senator. A New Hampshire native who arrived in Detroit in 1833, Chandler carried to Washington years of business acumen and hostility to slavery.[28]

Four years later, Republicans headed to Chicago for a national convention that surpassed its predecessors "in size, in enthusiasm, in noise, in wire-pulling, in self-righteousness, in lust for office, and in its blend of mass hysteria with idealistic fervor." Michigan Republicans supported New York senator William Seward for president. But when Abraham Lincoln won the nomination on the third ballot, Austin Blair, who led the Michigan delegation, seconded the motion and the choice became unanimous. A staunch abolitionist from an abolitionist family, Blair had settled in Jackson in the mid-1830s. "Slightly built, intense and nervous in manner," he had been a Free Soiler who supported giving blacks the right to vote. Despite favoring Seward, Blair, who soon received his party's nomination for governor, pledged to fight for Abraham Lincoln. He confidently predicted the Republican nominee would win Michigan by a 25,000 vote majority.[29]

During the fall campaign, Abraham Lincoln declined an invitation to visit Michigan, preferring the traditional practice of allowing others to do the presidential campaigning. Prominent out-of-state Republicans campaigned for Lincoln in Michigan, including Senator Seward who came to Detroit in early September. Enthusiastic Republicans came from all across the state to hear the candid New Yorker declare that federal government would defend freedom, which was "the general, normal, enduring and permanent condition of society." Later that evening, 3,000 torch-bearing Wide Awakes (a "political police force" that escorted and protected—if necessary—Republication candidates) induced Steward to give another speech, this time from the porch of Senator Chandler's home. According to the future Secretary of State, Lincoln was the best man to carry forth the cause of "freedom against slavery." When the votes were totaled, the Republicans had reason to be giddy. Lincoln captured 57.1 percent of the state vote, coming within 1,500 votes of Austin Blair's convention prediction.[30]

As the dust settled from the most important presidential election in the country's young history, Michiganians watched southerners wrestle with what one called "secession spasma." Republicans, as stated by the *Lansing Republican*, downplayed southern talk of slave states leaving the Union because secession was illegal. If states failed to return to the Union, the newspaper confidently noted that federal laws would be enforced "at the point of the bayonet." One Republican even hoped that a few southern states would leave the Union, albeit temporarily, because then, with the southerners gone from Congress, the Republicans could pass legislation previously blocked by the slaveholding states, which would lead to "accelerated prosperity" and make the United States "the foremost power and the happiest and most prosperous nation in the world." Despite extensive newspaper coverage about the secession movement, Michigan Republicans looked optimistically (and rather naively) to the next presidential election. In 1864, they dreamed of capturing states like Virginia—a state where the Republicans had received no votes in 1860. The *Lansing Republican* conceded these new states could not rival "the more radical standard of Republican sentiment" found in Michigan. However, "as long as these future Republicans supported the Lincoln administration's aim "to extend freedom, and to leave slavery to slave States, nothing prevents them from becoming hearty and useful auxiliaries; and such they will be." The *Lansing Republican* was only dreaming. When voters went to the polls in 1864 for the nation's next presidential election, the only men in Virginia voting for Lincoln's re-election were northern soldiers fighting and dying to preserve a nation torn by a bloody civil war.[31]

CHAPTER

9

The Civil War

The men drilling at Detroit's Fort Wayne were among the 90,000 Michiganians who saved the Union.

"No concession, no compromise—give us strife, even to blood—before yielding to the demands of traitorous insolence."

—U.S. Senator Zachariah Chandler in early 1861

On the evening of April 12, 1861, Sara and Carry Nelson had just finished their first musical piece at the Detroit Theatre. Suddenly, the theater manager rushed onstage with a telegram. It said that Confederate forces had opened fire on Fort Sumter, a fortress the U.S. government controlled in the harbor at Charleston, South Carolina. The audience sat stunned. Suddenly, the orchestra began playing "Yankee Doodle," and the theatergoers rose and gave three cheers for the Union.[1]

The Civil War had started.

Michiganians were not surprised that civil war had come to the nation. Several months earlier, Governor Austin Blair had declared that South Carolina's decision to leave the United States was "revolution and revolution . . . is treason, and must be treated as such. . . . It is not concession [to the South] that is needed now . . . it is patriotic firmness and decision." After Fort Sumter fell, Governor Blair announced "that patriotic citizen soldiery of Michigan will promptly come forward to enlist in the cause of the Union, against which an extensive rebellion in arms exists, threatening the integrity and perpetuity of the government."[2]

The governor was right. After hearing about Fort Sumter, Michiganians pledged their support to President Abraham Lincoln. All across the state people gathered at large meetings and adopted resolutions backing the president. "Old Glory floated everywhere," one witness reported. In Detroit, a large banner draped across the front of the post office read, "The Union—one and perpetual; what God has joined together let no man put asunder." The *Detroit Advertiser*, the state's leading Republican newspaper, advised, "There can be no more hesitation in the mind of any patriot as to the duty which the emergency imposes. The Star and Stripes must be sustained at all hazards and at every sacrifice." Lewis Cass addressed thousands of Detroiters declaring, "He who is not for his country is against her. . . . There is no neutral position to be occupied."[3]

—— Off to War

War fever mounted by the hour as Michiganians rushed to join the army. Less than a week after Fort Sumter fell, George Woodruff, a West Point graduate from Marshall, informed state officials, "Our people are prepared for the most prompt and energetic action of the government, and are already becoming impatient of delay in forwarding volunteers." When news of President Lincoln's call for troops reached farmers in Mecosta County, they stopped their threshers and headed for Big Rapids where troops were being formed. Near Battle Creek, 30-year-old Samuel Hodgman organized a company of volunteers, studied the manual of arms, and drilled his men each day. In Detroit, Uncle Sam's Cadets, the Detroit Invincibles, the Lafayette Guard (only French-speaking Detroiters), and the Silver Grey Legion (only men over 45 years old) were among the volunteer companies drilling all across the city. The Sherlock Guard drilled on Campus Martius, where one observer noted, "Although some were a little awkward on account of having had no experience in warlike details, [they were] a tough muscular set, and if they ever get a chance to fight, will doubtless make short work of it." Sometimes patriotism went too far. At one rally a state official was injured when a cannon was fired near his railroad car, breaking the window and showering him with glass. Yet, everyone was expected to support the war effort. As the *Battle Creek Journal* reminded its readers in late April 1861, "A man is either a patriot or a traitor . . . of the latter, he had better keep it to himself."[4]

Love of country explains why thousands of Michigan men—and a few women—joined the army. One Michiganian noted that he enlisted because "our rights, all that is clear to us as a nation, were in danger." Another simply added, "Our country needs us." Most Michiganians also believed the war would be neither long nor bloody. A Battle Creek woman told her brother who had joined the army, "I for one was glad when I heard of your decision to go . . . there seems but little fear of great loss of life from those craven fearstricken Southerners."[5]

—— "Thank God for Michigan"

President Lincoln asked Michigan to send one regiment—a total of 1,000 men. On May 1, the First Michigan Infantry was mustered into federal service. Its ten companies of 100 each came from nine different communities (Detroit, Jackson, Coldwater, Manchester, Ann Arbor, Burr Oak, Ypsilanti, Marshall, and Adrian). The First camped at Detroit's Fort Wayne, where it began learning military discipline, the use of firearms, and battle formations. On May 11, thousands of people gathered at Detroit's Campus Martius to watch the regiment receive its flags, which had been made by the ladies of Detroit. Two days later, the First left for Washington, DC. After the Michigan men reached the capital, the *New York Tribune* recorded, "No regiment that

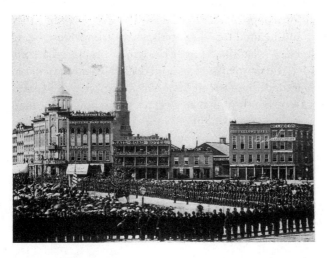

On May 11, 1861, the 1st Michigan Infantry Regiment gathered at Detroit's Campus Martius before leaving for Washington, DC.

has yet arrived has created such an excitement as the Michigan first." According to legend, a much-relieved President Lincoln greeted the arrival of the first western regiment to the nation's capital by simply declaring, "Thank God for Michigan."[6]

More regiments were soon organized, and each left the state in heroic fashion. In June 1861, the Fourth Michigan Infantry received its flags in a ceremony at Adrian. Colonel Dwight A. Woodbury told his men, "With our banner to cheer us, we will strive to do our duty as American soldiers." Woodbury then turned to his regiment and added, "Let each man remember that he has the honor of Michigan in his keeping." Another Michiganian remembered that when his regiment left Detroit "the girls were stationed at the windows waving flags and firing revolvers to cheer the men on to the great duty they had to perform." The Michigan men were also cheered as they traveled through other states. Perry Mayo of Battle Creek wrote, "We were nearly fed to death on the road through Ohio with pies, cakes, lemonade, and compliments. Flowers were showered on us at every [railroad] station." The regiment's first casualty was a man who was so busy hanging out the train window waving to the girls on the platform that his head struck a post as the train left the station.[7]

Besides cakes, cookies, and cool drinks, unexpected pleasures occasionally greeted the new recruits. Private Charles Robinson's regiment stopped in Jackson on its way to the nation's capital. As he later recalled, he was approached by "a fine, sweet-looking girl" who grabbed him and planted several kisses on his "trembling mouth." Momentarily stunned, Robinson regained his poise and "managed to get up enough to pay her back with the same kind of coin." As the unidentified girl released him, Robinson remembered, "I guess we both felt the better." Michigan men also made a positive impression as they traveled throughout the North. After the Fourth Michigan Infantry passed through Cleveland, a local Ohio newspaper wrote:

> When we see the splendidly armed and equipped regiments from Michigan pass through here . . . and compare their appearance with that of the regiments which recently left Cleveland, it makes us ashamed of Ohio. . . . Why is it that Michigan in the same length of time, sends regiments to the field prepared for service, while Ohio . . . sends from her camps as regiments, mere mobs of men, half uniformed, unarmed, and wholly without drill.

On another occasion, a Michigan soldier claimed that after marching through Cincinnati, he heard the local girls say, "Michigan boys were the prettiest that ever passed through the city."[8]

—— "We Fear Nothing"

Early camp life was exciting for the enlistees. One soldier recalled that the training was "like a picnic," especially for many of the men "who had been accustomed to hard work on the farm." But the Michiganians wanted to fight. The state's first regiments were camped around Washington, DC, in the early summer of 1861. The clamor of "On to Richmond," the capital of the Confederacy, was matched only by the soldiers' self-confidence. After a visit from the army's commanding general, one Michigan private observed, "We can whip our weight in wild cats. . . . We fear nothing."[9]

Soon the fighting started, and it quickly became clear that war was terrible. After fighting in the war's first big battle, Philo Gallup of Niles wrote home (in a singularly unique style) that the battlefield was "the awfulist site that i ever sawe [sic]." He went on, "It is a site that nere can bee for goten to see men slatered some of them ded some of them with there legs off some with an arm off some with now hed some with there face off."[10]

Michigan soldiers fought in all the Civil War's major battles. At First Bull Run, the Second Michigan Infantry covered the retreat of the defeated Union army. A year later, on the same battlefield, the First Michigan Infantry was ordered to assault a position held by Rebel artillery. The regimental chaplain watched as the officers "shook hands with each other in farewell." The charge failed and left sixteen of the unit's twenty officers killed or wounded. At Antietam, the Seventh Michigan Infantry was caught in an ambush that left 230 of its men casualties in thirty minutes. At Fredericksburg, the same regiment rowed across the Rappahannock River under intense enemy fire to drive the Rebels from the town so Union engineers could build pontoon bridges. At Chattanooga, the First Michigan Engineers and Mechan-

The 4th Michigan Infantry, as captured by famous Civil War photographer Matthew Brady.

ics set up a sawmill, cut lumber, and built a steamboat to open a supply line for a Union army that was trapped. The engineers also built a pontoon bridge that helped supplies get to the besieged Yankees. The Michigan Bridge, as it was called, led the army's commanding general to praise the regiment for its "skill and cool gallantry." At Spotsylvania, the Seventeenth Michigan Infantry went into battle with 225 men. By the end of the day's fighting, it had suffered 194 casualties. Finally, hundreds of Michigan men languished and many died in southern prisons, most notably Andersonville, aptly labeled by one Michigan survivor as that "dismal hole."[11]

—— Gettysburg: The War's Biggest Battle

At Gettysburg, Michiganians made some of their greatest contributions in helping the North win the Civil War.[12]

For three days in July 1863, 4,000 Michiganians were among the thousands of Americans who struggled in the war's largest battle. The fighting started when the Confederate army, led by General Robert E. Lee, clashed with the Army of the Potomac on the morning of July 1 in the south-central Pennsylvania town called Gettysburg. In McPherson's Woods, the Twenty-Fourth Michigan Infantry, part of the army's famed Iron Brigade, stubbornly held up the Rebels until overpowered by greater numbers. The Twenty-Fourth, largely a Wayne County regiment, started the day with 496 men. By evening, one of its surviving officers could muster fewer than 100 men. The regiment suffered 397 casualties—the most men lost by any northern regiment in the battle. Twenty-two of the regiment's twenty-five officers fell, including Lieutenant Gilbert Dickey, one of the first graduates of the Michigan Agricultural College, who was killed.

On the second day of the battle, the Rebels attacked both flanks of the Yankee army. General Alpheus S. Williams commanded the Yankees defending the Union right flank. Nicknamed Old Pap, the 52-year-old Detroiter used his men wisely in repulsing a series of determined enemy charges. On the Union army's left flank, northerners and southerners fought in places now simply known as Devil's Den, Little Round Top, the Peach Orchard, and the Wheatfield. Near the Peach Orchard, the Fifth Michigan Infantry, according to its commander, "stood up bravely under the storm of bullets sent against them." Some of the day's most brutal fighting occurred in the Wheatfield. Late in the afternoon the Rebels nearly captured the flag of the Fourth Michigan Infantry. As Colonel Harrison H. Jeffords, the regiment's

26-year-old commander from Dexter, rushed to save the flag he was shot in the leg and "thrust through with a bayonet." Jeffords died the next day.

On the third day of the battle, Lee's army attacked the Union center. Part of the day's fight occurred east of Gettysburg in fields defended by the Michigan Cavalry Brigade. The brigade, which consisted of four regiments of Michigan horsemen, was led by newly appointed General George A. Custer of Monroe. At age 23, Custer was one of the youngest generals in the northern army. Born in Ohio but raised in Monroe, Custer graduated from the U.S. Military Academy (albeit last in his class) in 1861 and served the early years of the war as a junior staff officer. Recognized for his battlefield courage, Custer and two other junior officers were promoted to brigadier general in June 1863 to inspire northern cavalrymen. As the southern cavalrymen advanced toward Custer's position, the Fifth, Sixth, and Seventh Michigan Cavalry regiments tangled with the enemy. In one charge, Custer led the advance, yelling "Come on, you Wolverines!" At a desperate point in the battle, Custer turned to the commander of the First Michigan Cavalry and ordered his men to charge. The Michigan men were outnumbered

George A. Custer led the Michigan Cavalry Brigade at Gettysburg.

and one officer feared, "We will be swallowed up." Suddenly, Custer placed himself in front of the Michigan regiment. According to one soldier, "With a fearful yell the First Michigan Cavalry rushed on, Custer riding four lengths ahead." When the blue and gray horsemen crashed into each other it sounded like "the falling of timber." After fierce fighting, the Confederates retreated. Custer later wrote, "I challenge the annals of warfare to produce a more brilliant or successful charge of cavalry."

After the cavalry fight ended, a much larger Rebel force attacked the center of the Union army line near a copse, or thicket, of tall trees. Stationed on this part of the field, the men of the Seventh Michigan Infantry anxiously watched and waited. When the Rebels got close, they fired, "mowing them down by scores," one Michiganian recalled. Captain Sam Hodgman of Climax recorded, "We stuck to our barricade and fought till they—what were left of them—were glad to come into our lines or skedaddle double quick." The Seventh's commander, Lt. Colonel Amos Steele, of Mason was among those killed repulsing Pickett's Charge. The Battle of Gettysburg—the largest battle ever fought on the North American continent—resulted in more than 51,000 casualties, a toll that included 1,111 Michiganians (200 killed, 653 wounded, and 258 captured or missing). Of the Michiganians who died on these fields, 177 are buried in the Gettysburg National Cemetery.

The fighting at Gettysburg had ended, but the next day, July 4, 1863, a group of Michigan men defeated a much stronger opponent in the little-known Battle of Tebb's Bend. Colonel Orlando Moore and 250 men from the Twenty-Fifth Michigan Infantry were stationed along the Green River in south-central Kentucky. Without warning, a Rebel force ten times larger approached. The Rebels demanded that the Michiganians surrender. A U.S. Military Academy graduate, Moore responded, "I am an American and the Fourth of July is no day for me to entertain such a proposition. I must there-fore decline." The Michigan colonel had selected a strong position and easily repulsed the attacking Rebels. The frustrated Rebels rode on, but the enemy general was so impressed with Colonel Moore that he sent him a note pro-moting him to brigadier general! (Later in the war, Moore was promoted to brigadier general, but through more "normal" channels.)[13]

—— The Generals

Custer and Moore were only two of Michigan's inspirational commanders. At least 73 other Michiganians rose to the rank of general, most notably, Orlando Willcox, Israel B. Richardson, and Alpheus S. Williams. Willcox was born in Detroit in 1823, graduated from West Point, and saw action in one of the Seminole Wars before leaving the army in 1857. Commanding the First Michigan Infantry Regiment, Willcox was wounded at the First Battle of Bull Run and taken prisoner. After a year in a southern prison, he was released, promoted to division command, and saw action at South Mountain, Antietam, Knoxville, and the Overland Campaign. Richardson was born in Vermont in 1815, graduated from the U.S. Military Academy, and served with distinction during the Mexican War. In the late 1850s, he left the army, mar-ried, and settled in Pontiac where he earned a reputation for being eccentric, some said "crazy." Orlando Willcox agreed Richardson was "slouchy, slovenly and absentminded," but possessed much-needed leadership skills. Richard-son led the Second Michigan Infantry to war and later rose in the ranks. At

Antietam, he commanded a division in heavy fighting at the Bloody Lane where a mortal wound ended a promising career. Possibly the most important Michigan general was Alpheus S. Williams. Born in Connecticut, 26-year-old Williams arrived in Detroit in 1836. He was not a career soldier, but a lawyer (among other professions) and had commanded troops that went to Mexico where he saw no action. At the beginning of the war, Governor Blair placed Williams in charge of recruiting, organizing, and training the state's volunteers. Later, Williams was given brigade command. At several key battles (Cedar Mountain, Antietam, Chancellorsville, Gettysburg, Atlanta, and Sherman's March to Sea and through the Carolinas), Williams held larger responsibility where the fighting was the heaviest. Among Williams's most notable contributions were his exceptional wartime letters, published in 1959 under the title *From The Cannon's Mouth*. As historian Albert Castel noted, Williams "contributed more to Union victory than any other Michigan general both by the battles he helped win and the defeats he prevented from turning into debacles."[14]

Another group who earned service recognition were 67 Michiganians awarded the Medal of Honor. These included Colonel Orlando Willcox for gallantry at Battle of First Bull Run and Sergeant Moses A. Luce of Adrian, who despite being wounded carried a seriously injured comrade through a hail of enemy bullets to safety at Spotsylvania and then kept him from bleeding to death. Other Michigan soldiers received the medal for capturing an

Two of Michigan's most accomplished Civil War generals included Orlando B. Willcox (left) and Alpheus S. Williams (right).

enemy flag—the most prized possession of the war. Tom Custer, the general's younger brother, received two medals for capturing flags on two separate occasions. Custer and Frank Baldwin of Manchester, Michigan, are among an elite group of Americans who have been awarded two Medals of Honor. (Baldwin received his second medal for actions after the Civil War.)[15]

Battlefield heroics captured newspaper headlines, but battlefield casualties accounted for only a small number of Michiganians who died in the Civil War. Many men died in battle, but diseases became the war's number one killer. Poor food, long marches, and inadequate sanitary habits led to sickness. Smallpox, typhoid fever, diarrhea, and pneumonia weakened many men who later died. According to Adjutant General Jonathan Robertson's postwar tabulations: Michigan sent 90,747 men to war, and of the 14,855 who died, two-thirds perished from disease.[16]

As the war dragged on, the earlier appeal of soldiering was lost amid the miserable conditions, battlefield setbacks, and the death of comrades. In December 1863, the Seventh Michigan Infantry earned a 30-day furlough, but only 160 of the 884 men who went to war in August 1861 remained with the regiment. Friends of one Calhoun County officer said he looked ten years older than when he had entered service two years earlier. The lingering effects of typhoid fever and the pain of leg wounds he had received at Antietam led Captain Sam Hodgman to admit that he was "pretty well worn." He soon resigned his commission and went home. Others refused to go home until the war was won. "We don't think we can whip everybody as we used to," one Michigan veteran conceded, but "still we are willing to try anything which occasion requires." Ira Gillespie of the Eleventh Michigan Infantry admitted he was "willing to quit soldiering [but only] as soon as our Union is restored."[17]

—— An Exciting Interruption

For all its discomfort and tragedy, the Civil War was an exciting interruption in the otherwise routine lives of many Michiganians. As the men traveled across the South, they saw people and places they had never experienced. One soldier, who saw the White House for the first time, wrote, "Its splendor exceeds by far anything and all that I ever saw before," while another thought the home of General Robert E. Lee and its surroundings on the south bank of the Potomac River "make the most beautiful spot I ever saw." At a dance in northern Virginia, Philo Gallup of the Second Michigan Infantry saw "some of the pretys [*sic*] girls. . . . I ever saw and good dancers they was to." A fellow Michigan soldier offered a different opinion, claiming that the Virginians "appear as tho' they had not got thoroughly waken up yet." Charles Haydon of Kalamazoo enjoyed the "morning sun reflecting from the white walls of the Capitol" and city's other buildings. The insightful Kalamazoo officer concluded that visitors to the capital

> will find three numerous classes of people, well marked & easily identified. . . . the first & most numerous class is composed of soldiers of ever rank, hue, Nation, uniform & branch. The other two great classes are politicians & prostitutes, both very numerous & abt equal in numbers, honesty & morality.[18]

One common wartime experience was foraging. When the Second Michigan Infantry camped in one small northern Virginia town, a member noted in his diary, "All the cattle & hogs & sheep that could be found were at once killed, in fact everything eatable was seized. The men would take bee hives off the stands & devour the honey & half the bees at the same time." On the way to Gettysburg, some soldiers of the 24th Michigan Infantry stepped out of ranks and stole a few geese. One of the regiment's drummers placed two geese in his drum. The colonel soon asked the boy why he was not drumming. The young man drew the colonel close and said, "Colonel, I have a couple of geese in here." The colonel straightened up and said loudly, "Well if you're sick and can't play, you need not." That night both the colonel and the drummer had roast goose for dinner. It is no surprise that Jan Wilterdink, a 22-year-old farmer from Holland serving with the 25th Michigan Infantry, noted, "The war makes a decent person forget his Christian upbringing."[19]

Campaigning in the South also gave Michiganians their first exposure to slavery. Many soldiers were shocked by what they saw. Captain John C. Buchanan of Grand Rapids wondered how slavery's "steady advance has been so long endured, countenanced & sustained." Back in Michigan, the state's small black community (6,000 out of 750,000 people) responded enthusiastically to the Emancipation Proclamation on January 1, 1863. Parishioners at Detroit's black churches adopted resolutions thanking President Lincoln, while condemning slavery for "brutalizing its victims" and making labor "disrespectable." Both black and white Detroiters raised the necessary funds to print and send copies of the proclamation to all Michigan soldiers. Republicans saw the Emancipation Proclamation as a "blow aimed at the rebellion [that would have] magnificent results." Critics continuously attacked it, claiming Lincoln violated his constitutional power, while predicting emancipation would "fire the Southern heart" and lead to "murder, lust and rapine upon the unguarded plantations of the South." Tragically, the violence precipitated by the proclamation occurred in Detroit. With the Emancipation and conscription occurring in the north in early 1863, disenchanted whites, especially the poor, blamed blacks for the war. On March 6, 1863, two nine-year-old girls (one white, the other black) accused William Faulkner, a Detroit black storeowner, of molesting them. The resulting riot left two blacks dead, scores injured, and extensive property damage in the black community. Faulkner was sent to jail, only to be released seven years later when the girls admitted they had lied.[20]

—— Blacks Answer the Call

Emancipation also renewed efforts to allow blacks to enlist. A year into the war, frustrated Detroit blacks reiterated they were ready "to buckle on our armor in defence of Liberty [and to] prove that we are not traitors, but willing to defend the land of our birth." In the wake of the March 1863 racial disturbance, Henry Barns, editor of the *Detroit Advertiser and Tribune,* intensified his campaign to "give the colored men of Michigan the chance they have been so long wishing for." An English immigrant, Barns was angered that 200 Michigan blacks had left the state to join the soon-to-be-famous 54th Massachusetts Infantry. The editor even sought and received Secretary of War Edwin Stanton's "every encouragement" to recruit a black regiment. In August 1863, the First Michigan Colored Infantry Regiment was conceived. Although blacks enlistees did not receive enlistment bounties, they responded enthusiastically. Barns accepted a commission as the regiment's colonel, acknowledging his lack of military experience would keep him from leading the men into battle.[21]

As with other black regiments, the officers in the First were all white and the enlisted men were paid less than their white counterparts. The regiment also faced racism in the form of barracks "unfit for human habitation," occasional clashes with whites, and inflammatory newspaper stories criticizing the black soldiers. According to the *Advertiser and Tribune,* stories in the *Free Press* "reported outrages perpetuated against the Colored Troops as outrages committed by the Colored Troops." Despite these distractions, many elements of the local community supported the regiment. The black ladies of Detroit presented the unit with a regimental flag, while Sunday church groups enjoyed dress parades. On one occasion, black leader Sojourner Truth brought "many gifts and food" from the people of Battle Creek. When on parade, the recruits showed "good proficiency in drill, stepping to the music of the drum like veterans." A supportive *Advertiser and Tribune* reported, "They make very cheerful, obedient soldiers and will be an honor to the State of Michigan."

In its first "campaign," the regiment toured Lower Peninsula cities where it was "well received." At Jackson, Governor Blair reviewed the men claiming, "this is the first time I ever saw Negro troops, and I am very proud of your general bearing." Mrs. Blair also assisted local ladies in preparing a meal for the soldiers. In Kalamazoo, the Democratic newspaper uncharacteristically conceded, "a more orderly or soldiery body of men has seldom been seen in our streets." Even in Niles, a hotbed of anti-war sentiment, the men received a 34-gun salute and enjoyed a community dance. Among the tour's highlights was a sixteen-mile march to Cassopolis. Farmers along the way offered foodstuffs and the area's many blacks residents cheered the regiment, while the unit's band, which boasted new instruments thanks to a financial gift from Detroit composer J. Henry Whittemore, earned "many accolades . . . at all the locations."

On February 11, 1864, the First Michigan Colored Infantry Regiment was mustered into federal service in Detroit. Six weeks later, the regiment left Detroit and arrived in the nation's capital where General Ulysses S. Grant reviewed the troops and called them "splendid." As expected, Barns resigned his commission and was replaced by Henry L. Chipman, a Detroiter and former lieutenant colonel of the Second Michigan Infantry Regiment. Transferred to the newly organized federal Bureau of Colored Troops, the First Michigan was redesignated the 102nd U.S. Colored Troops and for the balance of the war served in Florida, South Carolina, and Georgia. Much of the regiment's service involved picket and fatigue duty, but on occasion the men saw action. On November 30, the 102nd, brigaded with the 54th Massachusetts, tangled with a larger Rebel force near Savannah. As the fight raged, Lieutenant Orson W. Bennett led a small group of men 100 yards in advance of the Union lines to retrieve three abandoned federal cannon. For his actions, Bennett earned the Medal of Honor, one of two 102nd officers awarded such recognition during the war. After the war ended, the 102nd served as occupation troops in South Carolina before heading home, where it was disbanded. A total of 1,673 men had served in the 102nd; 12 had died in battle and 118 had died from disease. Fifty years after the war, one of the regiment's white officers, who had served with white units earlier in the war, offered a fitting legacy for the 102nd, "The blacks made good soldiers, and were very proud of being soldiers [and] there was no perceptible difference between them and the whites."

—— Women Go to War

Michigan women played important—but often overlooked—roles during the war. With the firing on Fort Sumter, women encouraged men to join the army. Then they changed gears, boasting that in the country's hour of need, they refused to let their men folk to "go upon their mission with their wants unprovided for." Women sewed up a storm. The wife of one prominent Detroit minister boasted how "her regiment" kept sewing machines "constantly running," making socks, blankets, towels, and havelocks (a covering for a hat to protect the neck from sunburn). They also made the flags the regiments carried into battle. In most stories about flags being presented to the new regiments, the women are thanked but remain anonymous. In the case of the Fourth Michigan Infantry, Mrs. Josephine Wilcox told the men they were all in this war together and promised that the women left behind "will follow you in our hearts, with our hopes and our prayers." Michigan women also organized aid societies, which provided medical care, clothing, food, and newspapers for Michigan soldiers. Late in the war, the association operated the Michigan Soup House near the front lines in Virginia where Michigan soldiers received hot meals. These groups also helped families back in Michigan whose loved ones were killed or seriously wounded in the war. In September 1864, a fundraising "sanitary fair" in Kalamazoo raised $10,000 for soldiers' aid.[22]

Women also worked as nurses, and 29-year-old Julia Wheelock of Ionia earned a reputation as "Michigan's Florence Nightingale." A college-educated teacher working in Ionia, Julia headed to Washington, DC, after receiving word that her brother had been wounded at the Battle of Chantilly on September 1, 1862. A futile search ended with the discovery that he had died. Rather than return home, she stayed in Washington, becoming an agent for the Michigan Soldiers Relief Association. Despite long days working in a soldiers' hospital, Wheelock spent evenings making pies—sometimes as many as 40 at one time—for the sick and wounded. Julia also kept one of the most detailed diaries written by a woman during the war. She met General Ulysses S. Grant ("very plain & unassuming"); saw the president at the Capitol ("Father Abe looks so careworn . . . he bears a load heavy enough to crush anybody"); and experienced the president's assassination ("I have scarce done anything but weep. . . . Truly a great and good man has fallen."). After the war, Julia's diary was published and entitled, *Boys in White: The Experiences of a Hospital Agent in and around Washington During the Civil War* (1870).[23]

Another Michigan woman who made a notable contribution was Evelyn Adams. During the middle of the war, Adams left Detroit for a job with the U.S. Department of Agriculture (USDA) in Washington, DC. Adams's prewar role with the *Michigan Farmer* (a weekly trade publication where she was an editor, columnist, and business manager) and endorsements from prominent state leaders helped her earn a full-time position with the newly created federal agency. Described by one contemporary as "a woman of large intelligence," Adams spent the balance of the war as one of the earliest female federal government employees, making an impressive $600 annual salary. She also volunteered for the Michigan Soldiers Relief Association and authored columns for the *Detroit Advertiser and Tribune*. Informative, sensitive, and possessing a touch of self-deprecating humor, Adams reflected on the uniqueness of her employment experience and life in the wartime capital. She also visited hospitalized Michigan soldiers and provided details of their conditions for readers back home; she wrote that Michigan soldiers talked with "flashing eyes and with eager motions of their wounded hands," [while] "their enthusiasm in General Grant is unbounded." After visiting "hundreds of these scarred and battered veterans," she heard only one complaint. One wounded soldier from St. Johns "didn't think it was half fair to be popped over in the way he was without having a chance to shoot once!" Adams also visited the White House and met President Lincoln:

> His hand takes mine, the eyes look down as kindly; he bows low and says, "How do you do?" in a tone that seems to demand a friendly reply. But no reply comes. My heart is on my lips, but there is no shape or sound of words. . . . Before I am fairly conscious that I have touched the hand and looked into the eyes of our honored Father Abraham, I find myself on the opposite side of the room. Doubtless if he had a thought about me it was, "What a stupid creature! Who does not know enough to give a name or answer a civil question?"

Adams remained with the USDA after the war, but suffered an illness, possibly contracted from working in the hospitals, that shortened her life.[24]

Although women could not enlist in the army, some went to war. Detroiter Annie Etheridge served as a combat medic with several different regiments, and as one contemporary wrote, "She shrank from no danger however great." Standing five feet, three inches tall, Annie possessed "a vigorous constitution and [was] decidedly good looking." Owning a horse equipped with saddlebags filled with medical supplies, she served on the battlefield.

After the Battle of Fredericksburg, a soldier wrote, "I saw one young lady in the very front of the battle dressing wounds and aiding the suffering where few surgeons dared show themselves. That girl is Annie Etheridge." At the Battle of Williamsburg, Brigadier General Philip Kearny saw Annie in action and proposed she be promoted to sergeant. Although the promotion never occurred (Kearny was soon killed in action), Annie later received the Kearny Cross, one of the war's earliest medals for heroism. Annie's impact on the battlefield went beyond binding up wounds. In a fierce fight, a Yankee artillery battery suffered heavy losses and the survivors considered abandoning their guns, until Annie rode up and offered words of encouragement. One eyewitness noted: "All the officers in the Army of the Potomac would not have as much influence

Annie Etheridge served as a combat medic and earned the Kearny Cross, one of the war's first medals for bravery.

over the men as did Annie." After the war, one observer concluded that if the government struck a gold medal to be given to a woman who distinguished herself on the battlefield "there can be little doubt that the united voices of the soldiers and of all the army nurses would assign the honor to Annie Etheridge, of Michigan." As the war ended, one Michigan sergeant recorded, "Noble Annie is with us to the last, and her brave womanly spirit breaks down, and scalding tears trickle down her beautiful bronze face as each of the boys bid her goodbye." After the war, Annie settled in Washington to work for the federal government and earned a pension in 1887. When she passed away in 1913, she was buried in Arlington National Cemetery.[25]

Sarah Emma Edmonds of Flint found a different way to serve. In the spring of 1861, Edmonds went off to war with the Second Michigan Infantry disguised as Frank Thompson. For the next two years, she served in a variety of capacities, most notably as a spy. Not surprisingly, her most effective disguise was a woman! When sickness would have led to hospital confinement and the inevitable disclosure of her sex, she deserted. Sarah survived a bout with typhoid fever but never returned to the ranks. Instead, she worked with a soldiers' relief agency and authored an account of her wartime experience entitled *Nurse and Spy in the Union Army*. This much-fictionalized autobiography sold well, and Edmonds devoted all the profits to soldiers' relief agencies. After the war, Sarah married, had three children (all of whom died in childhood), and adopted two boys. She also appeared at a regimental reunion where, after some convincing, her former comrades welcomed her, which made her the only female member of the veterans' Grand Army of the Republic. In 1884, she earned a pension and had the desertion charge erased from her service record. When asked why she had posed as a man, she explained, "I could only thank God that I was free and could go forward and work, and I was not obliged to stay home and weep."[26]

Elizabeth Bacon Custer of Monroe was among the war's best-known wives. Born in Monroe in 1842, "Libbie" Bacon was well-educated and valedictorian of her class. At a Monroe party on Thanksgiving Day in 1862, she met a young officer with local ties. Captain George A. Custer was smitten with Libbie, although she was not particularly impressed with Custer—nor was her father who forbade his daughter from exchanging letters with him. Custer persisted, and Libbie developed special feelings for the aggressive cavalryman. Following Custer's meteoric rise in the spring of 1863, the two lovers became secretly engaged. They won over Libbie's father and were married in February 1864 in Monroe. During the war's final year, George and Libbie lived together—sometimes in a tent—as Libbie eagerly sought to prove her superiority with the roughness of army life. When her husband's campaigning forced them apart, they wrote continuously; her nicknames for him included "my star" and "my hero," and his nicknames for her included "my rosebud" and "the idol of my heart." During the summer of 1864, when Libbie lived in Washington, she met President Lincoln, who commented that she was "the young woman whose husband goes into a charge with a whoop and a shout." When the war ended, General Philip Sheridan sent her the table that General Grant used at Appomattox to sign the surrender document with a note that read in part, "Permit me to say, Madam, that there is scarcely an individual in our service, who has contributed more to bring about this desirable result than your gallant husband." During the postwar, Libbie went west with her husband. Following his sudden death at the Little Big Horn in June 1876, she moved to New York City where she supported herself as a writer and speaker. Libbie's efforts to defend her husband from criticism that threatened to tarnish his reputation were rewarded in 1910 with the erection of a statue to her husband in Monroe. She never remarried.[27]

Unlike Annie, Evelyn, Sarah, and Libbie, most women stayed home during the war and ran the farms, raised young children, and worried about their loved ones in the army. Everywhere women filled the vacuum caused by the men who went off to war. In 1862, Detroiters debated if women should be allowed to replace male clerks in the stores. Women argued that storeowners needed to show their patriotism by allowing them to fill these jobs. Proponents for the change admitted female clerks would start out inexperienced, but they were "natural judges" of articles sold in stores and, given the "blessing of education in this country," most women understood math. A *Detroit Free Press* writer concluded, "It would take them no longer to make them good saleswomen, and even book keepers, than to transform an effeminate [i.e., male] clerk into a robust, well-drilled soldier."[28]

Women also shared their thoughts and experiences in letters to their men serving as soldiers. Unfortunately, most of these letters did not survive the war. One exception was the experience of newlyweds 21-year-old Melissa Hoisington and 26-year-old Ben Wells. The couple lived near Three Rivers, and in the summer of 1861, Ben (along with Melissa's father, her brother, and eleven other local men) joined the Eleventh Michigan Infantry. During the next two years, Ben saw action on the bloody fields of Stones River and Chickamauga, while surviving two severe bouts of sicknesses. After Ben read Melissa's letters, he sent them back to her, suggesting that if he survived the war the couple could someday sit on the porch and re-read their letters. Ben wrote two letters a week, Melissa less often—partly because of her busy schedule that included running the farm and raising a newborn. On one occasion, she beamed with pride over planting a field of potatoes, but later expressed self-doubt as she nursed her hands blistered from much hoeing. Two years after Ben had gone to war, Melissa reflected, "I have spent many gloomy and unhappy hours since you have been in the South. . . . Many times I have received a letter from you and would think that perhaps it was the last I would receive from you." She concluded, "I often think I never knew what trouble was until since the commencement of this horrid rebellion." Although she worried about Ben, Melissa knew the Union had to be saved. She told him, "Every true lover of liberty and the Flag of our Union" was needed to end the rebellion. Ben came home at the end of his three-year enlistment—aided by her less-than-subtle threat "to hunt me up another man" if he reenlisted. The Wells added two children to their postwar family. Melissa died at the age of

43, but Ben lived 50 years after his wife's death. There are no known pictures of Ben and Melissa Wells, but their letters tell a story many Michiganians experienced during the war years.[29]

—— Copper, Iron, and Wheat

The Civil War also had a generally positive impact on the state's economy. Among the state's natural resource industries, copper and iron ore production increased dramatically. In Keweenaw's copper fields, new mines opened, and some proved quite profitable, producing 70 percent of the north's copper needs for canteens, cannons, and uniform buttons. Iron ore production on the Marquette Range also increased from prewar totals (23,000 tons in 1858 to 297,000 tons in 1866). Much of the copper and iron ore easily passed through the Soo Locks, which played an important role in the first of several wars. Michigan iron ore also helped a burgeoning steel industry. The Bessemer Process, first introduced in the United States at Wyandotte in 1862, placed Michigan at the forefront of modern steel production. This success was attributed to the efforts of Eber Ward, Michigan's "first great captain of industry," who saw the possibilities of using iron ore with the new process for making quality steel inexpensively. Iron ore also contributed to railroad construction, which continued during the war, most notably a line from Marquette to Escanaba, which opened a Lake Michigan outlet for iron ore. Lumbering grew from 400 million board feet annually to 620 million board feet.[30]

Michigan farmers aided the northern war effort by increasing production despite a labor shortage. Turning to labor-saving machinery (which also facilitated state manufacturers), farmers harvested record yields of wheat, corn, oats, and rye that both fed the Union armies and played an important export role for the northern war effort. Wheat production doubled during the 1860s, and late in the war, one northern official described "the states of the Northwest the granary of Europe . . . and the chief source of supply in seasons of scarcity for the suffering millions of another continent." Manufacturing also grew during the 1860s (3,448 firms with 23,190 employees in 1860 vs 9,445 firms with 63,694 employees in 1870). Michigan manufacturers made an endless list of products, everything from reapers and railroad cars to shoes and tobacco products. Companies founded during the war—like the Detroit Bridge and Iron Works, the Detroit Stove Works and the Michigan Car Company—became postwar national leaders. With such growth, workers enjoyed an increase in wages; however, higher prices kept real wages down.[31]

—— Population and Politics

Michigan's population grew by 58 percent during the 1860s, partly aided by the Homestead Act where 6,000 settlers took up 760,000 acres. By 1870 the state's population neared 1.2 million people (having grown from 750,000 a decade earlier). Detroit remained the largest city with nearly 80,000 people, Grand Rapids was second (16,508) and Jackson was third (11,447). The expansion of the lumbering industry was reflected in the growth of Muskegon, Saginaw and Bay City, which all saw their populations quadruple during the 1860s. The state's black population had more than doubled during the decade to nearly 12,000 people. The top immigrant groups in 1870 were the Canadians (89,500), the British (86,200), and the Germans (64,100).[32]

Politically, Michigan remained a loyal Republican state during the war. In 1860, voters favored Abraham Lincoln by almost 25,000 votes (from 153,000 cast). During the 1862 midterm elections—a setback for President Lincoln's party—Michigan Republicans enjoyed their party's best showing in any state. Michiganians supported Lincoln's re-election again in 1864 by a wide margin, while the state's "boys in blue" gave the president a more than three-votes-to-one margin over former General George McClellan. Austin Blair, elected governor in 1860 and re-elected in 1862, earned accolades working with the Lincoln government, most notably meeting various troop requests. In 1864, Blair also was an enthusiastic supporter of allowing soldiers in the field to vote. Finally, as some Republicans sought to deny Lincoln's renomination in mid-1864, the governor favorably argued that such a decision meant a disaster and that he would lose the election.[33]

Senator Zachariah Chandler challenged Governor Blair as the state's leading political leader. Appointed to the U.S. Senate in 1857, the stalwart and outspoken Chandler (described by one historian as a "street fighter") provided northerners with backbone during the uncertain days of early 1861. As some spoke of compromise with the seceding southern states, Chandler claimed, "Without a little bloodletting this Union, will not be worth a rush." As president-elect Lincoln prepared to deliver his 1861 inaugural, Chandler offered, "No concession, no compromise—give us strife, even to blood—before yielding to the demands of traitorous insolence." On how best to handle secessionists, Chandler submitted, "The people of Michigan think the time has arrived to commence hanging & so think I." At First Bull Run, Chandler and several other fellow legislators attempted to rally the defeated Yankee army. (In something of an understatement, an observer noted the armed senator was "seemingly in a dangerous mood.") Months after the battlefield setback, Chandler proposed the creation of the Joint Committee on the Conduct of the War. He served on the committee throughout the war investigating military affairs, endorsing emancipation and the enlistment of black soldiers and, on occasion, annoying President Lincoln. However, the president might have thanked Chandler. In mid-1864, when some Republicans considered replacing Lincoln, the Michigan senator convinced frontrunner John Fremont to withdraw his name from consideration, an action that facilitated Lincoln's renomination. Chandler was controversial, but his support for the soldiers resonated with them. After the war, one soldier reflected, "The name of 'Old Zach' was the boast of our Soldiers around many Camp Fires and we felt we had a champion who would protect our interests, and defend our Record." Upon the senator's passing in 1879, one Detroit newspaper offered an appropriate eulogy: Chandler was "among the men of strong frames, sinewy arms and pugnacity of spirit."[34]

Chandler's colleague Jacob M. Howard worked more quietly in the Congress, but just as effectively. A Detroiter and former Underground Railroad agent, Howard entered the Senate in early 1862, replacing Kinsley Bingham who died in office. One of the Senate's better constitutional lawyers, Howard counted among his most notable accomplishments drafting the 13th Amendment that abolished slavery. A firm believer in executive reconstruction and punishing the South, Howard served on the Joint Committee on Reconstruction, where he played a key role in directing the senate passage of the 14th Amendment, which defined American citizenship.[35]

—— Victory and Tragedy

The Civil War finally ended four years after it had begun. Upon hearing of the surrender of Lee's army at Appomattox in April 1865, Private David Lane of Blackman wrote, "Everyone is wild with joy. . . . My glad heart cries, 'Hosanna! Hosanna in the Highest, the Highest.'" Another Michigan soldier remembered that when his regiment heard of the war's end, "the greatest uproar imaginable took place. It seemed as if the men could not make noise enough."[36]

The tragic assassination of President Lincoln a few days after Lee's surrender put a damper on the army's celebration. Corporal James Greenalch of Flint could scarcely think of the president's death without his eyes "being

Thousands gathered in Campus Martius in late April 1865 for an elaborate funeral ceremony marking the death of President Abraham Lincoln.

blinded with tears." Blaming the assassination on the Rebel leaders, Greenlach vowed that if the war continued, "the troops are determined not to take prisoners." Back home, many Michigan towns held elaborate funeral ceremonies honoring the slain leader, and the most elaborate observance occurred in Detroit. On April 25, a two-mile-long "moving panorama" of public officials, civic groups, and religious leaders marched through the city. The streets were lined with spectators and building fronts were draped in black crepe. The procession also offered a special hearse built by local craftsmen. Drawn by two black horses, the car was heavily draped in black cloth. An immense golden eagle looked down on an empty coffin. Large black plumes waved from each corner of the car. A shield carried the national motto with the letters "A.L." in silver-cloth lace were woven in the dark background. When the procession reached Campus Martius, a crowd estimated at 30,000 people sang a newly composed piece simply called the "Dirge." A few days later, the Twenty-Fourth Michigan Infantry served as the military honor guard for Lincoln's funeral in Springfield, Illinois.[37]

Even the death of a beloved president could not stop Michiganians from expressing happiness over the war's end. In late May, tens of thousands of Union solders gathered in Washington, DC, for the Grand Review. For two days, the eastern and western veterans paraded down Pennsylvania Avenue. George Custer stole the show one day when his horse spooked after a spectator tossed a bouquet of flowers at the famed general. An excellent horseman, Custer gained control of his horse and "the crowd cheered and applauded his horsemanship, with some grumbling that the incident was typical of the flamboyant cavalryman." Evelyn Adams watched the review and authored one of her best *Detroit Advertiser* columns. She wrote that, looking into the

> iron faces of these men, . . . no one can look at troops like these without feeling sure that an enemy country, through which they have once marched, must be pretty thoroughly conquered. They are not men to march without a purpose, and certainly not the ones to leave till that purpose is accomplished.[38]

One battle-hardened veteran regiment not in Washington for the Grand Review was the Fourth Michigan Cavalry. Two weeks earlier, these veterans, who had left the state in the fall of 1862 and fought at Stone's River, Chickamauga, and Atlanta, had been ordered to pursue a fleeing Jefferson Davis, president of the Confederacy. On May 10, the Michiganians, led by Colonel Benjamin Pritchard, a University of Michigan Law School graduate from Allegan, fell on the unsuspecting Rebel leader and his entourage near Irwinsville, Georgia, and easily captured him. Pritchard and a squad of men escorted Davis to Fort Monroe where he was incarcerated. The Fourth may have missed the parade, but they later shared in reward money set aside for Davis's capture. As for Pritchard, he returned to Allegan, fathered two children, and years after the war served as state treasurer.[39]

As the veterans began arriving home, they were joyously met and usually feted and fed before returning to their loved ones. But not all Michiganians came right home. The Michigan Cavalry Brigade, which ended the war with more battlefield casualties than any other northern brigade of cavalry, was sent west to fight "against a new enemy, one most of them had no reason to hate, much less a desire to fight: the American Indian." The brigade (except for those men who deserted when they learned of their destination) was sent to Fort Leavenworth, Kansas, and tangled with Indians, watched Mormons, took casualties, and longed for home. When finally mustered out of federal service in early 1866, these men were stationed at Salt Lake City, Utah, and forced to pay for their own way back to Michigan. Months later, a special act of Congress reimbursed them.[40]

By June 1866, the last Michigan units were mustered out of federal service. On Independence Day, the colors of these battle-hardened regiments were formally presented to Governor Henry Crapo at a ceremony in Detroit. The veterans marched down to Campus Martius, where General Orlando Willcox addressed them: "Now that the dark curtain is lifted, and the sun of victory breaks through in meridian splendor, I have more confidence than ever in our destiny. . . . We have tried to do our duty, and we have done no more than that duty which every citizen owes to a free and fraternal government." Willcox symbolically surrendered the flags to the governor and added, "We shall ever retain our pride in their glorious associations, as well as our love for the old Peninsular State."[41]

CHAPTER

10

Logging the Forests

"Shanty boys" proudly shared their accomplishments with photographers.

"Daylight in the Swamps!"

—Reveille call in the logging camp

When the pioneers settled Michigan during the 1830s, they discovered such an abundance of trees that it was said that "a squirrel could travel on tree branches across the state without ever touching the ground." As loggers depleted the eastern forests, they discovered Michigan's virgin forests, and within a few years, logging exceeded all expectations. Early estimates (which proved quite low) put the pine timber volume at 150 billion board feet—an amount large enough if sawn into lumber to build a floor over all of Michigan's land mass "with enough left over to cover Rhode Island." From the 1850s through the late 1890s, Michigan led the nation in lumber production. In dollar value, Michigan lumber exceeded the value of California gold by more than a billion dollars—even during a time when a thousand board feet of quality pine had a value of thirteen dollars. (A board foot is a piece of lumber one-foot square and one-inch thick.) Yet, Michigan's lumbering era also was "a free-for-all rivaling that of the 'Wild

156

West,' driven by basic greed, raw emotion, and the expediency of the moment."[1]

The logger's favorite tree was the white pine. The biggest ones, called cork pine, stood up to 200 feet tall with five-foot diameters, possessing a low-pitch content and few branches, while producing exceptional knot-free lumber. About 20 percent of Michigan's pine was cork pine—mostly located in the central Lower Peninsula in a band roughly north of the Grand River and south of a line from Manistee on Lake Michigan to Oscoda on Lake Huron. (Today, a few cork pine "survivors" can be found at Hartwick Pines State Park at Grayling and Estivant Pines Nature Sanctuary near Copper Harbor.) Besides the preferred cork pine, loggers were drawn to white pines that stood 80 to 100 feet tall with one- to three-foot diameters, and the smaller red pine. Initially, they largely ignored hardwoods like oak and maple.[2]

—— The Logging Process

Logging operations began with a "timber cruiser," who identified the best trees available for cutting. Before heading into the woods, he visited the U.S. government land office and reviewed the surveyor's maps and notes to learn where the best trees might be located. Armed only with a compass and maps, the cruiser hiked into the forest. His tasks required not only identifying quality stands of trees but also estimating board feet, assessing benefits and obstacles to moving the logs, and locating surveyors' stakes. The cruiser also worked quickly and quietly in a highly competitive environment. After scouring the forests, he raced back to the land office hoping to purchase the land. David Ward earned a reputation as one of the more successful timber cruisers. After discovering "a promising stand of pine" near the Au Sable River, he walked 80 miles to the Tobacco River, paddled a canoe another 80 miles to Saginaw, took a stagecoach to the nearest depot, and then took a train to Detroit (to meet with his employers) before taking another eighteen-hour carriage ride to Lansing and finally another stagecoach to the land office in Ionia. He won, but another cruiser arrived only a few hours later.[3]

Forests, like most government land at the time, usually sold at $1.25 an acre. Yet, timber could be easily poached from government or privately owned land, and disreputable loggers stole the trees without any fear of prosecution if caught. Some loggers used a "round forty" strategy—purchasing a 40-acre parcel and cutting it and the lands "around" the parcel. Loggers also exploited provisions of the Homestead Act of 1862, which allowed a settler to "homestead" 160 acres at no cost if he built a small house and remained on the land for five years. Loggers paid employees to file a homestead claim and a crude structure might be added before the land was cut and abandoned. The law specified the structure had to be "fourteen by sixteen." A packing crate sufficed and a whiskey bottle jammed into a hole met the "glass window" requirement. If challenged by federal land agents (a rarity), the "owner" could claim the law did not specify whether inches or feet. According to author Robert W. Wells, "Fully 90 percent of the 'homesteads' in the prime pinelands are estimated to have been bogus." According to one authority, "the problem of how to keep people from stealing pines was not really solved until there were no more pines worth stealing."[4]

—— The Logging Camp

When a logging company prepared to cut the trees, it established a temporary camp on the site to house its crew. The log-cabin buildings included a barracks, a cookhouse, a blacksmith shop, and a stable. A foreman, called the "bull of the woods," managed the camp and understood all aspects of the logging operation. Large camps employed as many as 100 "shanty boys" (the term *lumberjack* came into use after the 1870s) who lived in the crowded barracks.[5]

The barracks, which reeked from an assortment of odors, offered double-decked bunks filled with straw or conifer boughs (soon infested with lice and bedbugs), and a gunnysack packed with straw served as a pillow. A pot-bellied stove provided heat and candles or kerosene lanterns gave limited light. Latrines or washrooms ("if they existed at all") were simple or "a luxury the early shanty boys considered quite unnecessary." One Saginaw merchant claimed, "I can smell a shanty boy a mile downwind." Only a slight exaggeration since the logging camps offered no bathing facilities "and if the shanty boy bothered to wash his clothes—not all considered this advisable—it was in a futile effort to discourage vermin, not from any enthusiasm for cleanliness." It is no surprise the barracks were a breeding ground for infectious disease. Shanty boys, who earned about one dollar a day, received their pay at the end of the six-month cutting season. In a day before worker's compensation or safety rules, shanty boys injured on the job had to rely on their own resources to recover.[6]

The camp's central building was the cook shanty and mess hall where the men ate breakfast and dinner. Besides making the meals, the cookee—who could make or break a camp—got the boys up by making "as much noise as necessary" after the traditional morning pronouncement of "Daylight in the swamp," which was accompanied with blasts from a tin horn called a "gaberlel" or beating a "gut hammer," a triangular piece of iron. Each shanty boy had a marked place at the mess table and, working under the belief that talking during a meal "could erupt into a fight," conversation was prohibited at meals. According to one shanty boy, "A man could be discharged quicker for any disorder in the dining room than for almost anything else." Given the isolation of many camps, food consisted mostly of staples (dried beans, rice, dried peas, salt meat, potatoes, and coffee) that kept indefinitely. Cooks also baked, especially breads and desserts. Fresh vegetables might augment the menu, while some camps assigned a man to provide fresh venison.[7]

After dinner, shanty boys relaxed, dried their wet clothes, shared exaggerated stories, and played games. In one game, two men stood about five feet apart with a long pole on their shoulders. A man sat perched on the pole with his hands on his hips and legs crossed. Armed with a straw-filled gunnysack, another shanty boy hit the man, hoping to knock him off the pole. The game "caused much merriment." Another game involved one man bending over as another shanty boy kicked him. The man being struck had to guess who kicked him. If he guessed wrong, he took another boot. A French-Canadian recalled the game provided "great sport." New arrivals also needed to be initiated. One newcomer at a Manistee camp was told to remove his coat, get on his knees and gaze through the sleeve at a black dot on the ceiling. As he looked "a pail of water came through his sleeve, and all but drowned him." One "well-liked" greenhorn was greeted upon his return to camp by veterans who tossed him in a blanket before dropping him in the potato bin and dancing over him. New shanty boys also might be asked to sing, dance or play the mouth organ, while the veterans mocked their efforts. Alcohol was prohibited in the camp and at 9:00 PM it was "lights out."[8]

The lumber era produced some of Michigan's most colorful workers. Shanty boys were male, young, and often immigrants. French-Canadians represented the largest group, and one study indicated that 75 percent of Canadians coming to the United States for seasonal work were shanty boys, which helps explain a Canadian government concern about this exodus across the border. Scotland was well represented, and one camp's payroll had so many "MacDonalds" they were separately entered by their first names: Big Dan, Black Dan, Curley Dan, Dirty Dan, and Dan-with-the-Gold-Watch. Germans and Scandinavians also worked as shanty boys, as did farmers, since the logging and farming seasons did not conflict.[9]

Most photos of shanty boys lack even the most basic identification.

Foremen even used nationality in assigning jobs. French-Canadians "were too volatile to handle oxen or even horses, but were cocky daredevils well suited for river drives. Germans were considered too phlegmatic and cautious to ride logs, but they were steady and dependable. The Indians were best kept in a separate crew. . . . otherwise the fights, which were a form of recreation in the woods, might get out of hand as old enmities surfaced." Shanty boys also earned a reputation for being tough. One observer recalled "Jim, Pat, Tom, and Jack Roach, of Roscommon . . . . could whip an army." Although shanty boys "were a tough and agile breed, willing to work hard under miserable conditions, content with enough pay to finance a brief springtime fling," there were exceptions. Ontario native Robert Dollar started as a shanty boy. Instead of spending his wages on springtime revelry, he bought a few acres of pineland and continued expanding his holdings until starting a logging company and sawmill in the western U.P.[10]

Logging camps were almost exclusively male domains, and most shanty boys were single. Women never worked in the forests, and married shanty boys left their wives back home. An exception to the rule might be a married foreman or timekeeper whose wife worked as the camp cook. Foreman Jack Mitchell's wife (whose first name remains unknown) spent 35 years as a camp cook. Described as "a strong, fearless woman, able to handle any job or situation," Mrs. Mitchell rose at 3:00 AM to prepare two daily meals for up to 100 men. With two assistants, she also cooked a "mobile" lunch of stew, stewed prunes, cookies, and coffee that the men ate in the forests.[11]

—— Marking the Logs

Because pine logs were prone to insect infestation during warm weather months, logging was a winter activity that began well before dawn. After eating a hearty breakfast, the shanty boys headed into the forest. Using double-edged axes and crosscut saws, they felled only the largest trees. Next, they removed the branches and cut the fallen trees into shorter logs. Teamsters stacked the logs on horse-drawn sleighs and slid them to the banks of the frozen rivers and creeks. Water sprinkled on the snow-covered roads left them icy, which made the job easier, but more dangerous. (Sand placed on down grades prevented the sleighs from going too fast.) The logs were stacked along the banks of frozen rivers and streams in piles called "rollaways," where they received a state mandated "log mark" identifying ownership. The company's "hammer man" placed the mark on one end of the log and his number at the other end of the log. If the log was improperly marked, he was held accountable. Registered with the government, log marks consisted of a combination of letters, numbers, and shapes. One study that claimed that there were more than 3,500 different Michigan log marks also noted that this was "only a fraction of those that were used" by Michigan loggers. (According to one source, at the height of the logging era, a standing offer of $50 existed for anyone "who could design a mark of three letters in any arrangement that had not yet been used before." It is unknown if the offer was ever redeemed.) Despite the log marks, thieves still stole logs, cutting off the ends and remarking them. If such theft was discovered, it cost the guilty party $25 per log and possible jail time.[12]

—— Riding the Logs

During the springtime, logging season climaxed with the river drive, which attracted great local attention. For owners and shanty boys it meant cash; for residents along the waterways it offered a spectacle that one observer

Skilled "river hogs" literally rode the logs to sawmills at the river's mouth. This was the most dangerous job in the industry but also earned the highest salaries.

described as "a noise that was a symbol of prosperity, progress, and break in the monotony." Those most eager for the river drive were its stars—the "river hogs." Michigan's many rivers and creeks, coupled with white pine that floated, made log drives an important part of the industry. The Tittabawassee, Manistee, Au Sable, Muskegon, Menominee, and Manistique, as well as many other lesser rivers and creeks, played such a key role in the logging era that an 1853 Michigan court ruling opened the waterways for all loggers to use. (Despite this law, which was designed to prevent a company from monopolizing a waterway, sabotage and dirty tricks occurred in the competitive world of logging.) Before a river or stream could be used for a log drive, crews cleared the waterways of impediments (fallen trees or rocks) to minimize logjams. Hastily constructed dams, especially on tributaries, regulated water flow and kept the mass of logs moving. Melting ice on the rivers in the late spring signaled the beginning of the log drive.[13]

The river hogs, who earned the highest wages paid to loggers, were divided into three crews. The "driving crew" kept the logs moving and out of the backwaters, sometimes a distance of up to ten miles on the river. The "jam crew" stayed close to the head of drive, preparing to come to the rescue if needed. The "sacking crew" brought up the rear, steering wayward logs back into the drive. (About 10 percent of the logs failed to get to the mills.) The rear crew required the least skill since "its chief attribute [was] a willingness to stay wet and to lift and shove logs when the boss gave the word." On the river, the "boss driver" (also called the "head push") kept the logs moving. With or without using his fists, he "had to command the respect of as unruly a group as could be found anywhere." Companies preferred their river hogs to be French-Canadians since the job "demanded a devil-may-care attitude and the surefootedness of a squirrel." The most skillful river hogs worked with the jam crew—the most dangerous job on the river. A river hog "was a man who could demand respect. He was rough. He was tough. He was rugged. And when he made his brag, people listened."[14]

The log drive began by prying key logs from the rollaway, which sent the mass of logs tumbling from the riverbanks into the rushing waters. The cascading of hundreds of logs into the river was both exciting for bystanders and dangerous for the men responsible for starting the chain reaction. Once the logs reached the water, river hogs wearing spiked caulk boots for firm footing and carrying a "peavey" (a spike-tipped pole) walked among the mass of moving logs.[15]

Hung-up logs and jams tested the skills of these daring men. Jams were expected, but for company owners they threatened financial ruin, and the head push had to clear them quickly. Getting the mass moving again required identifying troublesome logs and carefully removing them. A river hog chosen to dislodge the log would make his way ("picking his footing like a cat") to the middle of the jam and a suspected key log causing the problem. Using an axe, he notched the log so it broke, releasing the jam. Sometimes, the river hogs used a "flyboom" to reduce the potential damage caused by a jam. The boom was a log chain strung across the river, stopping the mass of logs until the downriver jam was cleared. In desperation, the river hogs even resorted to using dynamite. One of the worst logjams occurred on the Grand River in Grand Rapids during the summer of 1883. The ten-mile-long bottleneck destroyed the city's iron bridges before being cleared. The men chosen to break up the jam were well paid (up to five dollars a day), but danger and death might be right around the next river bend. The death of a river hog did not slow the drive since the logs always came first.[16]

The arrival of the log drive, especially in smaller mill towns, was a cause for celebration. As residents turned out, one settler recalled, "The river became a mass of sluggish bodies, rolling this way and that, grumbling all day and night."[17]

Once the logs reached the river's mouth they came under the jurisdiction of the boom company, whose workers sorted the logs by their mark. The Tittabawassee Boom Company, the state's largest, owned twelve miles of booms and delivered 11.8 billion board feet of logs to Saginaw mills. In 1890 the company moved logs belonging to 99 different companies. On the west

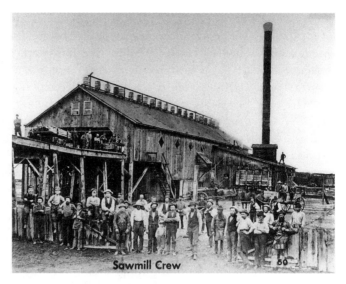

Sawmill Crew

Barrels sitting on this sawmill's roof were part of its fire-suppression system.

side of the state, the Muskegon Boom Company delivered 10 billion board feet of logs to sawmills. Boom companies proved less important in the Upper Peninsula where rivers played a minor role in the logging operations.[18]

—— From Logs to Boards

Once sorted, the logs headed to the sawmill. Usually located at the mouth of the log-driving rivers, the sawmills underwent many technological changes during the lumbering era. Waterpower gave way to steam, which greatly increased a mill's cutting capacity. In 1837, Michigan boasted 435 sawmills; 35 years later, that number had grown to 1,600. Saginaw-Bay City, Muskegon, Manistee, and Menominee hosted the greatest concentration of sawmills. In the early years of logging, sawmills averaged 3 million board feet annually. By the early 1880s, sawmills averaged 10 to 20 million board feet annually, although about 10 percent of the state's mills had a capacity of 20 to 50 million board feet. However, size was not a major factor. In 1883, mills cutting less than 10 million board feet represented half the state's mills. Peak-year board-feet production numbers from sawmilling communities are mind-boggling: Alpena (215 million), Cheboygan (127 million), Muskegon (665 million), Manistee (300 million), Grand Haven (192 million), and Saginaw-Bay City (more than one billion). Michigan sawmills peaked in 1888 cutting 4.2 billion board feet. Sawmills were usually two-story structures. A conveyer belt lifted the logs to the saws on the second floor. The rough boards moved by a conveyor belt to machines that edged them and cut them into specific dimensions. Refuse pieces fell from the conveyors to be burned. Finished boards were stacked for drying before being loaded onto shallow-draft boats (called "hookers") and shipped to a lumber-thirsty market. Michigan lumber built the cities of Chicago (especially after the 1871 fire), Milwaukee, Cleveland, Buffalo, and New York. Mills also cut millions of shingles, staves, pickets, and railroad ties. Michigan manufacturers of furniture, railroad cars, wagons, and ships, as well as Upper Peninsula mines (nicknamed "Michigan's underground forests") also consumed vast quantities of lumber.[19]

Sawmills cut logs using several different saws—circular, gang, and band. The circular saw was a single large blade but flawed because teeth broke off becoming deadly projectiles. The early circular blades also wobbled as they cut through the logs, producing boards that "more readily resembled washboards than lumber." However, improvements increased the popularity of circular blades. Gang saws, a "rack of large thick saws set in a vertical frame" that oscillated up and down, cut only on the down stroke. Capable of cutting two or three logs simultaneously, gang saws "became the monstrous giant of the mill," but they generated much waste. The most efficient saw was a band saw—a thin steel belt fourteen inches wide with teeth on one edge running on two wheels cutting a single board at a fast speed. Regardless of the saws used, mills generated enormous amounts of sawdust. One estimate claimed one board in four was lost in sawdust. Sawdust covered muddy roads and filled swamps and even mattresses. Cheybogan mills disposed of their sawdust creating a twelve-acre hill that impressed tourists.[20]

—— Technological Advances

Besides sawmill improvements, other technological changes greatly affected the logging industry.

Silas C. Overpack of Manistee invented one of the "most outstanding and picturesque" inventions to haul logs. Overpack's "Big Wheels" provided a comforting solution when loggers experienced snowless and warm winters.

Silas Overpack's "Big Wheels" allowed loggers to move logs during times when an absence of snow posed a handicap.

Introduced in 1870 and manufactured in Manistee for about 65 years, the Big Wheels stood ten feet tall with a sixteen-foot tongue:

> For hauling, the wheels were run astride a pile of four or five logs on a skid. The tongue was raised to a vertical position, and a heavy chain was slipped under the logs and fastened to hooks on the top of the axle. When the tongue was pulled down parallel to the ground, the logs were raised from the skid. A second chain around the forward end of the logs was attached to the tongue to hold it down. The driver sat on a board which extended back from the axle. One team of horses or oxen could draw a load of logs slung under the axle of the big wheels.

Overpack's invention weighed a ton and allowed loggers to handle logs "as cheaply during the summer months . . . as they could with sleighs in the winter time." Big Wheels, which earned a blue ribbon at the 1893 Columbian Exposition in Chicago, saw service throughout the United States and abroad.[21]

Railroads, however, had an even greater impact on the logging industry than the Big Wheels. Loggers started adapting railroads to move logs out of the Michigan forests during the 1850s. In 1857, the Blender Lumber Company used a standard locomotive to move cut logs from a 2,500-acre stand of timber to the Grand River near present-day Grand Valley State University. "Old Joe," the engine's name, made several runs a day, carrying logs totaling up to 100,000 board feet. When the company ceased operations in the late 1860s, its railroad had moved 40 million board feet of logs.[22]

A more comprehensive effort to merge log cutting and railroads began in the late 1870s after Winfield Scott Gerrish saw a narrow-gauge locomotive at the 1876 Philadelphia Exposition. Running a logging operation in Clare

Railroads radically changed the logging industry by allowing year-round logging. This image was taken at Antrim in the mid-1890s.

County, Gerrish returned home and built a six-mile, narrow-gauge railroad that earned him rewards and recognition during a mild winter. Gerrish's efforts triggered an explosion of logging railroad construction. By 1882, 32 narrow-gauge logging railroads were operating in Michigan forests; that number increased to 89 just a few years later. The Russell Wheel & Foundry (Detroit) and the Butterworth & Lowe Company (Grand Rapids) both produced thousands of logging cars, while at the same time Ephraim Shay, a Cadillac lumberman, invented a small powerful locomotive that easily climbed steep grades. The Shay locomotive—soon used by dozens of logging companies—impressed loggers who "contended that these locomotives could do everything except climb trees." As narrow gauge railroads grew increasingly popular, standard-gauge railroads moved more logs and built logging spurs. In the late 1880s, the Detroit, Mackinac, and Marquette Railroad carried logs from Seney to St. Ignace. Elsewhere in the U.P., main lines carried logs used to shore up mine shafts, fabricate maple flooring, and make charcoal for iron ore smelters.[23]

—— Deadly and Destructive Fires

Railroads also contributed to one of the great tragedies of the logging era—fire. Fueled by the stumps and branches (called "slash") that had been left behind, fires raced across the state annually with a devastating effect on the people, animals, and land. Once the slash dried (as much as 200 tons per acre), it only needed a spark, sometimes provided from a passing locomotive's smokestack. Other times, settlers started the slash on fire to clear the land for farming. However, sometimes the fires kept burning. As a result, "during the summer and early autumn the skies of late-nineteenth century Michigan usually were obscured by smoke. The sun rarely was seen in a clear sky." One Saginaw-area youngster recalled the smoke being so dense that children from outside the city "lost their way in coming and going from school." Children playing hide-and-seek lost track of anyone standing out in the open more than sixty feet away.[24]

One of Michigan's first memorable forest fires occurred in October 1871. Following an exceptionally hot and dry summer, the conditions proved ripe for fire. The fires started in the Upper Peninsula where one Menominee woman recorded, "everyone had a feeling of uneasiness and premonition for weeks." Fires devastated northeastern Wisconsin and jumped across the state line into the Upper Peninsula. Josephine I. Sawyers, who lived in Menominee as a little girl, recalled "where the fire struck, it was so sudden and fierce that everything caught at once." Everything burned, including the sawdust in the streets. Sawyers recounted two young girls who survived the fire hidden in the mud and water beneath a tree trunk, while Sawyer's brother-in-law stumbled across a group of desperate people "blind from smoke and heat and badly blistered." He roped them together and they stumbled along, often "burning their feet in hot ashes," to safety.[25]

Beyond Menominee, the Great Michigan Fire (as it was called) burned areas in the Thumb (leaving the residents in large areas of Huron and Sanilac Counties homeless), as well as the Saginaw Bay area, the Au Sable River valley, and lands around Roger City and north of Lansing. Led by Professors Robert Kedzie and Manly Miles, Michigan Agricultural College (MAC) students battled fires round-the-clock for two days and saved the East Lansing campus. An appreciative faculty rewarded the fledgling firefighters with an oyster dinner. The fires also hit the Lake Michigan coast between Holland and Manistee. Winds fanned fires burning in piles of sawdust and, within a few hours, Holland lay in ruins. A local observer noted that "Holland was and is . . . no more. The city as city, is gone, and scarcely one small row of houses on the outskirts remain. All factories and businesses have been swept away. . . . The scene is heart-breaking." On a positive note, Hope College students, who had left church services to form an impromptu fire brigade, saved the school's buildings. Farther north, fires near Manistee caused $1.2 million in property losses. The October 1871 fires even disrupted shipping as "a blanket of smoke" lay over Lake Michigan, while a "rain of burning embers" forced crews to water down their ships' wooden decks to keep them from bursting into flames. The Great Michigan Fire losses were poorly recorded, but the state claimed 3,000 homeless families and an estimated 2.9 million acres (more than 3,900 square miles) destroyed. Despite the unprecedented destruction, nothing was done to prevent another devastating fire. Dr. Robert Kedzie at MAC predicted the unchecked harvesting of trees without replanting promised greater conflagrations. He was ignored, and his prediction came true ten years later.[26]

The September 1881 Thumb fire remains, more than a century later, one of the worst fires in American history. The summer was exceptionally hot and dry, and by September most of the streams in Huron County had dried up. A Bay City newspaper reported that the Thumb was as "dry as a man after eating salt mackerel." Logging had peaked in the Thumb, leaving behind extensive cutover lands covered with slash. Monday, September 5 proved to be "the worst day in the history of the Thumb." Fanned by southwestern winds that increased in velocity, fires started burning all across the area. According to the local newspaper, "It was absolutely impossible to see one's hand before his face. We have never seen the darkness of night which exceeded it." Parisville lit its lamps at noon, but 90 minutes later, "a solid wall of flame," up to 100 feet tall, shattered the darkness. In Bad Axe, the wind "increased to a hurricane, and . . . with a horrible roaring, bore the insatiable flames with the speed of a race-horse." The fires destroyed most buildings except the stone courthouse where several hundred desperate and frightened residents sought sanctuary. Flames leveled Ubly and Sand Beach (present-day Harbor Beach) to ashes before the winds turned and spared Port Austin. To escape the smoke and flames, residents hid in wells or covered themselves in plowed fields with wet blankets or carpets. Man and animal fled into Lake Huron. The next morning, one survivor found himself standing next to a bear who he claimed was "as a gentle as a kitten." The Thumb fire left more than 280 people dead and 15,000 homeless, destroyed 3,400 buildings, and consumed one million acres. Half of those who perished died in a 30-mile stretch between Sand Beach and Port Austin. On a most somber note, the fire destroyed the area's sawmills and lumber, creating a shortage of coffins and forcing grieving families to bury more than one person in a single coffin. Shortages of food, clothing, and medical supplies led to enormous relief efforts, including the first disaster relief operation for the newly organized American Red Cross. If tragedy can have a shining lining, the fire had cleared the timber waste and left behind agriculturally rich soil for the future planting of navy beans and sugar beets.[27]

Devastating fires continued each year, with more notable fires in Ontonagon (1896), when a "monster tidal wave of flame," according to one witness, leveled the western U.P. town, left 2,000 homeless, and burned 228,000 acres; in Metz (1908), which left 43 dead, including 16 travelers on a derailed train; and, in AuSable-Oscoda (1911), which charred hundreds of thousands of acres. All this devastation spurred some positive changes, including the opening of forestry schools at Michigan Agricultural College (1906), the University of Michigan (1915), and Michigan Technological University (1936).[28]

—— Lumber Barons: Good or Evil?

By the later years of the nineteenth century, many Michigan cities and towns had residents who enjoyed great wealth from logging. Benefiting from an ostentatious lifestyle, they earned the nickname "lumber barons." Besides displaying their wealth in large mansions (many of which are gone today), some lumber barons entered politics, understandably as members of the Republican Party. Among the most prominent lumber baron politicians were Governors Henry Crapo (1865–69) from Flint, David H. Jerome (1881–83) and Aaron Bliss (1901–04) from Saginaw, and U.S. Senators Francis B. Stockbridge (1887–94) of Kalamazoo and Thomas W. Ferry (1871–83) of Grand Haven. Russell Alger of Detroit, who also served as Governor (1885–87) and in the U.S. Senate (1902–07), became Secretary of War (1897–99).[29]

Although lumber barons grew wealthy in an age of few controls on their business operations or the accumulation of wealth, some made major contributions to their cities even after the logging era had ended. Among the best known was Charles H. Hackley. Born in Indiana in 1837, Hackley arrived in Muskegon in 1856 with only a few dollars in his pocket. By 1888 he was a millionaire—one of 40 lumbering millionaires in Muskegon at the time. When logging ended in Muskegon in the 1890s, Hackley worked with some success to find new businesses to replace the closed sawmills. Hackley died in 1905, but he left one-third of his estimated wealth of $18 million to his hometown. Declaring "it is crime to die rich," Hackley added, "A rich man to a great extent owes his fortune to the public. He makes money largely through the labor of his employees." Appreciative townsfolk even discussed changing the city's name to Hackleyville. More than a century after Hackley's death, his name still adorns institutions in Muskegon, including a library, a hospital, his historic home, and an athletic field. In 2009, a life-sized sculpture was dedicated to him in downtown Muskegon.[30]

—— Logging Folklore

Michigan's logging era also contributed to the state's folklore. Two of the more notable stories involved the infamous town of Seney and shanty boy Paul Bunyan.

Located in the central Upper Peninsula, Seney earned "the reputation of having out-cut, out-logged, out-fought, out-drank and out-sported the rest of the world in its heyday." Each spring the nearby logging camps turned loose hundreds of thirsty and bored shanty boys who poured into the town of 3,000 people "wild for whiskey, the fighting and the women." If legend can be believed:

> Few places of its size ever had so many picturesque characters as this mad community. . . . Bona fide lumberjacks seeking the easy money which the jacks spent recklessly, gamblers, procurers, loose women, refugees from the law and a few business men. . . . Seney in the early days was a much abused town. 'Once tough, always tough' seemed to have been her fate. It became the gathering place of some of the toughest elements in the north.

Despite wild stories with even wilder personalities, the accounts of Seney's wickedness were greatly exaggerated.[31]

The first appearance of Paul Bunyan, the legendary giant of the woods, in print occurred in *The Detroit News-Tribune* on July 24, 1910. Reporter James MacGillivary's "The Round River Drive" (along with an illustrated drawing by staff artist Joseph L. Kraemer) showed a group of shanty boys sitting around a campfire sharing a story that included a character named Paul Bunyan. MacGillivary's widely circulated story led to sequels that not only added other colorful characters, but increased Paul's size, while making him the story's central character. Around 1914, *The American Lumberman* magazine carried a series of articles featuring "a consistent image" of Paul Bunyan as "a goliath sized lumber boss of great might and expertise, but one of very human character." In 1946, a collection of stories filled a small volume entitled *Paul Bunyan of the Great Lakes*. Author Stanley D. Newton gathered stories, many from the Upper Peninsula. In one entitled, "How Tall Was Paul?" Truthful Tom, the Irish logging camp cook, recounted climbing a twelve-foot ladder "while Paul sat down" to measure the lumberman's neck, which measured 39 inches. It took 70 yards of cloth to make Paul a pair of blue jeans. Tom also remembered the time when Paul's boots needed resoling. Tom spliced together about 100 half soles to fix one boot. Having run out of leather, Tom made up a batch of flapjacks (using 500 pounds of flour) that he spliced "together carefully" to resole the other boot. Months later, a delighted Tom learned the flapjack sole outwore the leather one. As Tom's efforts confirmed, Paul "was a big man."[32]

Maybe Carl Sandburg (who lived in Michigan from 1928 to 1945) offered the best explanation of who "invented" the mighty shanty boy. Writing in 1936, he observed:

> Who made Paul Bunyan, who gave him birth as a myth, who joked him into life as the Master Lumberjack, who fashioned him forth as an apparition easing the hours of men amid axes and trees, saws and lumber? The people, the bookless people, they made Paul and had him alive long before he got into the books for those who read. He grew up in shanties, around the hot stoves of winter, among socks and mittens drying, in the smell of smoke and the roar of laughter mocking the outside weather.[33]

By the early years of the 20th century, Michigan's lumber boom had passed. The last large tract of pine, about 400 million board feet in the Manistee River watershed, was cutover between 1900 and 1912. By 1920, the boom also ended in the Upper Peninsula. Many lumbering communities struggled economically as sawmills closed and companies moved westward to find new forests to cut. Years earlier, in the midst of the logging era, a speaker at a forestry convention noted that the ax had become "one of the worst enemies of the people" as it hastened the destruction of the state's forests "to produce a crop of millionaires." But little was done to curb the mania of cutting the timber as quickly as possible. According to forestry professors Donald I. Dickman and Larry A. Leefers, Michigan's logging era was "a juggernaut of laissez-faire out of control." In their haste to move on to new cutting sites, loggers gave no thought to the lands they were leaving. "Cut and get out" was their motto.[34]

The expanding use of railroads created even greater damage since removing trees caused erosion problems that not only affected the land, but the wildlife. Animals disappeared, some permanently, like the grayling, a popular game fish. Unchecked fires killed people, destroyed towns and farms, and damaged the soil, which is still in the process of recovering. Beyond the environmental issues, there was the saga of the "cutover lands" (as they were called). Initially sold to pioneer farmers (usually at a low price), the nutrient-deficient, sandy land could not sustain productive farming and usually reverted back to the state for non-payment of taxes. Finally in the 1920s, efforts at reforestation and fire control gained momentum and led to the creation of national and state forests. (Today, Michigan is home to three national forests.) During the 1930s, the enrollees of the Civilian Conservation Corps undertook many projects (not the least of which was planting nearly 500 million seedlings) that helped these badly damaged lands begin a rebirth.[35]

In 1929, two U.S. Department of Agriculture economists determined that during the state's logging era more than 33 million acres (92 percent) of Michigan's original forest had been cut or destroyed. Shanty boys had felled 244 billion board feet, fires had devoured 77 billion board feet, and land clearing had consumed 35 billion feet. Only 27.5 billion board feet of the virgin forest remained—three-quarters in the Upper Peninsula—and that soon was cut.[36]

In less than a century, Michigan's "inexhaustible" forest had disappeared.

CHAPTER
11

Mining
Michigan

Mining was demanding, dirty, and often dangerous.
During the early years, candles provided miners with
the primary source of light.

"There can scarcely be a shadow of a doubt [the
Keweenaw Peninsula] will eventually prove of great
value to our citizens and to the nation."

—Douglass Houghton, 1841

On February 21, 1836, Michigan Senator Lucius Lyon acknowledged the
possibility that Congress would offer Michigan the western Upper Peninsula when granting the contested Toledo Strip to Ohio. Besides the Lake
Superior fisheries, Lyon predicted "the copper mines supposed to exist" in
the western U.P. promised future wealth. "Within twenty years," he predicted,
these lands would be worth "more than forty millions of dollars," adding that
"even after ten years the State would not think of selling it for that sum."
Lyon represented an opinion held by a few Michiganians, and he suffered
criticism, even being accused of "selling Michigan out." Although most Michiganians despaired over the eventual loss of Toledo in favor of a "region of
perpetual snows," Lyon's prediction came true. Less than a decade after
Michigan's admission to the Union, the western Upper Peninsula, especially

174

the Keweenaw Peninsula, promised great wealth. But achieving it would not be easy.[1]

As early as 5,000 BCE, Native Americans used Michigan copper to make tools and weapons to replace stone implements. The copper also was traded and "nearly all" of the copper used by prehistoric Indians living in the east probably came from the Keweenaw Peninsula—a land mass that juts into western Lake Superior. Centuries later, French missionaries noted the presence of copper, and on two occasions the French demonstrated an interest in mining copper. When visiting the Ontonagon River in 1765, British trader Alexander Henry found "an abundance of virgin copper" on its banks that "required nothing [more] but to beat [it] into shape." Copper spoons and bracelets used by the Indians also intrigued him. A few years later, the British mined copper near Ontonagon, but the "largely hit-and-miss operation" failed. Serious mining efforts awaited the arrival of the Americans.[2]

As early as the presidency of John Adams, Americans expressed interest in Keweenaw copper. Although a congressional resolution authorizing an 1801 expedition to the Keweenaw was aborted, an army surgeon at Fort Mackinac believed rumors that Keweenaw copper promised "an inexhaustible source of wealth." In 1810, Dr. Francis Le Baron urged the Secretary of War to conduct an official investigation, explaining "that valuable & necessary Metal is growing daily in greater demand." La Baron sent copper samples east but, despite his enthusiasm, nothing came of the effort. Matters accelerated when Territorial Governor Lewis Cass proposed examining Keweenaw copper deposits during his 1820 Lake Superior expedition.[3]

Paddling along the southern shore of Lake Superior, Cass's expedition noted the Grand Sable Banks and the Pictured Rocks ("two of the most sublime natural objects in the United States," according to Cass). Along the way, the expedition's mineral expert, Henry Schoolcraft, who had earlier explored Missouri's lead mines, collected mineral samples and recorded his findings. Among the journey's highlights was a visit to the "Ontonagon Boulder," described by one expedition member as "the enormous mass of copper so much spoken of in the civilized world." Traveling up the Ontonagon River about twenty miles, Schoolcraft reached the boulder "after great exertion." (Cass abandoned the challenging final leg of the journey.) One expedition member expressed disappointment with the boulder's size (about four feet wide), describing it as "a mere stone, a large pebble." After making observations and hacking off small specimens "with much difficulty," Schoolcraft rejoined Cass. The expedition continued into Wisconsin, over to Lake Michigan and then returned to Detroit—122 days and 4,000 miles later.[4]

Schoolcraft reported that the region "contains very frequent, and some extraordinary imbedded masses of native copper." The Ontonagon Boulder had been disappointing, but he believed it "may still be considered one of the largest and most remarkable bodies of native copper upon the globe." These reports led the government to acquire by treaty mineral rights from the Indians, while facilitating dreams of future mineral wealth. A February 1823 Detroit newspaper story predicted Keweenaw copper "will create an active and profitable commerce on Lake Superior." Less than a decade later, Schoolcraft headed west again, but this time he took a trained mineralogist with him—a man who earned the title "father of copper mining in the United States."[5]

—— The "Little Doctor" Comes West

According to historian David J. Krause, Douglass Houghton and Keweenaw copper "have come to be almost synonymous." Born in upstate New York in 1808 to Jacob Houghton and Mary Lydia Douglass, Douglass Houghton earned his bachelor of arts degree in an amazing six months, focusing on science, especially geology. Houghton remained at the Rensselaer School in Troy, New York, as an assistant professor in chemistry and natural history. He also studied medicine and later earned a physician's license. But Houghton's real passion of geology changed his life dramatically. In late 1830, Detroit's leading citizens approached Amos Eaton, Houghton's mentor and the nation's leading scientific educator. They sought a scientific lecturer. Eaton suggested the 21-year-old Houghton, who arrived in Detroit in November 1830. Houghton possessed "a quick, nervous demeanor, [was] a great storyteller, always courteous, at home with all social classes"; his lectures sold out and crowds were turned away. Prominent citizens gathered around the "Little Doctor" (so nicknamed because he stood only 5' 3" tall) "like bees around honey," while those closest to him fashioned themselves "the Houghton boys."[6]

After lecturing in Detroit, Houghton planned on returning to New York, until Henry Schoolcraft asked him to serve as the physician/naturalist on an expedition north. Houghton agreed, and during the summer of 1831 he traveled to the Upper Peninsula. The 72-day, 2,000-mile expedition left Detroit in June and stopped at the Sault before heading west to the Keweenaw. They paddled around the tip of the Keweenaw, collecting specimens and examining rock formations before visiting the Ontonagon Boulder. Houghton returned from the rock with "some large samples and a mind brimming with ideas." Word of the expedition prompted a Detroit newspaper to boast how the discovery of "a new and extensive copper mine" on the Keweenaw "will undoubtedly become a source of wealth to the country." The expedition also mobilized Detroiters to petition to Congress to build a canal around the Sault rapids to improve shipping for "the opening and working of the extensive copper mines on, or near the river Ontonagon." The Soo Locks were still more than twenty years away, but Houghton's *Report on The Existence of Copper in the Geological Basin of Lake Superior* received great exposure and revealed extensive copper riches existed in the western Upper Peninsula.[7]

Houghton sought an appointment as a U.S. Army doctor until Schoolcraft asked if the Little Doctor might join him in his quest to find the source of the Mississippi River. Once again, Houghton agreed. They stopped on the Keweenaw where he collected more copper samples. In a letter appearing in a Detroit newspaper about the expedition's progress, Houghton predicted—in what later became an understatement—how these new finds might influence the "coming prosperity" of the Lake Superior region. After several quiet years when Houghton married, retired from medicine, and earned wealth dabbling in real estate, his life took another unexpected turn after Michigan joined the Union in 1837.[8]

During the 1830s, Michigan, like many states, conducted a geological survey that provided the necessary information to promote economic development and attract new settlers. Geological surveys required a state geologist. Less than one month after Michigan joined the Union, Governor Mason signed into law a geological survey act and appointed Houghton as the state's first geologist—a position he called "one of the most important jobs in state government." Although Houghton spent the first several years focused on the state's salt deposits, by 1841 he was in the western Upper Peninsula where his investigations led him to report, "There can scarcely be a shadow of a doubt [that the district] will eventually prove of great value to our citizens and to the nation." Houghton's 1841 annual report, known simply as "the copper report," became "the founding document of the subsequent copper rush." The *Detroit Daily Advertiser* noted in May 1841 that "Dr. Houghton has submitted a mass of valuable and interesting matter which cannot but excite the earnest attention of every class of readers."[9]

—— The Ontonagon Boulder

As the Copper Rush began, the federal government acquired the western Upper Peninsula from the Indians under the 1842 Treaty of La Pointe. The Ontonagon Boulder also returned to the news as a Detroit businessman hoped to turn Michigan's most famous rock into a money-making adventure. In 1841, Julius Eldred visited the Ontonagon River and purchased the rock from a local Indian chief for $150. The following year, he returned to

The Ontonagon Boulder is shown on display at the Seaman Mineralogical Museum.

determine how best to move it. A year later, as Eldred prepared to move it, he discovered others had claimed the rock, forcing him to buy it again—this time for $1,365. Through a dense, hilly forest, his team of twenty white men and Indians hacked a four-mile road and "with very great effort" used a capstan to raise the rock and load it onto a railroad-like flatbed. Pushing and pulling, they took up the track from behind them every 50 feet and re-laid it, finally reaching the river. The boulder was placed on a raft that negotiated a low river, before reaching Lake Superior and a sailing ship. At the tip of the Keweenaw Peninsula, the U.S. mineral agent congratulated Eldred on "one of the most extraordinary performances of the age," before seizing the boulder. (The Secretary of War even gave the agent permission to use troops since "the object is really one of great importance to the scientific world.") Eldred accompanied the boulder to Detroit where he delayed the federal government temporarily, while charging a quarter to see the famous rock. Finally, the boulder traveled under government protection east via the Erie Canal. Eldred pursued ownership claims unsuccessfully, but in 1847 Congress compensated him $5,664.98 for the mass of copper that weighed 3,700 pounds and was valued at $600. After years at the War Department, the Ontonagon Boulder was moved to the Smithsonian Institution. In the 1990s, Indians demanded its return, claiming it had sacred value. The federal government disagreed, and the boulder remains in the collection of the National Museum of Natural History.[10]

—— Copper Rush Begins

The publicity from Houghton's copper report and the travels of the Ontonagon Boulder precipitated the Copper Rush—America's first mineral boom, predating the famed California Gold Rush by several years. During the summer of 1843, a U.S. Mineral Agency office opened at the tip of Keweenaw Peninsula, soon the site of a chaotic settlement called Copper Harbor. Following established precedents, mining permits covered nine square miles (later reduced to one square mile). The lessee received one year to explore the site and three years to mine it; renewals gave the explorer ten years to develop the site. The government received a royalty of six pounds of copper for every 100 pounds extracted; after three years, that figure increased to ten pounds.[11]

Prospectors arrived at Copper Harbor with a small tent, two blankets, a frying pan, and hopes of "striking it rich." John H. Forster, a Copper Harbor visitor, reported in 1846: "Card playing, the use of the 'flowing bowl,' and some good fighting with fist and pistol, were the social amusements of this conglomerate community. . . . It was a common saying that there was no Sunday west of the Sault." Another early settler added, "The country is bleak, barren and savage, without any signs of cultivation or civilization except the appearance of bedbugs and whiskey; rats and cockroaches have not yet come up, but are expected. It is the land of dirty shirts and long beards." In 1844, the federal government built a fort at Copper Harbor, according to the official explanation, "to countenance the miners and protect them, and to encourage the migration of the Indians from Michigan when the time for their removal comes." Built on Lake Fanny Hooe, the fort was named after Secretary of War William Wilkins and garrisoned by two companies of U.S. infantry. As one veteran miner concluded shortly after arriving at Copper Harbor, "A country of this character will require a great deal of labor and privation as well as capital, and at least two years to determine its character as a copper region." How right he was! Prospectors faced a hostile terrain of cedar thickets and swamps. (It took two days to travel the six-mile width of the Keweenaw Peninsula.) Unparalleled winter isolation—when Lake Superior froze and no supplies or mail reached the Keweenaw—was followed in the spring with the arrival of pesky black flies called "Keweenaw eagles" as a tribute to their ferocity.[12]

As the Copper Rush peaked during the summer of 1845, Dr. Houghton "achieved the pinnacle of his personal fame." When visiting a mining encampment "he was immediately hailed. . . . His small, boyish figure was easily recognizable among the burly frontier adventurers." Although Houghton's future looked bright, on October 13 he and four other men left Eagle Harbor in a small boat. Following several stops, they started back after sunset. Suddenly, the weather changed and high winds and heavy seas lashed the boat swamping it. Houghton and two other men perished. One of the survivors later reported that Houghton had rejected suggestions to head to shore before conditions worsened. He also refused to wear a life preserver. Houghton's body was retrieved the following spring and buried in Detroit. Seventy years later, a monument featuring an assortment of different Keweenaw rocks was erected in Eagle River in honor of "the father of copper mining in the United States."[13]

—— Mining in Earnest

Early mining operations required sinking a shaft next to the vein of copper. Miners descended underground in buckets or climbing ladders, using candles as their primary source of light. Swinging seven-pound hammers and chisels, miners bored holes in the rock and then filled them with black powder. After the explosion, they hauled away the rock in wheelbarrows. A windlass (operating under horsepower) brought the rock to the surface where it was crushed to separate the waste rock from the copper. As early as the 1850s, the introduction of steam power improved these efforts. Miners earned $1.50 a day.[14]

It soon became apparent that the individual miner would enjoy little success on the Keweenaw. One Keweenaw company operated for five years before going bankrupt after spending $2.5 million but paying investors only $20,000 in dividends. Regardless of the risk, there was no shortage of investors. By the end of 1845 the Keweenaw boasted 45 organized mining companies. Of the twelve companies extracting copper, the Cliff Mine stood above all the others. In late 1844, the Pittsburgh and Boston Copper Harbor Mining Company struck it rich with the discovery of a massive vein of copper near the village of Eagle River. The company paid a stockholder dividend in 1848 as the Cliff became the Western Hemisphere's first successful copper mine. With a few

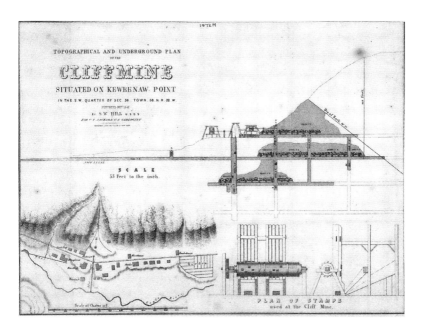

The Cliff (circa 1847 topographical map) was among the most successful Keweenaw Peninsula copper mines.

exceptions (the Minesota [sic] on the Ontonagon River and the Quincy and Pewabic near Portage Lake), the success at the Cliff was not duplicated anywhere on the Keweenaw. By the time the Cliff played out shortly after the Civil War, it had paid its stockholders $2.3 million in dividends on a total investment of only $110,000. Elsewhere on the Keweenaw, most companies failed, and their miners headed west to strike it rich in the California gold fields. *New York Tribune* editor Horace Greeley, who served as a director of the Northwest Copper Mining Association, observed after years of investment and little financial gain: "All I ever realized by mining was a conviction that digging . . . [copper] is a fair business for those who bring to and invest in it the requisite capacity, knowledge, capital, experience, perseverance, and good luck, and that the rarely encountered 'big strikes' are as one to a million."[15]

The Copper Rush was over within a few years. Conditions on the Keweenaw changed so drastically that the army vacated Fort Wilkins and sent its soldiers to fight in Mexico. Despite a rocky start, the Keweenaw copper mining continued and contributed to the northern war effort during the Civil War. Yet, the industry's greatness lay after the war.

—— Postwar Boom

The copper boom after the Civil War occurred in Houghton County in the middle of the Keweenaw Peninsula, especially around the town of Red Jacket (better known as Calumet). The merger of the Calumet Mining Company (formed in 1861) and the Hecla Mine (opened in 1866) greatly changed mining dynamics on the Keweenaw. Boston investors, including Alexander Agassiz, the son of the noted naturalist Louis Agassiz, combined the two mines to form one massive conglomerate—the Calumet and Hecla Mining Company (C&H). By 1872, C&H increased its share of Michigan's copper production to 65 percent, half the nation's copper during the 1870s. The success C&H enjoyed was aided by improvements to Portage Lake, which allowed Lake Superior vessels to dock at Houghton and Hancock—two cities that took shape in the early 1860s. The dredging of the Portage Entry also allowed smelting and stamping operations to open elsewhere along Portage and Torch Lakes.[16]

Keweenaw copper production grew rapidly from 12 million pounds in 1860 to more than 200 million pounds annually by the turn of the century. Until 1887 Michigan produced more copper than any other state. Although Keweenaw copper mines peaked in 1916 (producing 266 million tons), Minnesota and Arizona mines surpassed Michigan. As late as 1904, Keweenaw mines produced about 25 percent of America's copper.[17]

Although no longer leading the nation, Michigan copper communities flourished, especially Calumet. Throughout the late nineteenth century and into the twentieth century, the rich Calumet & Hecla mines paid stockholders $150 million. C&H's Boston owners used those profits to build Harvard University and fund the Boston Symphony, while Keweenaw residents owned less than 5 percent of the C&H stock. But the company did not neglect Calumet, offering its workers a paternalistic environment that included more than 1,700 company houses renting for as little as five dollars a month. C&H also provided bathhouses (a miner's family bathed for free, while miners paid 2½ cents), a library (with 3,000 volumes), a modern hospital, and schools, as well as pension and medical benefits, including death benefits for widows and families of miners killed on the job. Employees could even graze their cows on C&H pastureland at no cost. Although C&H owned everything—most notably the land on which Calumet stood—the city prospered. The city offered its more than 30,000 residents electricity, telephones, streetcars, and stores selling fine wine, furs, and jewelry, as well as one of the "nation's most renowned" opera houses that attracted some of the leading performers of the time: "When times were good, C&H was good to Calumet. When times were not so good, C&H was free to act in its own best interests."[18]

—— The Copper Strike of 1913–14

As the Industrial Revolution transitioned America from an agricultural nation to one of the world's leading manufacturing powers, a small group of men controlled the country's natural resources. To improve productivity and increase profits, corporations introduced new machines. At the same time, many of the immigrants coming to America performed the backbreaking labor in miserable and unsafe conditions with little prospect of upward mobility. At the turn of the century, the United States had the highest death rate for workers among industrial states and no worker's compensation for men injured on the job. During the early years of the twentieth century, Keweenaw Peninsula mines averaged up to 60 underground deaths a year. At the same time, wages rarely kept up with basic expenses. When workers sought to improve their conditions—like asking for a pay raise—they were met with strong resistance. They had no rights. There were strikes—some violent—and the workers won a few concessions, but not many. The giant corporations who possessed the wealth and power to fight a strike for months, imported strikebreakers, hired detectives, carried the battle to court with highly paid lawyers, influenced politicians, and "if necessary, shut down plants completely to force workers into submission." According to writer Jerry Stanley, the Industrial Revolution's double standard was "when corporations pooled their money to control an entire industry, it was a skillful business move; when workers tried to combine their numbers into a union it was considered a conspiracy." In 1913 all these issues converged in the Copper Country, exploding into a nine-month strike that "pitted neighbor against neighbor; brought malice, mayhem, and murder; and left a badly divided community in its wake.[19]

By 1913, C&H experienced a decline in profits. The average mine depth was 4,000 feet, double what it had been 30 years earlier. In 1874, every ton of ore produced 97 pounds of copper; by 1913, one ton of ore produced 25 pounds of copper. To increase productivity, the company turned to the one-man drill—already used in western copper mines and "the first major cost-saving innovation in rock drills since power drills had largely replaced hand drilling in the early 1880s." A 150-pound drill was mounted on a heavy iron post and operated by one man. However, if the post was struck by debris or

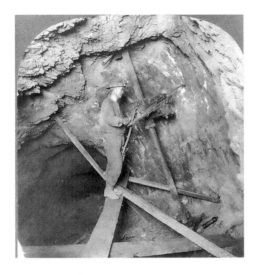

Nicknamed the "widow maker," the one-man drill contributed to miner unrest and precipitated one of Michigan's worst labor strikes.

collapsed from any cause, the miner was doomed, since the nearest man was several hundred feet away. As one miner recalled, "Even before the one-man drill, we lost maybe a man a week in those mines." The miners nicknamed this new tool "the widow maker," and newspapers carried frequent stories of men who died using this tool. Besides the one-man drill, miners had other grievances. For an eleven-hour day, they earned $2.50. Between 1907 and 1913, 3,000 workers quit C&H because of dangerous and unhealthy working conditions. As one miner observed: "In all these years that I have been working for this company we have been treated more and more like slaves. . . . The company drives us about like mules."[20]

Calumet & Hecla did not fear its workers, mainly because it had successfully played the various ethnic groups off each other. But the one-man drill, working conditions, and the efforts of the Western Federation of Miners (WFM) changed the dynamics of the situation. Although the WFM was a western union, it had worked to organize Michigan miners, and by 1913 it counted more than 9,000 Keweenaw workers as members. Mine managers blamed the labor unrest on the WFM and vowed its destruction. Besides concerns over a wage increase and adoption of the one-man drill, mine operators viewed the WFM with "a genuine fear of socialism."[21]

During the summer of 1913, miners proposed a pay raise (to $3.50 a day), a shorter workday and a return to the two-man drill. Management refused to meet with the miners, with C&H general manager James MacNaughton telling the WFM: "The grass will grow on your streets before I'll ever give in." The ensuing strike led Governor Woodbridge Ferris to send in the National

Annie Clemenc rallied miners during the Copper Strike of 1913–14.

Guard (nearly 3,000-man strong) to Calumet four days after the strike began. In a few days, all the mines closed and strike leaders claimed that 16,000 miners had joined the protest.[22]

Women played a central role in the strike, most notably one who earned national fame as a "modern Joan of Arc." Annie Klobuchar Clemenc (pronounced Clements) was born in 1888 in Calumet as the oldest of five children in a Croatian immigrant family. Her father had a job in the mines, and her mother worked as a cook and maid. On the third day of the strike, Clemenc hoisted a massive American flag and led a march of several hundred strikers down Calumet's main avenue. It started something, and each morning hundreds of miners, their wives, and children lined up behind Clemenc and paraded the several miles to the mines. On Sunday mornings, the marchers wore their best clothes, and "Annie was joined at the front of the line by two young girls dressed in white, who carried the ends of streamers that fell from the tip of the flagstaff." Although the flag and its flagstaff weighed much, Clemenc claimed, "I love to carry it." These marches offered labor unity and a daily sign of defiance.[23]

However, neither the marches nor Clemenc's determination deterred C&H. They organized the nonstriking elements, like Calumet businesses, into an organization called the Citizens' Alliance. If a business did not oppose the strike, it faced economic ruin since C&H controlled the Copper Country banks. The Citizens' Alliance set up roadblocks to stop the marches, but the miners went around them. C&H also hired eastern thugs, recruited from the New York City slums. Called "waddies," the strikebreakers were given complete authority and openly carried guns. There was more violence between the strikers and the Guard and the waddies. When Governor Ferris visited Calumet in August, he declared the miners "have real grievances and grounds for complaint." Ferris removed most of the soldiers and appointed a judge to seek a solution. Judge Alfred Murphy concluded the one-man drill was here to stay and C&H was "arrogant and unfair." The strike also received national attention. Lawyer Clarence Darrow came to the Copper Country and represented strikers. Mother Jones, a champion of labor and one of the most famous women of the times, marched with Clemenc three times. In August, the 83-year-old champion of labor addressed a crowd of 2,000 strikers and told them not to carry guns like the company thugs, but "use your fist and black his two eyes, and then he can't see to shoot you."[24]

As summer turned into fall, some miners returned to their jobs. At the same time, a shortage of workers led to the hiring of a new work force, which angered strikers. Mediation efforts failed, as C&H manager MacNaughton told U.S. Department of Labor representatives he "knew of nothing to arbitrate." A company attorney added they "were determined to drive the Western Federation of Miners out of the copper fields, if they had to fight all winter to do so." Sometimes, the union worsened its position. The early December murder of three miners by WFM ruffians prompted mass rallies denouncing the union as a socialistic "enemy of the home, community, law and order, good citizenship, good morals, and the church and 'the enemy of the gospel of Jesus Christ.'" When a local minister asked the throng of anti-strikers "What had the WFM cared for laboring men?" the audience responded, "Nothing, Nothing!" Despite a C&H ultimatum to return to the mines by December 19 or be permanently replaced, some miners resisted—although the prospects for success had dimmed. C&H also threatened to evict strikers from company houses or quadruple their rent. The Citizens' Alliance also attacked the WFM in a variety of ways, including circulating a publication called *Truth* that challenged union claims.[25]

—— Christmas Eve Tragedy

With the Copper County facing a civil war, Calumet women planned a Christmas party for the children of the striking miners. On December 24, 500 children and 175 adults gathered on the second floor of Calumet's Italian Hall to sing carols and receive gifts. Suddenly, a cry of "fire!" panicked the gathering, and the mass exodus from the building led to "an avalanche of terrified men, women, and children" down the stairwell:

> Those who fell first could not regain their footing and were trampled to death. Boots came down on a child's head or smashed a breast. On they came, hurtling down, grasping, clawing in efforts to get out while others behind them fell (some descending head-first) upon them. The more agile leaped down upon the others wedged in the mass of bodies below. Arms and legs meshed as body piled upon body. Within minutes, the stairway was tightly blocked. At the bottom, children were 'jammed into one solid mass from which no one could emerge.'

There was no fire, but 73 people (64 children) died in the stairwell that day. Numerous witnesses swore the man yelling "fire" wore a Citizens' Alliance button. A few days after the tragedy, thousands gathered to bury their dead. The logistical arrangements (acquiring enough coffins and digging so many graves) proved challenging. Services were held in six churches, and then a mournful, silent procession "punctuated by sobbing and crying" and led by Annie Clemenc carrying the American flag, made its way to the local cemetery. Although the Citizens' Alliance offered the victims' families financial assistance, they refused.[26]

Matters intensified when Citizens' Alliance vigilantes beat up and shot WFM president Charles H. Moyer, placed him on a southbound train, and told him never to come back to the Copper Country. The attack on Moyer made national news and even led to a congressional investigation. The chairman of the committee, a Colorado Democrat, claimed that "the Copper Country was a little kingdom with James MacNaughton reigning over men who were practically serfs but not oppressively treated and that little could be done to end the strike." Although no official report was issued, one congressman added, "We have found things to criticize of course but, on the whole, the men are far better off than two-thirds of the workingmen of the country."[27]

The Copper Country strike dragged on through the winter until April 12, 1914, when striking miners voted 2-1 to end the walkout. Workers could return to the mines but first they needed to hand in their union card.

Hancock's Quincy Mine (circa 1915) is a national historic landmark today.

Thousands headed south to Detroit to the auto industry and the Ford Motor Company's five-dollar workday. Those who stayed earned an eight-hour day, a three-dollar workday, and promises of improved grievance procedures. But the one-man drill remained.[28]

According to historian Arthur W. Thurner, the Copper Country strike "influenced all future life in the Keweenaw Peninsula." Among the costs: Nine men died from gunshot wounds and 26 others survived their wounds; 168 were beaten, hundreds were terrorized, and "many families were vulnerable to pressures from neighbors." Authorities searched homes "ruthlessly" and often without warrants, while gatherings turned into riots, and "the grimmest and saddest memory" was the Christmas tragedy at Italian Hall. The financial cost left the WFM with "enormous debts," while "the loss in mining company income ran into the millions, and the loss in wages, was enormous." Annie Clemenc left Calumet for Chicago where she married a Chicago newspaper reporter who had covered the strike. In 1984, Italian Hall fell to the wrecking ball, but the archway remains as a memorial to one of the worst tragedies in Michigan history.[29]

Copper mining continued on the Keweenaw for many years after the strike. A rise in copper prices during World War I was followed by setbacks during the early 1920s and again during the Great Depression. Miners finally received the right to collective bargaining under the guarantees of the 1935 Wagner Act. While costs made underground mining prohibitive, reclamation efforts of tailings (refuse remaining after processing) kept the industry alive. C&H finally closed its Keweenaw operations in the late 1960s.[30]

—— Iron Ore Discovered

At the same time copper was being discovered and explored on the Keweenaw Peninsula, about 100 miles to the east, the discovery of iron ore greatly affected another part of the Upper Peninsula. On September 19, 1844, near present-day Marquette County's Teal Lake, William Austin Burt and his surveying crew watched as the needle of their compass fluctuated wildly. Burt called out, "Boys, look around and see what you can find." Burt's accidental discovery of the Marquette Iron Range contributed enormously to America's future Industrial Revolution.

Fifty-two-year-old William Austin Burt had been running lines and exploring the wilderness as a U.S. deputy surveyor for eleven years when he and his party encountered iron ore. Although quiet and unassuming, Burt was an articulate conversationalist, ingenious inventor, knowledgeable woodsman, and determined surveyor with an obsession for accuracy. Born near Boston in 1792 (in a family that arrived from England in 1638), Burt pursued an esteemed vocation practiced by George Washington and Thomas Jefferson. Settling north of Detroit in 1824 and elected Macomb County surveyor in 1831, Burt soon received an appointment with the federal government. Experienced surveyors knew the key to making money under the government contract system was to perform the greatest amount of work in the shortest amount of time. This method also generated inaccurate surveys. An exception to this practice, Burt's "attention to detail did cause him to lose money." But the result, according to the U.S. surveyor general, was "the most satisfactory work I have yet met with." While working in the U.P., Burt invented the solar compass to compensate with the minerals that deflected the needle of a magnetic compass and produced errors. Burt's invention greatly aided surveyors for years, especially working in the mineral-rich western United States.[31]

The year after Burt's discovery, the Jackson Mining Company (named after Boston geologist Charles T. Jackson, not the Michigan city where the company originated) set up the Jackson Mine about half a mile west of where Burt's surveying party made their discovery (near the present-day city of Negaunee). The company purchased a square-mile piece of land for $2.50 an acre, and the following year collected 300 pounds of ore that it sent downstate. They also set up a forge to process their ore about three miles from the mining site. The fires heated the chunks of ore, which were then hammered into "blooms" four inches square and two feet long. On February 10, 1848, the Jackson forge produced its first bloom, which was hauled over a crude road to Lake Superior and sent downstate by boat in the spring.[32]

The iron ore industry had come to Michigan. Other companies followed Jackson, and within a few years ore docks were built at the present day port city of Marquette. In 1855, companies working the Marquette Range shipped 1,449 tons downstate. But shipping blooms or high-grade natural iron ore required portaging the rapids at Sault Ste. Marie—an expensive, time-consuming and labor-intensive process. It cost $200 to send a ton of processed ore to Pittsburgh that had a market price of only $80. The situation changed dramatically when the Soo Locks opened in mid-1855 and the volume of ore shipped increased exponentially, as shipping costs decreased rapidly. In 1857, 26,184 tons of ore passed through the locks and costs dropped almost in half.

By the eve of the Civil War, new forms of transportation and loading techniques, coupled with the extraction of more iron ore, cut downstate shipping costs considerably.[33]

—— Postwar Expansion

During the years after the Civil War, America's Industrial Revolution flourished as railroads, iron ships, factories, and skyscrapers demanded iron ore and steel. New discoveries in the western U.P. propelled Michigan to become the nation's leading iron ore producer—a position it held until superseded by Minnesota in 1900. But iron mining, which had been largely a quarrying operation during the early years, now required sinking shafts into the ground as had been done in the Copper Country. The Menominee Range first shipped ore in 1877 from an assortment of mines of varying size. The most notable was the Chapin, among the greatest iron mines in the Upper Peninsula. In 1900, the Chapin's most productive year, it became Michigan's first iron mine to exceed one million tons. During the 1890s, iron mines along the eastern range of the Menominee employed 4,000 miners, and the city of Iron Mountain (home to the Chapin Mine) was nicknamed "The Payroll City of the North." The Chapin was also home to the Cornish Pump, the "largest of its kind in the United States." As the mines went deeper underground, wetness posed problems. Installed in January 1893, the 725-ton Cornish Pump pumped five million gallons every 24 hours. The Chapin closed in 1932 when costs outweighed the value of the iron ore extracted. A National Historical Landmark, the Cornish Pump survived and today is part of Iron Mountain's Mining Museum, which also boasts the largest collection of underground mining equipment in the country. Menominee Range mines totaled 300 million tons of iron ore, second to the Marquette Range.[34]

Farther west, Harvard geology professor Raphael Pumpelly pursued leads discovered after reading William Austin Burt's surveying notes. His effort led to the 1871 discovery of the Gogebic Range, Michigan's third iron ore range. During the 1880s, the arrival of railroads in the western U.P. aided the development of mines along this range that stretches into neighboring Wisconsin. During the mid-1880s, a dozen mines opened on the range's Michigan side. Other mines followed, including the Norrie-Aurora-Pabst near Ironwood, one of state's most productive. Production on the Gogebic peaked during the late 1910s, although the last Gogebic mine closed in 1966 after the range had produced 250 million tons of iron ore.[35]

—— Iron Ore Processing

Producers either shipped ore downstate for processing or they opened furnaces locally to remove the ore from the impurities of the excavated rock. More than 25 forges were built in the U.P. during the late nineteenth century, producing what was known as "charcoal iron." This process mixed crushed ore with charcoal and dolomite (limestone) and placed the mixture in a furnace stack. Blasts of heated air—blown into the stack by large steam engines—made the charcoal burn (hence the term *blast furnace*). As the ore sank to the bottom, it gradually melted. The impurities mixed with the limestone and floated to the surface. Tapholes took off the "slag" (waste products) and the molten iron was guided into channels in the sand floor and allowed to cool. The bars of iron, called "pigs," were separated and hauled to the dock for shipment. However, charcoal iron required vast quantities of hardwood to make the charcoal necessary for these forges. In 1903 it was estimated that the U.P. furnaces consumed 30 acres of hardwood daily to supply the kilns making the charcoal. By the early twentieth century, a shortage of hardwoods, coupled with higher costs, made it more profitable to ship ore in large ore carriers to smelters on Lake Erie and southern Lake Michigan that used coke (a high-sulphur product made from coal).[36]

One of the more intriguing Upper Peninsula furnaces was Fayette. In 1864 the Jackson Mining Company purchased 16,000 acres of hardwoods on the Garden Peninsula, intent on taking advantage of a new railroad connecting the Marquette Range and Escanaba on Lake Michigan. (Nearby limestone cliffs made the site even more attractive.) Marquette sent ore by rail to Escanaba and then by boat across the Bay de Noc (a three-hour journey). Two blast furnaces, a store, a hotel, workers' homes and support buildings, a narrow-gauge railroad (to bring in hardwood to the charcoal kilns), and shipping docks completed the settlement named after company manager Fayette Brown. Fayette grew to 500 people and over the course of 25 years produced 230,000 tons of iron—the second most productive U.P. iron ore smelter. But keeping Fayette economically competitive proved challenging, and operations closed in 1891. In 1959, the Department of Natural Resources acquired the site and, working with elements of the Michigan Historical Commission, developed one of the state's most picturesque museums. Equally important, the Michigan Iron Industry Museum in Negaunee (on the site of the first iron forge in the Lake Superior region) interprets the state's iron ore past, present, and future.[37]

One of the saddest moments in Michigan's iron ore history occurred in November 1926 at the Barnes-Hecker Mine near Ishpeming. First explored in 1907, the Barnes-Hecker site was developed ten years later by the Cleveland-Cliffs Iron Company, one of the Upper Peninsula's biggest mining concerns. Because the site was swampy, a concrete shaft lining and underground dams were built as safety precautions as the mine shaft sank deeper into the ground. The draining of wet areas near the mine provided a drier working environment, and in 1922, Cleveland-Cliffs began removing ore from Barnes-Hecker, which earned a reputation as a safe mine. However, late on the morning of November 3, 1926, explosions heard at the mine surface proved foreboding, a situation that worsened when only one of the several dozen workers in the mine reached the surface safely. Mud, rock, water, and debris rising from the mine floor greeted rescuers headed down the shaft to investigate. Fifty-one men perished in the state's worst mining disaster—an accident that also widowed 42 wives and orphaned 132 minor children. Cleveland-Cliffs compensated beneficiaries twice the maximum pension ($8,400) under the state's Workmen's Compensation Law. The exact cause of the cave-in was never determined, and the mine was never reopened.[38]

——Averting a Crisis

After World War II, the U.S. steel industry faced a crisis. Estimates indicated that Minnesota's iron-rich Mesabi Range would soon be exhausted. President Harry Truman challenged the industry to expand its iron ore resources, declaring, "We must make a diligent effort to discover new deposits. . . . And we must develop for the use of industry new technologies so that the vast deposits of low-grade ores . . . may be put to work." Ten years later, the industry successfully introduced a way to enrich traditionally uneconomical low-grade taconite. Although the industry successfully separated taconite from the waste rock, the

The discovery of iron pellets addressed a major industrial need.

resulting product had a consistency of baby powder and could not realistically be shipped. But mixing taconite with water and clay, and then balling it, left the "low-grade ore better than high-grade ore once used, and it did so in a way that saved energy and labor."

"Pelletization," which began on the Mesabi Range, came to Michigan at the Republic Mine in 1963. For a variety of reasons, iron ore pellets became "the preferred form of iron ore." At one point, the remaining mines on the Marquette Range (Empire and Tilden near Palmer) produced about one-quarter of the nation's iron ore pellets. But changes are coming. In 2014, the Empire Mine will cease operations. Some Empire employees will be transferred to the Tilden, which authorities claim has a 30-year plan. According to one mining official, "it's not like mining is going away."[39]

CHAPTER

12

Turn of the Century

The 1889 Detroit International Fair and Exposition allowed hundreds of Michigan companies to boast about their many accomplishments.

"I sort of feel it is in my bones that we are now preparing for a campaign on a food which will eventually prove to be the leading cereal in the United States, if not the world."

——W.K. Kellogg

In September 1889, thousands of Michiganians visited the Detroit International Exposition & Fair. Hailed as a "grand combination" boasting the state's agricultural and industrial successes, hundreds of companies—both small and large, producing everything from cigars to railroad boxcars—offered exhibits for the two-week extravaganza. Constructed on 72 acres of unincorporated land outside the city limits at the juncture of the Detroit and Rouge Rivers (present-day Springwells), the Exposition included a massive wooden exhibition building (designed as a European palace and boasting 200,000 square feet of exhibit space) and dozens of smaller cottage-size buildings where exhibitors showed off their wares. The fair proved so popular that exhibitors were turned away for lack of space. One visitor, who boasted the "class of goods and the varieties are almost bewildering," may have had the Detroit Soap Company cottage in mind, which was built entirely from "giant cakes" of the firm's popular Queen Anne soap. If manufacturing exhibits lacked appeal, there were sea lions, "Fiji Jim" (described as both a cannibal and a warrior), and a daredevil balloonist who took his act to 9,000 feet above the fair grounds and then jumped, missing Detroit entirely, although landing safely in nearby Windsor.[1]

The Detroit Exposition never rivaled Chicago's 1893 Columbian Exposition or its star attraction, George Ferris's massive passenger wheel, which was built largely in Detroit shops. But the Detroit effort demonstrated the changes Michigan and its leading city experienced before the arrival of the horseless carriage (still a decade away). Before the Civil War, manufacturing employed one percent of the state's population. By 1900—even before Henry Ford, Ransom E. Olds, and William Durant changed Michigan forever—that figure grew to 25 percent. As the sponsors of the Detroit Exposition boasted, the state's businessmen could "act in harmony," while its workmen could "execute with as much energy and skill" as any others in the nation. All across the state, Michiganians invented, produced, and marketed products for a national, even international, audience.[2]

—— Made in Michigan

Curiously, tobacco products ranked among the most valuable products coming out of Detroit factories during the 1880s. Although Michigan farmers did not grow tobacco, more chewing tobacco was processed in Detroit than anywhere else in the nation. Detroit's climate and production methods and the city's reputation as an "open shop" (where employers paid their workers a lower wage) explain the industry's success. One of the city's largest tobacco manufacturers, the firm operated by Daniel Scotten and John Bagley, employed 1,200 workers and enjoyed $4 million in annual sales. By 1900, Detroit's 300 tobacco manufacturers produced 40 million cigars annually, making it one of the nation's most important cigar-making centers. The city's top-ten leading producers employed more than 7,000 women workers.[3]

Detroit was also home to D. M. Ferry & Company, one of the world's largest seed houses by the 1880s. Employing 800 workers, the company shipped 50 million packages of seed to more than 80,000 merchants in 1883. The company also mailed tens of thousands of catalogs annually to farmers who ordered seeds by mail. Detroit's rich history of brewing beer began during the mid-nineteenth century. The first city directory, which appeared in 1837, listed two breweries. On the eve of the Civil War, that number had grown to "upwards of 40," including a brewery established by Bernard Stroh, who immigrated to Detroit from Germany in 1848. Stroh's "fire-brewing" process (using a direct flame rather than steam to heat the copper kettles of beer) allowed Stroh's to boast that its beer was more flavorful, while helping the company become one of the city's leading breweries.[4]

Iron ore and steel foundries also made major industrial contributions. By the 1890s, Detroit was among the nation's shipbuilding centers, relying on the iron and steel foundries in Wyandotte, which was one of the many accomplishments of Eber Brock Ward, "the steamship king of the Great Lakes" and the state's wealthiest person. Foundries also made Michigan a leading producer of stoves. On the eastern side of the state, the "big three" (Detroit, Michigan, and Peninsula) made Detroit the world's leading producer of iron stoves. By the 1890s, the 1,200 workers of the Michigan Stove Company, which claimed to be the world's largest, produced more than 76,000 Garland-brand stoves annually. By the early 1920s, Detroit firms produced 400,000 stoves annually. On the western side of the state, Dowagiac's Round Oak Stove (home to a popular marketing scheme that introduced customers to Chief "Doe-Wah-Jack") intrigued visitors with a gold-plated stove at the Columbian Exposition, while boasting it had already sold one million stoves nationally. Foundries also helped manufacture railroad cars. By the 1890s, the 9,000 employees of

Glazier Stove Company in Chelsea was one of Michigan's many stove companies in operation during the late 19th century.

Detroit's Michigan-Peninsula Car Company delivered 100 freight cars daily, ranking it first nationally and making it the city's largest industrial employer.[5]

Besides cutting down trees for lumber, Michiganians also made furniture, especially in Grand Rapids. The furniture industry began in the mid-1830s when individual craftsmen worked in small shops using hand tools to produce chairs, bedframes, and coffins. By the 1860s, a combination of skilled craftsmen, an abundance of hardwoods, waterpower of the Grand River, railroad connections, and a post–Civil War demand for furniture sparked a flourishing industry. As the single craftsman gave way to the factory-production system, new machinery, especially carving and dovetailing machines, helped the industry expand. Equally important, Grand Rapids manufacturers exhibited their furniture at the Centennial Exposition in Philadelphia and earned national recognition that led enthusiastic buyers to flock to Grand Rapids. "Made in Grand Rapids" took on considerable significance and, by the end of the century, 33 furniture manufacturers employing more than 6,000 workers satisfied an estimated 10 percent of America's furniture needs. At the same time, Grand Rapids office furniture attracted a national audience, and the Grand Rapids School Furniture Company (later called the American Seating Company) became the world's largest producer of public and institutional seating.[6]

Michigan's pharmaceutical industry grew substantially in the late nineteenth century. Formed after the Civil War, Detroit's Parke-Davis Company built the first modern pharmaceutical laboratory and developed the first systematic methods of performing clinical trials on new medications. During the early 1880s, Dr. William Erastus Upjohn, a University of Michigan Medical School graduate and a Hastings physician, also experimented with medicines. At the time, pills were made from a paste and coated with a sealant to prevent them from drying out. However, as a pill aged, it hardened and passed through the patient's system without dissolving. Upjohn created a new pill through a layering process:

> Using a revolving pan, the doctor introduced a starter particle and sifted medicinal powders over it, moistening them with a fine spray. The tumbling particle gradually accumulated a coating of powder, much the way a snowball begins to grow if rolled on the ground. This process produced a pill that required no binders and coatings. Since it was dry from the beginning, the "friable pill," as Dr. W. E. [Upjohn] dubbed his invention, did not harden with age, but could at any time be easily crushed or digested.

Upjohn patented his invention in 1885, left his practice, moved to Kalamazoo, and joined with several brothers to form a company to manufacture medicine. During the twentieth century, the Upjohn Company became one of the nation's leading pharmaceutical companies. Finally, Herbert Dow, a newly minted chemist, arrived in Midland in 1890. He rented a brine well and tested out a new process for extracting bromine—an important ingredient used in drugs and photography. After some initial struggles, Dow incorporated a chemical company that manufactured a variety of products, rivaling bromine producers around the world.[7]

Two truly unique industries were long shots. During the 1880s, 30-year-old Edward K. Warren managed a dry goods store in the small town of Three Oaks. Combining complaints he heard from female customers about whalebone stays in corsets with an awareness that the makers of feather dusters rejected many feathers, Warren invented "Featherbone," a product that transformed turkey quills into a stiffening agent superior to whalebone. Sophisticated promotion and marketing techniques kept Warren's invention at the forefront of women's fashions well into the next century. As turkey feathers rolled into southwestern Michigan by the trainload, the owners of the Plymouth Iron Windmill Company struggled with a good product that no one wanted to buy. As declining sales led the board of directors to contemplate liquidating the company, a local watchmaker visited the firm's manager with his latest invention—a strange-looking, BB-firing, metal air rifle. Lewis Cass Hough took the rifle, fired a couple of shots, and allegedly exclaimed, "That's a daisy." Hough offered an air rifle as a premium for every windmill purchased. While farmers wanted rifles, they did not want the windmills. Hough got the message. Changing the company's name to Daisy Manufacturing, he sold 50,000 rifles in the first full year of production, and with plenty of skilled marketing, Plymouth became the "air gun capital of the world."[8]

—— "Best to You Each Morning"

The Michigan manufacturing story would not be complete without telling the story about how America's breakfast-eating habits changed. Shortly after the Civil War, the newly founded Western Reform Health Institute in Battle Creek offered patients cures using water, sunshine, exercise, rest, and a healthy diet. In 1875, Dr. John Harvey Kellogg, a Battle Creek native and University of Michigan Medical School graduate, became the institute's director. He renamed the institute the Battle Creek Medical and Surgical Sanitarium (soon known simply as "the San") and promoted "methods of healthful living," especially in patients' diets. Dr. Kellogg told his patients, "Eat what the monkey eats—simple food and not too much of it."[9]

At the San, patients were served Granula, a mixture of dried, ground-up leftover bread, and Caramel Cereal Coffee, a coffee substitute made of burnt bread crusts, bran, and molasses. To make a healthy diet taste better, the sanitarium experimented with food. One day in 1894, the Kelloggs (John Harvey, his dietician wife Ella, and the doctor's younger brother William K.) ran a batch of cooked dried wheat through rollers, flattening each grain and then baking them. These early wheat flakes (later called "granose") were tough and tasteless, but patients at the sanitarium liked them.

The Kelloggs had invented the wheat flake, but it took one of their patients to explore the marketing possibilities of this new creation. Charles W. Post spent months at the San battling a bad case of indigestion. He never found a cure. After leaving the San, Post opened his own health spa

Kellogg's aggressive marketing made it the nation's leading producer of breakfast food.

in Battle Creek and experimented with health foods. He created a hot drink from wheat, bran, and molasses called Postum Cereal Food Coffee, and then introduced a dry cereal called Grape Nuts made from wheat and malted barley flour. Post claimed Grape Nuts was "the most scientific food in the world" because it prevented indigestion (as well as malaria and even loose teeth). Post formed the Postum Cereal Company in 1896, and the sale of Postum and Grape Nuts left him a millionaire.

Post's success led others to start cereal companies—more than 40 during the early years of the twentieth century. In 1902, one observer noted than everyone in Battle Creek "has gone daft over [the] food cereal business." Most companies failed. Frumenta Flakes were so brittle that the cereal's sharp edges cut the mouths of unwary consumers, and Norka Malted Oats spoiled on the grocer's shelves possibly because the gray flakes lacked visual appeal.

One entrepreneur who entered the boom late was William K. Kellogg. After leaving the San, partly because his older brother rejected the commercial possibilities of breakfast cereal, W. K. (as he was better known) invented corn flakes. Not satisfied to sell by mail order as was common at the time, W. K. wanted to sell corn flakes "by the [railroad] carload." After he set up a factory in Battle Creek capable of producing 4,200 cases of corn flakes a day, a sophisticated advertising strategy followed. Although a cautious man, Kellogg proved fearless when it came to advertising. Full-page advertisements in nationally distributed magazines "asked readers to demand that grocers stock his product." One particularly daring campaign suggested that female customers wink at the grocer "on Wednesdays and see what you get." The winker got a free sample of corn flakes. Despite the seemingly risqué nature of the advertisement, sales increased in New York City from two carloads monthly to a carload daily. On February 16, 1906, W. K. incorporated the Battle Creek Toasted Corn Flake Company. Three years later when the company changed its name to Kellogg, it sold more than one million cases of corn flakes. About that time, W. K. told an associate, "I sort of feel it is in my bones that we are now preparing for a campaign on a food which will eventually prove to be the leading cereal of the United States, if not the world." Few prophecies rang truer.[10]

—— Coming to Michigan

Many of the workers who fueled Michigan's growing industrial engine were immigrants who started coming to the state during the 1840s. Canadians were among the most frequent and earliest immigrants. Following the failed Canadian uprisings of the late 1830s (Patriot War), a migration across the border led one Toronto newspaper to worry that "the whole people appeared like 'swallows in autumn' preparing for their flight to the south." During the Civil War, so many Canadian and British soldiers joined the Union army that Canadian authorities feared army units stationed near the border would "melt away." During the postwar years, economic opportunities, especially in logging and copper mining, proved especially enticing for French-Canadians. By 1900, thousands of French-Canadians lived and worked in the Saginaw Valley and on the Keweenaw Peninsula.[11]

During the early years "no immigrant group contributed more to Michigan's growth and development" than Germans. Viewed by Michigan leaders as the "ideal settlers," Germans were the first "significant body" of immigrants to settle in Michigan. The state legislature actively recruited German immigrants and in 1845 Michigan became the first state to appoint a state emigration agent. Michigan also published *The Emigrant's Guide to the State of Michigan*, a 47-page guide in both English and German extolling the state's many attractions. Michigan also funded an emigration agent who worked out of New York City to steer Germans to Michigan. In 1861, the governor complimented efforts that had directed 1,500 Germans (who brought "a cash capital of $150,000") to settle in the state. Detroit, Ann Arbor, Saginaw, Bay City, and smaller settlements like Frankenmuth attracted German immigrants. In 1849 a visitor found the fledgling German settlement of Frankentrost (six miles north of Frankenmuth) so beautiful he was uncertain if he "was in America or Germany." During the Civil War, Germans composed the largest group of foreign-born males who joined the army from Michigan. This included two German militia companies (one from Ann Arbor and the other from Detroit) who served in the First Michigan Infantry Regiment.[12]

More than Germans found Michigan alluring. As the Upper Peninsula mines developed, the Cornish who had worked the world's underground mines in Cornwall, England, headed to Michigan, especially the Copper Country. They revolutionized U.P. mining methods while introducing the pasty, a meat-and-vegetable-filled pastry that won considerable fame. The Irish were also among the earliest immigrants, and they came primarily looking for jobs: "With few worldly possessions to tie him to a particular area and with little to offer but strong backs and a willingness to dig, shovel, and carry, the Irishman became an economic fixture in the mines and on railroad and canal construction crews." The Irish also brought "an intense Catholicism with them [and] came in contact with American culture much more quickly than other immigrants."[13]

Another early immigrant group were the Dutch, led by Albertus C. Van Raalte who changed his plans to settle in Wisconsin after becoming convinced Michiganians were "better educated, more religious, and more enterprising people." By 1860, the Holland Colony at the mouth of the Black River survived the "bitter days" (poor Indian relations and debilitating diseases) to boast a settlement of 2,000 people. Scandinavians also headed to the Midwest. Some found the Homestead Act guarantee of 160 acres appealing, while "others simply left to seek their fortune and escape parental control, military conscription, or political and religious persecution." Many headed to the Upper Peninsula copper and iron ore mines, and by 1900, Ishpeming was the state's center of Swedish Americans. Further west, many Finns settled in Hancock, where they founded Suomi College (present-day Finlandia University), the nation's only Finnish school of higher education. Highly literate,

Scandinavian settlers worked hard and possessed "the dream of finding great wealth."[14]

During the early twentieth century, the face of migration changed as eastern Europeans arrived in Michigan. Poles, who were escaping a society that held little promise, especially for the lower classes, found Michigan attractive because of an abundance of jobs requiring "little besides the ability to dig, lift, and haul." By 1920, Poles were Detroit's largest single ethnic group with nearly 20 percent of the city's population. Poles (and Italians, Hungarians, Russians, and Yugoslavs) provided workers necessary for the state's growing industrial economy. Detroit became the center of Polish culture, especially their Catholic churches and ethnic societies:

> In many respects, the Polish immigrant represented the ideal future citizen, in spite of the fact that various elements in the "older stock" had little use for him. The Pole worked hard; he sacrificed to save money either to buy property or to send a relative in the old country (sometimes both!); he craved the status that this money could bring; he agreed, however, all work and no play made one a dull fellow indeed; and he believed in (and in the second and third generation provided ample evidence to support) the American dream of mobility.[15]

Detroit became the center of culture for Polish immigrants. This is a Polish funeral procession in Detroit.

During the mid-1920s, a national debate, often mired in "distorted ethnic theory or more specifically Anglo-Saxon superiority," led Congress to establish immigrant quotas. Most of Michigan's congressional delegation supported slowing immigration. In more recent years, Michigan has become home to a number of Hispanics, many who traditionally provided the labor to harvest the state's fruit and vegetables. Another recent immigrant group are Arabs, who made Dearborn one of the leading Arab-American communities in the United States. Notable Arab Americans with solid Michigan connections include presidential journalist Helen Thomas, radio personality Casey Kasem, actor Danny Thomas and his actress daughter Marlo Thomas, former U.S. Energy Secretary and U.S. Senator Spencer Abraham, and Rima Fakih, Miss USA 2010. Dearborn is also home to the Arab American National Museum.[16]

—— War with Spain

In mid-1898, as U.S. Secretary of State John Hays labeled the ongoing conflict with Spain a "Splendid Little War," Private Martin Hoban of the 34th Michigan Infantry, then stationed in Cuba, admitted in a letter, "I do not wish we had stayed home, but I am ready to go now at any time." In his two weeks on the Spanish island, Hoban experienced rain, thunder, and lightning "all the time." On a more somber note, his "first sight" of Cuba was the burial of two Michiganians from a fellow regiment.[17]

During the spring of 1898, Michiganians watched as American outrage over Spanish atrocities in Cuba (some real and other fabricated by the U.S. press) steered the United States and Spain closer to war. In April, President William McKinley reluctantly asked Congress for a declaration of war. It eagerly concurred, and Michigan's congressional delegation enthusiastically supported going to war. A call for volunteers led Michigan Governor Hazen Pingree to transfer the state's National Guard units to fill the federal quota of five regiments of infantry. However, the army required that the men volunteer individually and most did. The 1,000-man regiments, numbered 31 through 35 (following a sequence begun during the Civil War), gathered south of Brighton at a camp named for State Adjutant General Charles L. Eaton. At different times, the regiments left for the front, although only the 33rd and 34th saw duty in Cuba, and only the 33rd saw any fighting.[18]

Besides Private Hoban, Dr. Victor C. Vaughn recorded his thoughts about serving in Cuba. A 47-year-old University of Michigan medical profes-

COL. GARDNER & STAFF

These officers of the 31st Michigan Infantry served in the Spanish-American War.

sor, Vaughn had opposed the war and had been chosen to urge students to stay in school and not join the army. Suddenly seized by a burst of excessive patriotism, Vaughn gave "a rousing enlistment speech" that led the governor to offer him a surgeon's commission with the 33rd Michigan. As Vaughn later explained, "Some enlist because they like the soldier's life, some enlist for patriotic reasons, but I received my commission because I talked too much." In his postwar memoirs, Vaughn recalled being shocked by his experiences. He could "hardly believe" the Cuban rebels who were "a rabble of half-clothed, half-starved men, women, and children." Cuba also introduced Americans to crabs "as large as a man's fist." At night, the crabs crawled over the sleeping soldiers and Vaughn wryly noted, "their presence did not favor unbroken rest." More seriously, Vaughn remembered Spain's greatest weapon—disease. On the transport to Cuba, Vaughn "had never seen finer looking, more intelligent, cleaner young men." But after a few weeks in Cuba, those same men arrived at the hospital with sunken cheeks, glazed eyes, wrinkled skin, and "the fine glow of youth and health replaced by a cadaverous coppery hue." Even simple questions like a soldier's name came "slowly and stupidly [since the] brain was benumbed and paralyzed by the plasmodia of tropical malaria." More than 90 percent of the 209 Michiganians who died in that "Splendid Little War" perished from disease.[19]

Two other Michiganians who played commanding—and controversial—roles in the war included U.S. Secretary of War Russell Alger and General William Shafter. Alger was a wounded Civil War cavalryman who had ridden with Philip H. Sheridan and George A. Custer and who settled in Detroit and made a fortune in the lumbering business after the war. After serving a term as Michigan governor, he joined President McKinley's cabinet in March 1897. However, Alger endured intense criticism for an army poorly prepared for the war with Spain. These charges even led to a new word (*Algerism*), meaning "incompetence." A presidential commission appointed at Alger's request looked into the many accusations. After interviewing nearly 500 witnesses over the course of more than three months, the commission determined that congressional neglect created many of the shortcomings that were beyond the War Department's control. Accord-

U.S. Secretary of War Russell Alger during the Spanish-American War.

ing to a later-day observer, Secretary Alger's agency "had met the emergency with earnestness and energy and in doing so had effected one of the marvels of history." Despite the vindication, the embattled secretary resigned in August 1899. Appalled at the disgraceful way Alger had been treated, Detroit gave this former battlefield hero a "big homecoming reception," while the state legislature soon returned him to the capital as a U.S. senator. Alger (and other Michiganians) felt he was made a scapegoat for an easy war that had so many logistical problems. (In many respects, the Spaniards posed the least of the problems.) In his memoirs, Alger pointed out that "the governmental machinery was altogether inadequate to immediately meet the emergency." He was right. The ten-fold growth of the army in just a few weeks revealed the War Department's inadequacies and inefficiencies. One sympathetic later-day observer concluded that Alger "meant well," adding that had he "been incompetent, as he has so often been pictured, the system would not have worked well at all." At the same time, Alger's ineffectiveness as secretary "hardly excuses him to reflect that it is remarkable that things weren't worse."[20]

William Shafter of Galesburg joined the army in the summer of 1861 as a junior officer and saw plenty of action; at the end of the Civil War, he was a colonel commanding a regiment. Following the war, this former teacher remained in the army. In the months immediately leading up to the Spanish-American War, Shafter bought a California farm, accepted the Medal of Honor for actions 33 years earlier on a Virginia battlefield, and received a "long overdue" promotion to brigadier general. In 1897, he received orders to command the Department of California, more than 2,000 men who occupied a dozen posts with headquarters at San Francisco's Presidio. With the declaration of war against Spain, Shafter headed east to lead the American invasion of Cuba. But even Shafter's biographer concedes the general "seemed a wholly illogical choice" to command the largest U.S. expeditionary force to date. Nearly 63 years old, weighing about 300 pounds, and suffering from varicose veins and severe gout, Shafter reminded one newsman of "a floating tent." A loyal and capable soldier, Shafter was chosen partly because the anticipated land campaign in Cuba was of little significance in what American officials viewed as a naval war. As important, Shafter had no political ambitions, much to the relief of President McKinley and other prominent decision makers. Despite a campaign plagued by confusion on numerous fronts, neverending logistical nightmares, lousy weather, little inter-service cooperation, and tropical diseases that knew no cure, Shafter led the Americans to victory. Certainly, the Americans were aided by Spanish misfortune and ineptitude, but the postwar opinion that Shafter "blundered his way to victory" is at best unfair. Despite all the general's faults, Shafter "had won a significant and rapid victory with minimal loss of life."[21]

Michigan's role in the Spanish-American War was more than soldiers. The Michigan Naval Brigade, a part-time, volunteer force of men from Saginaw, Benton Harbor, Detroit, Ann Arbor, and Hancock (three-quarters of the brigade's 281 men were college graduates, including 46 who were faculty, students, or alumni of the University of Michigan) also went off to war. Stationed aboard the USS *Yosemite*, a converted commercial steamer that lacked any armor plating, the brigade saw its first action landing U.S. Marines at Guantanamo Bay, who raised the first American flag on the Spanish-held island. Two weeks later, the *Yosemite* formed a one-ship blockade of San Juan harbor on the nearby Spanish island of Puerto Rico. On June 28, the outgunned and outnumbered Michiganians faced a daunting challenge from the Spanish ships in the harbor. One Michigan sailor described what followed:

> The enemy ships immediately opened fire on us. The *Yosemite* was quickly bracketed by exploding shells. We were trapped. Our only option was to attack. Swinging sharply, we dashed recklessly toward the Spaniards— straight in the face of heavier guns. As soon as we came within range, a

savage whirlwind of fire swept with perfect accuracy from our broadside batteries. . . . Our fire was too rapid and accurate for the enemy vessels to withstand.

The *Yosemite* crippled two larger Spanish ships and chased two others away, while going untouched and suffering no casualties. When war ended the following month, the Michigan Naval Brigade returned home to "a tremendous reception."[22]

Another Michiganian who served in Puerto Rico was Ellen May Tower. Born in Byron and the daughter of a Civil War veteran, Tower graduated from the nursing program at Detroit's Grace Hospital in 1894. With the outbreak of the war, she offered her nursing skills to the army, and by late September 1898, Tower was comforting American soldiers in Puerto Rico. However, a few weeks later, she contracted yellow fever and died on December 9, one day before the war officially ended. Her remains arrived in Detroit in mid-January 1899 where she lay in state as thousands paid their respects. Her casket was taken to Byron under military escort and given "the first military funeral ever accorded a woman in Michigan."[23]

One notable postwar tribute occurred well after the troops had arrived home. On May 30, 1899, Mayor Edward K. Warren proudly announced to citizens of his small town of Three Oaks that they had won a national fundraising campaign. "Three Oaks Against the World" (so named by Warren) raised $1,132.80 (more money per capita than any other American city) to fund a national monument for soldiers who had died in the recent war. The victors received a cannon captured by Commodore George Dewey after he defeated the Spanish fleet in Manila harbor. "Enthusiasm was at a boiling point in every man, woman and child," the *Three Oak Press* boasted. The victory was "a 4th of July, Memorial, and circus day rolled into one." The subsequent celebration even left the farm horses prancing "like thoroughbred chargers." An October 1899 dedication featured President McKinley, but not the cannon, which had not yet arrived. But all was not lost since Mayor Warren had a special commemorative silver spoon struck for the occasion and presented it to the First Lady. The Dewey Cannon, as it was called, arrived months later in time for a second dedication. The celebrated Admiral Dewey was in Michigan during the dedication, but could not fit Three Oaks into his schedule, prompting an indignant *Chicago Tribune* to observe, he "will never know how much he missed." The proud citizens of Three Oaks turned out on June 29, 1900. Following a parade, singing, and speeches, the push of a button sent an electric signal to a tent covering the celebrated cannon. Slowly, the tent opened, and each section fell to the ground to form an eight-pointed red, white, and blue star. As the Dewey Cannon became visible, the crowd of 10,000 went "nearly mad with cheering."[24]

—— Presidential Assassin

Leon Czolgosz was born in Alpena, Michigan, in 1873 to Polish immigrant parents. When Czolgosz was five years old, his family moved to Detroit. During his teenage years, Czolgosz lived in Ohio and Pennsylvania. Considered the best-educated child in a large family, Czolgosz had little to show after years of laboring in the factories and fields. The loss of his mother during the birth of her eighth child, coupled with witnessing and experiencing worker exploitation, help explain Czolgosz's turn to anarchism. On September 6, 1901, the 28-year-old disgruntled laborer shot President William McKinley after standing in a receiving line at the Pan American Exposition in Buffalo, New York. His trial, which began a week after McKinley died, lasted only a couple of hours before the jury (who all had determined Czolgosz's guilt before their selection) pronounced him guilty of first-degree murder after deliberating only 31 minutes. Prior to his execution on October 29, 1901, Czolgosz calmly declared, "I killed the president because he was the enemy of the good people—the good working people. I am not sorry for my crime." Czolgosz' remains were secretly buried in an unmarked grave in New York.[25]

—— "Potato Patch" Pingree

With the Spanish-American War behind them, reforming Americans looked inward to end political corruption, improve governmental efficiency, regulate business to expand competition, and enrich the lives of the less fortunate. Michigan was not a leader in what became known as the Progressive Era. Yet, one Michiganian earned recognition as a "pre-Progressive" reformer—a man who fought for changes and principles championed by later-day Progressives. Hazen S. Pingree, a Maine native and a Union army veteran who survived the rebel prison at Andersonville, arrived in Detroit after the Civil War. He started a business making shoes and, 20 years later, with annual sales exceeding one million dollars, Pingree was one of the country's largest shoe manufacturers.

By the late 1880s, Detroit was the nation's fourteenth largest city but was plagued by issues of graft, bribery, and fraud. In 1889, Detroit businessmen drafted a reluctant Pingree to run for mayor on the Republican ticket. A poor public speaker who described honesty as his primary qualification for office, Pingree offered Detroiters "an impressive figure—a large man, six feet tall, erect in carriage and firm of step" who they came to like. After narrowly winning the election, he initiated a campaign of urban reform, incurring the enmity of the men who had urged him to seek public office who saw him as "a traitor to his class." Pingree battled against privately owned utilities, seeking better service and lower and fairer prices. In the process, he advocated both public regulation and municipal ownership of the utilities. According to historian Charles R. Starring, Pingree "had a strong conviction that the underdog, the poor man, was mistreated by the special interests, who used government to continue and strengthen their strangle hold." He compared corporations to a bee standing before a hive "taking away from the real workers all their honey except just enough to keep them alive." When corporate wealth "became greedy and monopolistic," Pingree argued, "It should be regulated in the public interest."[26]

As mayor, he also sought to relieve the distress of the worsening conditions of the Depression of 1893 and disprove "the popular notion that the unemployed were congenitally lazy" by allowing desperate Detroiters to plant family gardens on vacant municipal land. Pingree's program, called "The Agricultural Scheme" but known more simply as "Pingree's potato patches," started in mid-1894 with the common council establishing a seven-member volunteer Agricultural Committee who supervised the project. The committee set off the plots (reduced to one-quarter acre because of the program's

Mayor Hazen Pingree (behind the plow) received national recognition when he introduced a program to assist unemployed Detroiters.

popularity) and, working with experts from D.M. Ferry Seed Company, the Michigan Agricultural College, and the engineering staff of the Detroit Water Board, provided a salaried foreman who supervised the planting. The committee even provided manure from the city's streets to enrich the plots. In the fall of 1894, 945 families working on 430 acres harvested 40,000 bushels of potatoes and large quantities of beans, squashes, and pumpkins. One Detroit reporter boasted, "Far as the eye can reach they spread, uneven, diversified, and incongruous . . . just one great big, nodding, smiling potato patch." Pingree's potato patches, which saved Detroiters from starvation and malnutrition, continued until 1901. In Indianapolis (one of several cities that followed Detroit's lead), the local newspaper noted, "Detroit's garden patches have turned out better than all expectations, and Mayor Pingree has proved to be 'no small potatoes.'"[27]

Eager to expand his power base, Pingree sought the Republican gubernatorial nomination. Pingree's popularity with voters (he was re-elected mayor three times), coupled with fears that Michigan might slip from the Republican ranks in the 1896 presidential race and Pingree's threat to run as a third party candidate if denied the nomination, placed him on the Republican ballot. He easily won the governor's seat and in the process helped William McKinley earn the state's electoral vote. Despite their initial reluctance to Pingree's candidacy, his Republican opponents hoped that sending the reformer mayor to Lansing "might finish him."[28]

They were right. The success Pingree enjoyed in Detroit could not be duplicated as governor. The "Immortal Nineteen," a group of conservative Republican senators, repeatedly blocked Pingree's progressive initiatives, including making railroads pay their fair share of taxes. Among the state's richest corporations, railroads were virtually tax exempt, paying no tax on their real estate, buildings, and equipment. Five previous governors (all Republicans but one) had proposed this change but failed when confronted by the railroads' powerful lobby. Despite voters' support of this initiative, Pingree encountered Senate resistance. The governor also failed to implement a statewide primary or provide cities with home rule. After two terms as governor, a frustrated and exhausted Pingree left office and labeled his political opponents "old fogies, reactionaries and hypocrites." According to one supporter, Pingree's enemies "dogged him everywhere, as always is the case when men in public or private who are worth while (sic), assail the established order, no matter how bad the established order may be." In a departing speech, Pingree predicted "a bloody revolution" if the "present system of inequality" was not changed. Shortly after leaving Lansing, Pingree contracted an illness while traveling abroad that ended his life. Following an elaborate funeral, he was buried in Detroit. Although historians of the Progressive Era have often overlooked Pingree's efforts, according to biographer Melvin G. Holli, his "role as an advanced, pre-Progressive reformer in public office was unmatched during his decade in either Michigan or the nation."[29]

Michigan governors who succeeded Pingree enjoyed some notable Progressive accomplishments. Fred Warner, who served three-consecutive terms (1904–10), used "constant prodding" to convince the Republican legislature to adopt reforms, including a "workable" state primary law, regulation of insurance companies, and the establishment of a state Labor Department that focused on factory safety measures. Under Warner's leadership, the state adopted a new constitution, which relaxed earlier restrictions on state action but rejected more substantive changes like women's suffrage.[30]

—— Chase Salmon Osborn

Warner's successor, Chase Salmon Osborn, introduced Michiganians to a "New Deal" (a term later borrowed by Franklin D. Roosevelt). Despite serving only two years as governor, Osborn remains one of the state's most intriguing chief executives. In his autobiography, Osborn noted that because of his "independence and temperamental Liberalism, he was charged with being erratic, not a few called him crazy, and everybody agreed to the fact that he would not stand hitched." Biographer Robert M. Warner added to Osborn's self-analysis, writing, "There was in [Osborn's] long and highly complex career an absence of orthodoxy and conformity which was both baffling and refreshing to friend and foe alike."[31]

Born in Indiana in 1860 and well educated for the era, Osborn arrived in Sault Ste. Marie in 1887 as owner of the *Sault News*. After several years as a successful newspaperman, he ventured into politics when he was appointed state game and fish warden, a position suitable for Osborn's love of the outdoors. An ardent wildlife conservationist, Osborn proved "more efficient and energetic in enforcing the laws than any of his predecessors." Osborn next served as state railroad commissioner and, after personally inspecting Michigan's 11,000 miles of track, he advocated more effective railroad regulation (at a time when railroads were the predominant means of travel). Osborn even took the more extreme position that railroads should be government owned. Osborn also traveled the globe—in some cases exploring new iron ore deposits—an endeavor that earned him considerable wealth.[32]

In 1910, Osborn challenged incumbent Republican Governor Fred Warner. A "natural campaigner—energetic, colorful, egotistical, but very warm hearted," Osborn, according to one supporter, "by sheer force of personality . . . he won men over or wore them down." In Michigan's first major automobile campaign, Osborn traveled 12,000 miles and gave hundreds of speeches. Policies that aligned with the then-popular Progressive movement, combined with attacks on Warner, won Osborn the Republican nomination and then, the general election.[33]

Although the Republicans held strong majorities in both state houses, Osborn struggled getting his Progressive agenda adopted. According to one contemporary observer, the House lacked leadership, while "some of the members lacked other things, mostly brains and decency." Factionalism plagued the Senate, as well as some senators who simply were "generally anti-reform and usually hostile to the new governor." Despite some heated struggles, the list of Osborn's accomplishments included passage of Michigan's first workmen's compensation law, expanded business regulations revisions to the tax laws, and improved popular government through the adoption of a presidential primary and moving the state closer to women's suffrage.[34]

Osborn also took an interest in national politics, and 1912 proved to be a decisive year for the Republicans. Incumbent President Robert Taft sought re-nomination but had to fend off a challenge from his mentor, Theodore Roosevelt. Osborn's chief adviser, Frank Knox, had ridden with Roosevelt's Rough Riders in Cuba, and this brought the governor and Roosevelt closer together. Osborn led the Roosevelt movement, which resulted in considerable infighting in Michigan. Bedlam prevailed at the state Republican convention as delegates from both sides grappled with each other, forcing the police and militia to establish order. Michigan Republicans sent two slates of delegates to the national convention, but the Roosevelt delegates went unseated. Denied the Republican nomination, Roosevelt organized the Progressives (or Bull Moose) party. A committed Progressive but also a faithful Republican, Osborn struggled. He first offered his support to Democratic nominee Woodrow Wilson before ultimately returning to Roosevelt. In the general election, Michigan voters supported Roosevelt—the first time since 1856 that the state's electoral votes did not go to a Republican. The divided Republican ticket also allowed Democrat Woodbridge Ferris to win the governor's race. The state's last Progressive era governor, Ferris had established a school of higher education in Big Rapids in 1884 (present-day Ferris University). In his four years in Lansing, Ferris successfully added the initiative, recall, and referendum—all-important Progressive initiatives—to Michigan's constitution.[35]

One additional footnote from the 1912 presidential campaign occurred when Roosevelt toured the Upper Peninsula. Thousands turned out, giving the energetic former president, according to one newspaper, "the royalest welcome ever offered by the Upper Peninsula to a great man." One exception was George A. Newett, publisher of the Ishpeming *Iron Ore*. After hearing Roosevelt rail against President Taft, Newett editorialized that "Roosevelt lies, and curses in a most disgusting way, he gets drunk, too, and that not infrequently, and all his intimates know about it." The outraged Roosevelt filed a libel suit against Newett and sought $10,000 in damages. The jury trial was held in May 1913, and Roosevelt disavowed drinking alcohol "except under a physician's advice." The list of witnesses testifying (in person or via afidavit) that they had never seen the former president drunk included Admiral George Dewey. Overwhelmed by Roosevelt's aggressive presentation, Newett admitted, "I am forced to the conclusion that I was mistaken. I am unwilling to assert that Mr. Roosevelt actually and in fact drank to excess." After the publisher's declaration, Roosevelt acknowledged, "I have achieved my purpose," and he asked the jury, who found Newett guilty, to award only a nominal sum. They fined him six cents—the cost of a good newspaper.[36]

As for Osborn, he had announced his intent to serve a single term as governor. Interspersed with other political ventures (which all proved unsuccessful), Osborn continued traveling ("he covered nearly every corner of the earth") while making money as "the iron hunter." In his later years, Osborn "ran a constant stream of Liberalism and reform tempered somewhat by personal eccentricities." He pursued two major projects—making Isle Royale a national park (achieved in 1940) and linking the straits by a bridge (achieved after his passing in 1949). While biographer Robert Warner concludes that Osborn befriended "the great, the highly placed, the powerful, [and] the wealthy . . . his affection and his labors were with the ordinary citizen." Equally significant was a letter Governor Osborn received from a constituent who wrote, "You have did [sic] well for the common people. . . . The other class provide for themselves, *you* have *cared* for us."[37]

CHAPTER

13

Birth of the Automobile

Henry Ford poses with his 1896 quadricycle, already well on his way to fame and fortune.

"I will build a motor car for the great multitude."

—Henry Ford

At 11:00 PM on March 6, 1896, Charles King, a 32-year-old mechanical engineer, seated himself in an open carriage. The carriage looked like most other vehicles on Detroit's streets, except there were no horses pulling it. King's "horseless carriage" moved down Woodward Avenue to the surprise of the few pedestrians on the street that evening. The next day, a local newspaper noted that King's "most unique machine" was powered by a gasoline engine that "went at the rate of five or six miles an hour at an even rate of speed." The son of a mother who came from an old Detroit family and a military-career father, King is credited with driving Michigan's first horseless carriage after visiting Chicago's 1893 Columbian Exposition where he saw a gasoline-powered engine. King remained involved in the automobile industry but never headed his own manufacturing company. But the horseless carriage had come to Michigan and the state would never be the same.[1]

214

The arrival of the automobile affected the daily life of the twentieth-century American to a greater degree than any other technological development. It was not so much the speed of the automobile, but its flexibility that marks its chief significance in the history of transportation. The automobile directly affected the economy by absorbing vast amounts of capital and employing tens of thousands of workers. It spawned a host of ancillary industries, greatly influenced the growth of the cities and the suburbs, and revolutionized life on the farm. Culturally, the automobile influenced everything from architecture to dating habits. Finally, and most important to the Michigan story, within a few short years after the early Michigan inventors introduced their contraptions, the manufacture of horseless carriages (later "automobiles") found a home in Michigan.[2]

The horseless carriage story starts with the French and the Germans who attached steam, gasoline, and electric engines to carriages as early as the 1870s. In the United States, Charles and Frank Duryea of Springfield, Massachusetts, became the first Americans to manufacture horseless carriages when the Duryea Motor Wagon Company produced thirteen cars in 1896. In Michigan, Albert and Louis Baushke, brothers in Benton Harbor who operated a carriage company (one of 125 similar companies in the state), announced in late 1895 the formation of a company to manufacture horseless carriages. With each passing day, enticing stories filled the local newspaper about how the manufacture of horseless carriages would "bring new fame" to this southwestern Lower Peninsula city. Ten weeks after the earliest reports, shocked readers of the *Benton Harbor Palladium* learned that the Baushkes' horseless carriage was "a subject of ridicule and a spectacle of failure." Although the Baushkes stumbled, they "deserve attention and sympathy," according to historian George May, because they belonged to "a long list of unfortunate Michiganians" who tinkered in a host of Michigan towns (Albion, Grand Rapids, Charlevoix, and Fowlerville, among others) by unsuccessfully fiddling with gasoline-powered vehicles.[3]

Several months after Charles King shared his invention with the world, he joined another Detroit inventor whose accomplishments would later earn him international recognition. In the early morning hours of June 4, 1896, Henry Ford, drove his "quadricycle," built with the assistance of men like Charles King, out of a shed behind his home on Bagley Avenue. (Careless planning did require Ford to use a sledgehammer to "widen the door" to get his machine out of the shed.) Born in Dearborn in 1863 to parents who immigrated from Ireland, Ford could have been a farmer. In fact, he claimed that his initial interest in machines stemmed from his dislike for hard physical labor on the farm. When Ford and his father drove their horse and wagon into Detroit in 1876, they saw a huge, self-propelled steam-threshing machine. Years after Ford had become the world's best-known automaker, he kept a picture of a steam thresher as inspiration. After leaving the farm, Ford used his natural mechanical abilities in various jobs including a well-paying engineering job with Detroit Edison. But it was a visit to the Chicago world's fair where he saw internal combustion gasoline engines that changed his life dramatically.[4]

—— The First Automaker: Ransom E. Olds

Another early Michigan inventor introduced his horseless carriage during the summer of 1896. Born in Ohio in 1864, Ransom E. Olds moved with his family to Lansing in 1880. Olds worked in his father's engine repair shop where the family's steam engine proved so popular that it was put into production. The younger Olds attached steam engines to wheeled vehicles, but he remained unconvinced steam was the answer, especially after seeing the gasoline engines at

By the time these Oldsmobiles (including the famed Curved Dash, second from left) lined up for this 1906 picture, inventor Ransom E. Olds had moved on to form REO Motor Car Company.

the 1893 world's fair. On August 11, 1896, Olds drove his gasoline-powered carriage through the Lansing streets. The newspaper reporter who accepted Olds' invitation to join him that summer night commented on the "the beauty of the vehicle." Dark green with "dainty red trimmings" and powered by a five-horsepower engine, Olds' 1,000-pound invention passed all the endurance tests and reached a speed of eighteen miles per hour (one report claimed twenty-five miles per hour). A satisfied Olds reported that the vehicle was "noiseless and light running, yet perfect in every details as regards wear, stability and carrying capacity."[5]

In August 1897 several of Lansing's leading businessmen, including Edward W. Sparrow, one of the city's wealthiest entrepreneurs, joined Olds to form the Olds Motor Vehicle Company for the purpose of "manufacturing and selling motor vehicles." However, the company's financial success had more to do with the popularity of Olds engines than with horseless carriages. A need for more capital led Olds to accept an offer to move to Detroit. The newly named Olds Motors Works opened in early 1900 with 100 men building as many as eleven different models ranging in price from $1,200 to $2,750. "After a long sleepless night," as Olds remembered, he decided to produce an inexpensive, one-cylinder runabout that weighed 600 pounds and cost $600. Olds claimed he wanted a vehicle so simple to operate "that anyone could run it and the construction such that it could be repaired at any local shop." The Oldsmobile Curved-Dash Runabout, which had a curved front much like a sleigh, proved popular and orders poured in. Although a factory fire temporarily slowed production, between 1902 and 1905 annual totals increased. By the end of 1903, Olds had produced more than 8,000 Runabouts.[6]

Among the early highlights of the Olds operation was an endurance drive by 21-year-old Lansing native and test driver Roy D. Chapin. On October 29, 1901, Chapin left Detroit for New York City in a Runabout. Olds did not have a New York City dealer and hoped the publicity from this test might introduce his vehicle to an eastern audience. Chaplin traveled across Ontario, western New York, and down the Hudson Valley, arriving on November 5. He had traveled 820 miles and the Runabout had consumed 30 gallons of gas and 80 gallons of water. Despite terrible road conditions and numerous repairs, Chapin's journey was later compared to Lindbergh's flight across the Atlantic and hailed as "testimony to the image-building ability of the Olds company." Chapin did not set or break any endurance records for horseless carriages, but Olds found a New York City dealer who ordered 1,000 Runabouts ("an astronomical number for the time").

The dealer sold 750 the first year and "that helped greatly to make the curved-dash Olds the most talked-about car in America."[7]

In 1905 the Olds Motor Vehicle Company closed its Detroit plant and focused all its operations in Lansing. By then, Ransom Olds had left Oldsmobile. Disagreements over model production and company management had led the board to sever the company's relationship with him. Required to leave his name with the original company, Olds orga-

President Roosevelt (rear left) with Ransom Olds (front left) visiting the Michigan Agricultural College in 1907.

nized a new Lansing-based operation called REO Motor Car Company that soon outsold the cross-town rival he had founded.[8]

Olds became the first Michiganian to produce automobiles in any significant numbers and the first to prove that great profits could be made manufacturing horseless carriages. Even more important, he inspired an assortment of other automakers. The list included Henry M. Leland, a machinist who produced transmissions and engines for Olds and later organized the Cadillac Automobile Company; Jonathan Maxwell, whose company formed the basis for the Chrysler Corporation; Robert C. Hupp, who started with Olds as a common laborer before launching his own company; Roy Chapin, who helped form the auto company backed by Detroit department store magnate, J. L. Hudson; and, John and Horace Dodge, who made transmissions for Olds and Henry Ford before founding their own company.[9]

—— Henry Ford and His Model T

By the time Olds returned to Lansing, Henry Ford had formed his own company. But producing cars did not come easy for Ford. After selling his first horseless carriage, he focused on an improved model. Exhausting all available capital, Ford formed the Detroit Automobile Company in 1899; the venture collapsed the following year without having producing anything. Ford knew nothing about manufacturing a car and, more important, he remained obsessed with improving the product *before* manufacturing it to sell. Ford also grew distracted by a new hobby—car racing. On October 10, 1900, after winning a race in Grosse Pointe that featured America's top racer, Ford gained national exposure and financial backing to found the Henry Ford Company. But in a few months, Ford left; he either was fired or quit. The investors wanted cars, and Ford was not ready to make them. This company became the basis for the Cadillac Auto Company.[10]

In mid-1903, Detroit coal dealer Alexander Malcomsom financed the Ford Motor Company. A month later, as the first Ford Model A was being prepped for shipping, Ford's perfectionism threatened to derail the fledgling endeavor. Business manager James Couzens, a no-nonsense Canadian who had arrived in Detroit as an 18-year-old in 1890 and worked for Malcomson as clerk, insisted the cars had to be shipped to bring in the necessary funds to continue production. Couzens even helped crate the cars and load them onto freight cars. When some mechanical problems developed and Ford wanted to halt future shipments, Couzens refused, preferring to

In 1908, Ford introduced the Model T (a 1909 model here). Within a few years, the car's popularity made Ford the nation's leading auto producer.

send mechanics to the customers. He warned Ford, "Stop shipping and we go bankrupt." Sales continued and the Ford Motor Company was on its way to success.[11]

The Model A impressed customers, but the Ford Motor Company was only one of fifteen Michigan companies producing autos in 1903. Trade publications briefly mentioned the new firm, while local newspapers gave it a fleeting back-page citation. Over the next several years, Ford introduced eight models (A, B, C, F, K, N, R, and S). However, sales of nearly 6,400 cars in the twelve months ending in July 1908 ranked it fourth among auto producers. Then Ford introduced the Model T, which quickly separated the Ford Motor Company from the other automakers.[12]

In early 1908, the Ford Motor Company sent advance information to its dealers about the upcoming latest model. The response was overwhelming. One Detroit dealer admitted, "We have rubbed our eyes several times to make sure we were not dreaming," while another contended the new model "is without doubt the greatest creation in automobiles ever placed before a people." Introduced in October 1908, the Model T offered "several attention-getting innovations," including placing the steering wheel on the car's left side (a feature all other American automakers soon adopted) and an enclosed power-plant and transmission. These mechanical features, coupled with the original price of $825, led the Ford Motor Company to boast, "No car under $2,000 offers more and no car over $2,000 offers more except in trimmings." Although the car came in one color (black paint dried quicker, allowing more cars to be built), the price dropped to $360 by 1916, leading Ford to claim that he had "gained 1,000 new customers for every dollar the car was reduced in price." The Model T was a car for the common man and lived up to Henry Ford's boast:

> I will build a motor car for the great multitude . . . constructed of the best materials, by the best men to be hired, after the simplest designs that modern engineering can devise . . . so low in price that no man making a good salary will be unable to own one—and enjoy with his family the blessing of hours of pleasure in God's great open places.[13]

The Ford Motor Company introduced the Model T with the "most energetic" campaign that the American automobile industry had ever witnessed for a new product. In "unprecedented scale," the company issued news releases, photos, and sketches about the Model T to all the nation's media. The success proved phenomenal. Six months after introducing the Model T, the company temporarily discontinued taking orders because it could not keep up with the demand. By 1914, Ford Motor Company sold 250,000 Model Ts annually. The Model T appeared everywhere. According to one American newspaper, the Model T had beaten the Stars and Stripes and the U.S. Constitution "in carrying civilization into the wild places of the world." Models Ts helped build a railroad in Siberia, crossed China's demanding Gobi desert, and intermixed with elephants and camels in India. By mid-1914, 550,000 Model Ts logged more than ten million miles daily. The car also grew in popularity as it entered in hundreds of climbing tests and other reliability-endurance runs all across the nation. To help make sure the consumer did not miss these successes, the company introduced the *Ford Times*, a free slick magazine that eventually reached a circulation of 900,000. With the Model T, the Ford Motor Company backed up its claim to "put America on wheels." The car was cheap, and many repairs required nothing more than a pliers or screwdriver. Affectionately nicknamed the "Tin Lizzie" because it rattled (although it was not made of tin), the Model T became a national institution.[14]

As Model T sales steadily grew, the Ford Motor Company needed to enlarge its manufacturing operations. Ford selected Highland Park, a small town about six miles northwest of downtown Detroit, and turned to Albert Kahn, a young, up-and-coming architect who specialized in industrial design. Arriving in the United States from Germany in 1880 when he was eleven years old, Kahn devoted his life to drawing and in 1896 opened Albert Kahn Associates in Detroit. Commissioned by the Packard Motor Car Company to design a factory in 1907, Kahn revolutionized factories by using reinforced concrete and steel rods rather than wood in walls, roofs, and supports. He achieved his goal of acquiring more workspace and quickly became Detroit's preferred automotive building architect. Ford's collaboration with Kahn created "the world's largest auto factory, Michigan's biggest building under one roof, and the most artistic factory of its day—in architecture, shining cleanliness, and harmonic arrangement." Standing four stories tall and three football fields long, the plant had more than 50,000 square feet of windows, earning the nickname "Crystal Palace." An abundance of windows greatly improved lighting inside the factory and allowed machines to be placed closer together, which improved efficiency. The many vents in the roof also provided fresh air. According to Ford Motor Company historian Douglas Brinkley:

> Overall, the building's design relied on logic: raw materials were delivered to the top floor, and as they were forged and machined into finished parts, made their way down through the floors through more than a thousand openings Ford and Kahn had incorporated for chutes, conveyors and tubes.

One later-day observer succinctly observed, "Kahn created a new way of working," which explains why he ended up designing 1,000 buildings for the Ford Motor Company. When Kahn died in 1942, he had earned the nickname "The Man Who Built Detroit."[15]

The Ford Motor Company boasted about its Highland Park factory as the "wonder of the automobile world" and readily provided guided tours—even to competitors who were "generous in their praise." One local automaker

Ford's Highland Park plant (here in 1923), designed by Alfred Kahn, revolutionized the production of cars.

"concluded that no other automobile factory in the nation had a better production setup." The manager of Germany's Benz Company maintained, "The Ford plant is the most remarkable in the world," while the head of the French Renault Company claimed the plant was "the best organized" auto plant in the United States. Local residents also took pride in Highland Park, confident that the fledgling automobile industry would greatly alter Detroit's future.[16]

Although the Model T did not change, Ford upgraded production methods constantly by adding at least one new machine or tool every day throughout the car's production years. However, according to historian Brinkley, the biggest single change at Highland Park "spread like kudzu throughout the plant . . . [and] eventually through the entire world of heavy industry." According to one story, the Ford Motor Company began experimenting with the assembly line following a suggestion from a Ford foreman who had visited a Chicago meat packing plant. At every stop along this "disassembly" line, knife-wielding butchers efficiently and quickly carved away at a hanging carcass. Ford experimented with the idea and reduced production time for making magneto coils (the electrical part that sent the spark to the plugs) on an assembly line from twenty to thirteen minutes. Eventually, the moving assembly line reduced the building of a Model T from thirteen hours to ninety minutes. The assembly line also allowed production to double every year for a decade after 1913, while the price of the Model T dropped by two-thirds.[17]

Ford did not invent mass production; but by adapting techniques previously used in manufacturing a complicated product like an automobile, he had a startling impact on the American auto industry: "The first experiments with the moving assembly line changed Ford Motor Company—for good and ill—from a fine, successful car company into the greatest industrial enterprise in the world, and from a high-quality workshop into an unskilled-labor mill." But the "sheer systematic toil" of the assembly line worsened worker turnover. In seeking a solution, Ford implemented the "most audacious business innovation yet."[18]

—— A Revolutionary Declaration

On January 5, 1914, company treasurer James Couzens held a small press conference announcing that the company would "inaugurate the greatest revolution in the matter of rewards for its workers ever known in the industrial world." Besides reducing the working day from nine to eight hours, even the lowest paid worker would earn $5 a day. The three reporters invited to the announcement sat in stunned silence. The action doubled the average auto industrial wage—and even more so for other industrial wages, like steel workers who averaged $1.75 a day. The $5 day originated with Couzens since it fit his personality. He insisted on $5, although Ford argued for a lower daily wage. When Ford finally agreed, Couzens quickly formalized the decision to prevent Ford from rethinking it. The reasons behind the revolutionary decision were varied. Certainly, the Ford Motor Company could afford the monetary outlay, but other goals lay behind the decision. According to Brinkley:

> Everyone seemed to perceive the $5 Day a little bit differently. To Henry Ford, it was an enormous risk that would turn into the single greatest publicity coup in American history and the keystone of his lasting legend. To James Couzens, it was an act of defiance and benevolence at the same time, one that would show just how unlike other companies Ford Motor really was. To [employment] manager John Lee, the $5 Day would hone a new type of auto worker, one who was relaxed, confident, and motivated—and that, as Lee put it, "is the most powerful economic factor that we can use in the shape of a human being."[19]

The Ford announcement generated an unprecedented amount of free and positive publicity. In what Ford historian David Lewis calls "the biggest news story to have originated in Detroit up to 1914," the $5 day made front-page news in "every" newspaper in the nation and thousands of others abroad. During the week following the announcement, New York City newspapers carried 52 mostly front-page columns, while other newspapers hailed it as "an epoch in the world's industrial history," "a magnificent act of generosity," and an "economic second coming." The story received more than two million lines of favorable copy, and news clippings filled more than 1,000 pages of Ford company scrapbooks. One national paper declared, "If there were more Henry Fords in the ranks of capital, there would be fewer Calumets" (a direct reference to the terrible strike that was going on in the Keweenaw). Years later, a noted French intellectual concluded what Ford did with the $5 workday "contributed more to the emancipation of workers" than the Russian Revolution of 1917 because "he took the worker out of the class of the 'wage-earning proletariat' . . . [and] made every worker a potential customer." Although 90 percent of the newspaper stories were positive, the financial and conservative press viewed the $5 workday as an economic blunder, even criminal. Industrial leaders, especially automakers, described it as "foolish," "an economic mistake," and something destined to create labor unrest. Conversely, the general public found "Ford's scheme a source of hope and inspiration," leading thousands of men to arrive at Highland Park the day after the announcement. When told there were no jobs, scuffles broke out, which forced the police to use water hoses to disperse the crowd. Those who could not get to Highland Park sent letters. According to the *Ford Times*, "It rained letters," thousands of letters addressed to Henry Ford seeking jobs. In the South, black sharecroppers now had another reason to head north, hoping to escape disenfranchisement, discrimination, and poverty.[20]

Lost in the enthusiasm for Ford's revolutionary policy was the "fine print" attaching conditions that required workers "to meet certain criteria." Qualifying categories included: (1) married men "living and taking good care of their families," (2) single men, 22 years and older "of proven thrifty habits," and (3) men or women under 22 years of age who provided "the sole support to some next of kin or blood relative." Ford investigators started by administering "a somewhat intimidating evaluation process." One Ford employee later remembered, "They went to my home. My wife told them everything. There was nothing to keep from them. Of course, there was a lot of criticism on that. It was kind of a funny idea in a free state." Because the background checks took months to gather, most Ford employees did not see their wages boosted until mid-1914. These investigations later evolved into the company's sociological department, which kept tabs on workers and, according to some, successfully drove any union talk underground.[21]

Immediately after the $5 day announcement, Ford's productivity shot up by 15 to 20 percent and, in some departments, by 50 percent or more. Daily average absenteeism dropped from 10 percent to 0.5 percent. According to Brinkley, even turnover, "that constant drain on employee morale and factory output," fell fast. More than 50,000 replacement hirings in 1913 had fallen to only 2,000 in 1915, despite a workforce that had expanded by 50 percent. The $5 day also "inspired such ardent goodwill" that Ford workers proudly displayed their company badges. Little surprise that Henry Ford later observed, "The $5 was the greatest cost-cutting move I ever made."[22]

Henry Ford also gained fame by challenging the claims of New Yorker George Selden, who had received a patent in 1895 for a gasoline-powered horseless carriage. In 1899, Selden assigned the patent's rights to the Electric Vehicle Company, which reached an agreement with various automakers that formed the Association of Licensed Automobile Manufacturers (ALAM) in 1903 to pay Sheldon and Electric Vehicle Company a royalty for each car the companies produced. Initially, ALAM denied the Ford Motor Company a license. At the same time, ALAM boasted that its members represented "the pioneers of the industry," and customers who purchased vehicles from non-licensed companies ran the risk of prosecution for patent infringement. The Ford Motor Company countered, arguing that the ALAM and the Sheldon patent holders represented a "trust" designed to stifle competition and exploit customers. The running battle lasted several years, and the Ford Motor Company "was frequently pictured as underdogs fighting for their very lives—and for every prospective car buyer" against the "automobile trust." Ford reassured owners (and prospective owners) he would support any Ford owner sued by the ALAM for buying an unlicensed Ford car. In September 1909, a federal court ruled in favor of the Sheldon patent holders. As many of the unlicensed automakers succumbed to the decision, Ford appealed it, earning accolades as "Ford the Fighter." In January 1911, the U.S. Circuit Court unanimously reversed the lower court ruling, determining Selden's original claims covered two-cycle gasoline engines, not four-cycle. Since the patent expired in 1912, ALAM accepted the ruling. However, Ford's success—a modern-day David over Goliath—greatly benefited Henry Ford, his company, and the Model T, which grew more popular each day.[23] By the eve of World War I in mid-1914, the Ford Motor Company stood as the world's largest auto producer.

—— Charming Billy Durant

In September 1886, William Durant accepted a ride in a horse-drawn, wooden cart built in Flint. Impressed with the smoothness of the vehicle's ride, the 25-year-old Durant, grandson to former governor and lumber baron Henry Crapo, traveled to Coldwater where a proposal to invest in the company led Durant to buy the wagon maker and move it to Flint. Even before the company had a factory, Durant started taking cart orders. According to biographer Larry Gustin, "Durant made it all look so easy. . . . He had a quick mind, dressed well and carried himself with an air of supreme confidence." By 1900, Durant-Dort had become the nation's leading manufacturer of wooden carriages.[24]

At the same time, the growing popularity of horseless carriages led several Flint businessmen to acquire the Buick Motor Company, a Detroit-based engine company with a growing reputation. David Buick, who had come to Detroit with his parents as a young boy in 1856, earned his first success as a plumber before turning to engines. The first Buick horseless carriage appeared on the Detroit streets about 1900 and soon attracted the attention of James H. Whiting, president of the Flint Wagon Works and "a closet car enthusiast." Whiting's group purchased Buick and moved it to Flint. Durant rejected Whiting's initial offer to invest in Buick. The wagon business was good, and he detested the smelly and noisy horseless carriages that spooked horses, caused accidents, and, according to Durant, "were to be sold to rich men for their foolish sons." However, a desperate need for investment capital led Whiting to try again. This time, Durant rode in a Buick and quickly viewed it as a "self-seller."[25]

—— General Motors Is Founded

Durant assumed controlling interest in Buick on November 1, 1904, and moved quickly. He entered a Buick into the 1905 New York Auto Show and starting taking orders for hundreds of cars almost immediately. Buick grew rapidly and, after a brief manufacturing stint in Jackson, Durant moved it to Flint where Buick expanded into a ten-factory complex that one expert hailed as the finest "in the Country for the manufacture and sale of automobiles." By 1908, Buick stood first among all American auto producers. Yet, Durant wanted more and pursued a suggestion made by Benjamin Briscoe. A Detroit sheet metal entrepreneur who supplied parts to various auto producers and presided over the Maxwell-Briscoe Company, at the time one of the nation's largest auto producers, Briscoe proposed merging Buick and his company. Durant saw merit in the idea and asked Briscoe to see if Henry Ford and Ransom Olds were interested in selling their companies. Negotiations in early 1908 collapsed over irreconcilable differences, most notably the nature of the new company and payouts in stock or cash. Ford and Olds insisted on cash (each asked from between $3 and $4 million, estimates vary) rather than stock in the new company, and Durant could not raise the cash. However, he would not be deterred. He moved ahead alone, creating the General Motors Company (GM) in September 1908. The new company was incorporated in New Jersey, which set no limits on the amount of stock a company might issue. According to Durant's longtime attorney, "what Mr. Durant desired most of all were large stock issues in which he, from an inside position, could dicker and trade."[26]

Within two years, GM acquired about 30 other companies. In most cases the transfers did not require much cash. Instead, Durant exchanged GM stock for the company he bought. Some companies offered a positive future.

Cadillac enjoyed "a wide reputation for quality," while Oakland (later Pontiac) produced a quality four-cyclinder car that won endurance tests all across the country. Durant also persuaded companies either to join GM or open branches in Flint. This included Albert Champion (later AC Spark Plug) and Charles Mott's axle. Not all acquisitions were a success. Durant paid seven million dollars for Heany Lamp Company—his "biggest blunder." Other disappointments included Welch, Cartercar, Ewing, and Elmore, which all flopped. Durant pursued the Ford Motor Company again, but with the Model T doing so well, Ford's price stood at $8 million. Once again, Durant could not raise the cash.[27]

On the surface General Motors appeared successful. An admiring Detroiter wrote, Durant "has the Napoleonic faculty of thinking out details beforehand. These things mean power. There is almost nothing he cannot do except rest." Certainly Durant worked hard. A story that Gustin, Durant's biographer, claims "caught the spirit of the whole of Durant's life" occurred one evening when Durant and his secretary W. W. Murphy headed to Detroit to catch a train. Delayed by a slow-moving tractor obstructing the entire road, Durant "gunned the car" around the hay wagon but veered through a ditch. Something snapped, prompting Murphy to ask, "What was that?" "Never mind," Durant responded as they continued on their way, "we're still running." But GM teetered on the brink of financial collapse. At the eleventh hour, eastern banks, impressed with the "money-making ability and sound-business practices" of Cadillac, provided the necessary funds to save GM. However, the terms left the bankers in control and relegated Durant to a powerless vice presidency. During the following weeks, Durant struggled as men who knew nothing about manufacturing "moved quickly to cut loose some of Durant's subsidiaries, consolidate others, and to straighten out the tangled financial affairs of Durant's loose-knit organization." An increasingly frantic Durant revealed in his notes, "The things that counted so much in the past, which gave General Motors its unique and powerful position, were subordinated to 'liquidate and pay.'"[28]

—— Chevrolet Arrives

Despite some writers who compared Durant to Halley's Comet (which had lit up the sky earlier that year), Durant vowed to control General Motors again. He organized a new company named after Louis Chevrolet, a former Buick engineer and racecar driver. As Chevrolet later recalled, Durant "was

Louis Chevrolet (standing
with no hat), here with W.C.
Durant (far right with derby
hat), engineered the Chevy
490, which allowed Durant
to resume control over
General Motors.

planning a comeback and told me, 'We're going to need a car.' So I built
it." Through a series of characteristic moves—acquiring other companies, re-
designing vehicles (especially introducing a car to compete with the Model
T), and moving manufacturing operations before settling in Flint, Durant
introduced the Chevrolet. (Durant adopted the company's famous "bow-tie"
logo after noticing it in a Sunday newspaper and liking it.) Durant introduced
the Chevrolet "Four-Ninety" in 1915. A "good-looking, easy-riding, well-made,
powerful car" with electric lights and an electric starter that cost only $490,
the car quickly became a winner as orders poured in at a rate of 1,000 a
day.[29]

The Chevrolet 490 was a winner, but Durant's company remained "a
pigmy" compared to GM, which sold 124,000 Buicks in 1916, and the Ford
Motor Company, which sold 735,000 Model Ts that same year. When Durant
lost control of GM, Charles Nash assumed control of Buick, and his success
there led to his promotion to GM president in 1912. But the bankers were
the power at GM and they remained "skeptical about the future of the automobile industry." They cut costs, but when they also suspended paying stock
dividends, it gave Durant an opening. Riding the success of the Chevy 490
and supported by financier Pierre S. Du Pont, Durant started buying up GM
stock—offering five shares of Chevy stock for one share of GM stock. In the
end, Chevy acquired General Motors, which observers likened to "Jonah swal-
lowing the whale."[30]

After making himself president of GM, Durant started acquiring other
companies to make GM the nation's auto leader. "For a time," as biographer
Gustin points out, Durant "appeared to be moving toward this end boldly but
with basically good judgment." GM acquired Delco with inventor Charles Ket-

tering and his electric ignitions that eliminated hand cranking a car; Hyatt Bearing Company, producers of some of the best auto roller bearings in the nation and its talented president Alfred Sloan; and Fisher Body, the nation's leading manufacturer of automobile bodies. Durant created the General Motors Acceptance Corporation (GMAC) to make it easier for customers to finance an auto purchase. Durant also bought an electric refrigeration company. Established in Detroit in early 1916, the Guardian Frigerator Company had a good idea but lacked direction and money. Introduced to the operation to persuade a friend to reconsider his investments in Guardian, Durant became intrigued and acquired the company for $100,000. He reorganized it and changed the name to Frigidaire. When fellow directors asked why, he explained that "cars and refrigerators are the same thing, boxes containing motors." Four years after Durant returned, General Motors was eight times larger than the company he had acquired in 1915. In 1919, corporate profits had quadrupled over the previous year.[31]

Durant did suffer setbacks. His venture into tractor manufacturing proved a costly failure. Despite Durant's opposition, GM also moved forward to build the world's largest office building—at a cost of $20 million—which further drained available capital. More seriously, Durant's style of running a complicated company of more than 86,000 employees as a one-man show, while ignoring suggestions from valued subordinates on how to improve managerial operations, led to growing criticism. According to his biographer, Durant still "believed more in his hunches than in the considered opinions of a staff of experts." Durant's style also frustrated the company's most trusted executives—men who were essential to General Motors. This active involvement with stockbrokers (Durant had an estimated 70 brokerages) "made it almost impossible" for his most capable executives to reach him or keep his attention. Meetings started late as executives sat idle while Durant left the room to take phone calls. On one occasion, a frustrated Walter Chrysler, who had worked miracles at Buick, demanded Durant explain his policies. Durant responded, "Walt, I believe in changing the policies just as often as my door opens and closes." Exasperated, Chrysler, who later described Durant as the automobile industry's "greatest man," left General Motors in 1919. Vice president Alfred Sloan, who "learned a great deal from Durant about how not to run a complex corporation," also contemplated leaving.[32]

In 1920, a postwar national economic setback sent GM stock spiraling downward. Durant responded by frantically buying GM stock to stabilize the price. It did not work, leaving Durant deeply in debt to GM. Pierre S. Du Pont stepped in and bought Durant's 2.5 million shares providing that he leave GM entirely. With no alternative, Durant left GM, formed Durant Motors, and produced a quality automobile until his continued fascination with the stock market and the Great Depression drove him into bankruptcy. Several years after Durant left GM a second time, a contemporary observer concluded that if Durant had stayed away from the stock market he would have been worth $500 million and still be running GM. However, as Gustin explains, "Durant had not created this empire by being prudent, or practical, or by listening to others. He had been daring, impulsive, erratic. He won big, and he lost big. But on balance, he created what has become the largest industrial corporation in history."[33]

As General Motors struggled to gain stability, the Ford Motor Company continued its dominance of the American automobile industry, controlling 50 percent of market share. Ford did undergo some changes, acquiring the Lincoln Motor Car Company—breaking with the policy that Ford only produced one model. Purchasing Lincoln probably came at the urging of Edsel Ford, company president and Henry and Clara's only child. Edsel also belonged to a group of company executives trying to convince the elder Ford that the Model T had outlived its usefulness. Henry Ford, who remained the company's powerbroker, could not be dissuaded. At the same time, the elder Ford battled stockholders because he limited dividend payments, arguing the extra capital should be used for expansion, most notably the massive River Rouge plant then under construction. After losing a court case over the matter, the stubborn Ford bought out the other stockholders by threatening to leave the Ford Motor Company and start a new auto enterprise. The stock buyback cost Ford $100 million. One founder who profited handsomely was James Couzens, whose $1,000 investment in 1903 earned him a tidy $29 million. Ford remained a hero to many Americans and was even seriously considered for the Republican presidential nomination in 1924, but according to historian John Rae, key executives who left the company believed that the Ford Motor Company "was controlled by an autocrat who acted on impulse rather than on any rationally conceived program."[34]

—— Alfred Sloan and the "Annual Model"

Ford's biggest challenge in the 1920s came from General Motors, led by Alfred Sloan. Connecticut born and a graduate of Massachusetts Institute of Technology, Sloan acquired the Hyatt Roller Bearing Company, which supplied quality ball bearings to both Ford and GM in the early 1910s. In 1916, Sloan accepted Billy Durant's offer to buy Hyatt, which made Sloan a wealthy man and a GM vice president. Working for Durant for five years taught Sloan, according to his biographer David Farber, that "managing a business . . . took more than inspiration, charm, and financial wizardry." Durant's departure also gave Sloan "the opportunity he needed to reveal his organizational and managerial genius." Elevated to president in 1923 (a position he held until 1937), Sloan resurrected and reconstructed GM by introducing a management system that worked so well other automakers copied it. In the process, Sloan turned GM into the world's leading automaker.[35]

Among the challenges facing GM was a growing market of used cars (also a problem for all automakers, including Ford), which led Sloan to introduce "a systematic change each year carefully calculated so that each new model would be recognizably different from its predecessors, but not so far different as to pose the threat that each year's model would be completely out of style a year later." The Sloan policy of what became known as the "annual model" also was associated with the notion of building a car so that it would last only a limited period of time. The automobile industry understandably rejected this notion of "planned obsolescence," and historian John Rae agrees that "much of what has passed for planned obsolescence has been due to normal wear and tear, frequently aggravated by inadequate maintenance, and some of it should be attributed to careless workmanship and inadequate quality control, not to intent." Sloan also hired William Knudsen, who had left Ford, giving the Danish immigrant an opportunity to salvage the Chevrolet Division, which GM considered dropping because of poor sales. In a few years, Knudsen worked wonders, tripling sales to more than a million vehicles and making Chevy the nation's leading passenger car by 1927. The challenge from Chevy led Ford to spruce up the Model T, but it only delayed the inevitable. Jokes like *"What does a Model T use for shock absorbers?" "The passengers"* no longer seemed funny. Buying cars on credit and a consumer demand for greater variety marked the end of the Model T, and the last one rolled off the assembly line in May 1927. The Ford Motor Company had produced more than 15 million Model Ts—a record that stood for years. Ford's new Model A replaced Chevy as the nation's most popular car but only for one year.[36]

—— Walter Chrysler

As GM and Ford struggled for supreme power in the auto world, Walter Chrysler worked quietly in the wings. After Chrysler left General Motors, he accepted Durant's gracious offer to buy his stock in early 1920—a transaction that netted Chrysler $10 million in cash. He also re-entered the auto industry,

Walter Chrysler (with 1912 Cadillac) moved to Flint and improved the sale of Buicks. In the mid-1920s, Chrysler launched the company that bears his name to this day.

accepting an offer to help the financially strapped New Jersey-based Willys-Overland Company. A Kansan who purchased his first car in 1908 (although he did not drive it for three months, preferring instead to study it), Chrysler was managing a railroad in Pittsburgh when a GM investment banker introduced him to Buick president Charles Nash. Despite a substantial pay cut, Chrysler accepted Nash's offer to move to Flint. In four years, Chrysler introduced a series of cost-cutting and efficiency changes that expanded Buick production substantially and elevated him to company president. When Nash exited GM, an equally frustrated Chrysler planned to follow but changed his mind for several reasons, including Durant's offer to raise his salary tenfold. Despite continued accomplishments, frustrations with Durant's management style eventually led him to leave GM.[37]

Willys-Overland ended up in receivership, but Chrysler accepted an offer to aid the financially ailing, Detroit-based Maxwell Motor Company. At Maxwell, according to historian Charles Hyde, the former railroadman "realized his long-delayed dream." In January 1924, Chrysler took the automobile world by storm when he introduced the Chrysler Six at the New York Auto Show. The stylish Six boasted an assortment of advanced features (a high-compression engine, hydraulic four-wheeled brakes, and balloon tires) in a mid-priced range that "propelled Chrysler onto the automobile industry's center stage." Reviewers lauded the car's "speed, power, riding stability, comfort, good looks, and reasonable price." Even the distinctive radiator cap, which featured the wings of Roman god Mercury, offered a subtle reminder of the car's speed—up to 70 miles per hour "with power to spare." Over the next several years, Chrysler overcame manufacturing challenges, incorporated his company, launched two new car lines (DeSoto and Plymouth), and moved aggressively to expand his corporation by acquiring the Dodge Brothers Car Company.[38]

John and Horace Dodge enjoyed success wherever they went. After growing up in Niles, Michigan, the two brothers (John was the eldest by four years) headed to Detroit to work as machinists before starting a bicycle shop in Windsor, Ontario, Canada, in the late 1890s. They moved back across the Detroit River in 1900, where their machine shop began providing parts to fledgling automakers, including Ransom E. Olds and Henry Ford. Between 1903 and 1913, the Dodge Brothers manufactured parts representing 60 percent of the total value of Ford cars. They made every part except the bodies, wheels, and tires. Eager to have their own nameplate, the Dodges severed their relationship with the Ford Motor Company in 1913. Even before their first car appeared, the brothers' positive reputation as producers of low-cost and high-quality parts prompted one industry publication to declare, "When the Dodge Bros. car comes out, there is no question that it will be the best thing on the market for the money." When the first Dodge, nicknamed Old Betsy, rolled off the line in November 1914, the local press hailed the car's "smartness, grace and power."[39]

The Dodge Brothers never rivaled the Ford Motor Company in cars sold. But their technological advances included adopting stronger, cheaper, and easier-to-paint all-steel bodies at a time when most automakers used wood or composite bodies. Dodge sales rocketed up to 145,000 vehicles in 1920. In

The Dodge Brothers (backseat) in their first car around 1914. John and Horace Dodge moved from making bicycle parts to creating a car.

that same year, tragedy stuck when the brothers fell victim to the influenza epidemic. John died shortly after contracting the illness. Horace struggled to recover, but the illness and the loss of his brother finally led to his death later that year. A Detroit newspaper editorialized, "It was not the mere physical fact of brotherhood that welded these two, John and Horace Dodge, together. . . . For the brothers loved each other as friends. They were friends."[40]

In July 1928, Chrysler purchased the struggling Dodge Brothers Company in a move that "became the core of a greatly enlarged and prosperous Chrysler Corporation." Chrysler sought the extensive network of Dodge dealers, "generally viewed as one of the best in the industry," to more easily market his low-priced Plymouth to compete with Ford and Chevy. The merger, hailed by one trade publication as "one of the most startling developments in many years," left General Motors, Ford, and Chrysler-Dodge producing nearly 75 percent of the nation's cars. The *Automotive Daily News* editorial writer may not have appreciated his contribution to the American lexicon when he noted that the merger meant that the "big three" dominated the American auto market.[41]

—— Why Michigan?

By the 1920s, producing motor vehicles in large numbers had been achieved. In 1921, American automakers built 1.1 million cars; by 1929, that number exceeded 5 million, and vigorous competition kept the price of an auto low. At the same time, there was a noticeable decline in auto companies. The 108 American companies making cars in 1920 fell to 44 in 1929. Smaller makers (Hudson and Maxwell & Durant in Michigan) had difficulty getting parts at reasonable prices, and they lacked the volume of sales to manufacture their own, while larger makers had their own parts operations or received concessions from independent suppliers. The mass consumption of the automobile in the 1920s stimulated the nation's economy and nowhere more than in Michigan, which boomed during the decade. In good economic times people bought cars; when the economy slowed, car purchases slowed, and it did not take much to impact Michigan. As the saying went, "When the nation sneezes, Michigan gets pneumonia."[42]

Five years after King, Ford, and Olds had introduced their horseless carriages, Michigan moved to the center of the nation's automobile industry. By 1904, companies located in Detroit produced more automobiles than elsewhere, and ten years later, Michigan firms manufactured 77 percent of the nation's automobiles. In that same year, an industry that had not existed twenty years earlier represented more than one-third of the state's entire manufacturing output.

No single reason answers the question "Why Michigan?" The list includes environmental factors (Michigan's geographical positioning in the center of the nation and its hardwood forests that contributed to its carriage and wagon industry) and a wealth of small-scale industrial enterprises that offered machine shop facilities and skilled laborers. Yet, some or parts of these advantages could be found elsewhere in the country. Certainly, automakers found Detroit's open-shop (anti-union) reputation appealing. Historian John Rae attributes the growth of the auto industry in Michigan to the concentration of a remarkable group of individuals who brought to the fledgling industry "exceptional entrepreneurial and technical talent." Native Michiganians (Ford, Olds, Chapin, Durant, and the Dodges) and men who relocated here (Packard, Leland, and Chevrolet) provided "the catalyst." Some had college educations, while others had not finished high school. Yet, they all had in common a dedication to the manufacture of motor vehicles, "to the point they preferred to go broke making automobiles than to get rich doing anything else." According to Rae, "the human factor" was decisive. Devoted and skilled men were "in the right place, at the right time, and with the right talents."[43]

CHAPTER

14

World War I

Several thousand doughboys (mostly Michiganians) were sent to Siberia to help put down the Bolshevik Revolution.

"The old army men tell us, that a soldier isn't a real one if he doesn't complain."

—Doughboy James Glenn Wilson of Bangor

As the Progressive Era rumbled on, Europe erupted into war in August 1914. Most Americans felt fortunate that the Atlantic Ocean separated them from the worsening death and destruction, but hundreds of young Michigan men joined Canadian military units—part of the British Commonwealth forces fighting the Germans. However, most Americans agreed with President Woodrow Wilson that this was not an American war. This attitude changed as Americans grew increasingly sympathetic toward the British and French, a relationship aided by Allied purchases of American foodstuffs and munitions, as well as a shrewd propaganda campaign that painted the Germans as cruel and ruthless militarists who raped and ravaged their innocent victims. Proposals favoring intervention or military preparedness led the nation's foremost auto manufacturer to suggest

236

an unorthodox plan to end the war that "proved to be his greatest personal disaster and one of the principal reasons for his popularity with the masses."[1]

—— Ford Says No to War

One year into the war, Henry Ford told a *Detroit Free Press* reporter that children needed to be taught that the "uselessness of war . . . [and] preparation for war can only end in war." Furthermore, Ford promised to "give everything" he possessed to stop war and prevent an arms buildup in the United States. The automaker claimed none of his Model Ts would be used for warfare. He described soldiers as "murderers" and said that only "militarists and money lenders" profited from war. Despite pleadings from his close friend and Ford Motor Company associate James Couzens that this harangue might produce a customer backlash, Ford could not be restrained. Instead, an irritated Couzens quit the company in outrage. Undeterred, Ford confronted Americans who demanded the United States enter the war by calling for a national referendum, arguing "the people who do the fighting and pay the war debts should have a vote whether they wanted a war or not." To the automaker, war was "a wasteful folly [that] . . . destroyed human and material resources and offered a stark contrast to the positive ethos of modern industrial production."[2]

In late 1915, Ford became the driving force behind a peace delegation sent to mobilize European public opinion and pressure the warring powers to come to the peace table. The automaker boasted his plan would "get the boys out of the trenches before Christmas." The genesis of this plan stemmed from an unlikely relationship between Ford and Rosika Schwimmer, a radical Hungarian Jewish pacifist. A renowned feminist, Schwimmer organized the International Congress of Women confident that women could find a way to end the war. Ford met Schwimmer in his office as a courtesy to a pacifist friend. After a second meeting, the automaker committed himself to Schwimmer's effort to end the war.

Throughout late November 1915, the media offered extensive, and generally positive, coverage of what became known as Henry Ford's "Peace Ship." However, as invited members (former Secretary of State William Jennings Bryan, Jane Addams, Thomas Edison, and William Howard Taft, among others) declined to join, critics labeled the effort an "ineffable folly" and an exer-

Anti-war "delegates" sailed with automaker Henry Ford on his "peace ship" in an attempt to stop World War I.

cise in "uselessness and absurdity." Despite the mockery, the *Oscar II* sailed from Hoboken, New Jersey, on December 5 with an assortment of unknown delegates and a considerable entourage of newsmen. At sea the situation worsened as delegates feuded among themselves and news stories presented the effort as "the first act of a comic opera." The Peace Ship unceremoniously docked in Oslo, Norway, on December 18. Just as quickly, an exhausted Ford sailed for home, while the delegates milled around ineffectively before dispersing. Once back in the States, Ford denied the effort had been a failure, asserting it had led to discussion of peace rather than war. Some earlier critics even congratulated Ford, including the *New York American*, which admitted if the nation's political leaders had "put forth one-tenth the individual effort that Henry Ford put forth, the boys would have been out of the trenches by Christmas." Ford also modified his earlier criticism of those responsible for war. "I don't blame an ammunition maker for making and selling ammunition," he surmised, "but I do blame the ignorant, thoughtless people who not only allow the manufacture of murder machines, but rob their stomachs, stultify their brains, and break their backs to pay for them." The Europeans, he argued, had not taken "enough interest in the government." Despite these pacifistic setbacks, Ford continued lobbying against U.S. preparedness and opposing intervention throughout 1916.

—— Entering the Great War

As the war dragged on, German policies resulted in growing American outrage. In early 1917, the Americans learned of a wild German scheme urging Mexico to ally itself with Germany if the United States entered the war. This absurd proposal—coupled with unrestricted submarine warfare—moved America closer to war. By sinking ships of all nations, including the neutral United States, the Germans risked expanding the war. However, they were confident they could starve the British into submission before an American army could be organized and reach Europe. The indiscriminate sinking of U.S. ships proved too much for President Wilson, who called Congress into a special session in early April 1917 to debate a declaration of war.

Plenty of Michiganians supported the president's actions. "If the president asks for war, Michigan will vote for war," the *Detroit Free Press* roared. Michigan's congressional delegation agreed. Congressman James G. McLaughlin (R-Muskegon), who disagreed with Wilson on most things, was "more than willing to aid" the president's efforts to stop German submarines. Even without a declaration, Congressman J. M. C. Smith (R-Charlotte) proposed fighting "like demons by every means known to modern warfare." Declaring American rights on the high seas were "the rights of peaceful people," Michigan senator William Alden Smith (R-Grand Rapids) argued that a failure to challenge German actions would lose Americans "the respect of liberty-loving people at home and abroad." Michigan leaders also called for universal military training.[3]

President Wilson's request for a congressional declaration of war against Germany overwhelmingly passed the Congress on April 6, 1917, by a vote of 82 to 6 in the Senate and 373 to 50 in the House. Only one Michigan congressman opposed going to war. The lone exception was Mark Bacon, a freshman Republican from Detroit. Although Bacon traced his German-American roots to the American Revolution and a relative who served in the Continental Army, his "no" vote on war undoubtedly contributed to his subsequent re-election defeat.[4]

As Congress prepared to declare war, talk of war flowed around the State Capitol. Governor Albert Sleeper proposed a $1 million loan "to send well-equipped troops to the front." The loan soon grew to $5 million and received rapid approval by the legislature. As in 1861 and 1898, Sleeper promised, "The people of Michigan are ready to give of their vast resources that American arms may triumph for American honor and the welfare of mankind."[5]

All across the state, many Michiganians expressed enthusiasm with the coming of war. In Ann Arbor, every engineering senior at the University of Michigan (except three) joined militia groups (a total of 23 squads) and trained on State Street. In East Lansing, 800 Michigan Agricultural College cadets, most with several years of military training already, waited eagerly "for the call of President Wilson for volunteers." Public schoolteachers proposed planting gardens in vacant lots to meet anticipated increased food needs, while Detroit women distributed literature to local factories encouraging workers to join the armed forces. "In the interest of patriotism" the Detroit YMCA invited "ambitious rifle men" to use its firing range atop its building at Adams and Witherell for target practice.[6]

Volunteering for service proved popular, and "all manner of applicants besieged the army recruiting offices." Much was made about a "full-blooded" Ojibwa chief from Frederick who joined the navy. The Michigan Naval Militia also mobilized, added new recruits, and prepared to ship out to the Philadelphia Naval Yard. A week after Congress's action, the 600-man strong brigade received a set of colors in a dramatic ceremony reminiscent of a similar presentation in May 1861 when the "boys in blue" went off to save the Union. Shortly thereafter, more than 150,000 Detroiters lined the streets from the naval armory to the train station to send their sailors off to war. At the station, the police "were swept aside as easily as if they were children" by friends and relatives who gave the sailors a heartfelt and tearful farewell.[7]

Those not going off to war expressed their enthusiasm in other ways. American flags decorated most cars and "nearly every business house in Detroit." Women and children of all ages pinned U.S. flags to their coats as they shopped the city's downtown businesses. In Ann Arbor, 5,000 people attended a mass rally where speakers reminded them the declaration of war meant "there will be but two classes in this country—those who are loyal to the American flag and American principles" and those who are "pacifists, pro-Germans, or traitors."[8]

Few Michiganians expressed fears about the coming war. A newspaper article entitled "Detroit's Position is Most Secure of World's Big Cities" argued that war would benefit the city's manufacturing sector. The author reasoned that, as "the leader in upwards of 20 separate industries" (including automobiles and stoves), Detroit need not fear any disruption in daily life. The only possible interruption would be an invasion, "which is beyond the dreams even of the champion jingoes." A leading Detroit businessman concurred, predicting that Detroit had the brightest future of any American city and "would continue to grow at its record pace."[9]

The purchase of liberty bonds to support the war effort often led to patriotic rallies like this 1918 parade in Grand Rapids.

Not all Michiganians favored war. Just days before the congressional declaration, German Americans rallied in Detroit and Frankentrost (Saginaw County) adopting resolutions criticizing President Wilson for pushing the United States into war with Germany. Elsewhere, the implementation of conscription to raise an army led ten drafted members of the Israelite House of David commune in Benton Harbor to seek conscientious objector (CO) status. The army tolerated the Israelites' refusal to shave their beards or cut their long hair but drew a line in the sand when the men refused any service because their religion rejected a "long term commitment to a war effort." Court-martials followed and the men were imprisoned at Fort Leavenworth, Kansas, for the duration of the war. In early 1919, the War Department released the men and gave them an honorable discharge.[10]

The mobilization of the National Guard left state leaders feeling vulnerable, especially to saboteurs or strikes at the munitions plants. Only a few weeks after the war's declaration, the state legislature created a home guard that was headquartered in East Lansing. According to Governor Sleeper, the 300-man mounted Michigan State Troops Permanent Force (more commonly called the Michigan State Constabulary) was the "best kind of an insurance policy that the state of Michigan can buy." Warning potential radicals "there would be no dilly-dallying," Constabulary commander Colonel Roy C. Vandercook used his troopers to suppress outbreaks of labor unrest all across the state. On May 1, 1918, the force officially changed its name to the Michigan State Police.[11]

—— Raising an Army

As the State Constabulary prepared to defend the homeland, federal dollars established major training facilities at Battle Creek and Mt. Clemens. Young fliers, including America's future ace Lt. Eddie Rickenbacker, learned their trade at Selfridge Field, named after the first American officer to die in an air crash. In September 1917, the first contingent of recruits arrived at Fort Custer, an 8,000-acre U.S. Army compound near Battle Creek.[12]

By the time Godfrey J. Anderson arrived at Fort Custer in late May 1918, the camp had grown to include hundreds of buildings. The 21-year-old Grand Rapids draftee recalled, "The camp seemed to extend for miles—a veritable city of barracks." For Anderson, and thousands of other Michiganians, army life was a shock. After getting settled in a barracks and receiving his equipment and uniforms, he recalled:

> We were lined up for our first drill in charge of a red headed foul-mouthed sergeant. He began by delivering a violent diatribe consisting mostly of threats, cussing, and obscenities, his voice at times rising almost to a shriek as he belabored us with vituperation and insult, referring to us repeatedly as bastards and sons of bitches. Whether all that was some form of army psychology, devised to intimidate new recruits and put them in a proper subservient frame of mind, I never knew.

Besides daily drill (especially gas-mask training) and calisthenics, Anderson experienced "peeling great piles of potatoes." Relaxation included reading, writing letters, shooting craps, or playing poker in a barracks "thick with tobacco smoke, and the noisy conversation on all sides [that] consisted largely of profanity, four letter words, vituperation, cussing of the army, and obscenity in general." Anderson survived basic training and then took a train east, followed by a monotonous thirteen days aboard a British troop ship to Liverpool highlighted by violent seasickness and food that he labeled as "simply execrable."[13]

Raising an American army posed great challenges. In April 1917, the federal government conscripted men aged 21–30 years old (later changed to 18–45 years old). In Michigan the pool of available men (380,000 under the first call, but later raised to 870,000) revealed that 40 percent of the initial 115,000 selected failed to pass their physical examination. The disappointing numbers led to expanding the draft pool. Eventually, 175,000 Michigan men served in the American Expeditionary Force (AEF). Thousands never completed their training or were not deployed before the war ended in November 1918. About 5,000 Michiganians died during the war, and another 15,000 were injured or wounded.[14]

The 32nd Division was one unit that played a major role in the AEF experience. Formed in July 1917 by combining Michigan and Wisconsin National Guardsmen into a single unit, the 32nd trained in Texas before arriving in France in February 1918. Two months later, the Midwesterners saw action, becoming the first American troops to set foot on German soil. By the end of the war, the 32nd earned the French nickname, *Les Terribles*, for its battlefield stubbornness and notable accomplishments. The first allied division to crack the famed German Hindenburg Line, the 32nd became known as the "Red Arrow Division" after adopting a shoulder patch with a red arrow shooting through a line. The division's greatest fight was the October 1918 Meuse-Argonne offensive where the 32nd suffered nearly 6,000 casualties. According to the division's postwar history, in three weeks of fighting, the 32nd

had encountered everything that troops in modern battle might be called upon to face. The struggle over the most difficult terrain that any soldiers in the great war were ever asked to conquer. There were commanding hills on which the enemy could make his stand, deep open ravines which he could sweep with machine guns and fill with gas, patches of weeds tangled with wire which were difficult to penetrate even when not garrisoned by the deadly Maxims of the Kaiser's machine gunners. There were open spaces on which the enemy had perfect observation, and which could be crossed only at the cost of a heavy toll of lives. . . . The enemy realized the importance of holding the line at this point. His positions were organized with every means that four years of experience in trench warfare had suggested.

The division's historian boasted the veteran German divisions who faced the Midwesterners had "all the advantages of combat," but were "completely beaten in every clash with the 32nd Division." Following the war-ending armistice on November 11, 1918, the 32nd served as occupation troops before arriving home in April 1919. The division suffered 14,000 total casualties—third among all AEF divisions.[15]

Another largely Michigan unit that saw action was the 85th Division. Organized in the summer of 1917 and trained at Fort Custer, the 85th (also called the Custer Division) headed overseas in July 1918. Unlike the 32nd, the 85th served as a "replacement division," dispersing its units to reinforce front-line units. James Glenn Wilson of Bangor, who served in the division's 328th Field Artillery band, kept a diary recording his wartime experiences. Although "rain, mud and war" greeted him upon arriving in France, when his troop train stalled going up a hill, an American engine came to the rescue; he confidently wrote, "bank on America for men and machinery." Many entries recorded the life of an infantryman such as, "We just keep moving, the leggings we wear are wet and caked with mud. My legs are so weary, but it seems there is always another hill to climb." Wilson added, "We do a lot of grumbling and growling, then we go right on with our duty. The old army men tell us, that a soldier isn't a real one if he doesn't complain." Shortly after the armistice silenced the guns on the Western Front, Wilson's band found itself in a bombed-out cathedral where they played the "Star Spangled Banner." "It was the best we ever played," he boasted. Both proud of his service and relieved he survived, Wilson reflected on his experience: "As we journey through the valleys and to the hilltops, we pass many things that make us think. For all over the hillsides are new crosses of wood for our fallen buddys. They are buried where they fell. More solemn yet. Many not yet buried. . . . We have walked long cold miles, we are weary and sad. The sights we have seen we will never forget. No! Never." After numerous concerts for the French people and three delousing inspections, Wilson's unit boarded a steamer and survived a massive Atlantic storm before arriving in New York City, where the band serenaded New Yorkers with *America*. In a final diary entry, he noted, "I am just glad the war is over, and the next stop is Camp Custer, and then to the good American soil at my farm house."[16]

On November 11, 1918, most Americans—either at home or in the trenches of northern France—celebrated the end of the Great War. For the 339th U.S. Infantry, a regiment of Michiganians stationed near the Russian city of Archangel, there was nothing to celebrate. Days of repulsing waves of Russian attacks had left 28 Americans killed and 70 wounded. When asked about their mission, one Michigan doughboy succinctly responded, "We fought to stay alive."[17]

—— The Polar Bears

The saga of these doughboys, better known as the "Polar Bears," began with the Russian Revolution. To get out of World War I, the Russians—much to the alarm of their British and French allies—signed a peace accord with the Germans in late 1917. This action, combined with concern over the Bolshevik Revolution, led the British to send troops to Russia supporting the anti-Bolsheviks. The British wanted American help, and President Wilson agreed, ordering 5,500 doughboys (90 percent of whom were Michiganians) to support the effort on the condition they not be used for offensive operations. Wilson also allowed the Americans to serve under British leadership—an unusual agreement that caused future problems. Back home, the president's decision received support. The *Detroit Free Press* explained that sending troops would end anarchy, establish a "responsible government in Russia," "secure guarantees for payment of national debts," and be in the "best interests" of the allies "in their future commercial relationships with Russia."[18]

On September 4, 1918, the American North Russian Expeditionary Force (its official name) arrived in Archangel, Russia. Placed under the command of British officers, the Americans were divided into smaller units and distributed

The Polar Bears, a largely Michigan component of doughboys deployed in Siberia, faced an abundance of unexpected challenges.

to distant outposts. More seriously, the British commanders, who were staunch anti-Bolsheviks, involved the Americans in offensive operations despite Wilson's earlier directive. The doughboys experienced a rough transition. Not only was their mission unclear, but they received inferior equipment. To save money, the Allied force was equipped with Russian rifles to eliminate the "expense of transporting a vast supply of American and British rifle ammunition." The Russian winter also made survival a challenge. Winter clothes arrived late and in short supply, forcing the Americans to remove boots from dead Russians to keep their feet from freezing. Campaigning also proved difficult. One Polar Bear recorded, "We would march a day, wet to the skin, and then have to sleep in our wet clothing. . . . It was worse when we were on outpost duty. We would not have fires, you knew if you moved, snipers would pick you off." Relations also soured between the Americans and the British.[19]

However, some Polar Bears remembered the occasional enjoyable experience. One Grand Rapids doughboy stationed deep inside Russia recalled celebrating Christmas so many miles from home. After setting up a Christmas tree in the building commandeered as a barracks, the men participated in a "singfest" accompanied by a three-piece orchestra (a violin, guitar, and banjo that "struggled through a couple of numbers"). The soldiers then received Red Cross Christmas stockings, "which included among other things a package of cigarettes, a cigar, and a can of pipe tobacco." According to Private Anderson, the cooks "had outdone themselves," preparing a menu that included rabbit, mashed potatoes, rice, and date pudding (with peppermint sauce) and chocolate layer cake. The doughboys "were pleasantly surprised" when some of the locals joined them. Anderson described the Russian girls as "bright and intelligent looking, fair and lovely, some even beautiful." The soldiers and the girls, who were "dressed in charming party dresses in the latest style," enjoyed an evening with those "lucky doughboys who could dance." The "only difficulty," he added, "was the language barrier, and about all we could do was to exchange smiles and such chivalrous courtesies as we could come up with, along with some desperate jabbering." After a pleasant and unexpected break from the war, Anderson recalled, "life again resumed its dreary course."[20]

As weeks dragged into months, U.S. officials seemed reluctant to bring the Polar Bears home. Discomfiting newspaper headlines like, "Washington is Fearful of Disaster," coupled with demands from loved ones for improved communications with their sons and husbands in Russia, met with official responses that "the matter was out of their hands" or "everything was being done to improve the situation." Concerned Detroiters finally mobilized. Letters from outraged citizens demanded that the men be brought home. The wife of one doughboy stationed in Russia noted, "How long must we people of this democratic land stand for this?" Another to the army's chief of staff pleaded, "For God's sake, say something and do something." The Michigan State Senate unanimously passed a resolution declaring, there was "no patriotic reason why" American troops should be in Russia, while U.S. Senator William Alden Smith presented a resolution from Grand Rapids citizens urging the Polar Bears be withdrawn "as soon as possible." At the same time, the secretary of war received a petition carrying more than 100,000 names demanding the troops be either recalled or reinforced. The secretary noted that British officials reassured the president that American troops were safe—a response that only further angered Michiganians.[21]

In early April 1919, the U.S. government finally announced the Polar Bears would be coming home, once the fifteen-foot-thick Arctic Ocean ice melted. The early contingent of Polar Bears who reached Detroit on July 3 were greeted with "cheers, crying and applause." Detroit's mayor conveyed the thoughts of many Michiganians when he declared that the Polar Bear story was one of "magnificent endurance, sacrifice and obedience." Mayor James Couzens added, "You fought doubts in your own hearts; doubts that Headquarters remembered your predicament, that the folks at home knew you still lived, that they had received your letters, that relief could ever reach you through the ice-locked sea. Your victory was a triple one—over self-pity, discouragement, and the enemy." Today, the Polar Bear saga is exceptionally well documented at Michigan's Own Military and Space Museum in Frankenmuth and at the White Chapel Cemetery in Troy where a large white polar bear sculpture stands guard over the remains of many Polar Bears.[22]

—— Industry Gears Up

Even before the doughboys headed overseas, industrial Michigan geared up to assist the Allied war effort. The Packard Motor Company, which started building trucks for the Allies shortly after the outbreak of the war, became the leading producer of trucks for the AEF by the war's end. Packard engineers also designed the Liberty aircraft engine produced by Ford Motor Company. William Durant shared Henry Ford's pacifist feelings, but General Motors (GM) also built Liberty aircraft engines. The Dodge Brothers produced "delicate recoil mechanisms" for French cannons, while the Withington Company in Jackson pressed and stamped the army's steel helmets, which were later painted and assembled at the Ford Motor Company plant in Philadelphia.[23]

Despite his earlier anti-war declarations, Henry Ford became a "fighting pacifist" as he produced a production miracle that included hundreds of submarines, tanks, and tractors. Ford contracted with the army to build a small armor-treaded vehicle called a Whippet at Ford's Highland Park Plant, but few saw active service before the war ended. The first Fordson tractor rolled off the Dearborn assembly line on April 23, 1918, and by Armistice Day, more than 26,000 had been produced. However, most arrived in Britain "too late to have any significant impact on wartime food production."

Ford also built submarine chasers for the U.S. Navy. The Eagle, a 600-ton, 204-foot-long boat constructed on the River Rouge, offered a revolutionary concept in boat building and did not "resemble anything else that floats," according to one naval officer. Ford launched its first Eagle in July 1918, and six more soon followed. Despite an 8,000-man workforce, Eagle production slowed, and the remaining boats were commissioned in 1919. It is hardly surprising that the Ford Motor Company star was the Model T, which became the "closest thing"

Trucks from Detroit's Packard Motor Company helped the Allies win World War I.

World War I offered to the Jeep of the next war. More than 125,000 Model Ts, many made by Ford Motor Company of England, served the Allied cause. Machine gun–laden Model Ts drove the Germans from their trenches in one sector of the Western Front. The Model T outperformed any other vehicle as an ambulance, most notably in the Argonne Forest, while the commanding British general in the Palestine theatre attributed Allied success to "Egyptian laborers, camels, and Ford cars." General Allenby commanded from a Rolls Royce, but he kept a Model T available as insurance.

— On the Home Front

Although the war only lasted eighteen months for Americans, Michiganians endured breadless and meatless days. Fuel shortages during the winter of 1918 caused schools and businesses to close for weeks. Michiganians also suffered from a deadly worldwide influenza epidemic that killed hundreds in Michigan in late 1918. Quarantine closed Camp Custer to visitors, while thousands of sick soldiers overwhelmed the base hospital. Churches and schools closed, and the fear of spreading the pernicious infection led Grand Rapids to cancel Christmas church services. For weeks, many Detroiters wore gauze masks hoping to avoid the flu, but "unfortunately, they did not."[24]

Michiganians took loyalty oaths, contributed to a *Detroit Free Press* tobacco fund that provided doughboys with superior American cigarettes, and stuffed Christmas stockings filled with everything from a toothbrush and chewing gum to playing cards and a compass. Detroit branches of various women's groups spent weeks putting together the city's quota of 11,000 stockings. For those in need of a last-minute gift idea for their doughboy overseas, the *Detroit Free Press* suggested soap, adding, "Don't forget that a trench isn't a snow-white boudoir."[25]

Students also stayed involved. When the draft age was lowered to eighteen years old, many males joined the Students' Army Training Corps (SATC). They were issued uniforms and received military training while continuing their academic studies at government expense. SATC enrollees numbered 1,200 at the Michigan Agricultural College and more than 4,000 at the University of Michigan. SATC also allowed smaller schools to remain open during the war.[26]

Americans also invested millions of dollars in "Liberty bonds." Even before the doughboys had reached France, Detroit newspapers carried full-page ads encouraging Michiganians to buy bonds to finance the war. One ad directed to older citizens argued:

> Few of us are destined for fame, [but] the things that make memory dear are not the deeds that we wore on the lapel of our coat for the world to see—but the victories won against ourselves, the resolutions made and kept, and the balance on the good side of the ledger of our conscience. . . . You can't sidestep duty without paying life's greatest penalty. That penalty is loss of self-esteem. . . [and] your duty [is to buy a bond]. If you spurn, now the greatest privilege of supporting your country in her crisis, you will never forgive yourself.

If subtlety did not work, scare tactics might. Accompanying an image of a menacing German soldier, another ad read in part, "Hell's own scourge is sweeping across Europe. . . . Obliterate the German ghouls 'over there.' Buy Liberty Bonds today so you won't have to pay tribute to the Kaiser later." Less than six months into the war, a letter from an anonymous young Lansing boy received much attention. Despite living with a dependent mother, which qualified him for a draft exemption, the boy refused, arguing his country needed him. The boy accepted his fate courageously but wondered why those who encouraged him to go to war (minister, grocer, banker, and even his fiancée) "will not take these bonds so the government can buy what is needed to preserve the lives of the soldiers on the field." He concluded, "I feel now that I would not care to return to a people whose patriotism consists only in the waving of flags and the singing of songs." The promotion must have worked. Michiganians exceeded the state's quota on the second bond drive by 140 percent.[27]

On April 6, 1918, the one-year anniversary of Congress's declaration of war, residents of the Oakland County community of Farmington held a "Patriotic Mass Meeting" to be among the first to buy bonds. Promotional incentives reminded potential purchasers that "your Uncle Sam has given you freedom, happiness and prosperity these many years past, and now that he is in 'straights' it surely is your duty, and should be a pleasure, to answer his appeal for help cheerfully and loyally." In case those words failed to motivate, purchasers had their names printed in the local newspaper. Farmington residents more than doubled their township's bond quota in just two days, earning a large "honor flag," with a red five-inch border and three three-inch stripes of blue across a white center. The flag flew atop a 100-foot pole on the town lawn.[28]

The home front also assisted the government in ferreting out slackers, spies, and draft dodgers. The American Protection League (APL), a private organization formed shortly after the United States entered World War I, worked with federal agencies, especially the Department of Justice, to identify potential threats to the war effort. Both male and female APL agents worked undercover and often in factories. They attended union meetings in hopes of identifying potential saboteurs, while conducting raids and detaining draft dodgers or German immigrants suspected of disloyalty. Almost 4,000 APL agents in Detroit (funded by prominent Detroit manufacturers) registered more than 30,000 complaints.

In one sympathetic postwar account, the Detroit APL provided "great assistance" to police by raiding theatres and dancehalls looking for draft dodgers, and boarded "every boat going up or down the river" to examine the papers of all passengers and crew. Detroit APL agents identified a local draft agent who took a bribe to keep a man out of the army, an action that led the agent to be sentenced to thirteen months in a federal prison. (Ironically he was sentenced on Armistice Day.) On another occasion, APL agents arrested a German navy officer who had been working in Detroit for six months. The man was jailed after confessing to "a line of information which, had the war continued longer, would have proven of the greatest importance." The national APL hailed the Detroit chapter as a "deadly efficient . . . machine of protection."[29]

—A Question of Loyalty

One disheartening aspect on the home front was the virulent sentiment directed toward German Americans. Despite a large, loyal, and well-established German-American population in the state, Michiganians viewed German Americans with suspicion, their contributions seemingly "overlooked or forgotten" and their constitutional rights violated. Some of these efforts were relatively innocuous, such as changing *hamburger* to "liberty sausage," *frankfurters* to "hot dogs," or *German measles* to "liberty measles." In Saginaw, *Germania Street* became Federal Street. In Kent County, the town of Berlin changed its name to Marne, the site of an Allied battlefield victory, while Germantown in Lapeer County became Loyal Point. Farmington's German Lutheran Church became St. Paul's Lutheran Church. Some stories even had a touch of humor. In April 1917, Theodore Valeski, a German Pole, told William Hallin in Hamtramck, "The American flag is a dirty rag and I can knock down seven Americans soldiers in a row." An irate Hallin punched Valeski, and then dragged him before a local judge. To the amazement of some, the German native judge fined Valeski fifteen dollars and "complimented Hallin."[30]

In time, the attacks became increasingly vicious. German language books were publicly burned in Menominee, while Saginaw schools stopped teaching the German language. Anyone of German heritage fell under suspicion. Even Henry Ford's personal secretary, Ernest G. Liebold, a Michigan native, saw his loyalty questioned after making the casual comment, "I think the Germans will quit before they are licked." Another Ford employee who came under fire was Carl Emde, a German-born, naturalized U.S. citizen whose work on the building of Liberty engines was deemed "impeccable." While critics admitted "nothing conclusive could be established" about Emde's loyalty, they asserted he needed to be replaced. Henry Ford stood by Emde—despite being publicly labeled a "Hun lover."[31]

One of the state's largest cities, Grand Rapids, was home to thousands of German Americans—about 10 percent of the city's population. While many German Americans supported the Allied war effort, any evidence of lukewarm support came under attack. Local editorials suggested that "if this land is good enough to live in," German immigrants should Americanize their names. The city's German language newspaper, *Germania*, lost so much advertising revenue that it discontinued service, while German language teachers were fired and the teaching of German stopped in public schools. Most of the city's German cultural organizations dissolved, and churches discontinued German language services. Under the guise of the 1918 Sedition Act, officials arrested a German barber for making pro-German statements. When asked how these actions denied German Americans their constitutional rights, a prosecutor in nearby Newaygo County responded, "We are prepared to act first, and look for explanation afterward."

As the war dragged on, attacks grew more violent. Enthusiastic students burned German books, while super-patriotic groups like the Liberty Committee confronted those whom they deemed disloyal. A mob lynched a Fremont man they labeled un-American. Just before he passed out, his attackers cut him down, shaved a German "cross" into his head, and painted the word *Hun* on his forehead. In Grand Rapids, a mob attacked the grocery store owned by a German American, painting it yellow and defacing the windows with slurs—ignoring the man's claim that he had just purchased a war bond.[32]

In Ann Arbor, University of Michigan Professors William H. Hobbs (geology) and Claude H. Van Tyne (history) led a local chapter of the National Security League, which advocated courses on patriotism and supported anything that promoted the Allies or disparaged the Germans. The League sought to rid the university of employees (everyone from professors to janitors) who failed to meet their "real American" litmus test. Early victims included members of the school's German department. In one outstanding case, several students accused Professor Carl Eggert of advocating support for Germany in his classroom. Eggert defended himself before the university's Board of Regents, although he was not allowed to question his accusers, including Professor Hobbs who had "a reputation for making wild and inaccurate claims." According to one regent, the hard evidence was less important. Instead, Eggert "was responsible for the impression that he was disloyal [and] his inability or unwillingness to negate it had rendered him useless to the university." The university dismissed Eggert, and more firings followed. The mere suspicion of disloyalty or refusing to purchase war bonds led to being sacked.[33]

As chairman of the UM History Department, Claude H. Van Tyne, a native Michiganian who had earned his bachelor's degree in Ann Arbor, had crusaded for a League program called "Patriotism through Education." The program hoped to arouse patriotic fervor in the country while crushing the Germans. This program proposed public lectures on the virtues of American democracy and a revised school curriculum "designed to instill into every student a pride of country and a hatred of adversaries." Van Tyne, who easily earned the governor's support to introduce patriotism courses in the state's public schools, envisioned two 30-minute sessions each week in Grades 7–12. The National Security League provided the necessary classroom materials. Ironically, Van Tyne's battle of democracy against tyranny duplicated a German program used in public schools "to train loyal citizens." The Michigan professor explained the Germans taught loyalty to an autocratic state, which was "ignoble," while his plan had "a very noble purpose" since it "would be spreading democracy." Van Tyne also argued that textbooks needed rewriting to lessen earlier antagonisms between the United States and Great Britain. Van Tyne finally stepped over the line when he attacked a publication endorsed by the chairman of the government's Committee on Public Information, an agency solidly committed to pro-Allied propaganda. Even before the war had ended, Professor Van Tyne devoted his full attention to his profession, which included later winning the Pulitzer Prize for his work *The War of Independence*.

Despite these vicious and fanatical attacks that contributed to a loss of cultural identity, many German Americans contributed to the American war effort. In 1918, the pastor of one German Lutheran church in suburban Detroit recognized that a proposed Independence Day celebration conflicted with the demands of his farming parishioners. He organized a Sunday, June 30 patriotic service. Festivities included hanging a 14-star flag (a star for each of the congregation's doughboys) on the altar and the singing of patriotic songs. Adopted resolutions reaffirmed the congregation's "undivided loyalty to this country," expressing "our sincere appreciation for the blessings of liberty," and pledging "ourselves anew to make every sacrifice and perform every service which will hasten the end toward which we as a nation are striving." The pastor (and the area's German community) won the support of the local newspaper editor who reminded his readers that "the German people of this section of the country are proud of their showing for Uncle Sam and their country." Elsewhere, St. Lorenz Lutheran Church in Frankenmuth sent 62 men into service, while town residents purchased $250,000 in Liberty bonds.[34]

—— Armistice Day

When the guns of the western front fell silent at 11:00 AM on November 11, 1918, Michiganians responded with understandable joy. "In practically every county auto parties laden with flags, horns, and enthusiasm scooted out into the country Paul Revere-ing the glad news to the awakening countryside," the *Detroit Free Press* reported. As police and fire trucks raced through Detroit's streets carrying the good news, "Everyone who owned a flag started a parade." Tons of confetti poured out of windows, while effigies of the German kaizer were dragged behind automobiles or hung from rooftops. Schools were closed and workers left their businesses—some after putting out a sign that read: "Too happy to work—closed." Detroit's Woodward Avenue hosted a block party as "every metal tub and every boiler" (even a bathtub) was tied behind streetcars or automobiles and dragged through the streets. Crowds filled city hall and cheered President Wilson and AEF commander General John Pershing. A man was lowered from a window down the side of the J. L.

Parades like this one in Grand Rapids for units in the 32nd Division greeted doughboys returning home in the spring of 1919.

Hudson building where a huge war map hung. As spectators on the sidewalk below watched and wondered, he drove a hole in the canvas and inserted an American flag over Berlin. Detroiters offered "a howl of appreciation." Outstate, Civil War veterans marched in Ypsilanti, work in the Copper Country was suspended, and thousands joyously paraded in Calumet, while Ann Arbor sponsored an impromptu parade where university medical students rode on a float around a table where the German kaiser was "industriously dissected." In Sault Ste. Marie, an effigy of the kaiser was riddled with bullets before being set ablaze, while in Kalamazoo, an overly enthusiastic sheriff released his prisoners so they could join the celebrating crowds. Most inmates never returned to the jail. The day's revelry turned tragic with several accidental deaths and some injuries. Responding to a request for "aerial entertainment," the army provided four planes to circle over Detroit. Each pilot tried to outdo the other as they thrilled the crowd by performing various loops and stunts. After "darting around the confining spaces" of the city's buildings, U.S. Army Lieutenant Clifford Morrow struck the flagpole on top of the Fyfe Building. His plane spiraled out of control, but Morrow gained enough control to crash it two blocks from Campus Martius, avoiding the celebrating throngs below. Miraculously, only Morrow died in the crash.[35]

More than six months later, the veterans of the 32nd Division arrived in Detroit where they were greeted with "Red Arrow Day." As 4,000 doughboys paraded through the city's streets and flags were waved "by the millions," Detroiters hosted an open-air ballroom for "Les Terribles." Dancing continued well into the night and only ended with the arrival of a rainstorm. Defeating Germany on the battlefield had been relatively easy for the Americans. However, success in a wartime-related reform known simply as Prohibition posed a more elusive challenge than all the kaiser's armies and submarines.[36]

CHAPTER

15

The Raucous Twenties

Detroit law enforcement officers admire a cache of alcohol captured in a raid, a common scene during Prohibition.

The U.S. government would have to employ an inspector for every man, woman, and child who crosses the ferry from Windsor to Detroit. It would have to line the shore for thirty miles with armed guards to hold up and search every craft that tries to land and then it would not begin to make serious inroads on the operations of rum runners. . . . Canada is the bootleggers' paradise and Detroit is their Klondike.

—*New York Times,* June 27, 1927

Besides an effort to "make the world safe for democracy," World War I also promoted two Progressive Era reforms—Prohibition and women's suffrage—that left a noticeable imprint on Michigan.

Although efforts to regulate alcohol in Michigan began before the Civil War, they enjoyed little success until the founding of the Anti-Saloon League in 1895. The league undertook a campaign to rid America of saloons, which one Michigan advocate pointed out contributed "so largely to human sor-row." Using an "economic argument," the League maintained saloons left workers inefficient, careless, and less punctual. Furthermore, scientific studies showed that alcohol slowed the brain and nervous system, leading to worker inefficiency. These conditions proved particularly detrimental for assembly line workers, which led automakers to become staunch prohibitionists. Automaker R. E. Olds hired detectives to report on the drinking habits of his workers, while the Ford Motor Company monitored the lifestyles of its workers. As Henry Ford explained, if a worker did not stop drinking, "we simply let him go." Increasingly, businessmen jumped on the "dry" wagon, especially as League studies showed that a sober citizenry meant "less crime, poverty, disease, and disorder and as a result less need for tax dollars to support prisons, police, hospitals, mental institutions, orphanages, and charitable organizations." By the eve of World War I, almost half of the state's 83 counties had voted to go dry, putting thousands of saloons and many breweries out of business.[1]

Churches also took up the Prohibition cause. In Detroit, 100 churches sponsored a visit by the nationally recognized evangelist William "Billy" Sunday, whose "Booze Sermon" condemned alcohol for destroying families and creating criminals. Described as "the Democratic convention, the circus, the World Series, the Chautauqua, and a declaration of war all rolled into one," the Reverend Sunday arrived in Detroit on September 9, 1916. Preaching 120 sermons to thousands of enthusiastic followers over an eight-week period, Sunday labeled booze "the blood sucker of humanity [and] God's worst enemy and hell's best friend." Sunday ended his Michigan visit in Grand Rapids, where he stood on a stage waving an American flag while an audience of 7,000 men vowed to make Michigan dry. The next day, November 7, they and thousands of other Michiganians went to the polls and overwhelmingly supported a constitutional amendment prohibiting "the manufacture, sale, keeping for sale, giving away, bartering, or furnishing [alcoholic beverages] except for medicinal, chemical, scientific or sacramental purposes" beginning May 1, 1918. The Michigan vote had national ramifications since no state east of the Mississippi River and no city as large as Detroit had gone dry. Joyous prohibitionists hailed their Michigan victory as "the beginning of the end for the liquor traffic in the entire country." Closing saloons would make Michigan a better place to live and would aid the war effort by feeding people grain that had been used for booze. In the process, brewers and distilleries became both enemies of temperance and "enemies of peace."[2]

—— The Prohibition Era Begins

Adopting Prohibition proved easier than enforcing it. In their zealousness
to outlaw saloons, moderates accepted "bone-dry" Prohibition. But closing
saloons did not reduce crime. At first, the problem came from the south as
smugglers used a variety of creative ways to bring booze from "wet" Ohio.
Train and bus travelers between Toledo and Detroit filled suitcases and bags
with booze, while others filled everything from dolls to hollowed-out loaves of
bread with whiskey. Hiding spaces in vehicles carried booze, and one enterprising Detroit mechanic modified gas tanks with two compartments—one
for gas and the other for booze. Along the Dixie Highway between Toledo
and Detroit (nicknamed the "Avenue de Booze"), police arrested hundreds
of smugglers and seized tens of thousands of bottles of booze headed north
to sell for four times their Ohio cost. On one occasion, the overzealous state
troopers placed two stops along the highway. If a smuggler sped through the
first stop, officers at the second stop dropped a telephone pole across the
road. Following an incident when a smuggler hit the pole going 70 miles per
hour, propelling him and dozens of bottles of whiskey into the air, the police
ended the practice explaining, "higher ups seemed to think it a bit informal."
(Amazingly, no one was killed.)[3]

More seriously, police grew careless interpreting the law, especially in
obtaining search warrants to raid private residences. One notable raid on
the home of the editor of Detroit's German language newspaper landed in
court and led the Michigan Supreme Court to declare prohibition and its
enforcement legislation unconstitutional. The court's February 1919 decision resulted in "The Great Booze Rush," a phenomenon that witnessed
"eighty cars a minute" racing into the city from Ohio "loaded with liquor."
The enthusiasm lasted less than a day until Michigan Attorney General Alexander Groesbeck secured a temporary injunction restraining anyone from
bringing booze into the state. The Michigan legislature followed with a more
stringent enforcement law that elevated violating prohibition laws to a felony,
allowing police to enforce the law using firearms, while not requiring them to
obtain a search warrant if they had reasonable suspicion. First-time violators
suffered a possible $1,000 fine and one-year imprisonment. The law passed
the House (82-6) and the Senate (30-0) without any debate and took immediate effect.[4]

As Michigan worked to enforce Prohibition, Congress adopted a Prohibition amendment to the U.S. Constitution. Both Michigan senators and eleven

of the state's thirteen congressmen voted for the Eighteenth Amendment. (The two exceptions were Detroit Democrats.) The Michigan legislature ratified the amendment on January 3, 1919, and two weeks later, Nebraska became the 36th state to approve it. Congress then approved the Volstead Act, an enforcement measure that outlawed intoxicating liquors—any beverage containing over 0.5 percent alcohol—with the exception of alcoholic beverages for medicinal, sacramental, and industrial purposes. When national prohibition went into effect on January 17, 1920, one smug temperance advocate maintained that only "traitors or Bolsheviks" opposed Prohibition. It would not be that simple.[5]

—— Border Problems

The issue of enforcing Prohibition turned to the international border with Canada. In early 1920, all Canadian provinces except Quebec chose to continue their wartime Prohibition experience. However, the Canadian federal government allowed distilleries and breweries to manufacture booze for export. More than two dozen breweries and sixteen distilleries operated in Ontario, including several of the largest located near the Detroit River. At the same time, Ontario residents—who could not purchase booze from retail stores—ordered it from Quebec through the mail for private consumption. Canadians quickly seized the obvious opportunity of quenching a growing American thirst. During the first nine months of 1920, Windsor and its nearby communities received 900,000 cases of booze. According to one estimate, 25 percent of Ontario residents living on the border engaged in the illegal liquor business.[6]

Canadian officials often looked the other way, since they collected millions of dollars in tax revenue. More important, the Michigan-Ontario border became a battleground as U.S. law enforcement agencies attempted to stop the flow of liquor into the country. Hardly a day went by without an article in a major newspaper or magazine highlighting the activities of the police or the bootleggers. Cases involving the violation of Prohibition laws also clogged the local court system as an estimated 75 percent of all alcohol imported into the United States during these years came through a 30-mile stretch from Lake Erie to Lake St. Clair. The Detroit River, less than a mile wide, could be crossed in a powerboat in five minutes, and the many islands, docks, and miles of deserted shoreline provided plenty of hiding places. After several years of trying to contain smugglers, a leading U.S. official noted, "The Lord probably could have built a river better suited for rum-smug-

These entrepreneurs, who tried crossing Lake St. Clair with a beer-laden truck, experienced one of the risks of smuggling alcohol into Michigan from Ontario.

gling, but the Lord probably never did." Mocking the newly opened tunnel between Detroit and Windsor, the porous border between the two countries was called "The Windsor-Detroit Funnel." According to one observer, Detroit had two industries: making automobiles and distributing Canadian booze.[7]

Law enforcement agencies faced determined smugglers committed to bring booze across the border. Boats of all sizes were used during warm weather. In winter, trucks replaced the boats to cross the frozen river. More ingenious ways included pulling whiskey-filled torpedo-like tubes across the river or even using electrically controlled torpedoes that carried 50 gallons of whiskey. Smugglers even laid pipes under the river and pumped alcohol from a Canadian bottling facility. Small-time smugglers used hot water bottles, rubber chest protectors, and even hollowed-out eggs. As a *New York Times* reporter observed after visiting Detroit in 1927:

> The U.S. government would have to employ an inspector for every man, woman, and child who crosses the ferry from Windsor to Detroit. It would have to line the shore for thirty miles with armed guards to hold up and search every craft that tries to land and then it would not begin to make serious inroads on the operations of rum runners. . . . Canada is the bootleggers' paradise and Detroit is their Klondike.

The attraction was money, and the profits were enormous. Windsor residents got rich, as did many Michiganians. By the late 1920s, the Detroit Board of Commerce reported the illegal booze business provided employment for 50,000 people and had an annual value of $400 million. The flow of cash money also involved organized crime, most notably Detroit's Purple Gang, whose customers included thousands of Detroit speakeasies and Chicago's Alfonse Capone.[8]

In 1925, an estimated 15,000 "blind pigs" or speakeasies (illegal drinking establishments) operated in Detroit (increasing to as many as 25,000 a few years later). One speakeasy even served customers in a building next to a Hamtramack police station. Residents who wished to avoid any risks associated with a blind pig made their own booze. Authorities estimated that 5,000 stills operated in Detroit in 1928. Besides beer and wine, "in thousands of warehouses, garages, vacant factories, attics, basements, and even in an abandoned church, heated corn mash produced hundreds of thousands of gallons of Detroit 'white lightning.'"[9]

—— An Unenforceable Law

No matter what officials did, they could not stop the flow of illegal booze. The fight raged for thirteen years, and law enforcement never got an upper hand in the battle. Part of the problem lay with inadequate funding. Seized rum-running boats left at an unguarded wharf on Lake St. Clair were soon back in action. Bribes also posed a major problem, and hundreds of officials went to jail for accepting money to close their eyes to the smugglers' activities. Since the annual salary of a U.S. Customs official was less than $2,000, it was no understatement when one agent reported being offered $1,500 a week just "to look the other way." He refused, but added that "the temptation was great!" Enforcement posed problems even away from the border. At first, the Jackson County sheriff arrested rumrunners who passed through his county from Detroit to Chicago. Then he had a change of heart, realizing there was money to be made if he just charged them a toll. If they refused to pay, he confiscated their car and sold the liquor to the local blind pigs. Under these circumstances, it is no surprise that the head of the Michigan State Police declared, "We could not enforce the prohibition law in Michigan if we had the U.S. standing army. As long as the people maintain their present attitude toward prohibition, the law is unenforceable."[10]

As the 1920s dragged on, it seemed increasingly clear the Prohibition war was lost. In May 1927, more than 400,000 cases of whiskey arrived in Detroit from Ontario distilleries, while in the twelve-month period ending in March 1928, 3.1 million gallons of beer arrived in Michigan from Windsor—and these figures did not include home brew. At best, authorities intercepted only 5 percent of the booze smuggled across the border.[11]

The desire to have a drink, coupled with enforcement issues, left the Detroit River particularly dangerous. Pleasure boats risked being caught in a crossfire between the "Prohibition Navy" and rumrunners. An increasing number of Michiganians also questioned the harsh laws enforcing Prohibition—and the attitudes of those enforcing them. According to the Wayne County Prosecuting Attorney Robert Toms, "the greatest obstacle" to enforcing Prohibition was the U.S. Constitution. Toms complained the court's liberal interpretation of the search and seizure thwarted efforts to enforce Prohibition. "Until the courts changed their interpretation of the law, it would be necessary to break the law to enforce it," he claimed. The severity of the punishments also led to concern. By the late 1920s, four-time Michigan offenders could receive life sentences. Finally, there were the stories about a double standard at work—everything from a Lapeer County Anti-Saloon League leader arrested for selling a variety of different homemade booze (he claimed the discovery by undercover agents was unfair), to stories about prominent state officials (including former Governor Fred Green) engaged in drunken revelry.[12]

—— Racism Rears Its Ugly Head

As law enforcement struggled with the losing battle of Prohibition, racism reared its ugly head. During the early decades of the twentieth century, Detroit grew rapidly as southern blacks and European immigrants arrived by the thousands. Between 1910 and 1930, the city's black population increased from fewer than 6,000 people to more than 125,000. At the same time, immigrants from Poland, Italy, and other mostly Catholic nations settled in the Motor City. Although racism had not been an issue in late nineteenth century Detroit, religious intolerance found some support. During the 1890s, the city served as the home for a national anti-Catholic organization. By the 1920s, many white Protestant Detroiters grew apprehensive watching their city become multi-ethnic, multi-religious, and multi-racial. Those who feared the change turned to the Ku Klux Klan, which burst onto the scene, especially in northern cities, during the early 1920s. On April 4, 1923, 8,000 Klansmen gathered near Royal Oak and listened intently as a Klan leader ranted about the superiority of white people.[13]

Klan enthusiasm reached beyond Detroit, and by the fall of 1923, "crosses blazed across Michigan illuminating people who were persuaded their flag and God needed them in the ranks of the Klan." While membership estimates varied (70,000 to 265,000), the Michigan Klan had more members than any southern state and ranked as high as seventh among all states. The Klan's magazine, *Fiery Cross*, even printed a Michigan edition. The legislature responded by banning masks at rallies, but that did not slow down the KKK. At a Christmas Eve rally in downtown Detroit, a masked Santa Claus led Klansmen (crowd estimates varied from 4,000 to 25,000) in the Lord's Prayer, while a cross burned on the steps of the Wayne County Building. In mid-1924, Klonvocations held near Jackson and in Lansing drew thousands.[14]

Some communities offered a resounding "no" to the Klan. One Upper Peninsula newspaper explained why the Klan received little enthusiasm in its town:

We have a few Jews in the Upper Peninsula, and our observation and knowledge of them is that they measure up most credibly as American citizens. They are good friends and good neighbors. . . . We also have a few Negroes in this peninsula and . . . they average up well as citizens. . . . As for Catholics, approximately one-third of the population of the peninsula are adherents of that faith.

A Newberry newspaper grumbled, "We have enough troubles around these parts without the Ku Klux Klan 'butting in,'" while local officials in both Mt. Pleasant and Traverse City denied the Klan permission to hold rallies on public land. The Mt. Pleasant Chamber of Commerce went further, urging "all loyal members and peace loving citizens to use their utmost influence to stop all efforts of the Ku Klux Klan "[15]

Not all communities took such bold action. On one occasion, a group of forty robed Klansmen arrived unexpectedly at a well-attended service at a Lansing protestant church. As historian JoEllen McNergney Vinyard recounts, "In a ceremony typical at sympathetic congregations, they paraded to the front of the church where their spokesman addressed the pastor, praised him for his patriotic principles, and then presented him with a Bible, a bouquet of white lilies, plus a silk American flag for the church." The Detroit Council of Churches even tacitly accepted the KKK's use of violence, tabling a motion to condemn the group's brutal tactics by a vote of 26 to 20.[16]

The Klan flexed its newfound muscle by supporting a KKK-leaning Republican candidate for governor and a measure outlawing parochial schools. Despite defeats on both fronts, the KKK also actively supported the write-in candidacy of Charles Bowles for Detroit mayor. One evening in mid-1924, thousands of Klansmen, chanting "Bowles, Bowles, Bowles," marched down Woodward Avenue to disrupt an anti-KKK rally, forcing the police to use tear gas and "flying wedges" to disperse the Klansmen. On the Saturday before the election, the Klan held its biggest Detroit rally, gathering an estimated 50,000 members in a Dearborn field where a large flaming cross lit up the evening skies. In one of the city's most contested elections, Bowles finished a close second place in a three-way race. Supporters argued that the city's decision to disallow certain write-in ballots cost Bowles the election. Some national observers shuddered at how a KKK-endorsed write-in candidate came close to becoming mayor of the nation's fourth largest city. Despite the electoral disappointment, the Klan hoped to recover some of its prestige as Detroit turned its attention to the issue of integrated neighborhoods.[17]

During the 1920s, the Ku Klux Klan claimed tens of thousands of members in Michigan.

——Segregation in Detroit

During the summer of 1925, one young black doctor declared, "We have decided we are not going to run. We're not going to look for any trouble, but we're going to be prepared to protect ourselves if trouble arises." With these firm words, Dr. Ossian Sweet prepared to confront the bigoted—and sometimes violent—world of segregated housing in Detroit. Sweet could not have anticipated the challenge that lay ahead.[18]

During the early 1920s, most Detroit blacks, who represented 7 percent of the city's population, lived in Black Bottom (ironically also called Paradise Valley), a ghetto on the city's near eastside of downtown that included only 1 percent of the city's housing. Besides extreme overcrowding where families shared apartments, living conditions in Black Bottom "pushed the limits of endurance. According to historian Kevin Boyle:

> There were houses in the central section of Black Bottom where the water cascaded through the ceiling every time it rained; houses where the walls were so sodden the tenants had to pull their beds into the center of the room so they wouldn't spend the night drenched to the skin; houses where the plaster on the walls had crumbled so that the wind whistled through the exposed laths; houses without glass in the window frames all winter long. Toilets stopped up and overflowed. Kitchen sinks spigots that spewed rust red water. And in half the houses of Black Bottom, there was no running water at all. To fill a cooking pot, a tenant had to prime the backyard pump. To relieve himself, he had to endure the outhouse fending off the swarm of flies in the summertime, the cutting cold in the winter, and the stomach-churning stench any time of the year.

Disease, especially pneumonia and tuberculosis, proved "a constant threat" because people lived too close and "no one was vaccinated." Then there was the matter of police harassment. During the first half of 1925, the police shot 55 black males, and some had even been executed.[19]

White Detroiters also intended to keep the city segregated. Realtors conspired to keep black families out of white neighborhoods, and in 1923, the Michigan Supreme Court gave its blessing to private restrictive covenants. House appraisers also "made it official practice to downgrade the value of any neighborhood that had even a single black resident." This practice made it difficult—if not impossible—for blacks to get a mortgage. Violence also proved an effective segregation tool. During the summer of 1925, at least five black families had been driven from homes purchased in white neighborhoods. The most spectacular incident involved Dr. Alexander Turner, one of the city's most prominent black doctors. Only hours after he moved into a white neighborhood, a mob ransacked his house and Turner narrowly escaped with his life. Rattled by the experience, he signed over the deed to the neighborhood's "improvement society" that same day.[20]

—— Ossian Sweet

Ossian Sweet, a native Floridian and a graduate of Wilberforce University (Ohio) and Howard University, arrived in Detroit in 1921. After setting up his practice, he met and married Gladys Mitchell, a native Detroiter, who had grown up in a white neighborhood where she experienced few racial problems. In October 1923, Dr. Sweet and his pregnant wife headed abroad for postgraduate studies in Vienna and Paris. A year later, the Sweets, with their young daughter (whose delivery had been denied at the all-white American hospital in suburban Paris), returned to Detroit. Upwardly mobile and rejecting Black Bottom, the Sweets bought a house on Garland Avenue in a white, working-class neighborhood a few blocks beyond a predominantly black neighborhood. The sellers, a light-skinned black couple, had received death threats when word leaked out about the sale. At the same time, white residents formed an "improvement society," proclaiming their intent to keep blacks out of the neighborhood.[21]

The day after Labor Day in 1925, the Sweets quietly moved into their new house as a white crowd watched silently from across the street. The next night, the crowd returned, turned into a mob, and started throwing stones at the Sweet home. The Sweets had come prepared. Haunted by an episode from his youth when a white mob poured kerosene on a black man and then cheered as the man burned to death, Sweet brought allies (his brother and several friends) and a supply of weapons to his new home. As the rocks continued to rain down on the house, shots rang out, leaving one white man dead and another wounded. The police, who had been on the scene but did nothing to control the mob, arrested the eleven people in the house and charged them with first-degree murder. Bail was denied, but Mrs. Sweet was released.[22]

The judge for the ensuing trial was 35-year-old Frank Murphy, who took the case despite noting, "Every judge on this bench is afraid to take this case.

They think it's dynamite." The National Association for the Advancement of Colored People (NAACP), which campaigned to end segregated housing and establish the rights of blacks to defend their homes, provided the Sweets with defense counsel. They hired Clarence Darrow, one of the nation's most skilled defense attorneys and a man who had "a long record of championing the rights of African Americans."[23]

To prove the Sweets had not been provoked, the prosecution offered numerous witnesses who claimed nothing unusual occurred outside the Sweet house that night. Darrow countered by exposing one witness who admitted rehearsing his testimony with police. Even more damaging, another witness saw "a considerable mob [between] 400 and 500" and learned from a white man in the crowd, "A Negro family has moved in here and we're going to get them out." The prosecution contended the trial had nothing to do with race. Darrow argued at great length the trial had everything to do with race. Benefitting from a sympathetic judge who admitted privately he wanted "the defendants to know that true justice does not recognize color," the famed attorney offered a powerful, spellbinding closing argument. Darrow concluded, "The question is what a colored man, a reasonable colored man with his knowledge of what mobs do and have done to colored people when they have the power," had done.[24]

After nearly seven weeks of trial, the all-white jury deliberated for three days and nights without reaching a verdict. Judge Murphy declared a mistrial as newspapers reported five of the jurors favored acquittal. Whites pressured the prosecution to refile charges against Ossian's brother, Henry, who admitted firing shots from the house that night. The second trial dragged into 1926 but offered no new evidence. Once again, Darrow provided the defense and a remarkable eight-hour summation that one sympathetic observer noted was "the most wonderful flow of words I have ever heard from a man's lips." After four hours of deliberation, the all-white jury found Henry Sweet not guilty.[25]

Darrow's successes "were surprising and important victories for integration," but predictions of a new era of improved race relations for Detroit proved premature. As for Ossian Sweet, tragedy hounded him. The Sweets' two-year-old daughter died of tuberculosis shortly after the second trial ended, and the disease soon took Gladys, as well as Henry. Dr. Sweet remarried twice, enjoyed a period of financial security, and lived in the Garland Avenue house for years without any further incident. But a loss of income, which forced him to sell his house to avoid foreclosure, contributed to his depression and undoubtedly led him to take his own life in 1960. While segregated housing did not magically end in Detroit, the activities of the Ku Klux

Klan disappeared from the front pages. By 1928, the Detroit Klan had only a few hundred members.[26]

During the 1920s, Republicans dominated Michigan government and the party's leading—and often controversial—figure was Alexander Groesbeck. Born in Macomb County and a graduate of the University of Michigan Law School, Groesbeck established a law practice in Detroit that flourished. After serving two terms as state attorney general, Groesbeck was elected governor in 1922. Critical of the state's inefficient and cumbersome administrative policies, Groesbeck initiated a reorganization of state government. He created the State Administrative Board, which included the governor and other department leaders. The board drew up a budget to guide the legislature in appropriations (the first time in Michigan history), set up a centralizing purchasing system so that the state could save money by buying wholesale, and devised a uniform accounting system. The governor also emerged with veto power over board actions, leaving him "the most powerful executive officer in the state government." The board also merged 33 independent or semi-independent agencies into five departments (Agriculture, Labor, Conservation, Public Safety, and Welfare). Groesbeck's many initiatives included centralizing road planning and construction financed by a new two-cent-per-gallon gas tax. The monies improved 6,500 miles of road and built 2,000 miles of hard-surfaced road, as well as Michigan's first superhighway. However, the frequent use of his veto power, combined with "his brusque manner and his no-nonsense attitude," led to comparisons with Italian dictator Benito Mussolini. Dissatisfaction among some Republicans, coupled with a rebellion among some Administrative Board members, led to Groesbeck's downfall. After being denied his party's nomination for a fourth term, he sought the governorship in 1930 and 1934 without success.[27]

—— Women Demand the Vote

The 1920s also marked a richly deserved victory for women, who finally earned the right to vote. The issue of women's rights in Michigan began as early as the 1840s when Ernestine L. Rose became the first woman to address the state legislature. A Polish native who migrated to the United States with her English husband in the mid-1830s, Rose spent three decades advocating women's rights. A year after her 1846 Michigan visit, a few state legislators responded favorably to the notion of granting women the right to vote. Most others, however, ridiculed the notion.[28]

Rose's actions inspired other women to pursue equal rights, including future leaders Susan B. Anthony and Elizabeth Cady Stanton. In 1848, women's rights advocates gathered in Seneca Falls, New York, where they adopted a "Declaration of Sentiments," which stressed women's rights. But little happened. In Michigan, the 1850 state constitution granted women the right to own property but ignored the issue of voting.[29]

After the Civil War, black males received the right to vote under the Fifteenth Amendment, an issue that angered some women. Black leader Sojourner Truth, who moved to Battle Creek in 1857, declared, "There is a great stir about colored men getting their rights, but not a word about the colored women. . . . I am for keeping the thing going while things are stirring; because if we wait till it is still, it will take a great while to get it going again." Truth even tried voting in the 1872 presidential election but was turned away. A year earlier, two Michigan women did vote—Mary Wilson in Battle Creek and Nannette B. Gardner in Detroit. The details about Mary Wilson are unclear, but Mrs. Gardner was a wealthy widow who "convinced an alderman that he should register her because she had no husband to protect her interests." On election day, Gardner voted, giving the election inspectors a vase of flowers as a token of appreciation. She also voted in future elections although "no other woman was able to get herself registered."[30]

In 1884, various state suffrage organizations gathered in Flint and created the Michigan Equal Suffrage Association (MESA)—Michigan's first statewide suffrage association. Over the course of the next three decades, the MESA educated Michiganians about the merits of enfranchising women, while countering the claims of anti-suffragists. Working out of offices in most large Michigan cities, suffragists gave speeches, picketed the state capital, and handed out pamphlets at fairs and parades, while advertising through banners, postcards, pins, and playing cards. They also lobbied elected officials with varying success. In 1886, both the Republicans and Democrats rejected a suffragist request to address the parties' state conventions. On several occasions, the state House supported a bill giving women the vote in municipal elections, only to see the measure rejected by the state Senate. Finally, in 1893, the bill passed both houses, but included an educational requirement that did not exist for men. In the same year, the Michigan Supreme Court struck down the law, arguing that the legislature did not have the power to create "a new class of voters."[31]

Although the court's ruling proved a major setback, the suffragists vigorously lobbied the all-male delegates to the 1907 state constitutional convention, submitting a petition carrying 225,000 signatures (the vast majority from

Devoted Michigan suffragettes (like these women in Grand Rapids) lobbied fervently to enfranchise women.

women) hoping the new document would enfranchise women. By a vote of 57 to 38, the delegates rejected the idea. Opponents feared that placing equal suffrage in the constitution would lead voters to reject the entire document. The constitution, which voters later approved, gave tax-paying women the right to vote on "any public question relating to the public expenditure of money or the issuing of bonds."

The chance for success improved when Governor Chase Salmon Osborn convinced the legislature to place the issue on the November 1912 ballot. MESA staff members traveled the state distributing "more than three tons of suffrage literature and paraphernalia." They even provided trained poll watchers to watch for possible infractions or voter intimidation. The early returns seemed encouraging, but the final totals showed the amendment had been defeated by 762 votes. Upon closer examination, voter fraud ran rampant. Ballot boxes disappeared, ballots were burned before a recount could be held, tally sheets were misplaced and, in some districts, the total number of votes outnumbered registered voters.

The MESA ignored the election irregularities and worked to resubmit the ballot for the spring 1913 elections, while confronting an invigorated anti-suffragist movement. Formed in 1913, the Michigan Association Opposed to Woman Suffrage (MAOWS) believed that giving women the right to vote would tarnish a women's character, and leave women "demoralized" and suffering physically. According to the widely circulated MAOWS literature, women were unfit for political life since they were "unreliable, inconsistent and easily influenced." One MAOWS flier happily concluded, as "long as women make the men of the country they can afford to let these men make the laws."

Although MESA fought to counter these arguments, it was to no avail as male voters overwhelmingly rejected the ballot measure. Despite yet another setback, suffragists remained focused and convinced the legislature to place the measure on the ballot once again. In November 1917, male voters approved unrestricted equal suffrage by a 34,000 margin (of more than 400,000 votes cast). The success lay with the adoption of Prohibition that left the liquor interests disorganized and unable to focus on opposing the enfranchise measure as they had in earlier votes. Another explanation may have been the role of women working outside the home during these early months of U.S. involvement in the Great War. Regardless, Michigan joined New York as the only two states east of the Mississippi River that gave women full voting rights. Michigan women registered in great numbers and in March 1919, 50 percent voted in the spring elections.

As Michigan women headed to the polls, Congress sent the Nineteenth Amendment, which enfranchised women, to the states. On June 10, 1919, Michigan became one of the first two states to ratify the measure. In 1920, Michigan women voted for the first time in a presidential election. In that same year, a slate of women candidates, later nicknamed "the Petticoat Rulers," swept into office in Jackson—among the first cities to have a woman as mayor. As one Michigan historian of the women's suffrage movement concluded, "With national suffrage secure, women turned their attention to another issue—equal rights. One struggle had ended; another had begun."

—— Anna Howard Shaw

One leading national suffrage advocate with solid early Michigan connections was Dr. Anna Howard Shaw. Born in England, six-year-old Shaw and her family immigrated to the United States in 1853. Three years later, they settled in a log cabin in the northern Michigan wilderness "40 miles from a post office and 100 miles from a railroad." The pioneer experience was not kind to Shaw, and the bitter recollections of her youth in Michigan "make up the most powerful section" of her memoirs. After attending high school in Big Rapids and graduating from Albion College in 1875, Shaw earned theological and medical degrees and became the first woman ordained by the Methodist Protestant church. A powerful speaker, Shaw developed friendships with Julia Ward Howe, Mary A. Livermore, and Susan B. Anthony that led her to leadership roles with the National Woman's Suffrage Association (NWSA). The NWSA enjoyed years "marked by unprecedented progress" while she was president (1904–1915). Membership increased twelvefold to 200,000 members, "while the number of states with full suffrage grew from four to twelve, and the whole suffrage movement changed from an academic discussion to a vital political force arousing the attention of the entire nation." Shaw spoke in every state and before many state legislatures and congressional committees. She also earned accolades for serving as the chairman of the Committee of Women's Defense Work during World War I. Two episodes reveal her staunch feminism. As a minister she would not perform a marriage ceremony "in which it was insisted that the word 'obey' be used." Although opposing militant suffrage tactics, like the 1917 picketing of the White House, Shaw fought "a lively skirmish" with local tax collectors in her Philadelphia-area home in the days before women could vote, asserting that "taxation without representation was tyranny."[32]

—— The End of Prohibition

As the 1920s ended, the distractions of enforcing Prohibition—coupled with a worsening depression that hit Michigan severely in the early 1930s—led to a growing chorus demanding repeal of America's great temperance experiment. From Prohibition's earliest days, critics sought to revise the Eighteenth Amendment, especially the definition of "intoxicating beverage." A Michigan chapter of the Association Against the Prohibition Amendment (AAPA), which viewed Prohibition as a "dangerous over extension of the powers of the federal government," formed in 1921. The AAPA acknowledged temperance was "a good thing," but bone-dry prohibition "had produced a plague rather than a paradise." In 1925, the *Detroit Free Press* announced its support for repeal, labeling the Eighteenth Amendment "a fearful error" and determining that moderating Prohibition laws was the nation's "most pressing domestic problem." A growing chorus of prominent critics included Senator James Couzens, Governor Fred Green, and Henry B. Joy, president of the Packard

Motor Car Company, once an active Anti-Saloon League member. General Motors Chairman Alfred P. Sloan, Jr., also abandoned bone-dry Prohibition and argued that repeal promised a "real foundation [for] renewed prosperity." Newly formed women's groups, often led by Republicans, also added their voices calling for repeal. Inflexible dry critics included Congressman Louis Crampton (R-Lapeer), who argued bootleggers and criminals posed no real danger to the country. In Lansing, efforts in the state legislature to redefine intoxicating beverage failed, while in Washington all but two members of Michigan's congressional delegation continued to support bone-dry Prohibition.[33]

The Great Depression invigorated repeal advocates who maintained that ending Prohibition meant raising revenue through licensing and taxation, while guaranteeing manufacturing jobs as unemployment worsened. Repeal also meant Michiganians could stay home and drink, rather than cross into Ontario where Prohibition had ended. Repeal also promised a return to law and order, as well as an end to the federal government's abuse of states' rights. Repeal also might end the growing radicalism caused by the economic setbacks. Congressman Robert Clancy (D-Detroit), who labeled the Eighteenth Amendment a "grievous wrong," feared that rising unemployment numbers and Prohibition fed appeals for communism.[34]

In November 1932, Michigan—along with the nation—turned to the Democrats, who supported repeal. Early the following year, the Democratic majority in the Congress moved quickly, submitting the Twenty-first Amendment (repealing the Prohibition amendment) to the states. Michigan voters went to polls on April 3, 1933, selecting delegates (one from each legislature district) to consider the repeal. Ten days later, the delegates met in Lansing and ratified the repeal by a vote of 99 to 1. (The lone "dry" delegate was Eugene Davenport of Hastings.) Appropriately, Michigan became the first state to ratify Prohibition's repeal.[35]

As other states quickly ratified the Twenty-first Amendment, the Michigan legislature legalized 3.2 beer and wine and set May 11 as the date for legal consumption. However, a special exemption for the American Legion convention in Detroit allowed veterans to celebrate on May 10. Celebrate they did—drinking 300 half-barrels and 500 cases of Stroh's beer. The next day, Stroh's Brewery president Julius Stroh, who reassured Detroiters his company's beer was "equal, if not superior" to the beer it had once brewed, poured the first glass of legal beer in Michigan in fifteen years. The arrival of legal beer received little attention. Then again, it had never been too difficult to find a drink in Detroit during Prohibition.[36]

CHAPTER
16

The Great
Depression
and Growth
of Labor

Joyous UAW sit-downers mark the end of a 44-day
strike that revolutionized the auto industry.

"Government was conceived for the shielding of
men, women, boys and girls from economic and
social processes over which they have no control
with which they can't cope unaided."

—Detroit mayor Frank Murphy, November 1930

"We were desperate, just desperate," one Detroiter remembered. "We saw people's lives fall apart because they didn't have any money." The early 1930s was a time of enormous suffering and turmoil as thousands of Americans lost their jobs, life savings vanished as banks suddenly closed, families went hungry and lost their homes because mortgages could not be paid, and suicides increased and marriages foundered. Industrial Michigan faced unprecedented obstacles, especially in Detroit, which was the "hardest hit big city in the nation." The strains of the Depression, which also produced demagogues and threats of revolution, pitted Americans against each other and led many to wonder when—or if—the economic turmoil would end.[1]

274

For many Michiganians, especially autoworkers, the 1920s had been prosperous times. The American automobile industry flourished, and workers were well paid. Some observers, however, feared for the future, including Senator James Couzens of Michigan. Secretary of the Ford Motor Company before being elected mayor of Detroit in 1918, Couzens (a Republican appointed to the Senate in 1922) understood the problems caused when the auto plants closed each summer to prepare to build the new models. Many workers called these layoffs their "starvation vacation." As one autoworker remembered, "I don't know how the laid-off autoworkers with families to support managed to live during those payless weeks. There was no unemployment compensation to tide them over until they returned to work." Credited with inspiring the Ford Motor Company's five-dollar workday, Couzens believed that in a democracy a man had a right "to preserve himself and his family from suffering and want." He proposed that in times of economic depression

James Couzens was an automaker, politician, and philanthropist.

the federal government should create public works programs for the unemployed. He also recommended that the government establish an old-age pension for workers. Finally, the former automaker argued that the government needed to end the great frenzy of speculation that left the stock market unstable and invited disaster. In February 1927, Couzens predicted that "times are not too good and it is my impression that they will be worse before they are better." The lawmaker's suggestions were ignored, but his worst fears soon came true.[2]

—— The Great Depression

In October 1929, the stock market crashed, ushering in the Great Depression, which had a devastating effect on heavily industrialized states like Michigan. A cycle of economic collapse followed the crash. Workers lost their jobs because of industrial cutbacks. Industries could not hire workers because there was no market for their goods. There was no market because the workers had no money to buy goods. The workers had no money because industries could not hire them.

Few Americans escaped the effects of the Depression, especially in Michigan where one out of every six jobs was tied to the auto industry. Throughout the 1920s, auto production had grown, peaking at more than five million units in 1929. In 1930, American automakers produced three million vehicles; by 1932 the figure had fallen to 1.3 million. Poor car sales mirrored unemployment figures that grew to unprecedented levels. By the end of 1931, General Motors had laid off 100,000 Detroit workers from its pre-Depression workforce of 260,000 employees. In 1932, Ford Motor Company laid off two-thirds of its workers. By early 1933, nonagricultural unemployment in Michigan reached an unbelievable 50 percent. In Detroit alone, that meant almost 225,000 unemployed workers. One hungry Detroiter remembered standing outside a livestock slaughterhouse "vying with other children to catch the discarded cattle lungs." Despair was not confined to Detroit. One Depression youngster remembered her mother fashioning clothes from feed and flour sacks. "Shoes and outer wear were the hardest to come by" and coats, hats and gloves had to be shared "if they had them," she recalled. Farm foreclosures rose and by 1933 were the highest in the country. In the Upper Peninsula, copper and iron mines slowed production and laid off miners. As the price for copper kept dropping, the Copper Country economy collapsed "with terrifying swiftness." By the early 1930s, one-third of the families in Houghton County were without means of support, while Calumet's business district "was the site of bankruptcy and 'going out of business' signs."[3]

In the minds of many Americans, accepting financial support from a public agency was a disgrace. Poverty was a product of result of sloth and laziness, especially in a country like America that provided all the necessary opportunities to succeed. The Depression challenged this conviction. An increasing number of desperate and out-of-work Michiganians soon overwhelmed private charities and local government. In Flint, the local Methodist church fed more than a thousand people a day, many of them out-of-work autoworkers. The city's "existing structure of welfare could not adapt to the new demands placed upon it." Welfare costs in Grand Rapids increased from $3,000 per month to $60,000 in eighteen months. Before the crash, relief costs represented one or two percent of the city budget; by late 1930, it stood at one-third. Ann Arbor also struggled, and by early 1933 the city had reached its legal borrowing limit, and as the *Ann Arbor Daily News* reported, "City Welfare Fund Emptied." Eventually, 250,000 Detroiters (out of a population of 1.5 million people) ended up on the city's relief rolls. Grand Rapids, Muskegon, Ann Arbor, and Saginaw instituted work-relief programs, but they were quickly overwhelmed. The growing demand on private charities came at a time when contributions suffered markedly. Among Michigan's wealthiest citizens, Senator Couzens proposed creating a $10 million private relief fund and offered to contribute the first $1 million. Well-heeled Detroiters responded with a resounding "not interested" and even expressed displeasure at how Couzens had embarrassed them.[4]

As the nation's fourth most populous city, Detroit had the greatest problems. Fortunately, it also had a mayor who insisted on taking action. During the bleakest days of the Depression, Frank Murphy earned a reputation as one of Michigan's most active public servants. Born in Sand Beach (present-day Harbor Beach) in 1890, Murphy followed in his father's footsteps, becoming a lawyer after graduating from the University of Michigan Law School. During World War I, Murphy joined the U.S. Army, earned a commission as a lieutenant, and served in France. After the war, a stint as an assistant U.S. attorney, followed by a successful private practice, led him to seek a position on Detroit Recorder's Court, "the most celebrated court in the United States at the time." Finishing first in a field of candidates, Murphy spent six years on the court, establishing a reputation as a "a consistent advocate of the view that a judge should tailor the punishment to fit the criminal." Murphy also received national attention as a fair judge, most notably in the racially charged Ossian Sweet trials. One criminal court authority who thought municipal judges "a sorry lot," took exception with Murphy, observing, "You dignify and glorify our judicial system as do few men who I have ever known." Following the recall of Mayor Charles Bowles in July 1930, Murphy ran and won the office. According to biographer Sidney Fine, Murphy "brought a dynamism, vitality, and enthusiasm to City Hall that had been sadly lacking there and succeeded not only in restoring public confidence in the city's government but also in making it a focus of public interest." In less than three years as mayor, he addressed the despair in his city, declaring that "unusual times can be met with unusual measures."[5]

The new mayor registered the unemployed, while putting them to work selling apples and planting "thrift gardens." Murphy established "municipal lodges" in vacant factories (donated by automakers) for out-of-work and homeless males. A firm believer that government could help the jobless, Murphy argued that

> government was conceived for the shielding of men, women, boys and girls from economic and social purposes over which they have no control and with which they can't cope unaided. At no time has this high purpose of government required such emphasis as in these tragic hours which shifting industrial conditions brought about.

Murphy became a leading advocate of federal aid to cities to deal with the crisis. In the spring of 1932, he called a meeting of Michigan mayors. A few weeks later, Detroit hosted the first meeting of the National Conference of Mayors. The big-city mayors convinced Congress to approve a $5 billion federal work relief program that President Herbert Hoover vetoed. Claiming "prosperity was just around the corner," Hoover denied the federal government had a role in relief programs.[6]

As conditions worsened, the response from Michigan's state government proved discouraging. In October 1930, Governor Fred Green (R-Ionia) told President Herbert Hoover that creating an unemployment commission "would only emphasize the problem." Wilber Brucker, Green's successor, agreed with Hoover that caring for the unemployed should fall to private charity and local government. Insisting the state should not be involved in relief measures, Brucker (R-Saginaw) reassured the president in August 1931 that "the people of Michigan will take care of their own problem." Governor Green did form the State Unemployment Committee, an unwieldy body of 105 prominent residents who had no power and provided no direct relief to the unemployed, except for occasional declarations like, "The only remedy for unemployment is employment" and "Our forefathers conquered the wilderness, subdued the savage Indian, founded a republic in a monarchial world, settled the question of slavery, and developed social standards for our inheritance. Can we lick this depression? Sure! Let's go." Green also refused to call a special legislative session to handle the deteriorating crisis. One later-day critic contended Brucker's refusal to involve the state more directly in unemployment relief "showed timidity" and a lack of leadership. Under the circumstances, it is hardly surprising Murphy and Brucker "engaged in an acrimonious debate over the relief question." Even when he grudgingly approved Murphy's requests to borrow more money to handle the city's relief needs, the governor claimed Detroit "suffered mostly through its own generosity in establishing the dole."[7]

—— Ford's Tin Goose

Another industrial casualty of the Depression was the Ford Motor Company's efforts to build airplanes. The story began in 1885 when five-year-old William Stout stood on the beach with his father watching seagulls sweep over the water. "Some day men will fly like that," his father observed. "And can I?" the boy asked. "You might," his father said. "You might even become the first man to do it." William Stout never forgot the occasion, later claiming it gave him "purpose." Stout did not become the first man to fly. However, he did become one of America's most brilliant inventors, and his many inventions included America's first all-metal airplane.[8]

By his thirties, Stout had moved to Detroit where he worked as an engineer designing automobiles. At night, he made airplane models. Most planes at the time were bi-planes, but Stout believed that the future of aviation meant planes with one set of wings. In the early 1920s, Stout founded the Stout Metal Airplane Company and began raising money to achieve his dream. In a letter to Detroit businessmen asking them for $1,000 each, he made an unusual promise. He wrote, "For your one thousand dollars you will get one definite promise. You will never get your money back." Many businessmen sent Stout money, including Henry and Edsel Ford. A few years, when the Ford Motor Company purchased Stout's company, the entrance of the Fords into the airplane business was big news, with the *New York Times* declaring, "The man who revolutionized the automobile industry has assigned himself the task of popularizing the flying machine."

On April 13, 1925, Stout's single-winged plane, called the 2-AT (Air Transport), successfully carried a load of Ford automobile parts from the new airport at Dearborn to Chicago. More flights were added, demanding a bigger plane. Stout's next effort (3-AT) proved a technological disaster and led

Ford's Tri-Motor plane contributed much to American aviation in the early 1930s.

Ford to replace Stout as the plane's architect. Introduced in June 1926, the 4-AT was an unqualified success. The plane's three engines (a radical innovation) earned it the nickname the Tri-Motor. Its all-metal construction made it sturdier, and it was considered safer than other similar planes made of wood. The Tri-Motor revolutionized the fledgling American airline industry and soon airlines all across the world flew Tri-Motors built by the Ford Motor Company. In November 1929, a Tri-Motor nicknamed the *Floyd Bennett* and navigated by Richard E. Byrd was the first to fly directly over the South Pole. (Today, that plane is on display at The Henry Ford in Dearborn.) But as the Great Depression gripped the nation, the Ford Motor Company quit building planes. The last Tri-Motor was built in June 1933. According to William Stout, "his greatest contribution" to American aviation was involving the Ford Motor Company in aviation. Tri-Motor historian Donald Bowman added that the Fords "took the airplane out of the cow pasture, put it in the hangar, and gave aviation the prestige and confidence which launched the Air Age."

As the Depression entered its third year with no sign of ending, a vocal minority advocated revolution. On the morning of March 7, 1932, a protest of 3,000 unemployed men and women, which included some communists, focused on the Ford Motor Company under "the belief that Henry Ford could turn things around if he only would." Besides jobs, the marchers had a long list of demands that included "an end to the speed-up . . . no discrimination against black workers in job assignments . . . and the right of Ford workers to organize." Carrying banners that read "Give Us Work" and "We Want Bread Not Crumbs," the marchers reached the Dearborn city line without incident. The protestors defied an order not to cross into Dearborn, and the police responded with tear gas. When demonstrators started throwing objects, the police opened fire. The "Ford Hunger March" left five marchers dead and 60 wounded. Five days later, thousands of mourners quietly paraded down Woodward Avenue carrying red banners (one read "Ford Gave Them Bullets For Bread") and marched to the *Internationale*, the communist party anthem.[9]

A few months later, the federal government rejected a demand by World War I veterans to implement immediately (rather than in the proposed year of 1945) a one-time pension or "bonus" for military service. Veterans from all across the country marched to the capital and camped out in downtown Washington and in vacant federal office buildings. While the House of Representatives supported the proposed change, the Senate refused. Eventually, President Hoover ordered the U.S. Army to remove the veterans. Despite the president's directive to "use all humanity," Brigadier General Douglas MacArthur drove the veterans out with tanks, horses, and cold steel. The veterans left the capital vowing revenge, even revolution.[10]

Michiganians who gained national recognition during the Great Depression included Frank Murphy (left) and Father Charles Coughlin (right).

None of the demagogues who enflamed social unrest during the Depression exceeded the influence of Father Charles Coughlin, one of the nation's most colorful and recognizable figures of the 1930s. Born in Hamilton, Ontario, in 1891, Coughlin arrived in Michigan during the early 1920s, serving as a priest in churches in several communities. In 1926, he was assigned to build a Catholic church in the Detroit suburb of Royal Oak—a community with a strong anti-Catholic bias and an active chapter of the Ku Klux Klan. Despite these distractions, the Shrine of the Little Flower church, named for St. Therese, a French nun known as the "The Little Flower," opened at the corner of Twelve Mile Road and Woodward Avenue.[11]

Taking advantage of the growing popularity of radio, Coughlin broadcast his first radio sermon from the powerful transmitting signal of Detroit's WJR radio in October 1926. In a short time—especially after the stock market crash—he developed a loyal following that rivaled anyone in America. While his initial weekly broadcasts focused on religious themes, Coughlin moved into the political arena, taking positions on a variety of different topics. Over the following years, the "Radio Priest," as he was soon called, expanded his broadcast network, earning the reputation as a supporter of the suffering working people who attributed the Depression to the failure of capitalism.

"Tens of thousands of good Americans," he charged, "were convinced that they were the victims of an international conspiracy aimed at enslaving them." At the height of Coughlin's popularity, one-third of the nation faithfully tuned to his weekly radio broadcasts where he addressed the social, economic, and political issues of the day. As Coughlin attacked President Herbert Hoover and the free enterprise system, supporters sent him financial contributions to expand his church. He also received so much mail (80,000 pieces weekly in 1933) that the U.S. Postal Service opened a new post office in Royal Oak. As Coughlin's popularity grew, so did his political clout. He supported the efforts of Mayor Murphy in Detroit and urged his followers to vote for Democrat Franklin D. Roosevelt. Michiganians needed little encouraging as they swept the Democrats into office in November 1932 and gave all the state's electoral votes to a Democrat for the first time since 1852. Voters also selected a Democrat governor and gave the Democrats control of the state legislature—quite an achievement since eight years earlier there had been no Democratic legislators.[12]

—— The New Deal

A banking crisis faced newly elected governor William Comstock (D-Alpena). Banks that overextended their financial commitments during the 1920s struggled as the value of their investments in real estate, stocks, and bonds— purchased at inflated prices—plummeted during the early years of the Depression. Disposing of these holdings meant taking losses. This situation worsened as depositors withdrew funds to meet personal needs or because they questioned a bank's soundness. President Hoover's Reconstruction Finance Corporation loaned money to stressed banks, but a congressional requirement that these loans be publicized accelerated the depositors' decision to withdraw their holdings. On the morning of February 14, 1933, Comstock closed all the state's banks so they could reorganize. Over the next several weeks, both the federal and state government authorized examiners to clean up the banking mess. Comstock's actions closed 436 Michigan banks and trust companies. Almost half (207) reopened and their depositors suffered "no loss." Of the remaining banks, 170 reorganized and 59 were placed in receivership. Reorganized banks paid their depositors 93.8 percent of their monies, while closed banks paid 85.4 percent. More important, the newly created Federal Deposit Insurance Company (FDIC) was designed to protect depositors' future savings.[13]

The banking fiasco only worsened the unemployment situation, and President Roosevelt's New Deal (a term earlier introduced to the political lexicon by Michigan Governor Salmon Chase Osborn) moved to relieve the pressure. During the first 100 days of his administration, Roosevelt introduced sweeping legislation to deal with the many emergencies confronting a nation struggling to dig itself out of Depression. The newly established Federal Emergency Relief Administration worked with local entities, and by the summer of 1933, 640,000 Michiganians (out of a state population of 4.8 million) received some form of relief. The New Deal also put the unemployed to work. The Public Works Administration followed by the Works Progress Administration provided federal funds for a variety of projects—everything from large construction projects and road repair to fine arts programs that employed artists and sculptors. For example, federally funded projects on the Michigan State College campus in East Lansing included the construction of the Auditorium, Jenison Field House, and Abbott Hall. WPA projects elsewhere in the state included the Brockway Mountain Drive (destined to become "one of the most popular motoring destinations in the Midwest") and the Keweenaw Mountain Lodge (later listed in the National Register of Historic Places). The Federal Art Project subsidized unemployed artists who painted murals in post offices (48 in Michigan) usually portraying people "engaged in an occupation that was central to the town's livelihood." Many of the murals have survived to this day. The WPA spent an estimated $500 million in Michigan, hiring as many as 200,000 people at any one time.[14]

—— The Civilian Conservation Corps

One of the New Deal's most successful programs was the Civilian Conservation Corps (CCC). Five days after his inauguration on March 4, 1933, President Roosevelt outlined a conservation relief measure that recruited unemployed young men to work on federal and state lands for "the prevention of forest fires, floods and soil erosion." According to Roosevelt, the CCC would "conserve our precious natural resources," while placing "a vast army of the unemployed [into] healthful surroundings."[15]

The CCC arrived in Michigan on May 2, 1933, when 200 young men from Detroit reached an isolated spot in the Hiawatha National Forest west of Sault Ste. Marie. They set up tents and called the area Camp Raco. A program administered through a series of federal agencies, the CCC opened camps all across northern Michigan. During the next nine years, more than

100,000 Michigan males enrolled in the CCC. (Nationally, the CCC enrolled more than three million young men.) Most enrollees were unemployed, single, healthy, and between the ages of seventeen and twenty-three. Nicknamed "CCCers," the enrollees each received a set of clothes that included shoes, socks, underwear, a blue denim work suit, and an old army uniform for dress purposes. They also received a shaving kit, a towel, a mess kit, a steel cot, a cotton mattress, and bedding. Most important, enrollees earned thirty dollars a month; each man kept five dollars and sent twenty-five dollars home to help support his family. Permanent structures often replaced the tent camps from the program's early days. These camps (approximately 100 in the state) included several barracks, a mess hall, a bathhouse and latrine, and various service buildings. The simple buildings had lights, but few other amenities. Enrollees began their day with reveille at 6:00 AM followed by calisthenics after breakfast. They spent their days working, only returning to camp in the late afternoon where they either attended classes or visited nearby communities. Lights were out at 10:00 PM.

Working in national and state forests, CCC enrollees planted seedlings, fought forests fires, and built roads, trails, towers, and firebreaks to prevent future fires. The enrollees who fought the massive fires on Isle Royale in

Michigan's forests are part of a legacy that grew out of the 1930s when Civilian Conservation Corps enrollees planted almost 500 million seedlings.

1936, according to one contemporary observer, saved "some of the [island's] finest scenic spots." The CCC also improved hundreds of miles of Michigan's best fishing rivers and streams, conducted many wildlife projects (including transplanting moose to Isle Royale), and constructed an assortment of structures (some of which remain in use to this day in national forests and several state parks). The many projects of the CCC developed Isle Royale National Park and the Seney National Wildlife Refuge and revitalized the Michigan State Park system.

Yet, the CCC was not all work. During their free time, enrollees could earn a high school diploma or take college classes. The camps also offered sports teams. Camp Manistique's team "played high class" baseball, Camp Walkerville's weekly boxing matches drew crowds of hundreds of area residents, and the Camp Escanaba River orchestra performed concerts that could be heard on the local radio station.

The CCC ended in June 1942, and Michigan's CCCers planted almost 500 million trees (more than twice as many as CCC camps in any other state), built 7,000 miles of truck trails, and placed 156 million fish in lakes and streams. Equally important, the enrollees sent more than $20 million home to their families. The CCC improved the morale, health, and education of desperate young men, while giving thousands of American males some military-like experience that helped when many joined the armed forces during World War II. During the early 1980s, the state's conservation and forestry managers reflected on the CCC legacy. Howard Tanner, director of the Michigan Department of Natural Resources, characterized the accomplishments of the CCC as "perhaps never-ending," while Steve Yurish, regional forester for the Hiawatha National Forest, added, "We travel on roads built by the CCC, hike on trails, camp or picnic in recreation areas and enjoy fish and wildlife provided by water impoundments and erosion control projects. We can't begin to place a value on trees that were saved by fire fighting crews or the acres of trees that were treated in pest and disease control programs." Finally, Wayne K. Mann, forest supervisor of the Huron-Manistee National Forest, concluded:

> The tribute to the CCC workers is found everywhere. It is not a tribute of bronze and marble with flowery words—it is the miles of green productive forests filled with water, wildlife, majestic trees, and happy recreationists. The work of the CCC illustrates sound conservation practices and their toil has left a legacy for all Americans to enjoy.

—— Management versus Labor

In April 1935, *Business Week* magazine declared, "Depression is a forgotten word in the automobile industry, which is forging ahead in production, retail sales, and expansion of productive capacity in a manner reminiscent of the 'twenties.'" The nation's improving economy was evident at General Motors where the sale of cars between 1932 and 1936 expanded from 472,000 to 1.68 million. At the same time, the company's workforce doubled from 116,000 to 230,000. But the auto industry's return to prosperity also resulted in monumental confrontations that greatly altered the relationship between management and labor. Before the Depression, Michigan enjoyed an open-shop reputation. During the boom years of the 1920s, autoworkers earned higher wages than workers in most other industries and saw little need for unions. Labor grievances also were neutralized by "welfare capitalism" (paid vacations, life insurance, savings programs, recreational facilities, etc.). Furthermore, the nation's largest union, the American Federation of Labor, was craft-minded and not interested in "industrial unionism" (the unskilled and semi-skilled workers who built cars). The Depression introduced dramatic changes. As the assembly lines began humming again, seniority played no role in callbacks. According to historian Mike Smith, "Job security often depended upon the whims of the factory foreman, who had the power to hire and fire workers at will." Management also sped up the assembly lines "unmercifully to raise productivity and restore profit levels." One autoworker remembered, "The working conditions were dehumanizing. You couldn't talk to another worker—couldn't even say hello without getting fired." The wife of one worker complained that her husband was "a young man grown old from the speed-up." One GM worker grumbled, "You might call yourself a man if you was [sic] on the street, but as soon as you went through the door and punched your card, you was nothing more or less than a robot." Another complained, "It was a fast pace. . . . [the] water fountain wasn't over ten feet from me. If I worked for an hour and wanted a drink of water, I didn't have time to get it." As future labor leader Douglas Fraser later remembered, "There was no dignity. You couldn't question any decisions and you couldn't dissent."[16]

As autoworkers sought relief from the worsening situation, the 1933 National Industrial Recovery Act (NIRA), which allowed workers the right to bargain collectively, offered hope. Even after the U.S. Supreme Court struck down the NIRA, the 1935 National Labor Relations Act (better-known as the Wagner Act after its chief sponsor, Senator Robert Wagner of New York) reasserted a worker's right to belong to a union without management's interference. Automakers ignored the Wagner Act, confident that it would meet the same fate as the NIRA. They also employed brutal tactics to crush union sentiment, especially at the Ford Motor Company. Ford's tough guy was Harry Bennett, an Ann Arbor native whose chance meeting with Henry Ford led to his appointment as head of Ford's "Service Department." As Henry Ford's primary troubleshooter, Bennett reported directly to the elder Ford, who admired him like a son. At Ford's massive Rouge Plant, Bennett's 3,000-man force (called "the world's largest private army") suppressed union sentiment by instituting "a bloody reign of terror." Bennett acknowledged his men (thugs, ex-convicts, and former boxers) were "a lot of tough bastards," but Ford's workers disagreed with his assertion that "every goddam one of them's a gentleman." General Motors did not have a Harry Bennett. Instead, the world's largest automaker spent a million dollars between 1934 and mid-1936 employing fourteen private detective and security agencies and creating what a congressional committee called "the most colossal super-system of spies yet devised in any American corporation." According to one labor organizer, the only safe topics for conversation among GM workers were "sports, women, dirty stories, and the weather." Senate investigators concluded that frightened GM workers were "in no sense" free Americans.[17]

—— A Strike Heard 'Round the World

Despite plenty of obstacles, the newly formed United Auto Workers (UAW) secretly enrolled about 10 percent of the 47,000 General Motors workers in Flint by December 1936. Conceding that a strike against the world's largest automaker lay in the future, UAW leaders identified GM's most essential plants. (GM operated 69 plants in 35 cities.) They determined that closing Flint's Fisher Body plants No. 1 and No. 2 would "immediately cripple" GM. Realizing its paltry Flint membership could not sustain a conventional picket-line strike, the UAW chose a sit-down strike. Sit-downs had several distinct advantages. According to one labor operator at the time, "It permits the strikers to remain in comfort, even if somewhat bored, instead of tramping about on the picket line in the heat, cold, wind, and wet." Besides maintaining higher morale, a sit-down stopped production, prevented management from employing strikebreakers and lessened the chance for violence. As for the argument that sit-downs violated sacred property rights, one contemporary labor leader submitted, "Workers have not attacked property; they have 'sat down' faithfully by the side of the machines which are life and death to them, and guarded them." Ancient Egyptian workers had used sit-down strikes as had Europeans during the 1920s. Even the United States witnessed sit-down strikes, including two in Detroit earlier in 1936 where workers made modest gains.[18]

In late December, strikes at a GM plant in Cleveland, coupled with rumors that GM planned to move stamping dies from Flint's Fisher No. 1, prompted the UAW to act. On the night of December 30, 1936, UAW workers took control of the two Fisher plants. What lay ahead was known as the Flint Sit-Down Strike—the single greatest demonstration of organized labor's power during the Depression. According to one striker, most doubted GM could be beaten. But as he added, "many felt, with him, that his 'job was no good anyway so that if I had lost it I hadn't lost anything.'" Among the determined labor organizers who vowed the UAW would not lose in Flint were the omnipresent Reuther brothers, Walter, Victor, and Roy, West Virginia natives who had once worked for the Ford Motor Company before joining the UAW. According to one story, an employer familiar with Walter Reuther suddenly heard Victor on a bullhorn encouraging the sit-downers inside the plant. When told it was a different Reuther, he bemoaned, "How many of those Reuther bastards are there?"[19]

As one striker remembered, the sit-downers organized as if "we were soldiers holding the fort." Recognizing their actions were in the public eye, union organizers had all women workers (and many women worked in the upholstery shops) leave the seized plants to avoid any tasteless comments by anti-strike forces. The sit-downers organized themselves into fifteen-person "families," with each family given a specific "apartment" within the plants. They formed committees for exercise, security, entertainment, and defense. Men whiled away their boredom by attending educational classes, performing plays and musical concerts, or competing in everything from cards to roller-skating. At night, the workers slept on unfinished car seats. One reporter allowed into Fisher No. 1 reported:

> The place was remarkably neat and tidy, at least as clean as it is under normal conditions. Beds were made up on the floor of each [unfinished] car, the seat being removed if necessary. . . . I could not see—and I looked for it carefully—the slightest damage done anywhere to any property of the General Motors Corporation. The nearly completed car bodies, for example, were as clean as they would be in the salesroom, their glass and metal shining.

The number of sit-downers varied from a high of 1,000 to a low of fewer than 100 "as hopes for a settlement waxed and waned." When enthusiasm lagged in Flint, UAW members from Detroit and Toledo helped out. Women played an invaluable role "at times when the strike might have turned either way." Female workers and strikers' wives organized a Women's Auxiliary, while 23-year-old Genora Johnson, a mother of two children with a husband on strike, led the 350-member Women's Emergency Brigade, which promised to fight "with rolling pins, brooms, mops, and everything else we can get." Emergency Brigade members wore distinctive tams and a red arm band with the letters EM in white. Women also helped prepare meals (three a day) off site that were delivered to the plants. They also endured harassment by strike opponents. The wife of one striker remembered nighttime visitors standing on her lawn threatening, "'We're gonna bust in and we're gonna kill you.'"[20]

Caught totally unaware of the UAW's sit-down plan, the automaker quickly obtained a court injunction demanding the strikers vacate the plants. However, the issuing judge owned hundreds of shares of GM stock (valued at nearly a quarter million dollars), and the obvious conflict-of-interest derailed this effort. General Motors also endorsed the Flint Alliance, a newly formed group designed to turn public opinion against the sit-downers by labeling them as communists. Although the UAW had communists among its members, the sit-down strike "was a grass-roots revolt owing no allegiance to communist ideology or conspiracy." As Flint Sit-Down historian Sidney Fine concluded, the sit-downers were "transformed from badge numbers and easily replaceable cogs in an impersonal industrial machine into heroes of American labor."[21]

Violence also marred the sit-down. Two weeks into the strike, GM turned off the heat in Fisher No. 2. Later that cold January day, tear gas-wielding police officers stormed the plant. Sit-downers retaliated by opening up the water hoses and showering the attackers with pound-and-a-half door hinges. When the wind changed direction and blew the gas back into their eyes, the police withdrew. Making no better headway a second time, they retreated out of range, before opening fire on the sit-downers. By midnight the sniping ended and ambulances carted off the wounded, about a dozen on each side. The "Battle of the Running Bulls," so dubbed by the strikers because the "bulls" (police) fled, led Governor Murphy to act. Declaring "peace and order will prevail," he ordered hundreds of National Guardsmen to Flint. Although Murphy disapproved of sit-down tactics, he supported the Wagner Act and, as he had declared in his recent campaign for governor, "I am heart and soul in the labor movement."[22]

Aware that the nation was watching their every action, UAW Flint sit-downers maintained good behavior and strict discipline as they brought production at the world's largest auto company to a halt.

Calm resumed, but efforts to reach a settlement failed as GM refused to negotiate as long as the strikers held the plants hostage. GM enjoyed a slightly favorable rating in a national public opinion (53 to 47 percent), but as one striker remembered, "It started out kinda ugly because the guys were afraid they put their foot in it and all they was gonna do is lose their jobs. But as time went on, they begin to realize they could win this darn thing, 'cause we had a lot of outside people comin' in showin' their sympathy." Four weeks into the strike, the UAW duped the automaker again and took over a third Flint plant—Chevrolet 4, where all Chevy engines were made. As the sit-downers occupied Chevrolet 4, the Women's Emergency Brigade formed a human barricade "in front of the building with locked arms." Their revolving picket line marched to songs like "We shall Not be Moved" while the police looked on "rather sheepishly."[23]

The capture of Chevrolet 4 led to a second court injunction, demanding the strikers immediately leave the plants within twenty-four hours or face a $15 million fine. (One striker taunted, "If the judge can get fifteen million bucks from us, he's welcome to it.") Governor Murphy intervened, moving between the two contestants "like a jack rabbit." According to historian Fine, "The UAW had brilliantly executed its imaginative strike strategy. The union had regained the initiative, and the turning point of the strike had been reached." As General Motors succumbed to the pressure (it produced 151 cars during the first ten days of February), one of the Chevrolet 4 sit-downers accurately boasted, "We shure [sic] done a thing that GM said never could be done." On February 11, 1937, after sixteen hours of intense negotiating, the 44-day Flint Sit-Down Strike ended. Carrying American flags, the enthusiastic sit-downers poured out of Fisher No. 1 and then joined fellow strikers from the other occupied plants. That evening the victorious sit-downers and their supporters held a torchlight parade singing their new anthem, "Solidarity Forever." In the settlement, the UAW earned the right to organize GM workers. Although GM clearly lost, William Knudsen, one of its negotiators, added, "Let us have peace and make automobiles." By the end of 1937, the UAW boasted 256 locals and 375,000 dues-paying members. Years later, one sit-downer crowed they had let GM know "they couldn't be treated like dogs. . . . they [were] human beings."[24]

——Sit-Down Fever

The Flint Sit-Down Strike, which the British Broadcasting Corporation called "the strike heard around the world," set off a myriad of copy-cat strikes. The day after the Flint strike ended, the *Detroit Labor News* urged workers to strike "while the iron is hot, never resting, never stopping. . . . The iron is as hot as it will ever be. . . . Strike on!" Soon, sit-down strikes occurred in hotels, laundries, coal yards, restaurants, and department stores. As one Detroit cigar factory worker observed, "We figured, if [the auto workers] can do it, we can also do it." In April alone, Detroit experienced 100 different sit-down strikes. Some strikes lasted weeks; others were settled in a few days or even a few hours. Most were peaceful and led to higher wages and improved working conditions for workers. The Chrysler Corporation, the nation's number three automaker, surrendered after a seventeen-day sit-down. Elsewhere in Detroit, the lunch counter waitresses at Woolworths sat down for eight days and won a nickel-an-hour raise, union recognition, and a paid, annual vacation. Sit-downs became so common the *Detroit News* noted that "sitting down has replaced baseball as a national pastime, and sitter-downers clutter up the landscape in every direction." Despite causing some inconveniences, the strikers had plenty of support, as evidenced by 100,000 sympathetic demonstrators who rallied in downtown Detroit in late March.[25]

Sometimes the sit-downs offered an odd, even humorous, twist. When Detroit major hotels suffered strikes, chaos prevailed as operators shut down their elevators, while waiters and waitresses quit serving. At one hotel, the striking staff consumed food prepared for the abruptly cancelled banquets, giving one young waitress her first taste of caviar, which she acknowledged was

Richard Frankensteen
(center) is flanked by
Walter Reuther (right)
and Robert Kanter (left)
at what was called the
Battle of the Overpass.

"not so hot." The general manager and chief of sales of Fry Products staged a "counter sit-down" when his 142 employees went on strike. He earned the respect of sit-down opponents when he declared, "If they won't work, I won't work, and unless I work and sell, they won't have any work to do." *Business Week* magazine praised Walter L. Fry for the "safest and soundest management policies." Sit-downs spread so rapidly the Detroit and Wayne County Federation of Labor experienced a shortage of organizers, while the UAW headquarters suffered delays when deliverymen went on strike. The popularity of sit-down strikes led the *New York Times* to conclude: "Only a few months ago, we thought kindly of Michigan as our greatest producer of automobiles. And now what does she produce? Strikes, strikes, strikes."[26]

One automaker successfully avoided a sit-down and delayed the rush to collective bargaining. On May 26, 1937, Walter Reuther and Richard Frankensteen led about 50 unionists, both men and women, to the Miller Road overpass—the site of the Ford Hunger March five years earlier. Possessing a city permit, the unionists peacefully distributed UAW flyers to Ford workers arriving at the River Rouge complex. Without warning, Harry Bennett's security force attacked. According to investigators, the unionists were "knocked on and viciously pounded and kicked. . . . They were then raised in the air several times and thrown upon their backs on the concrete." Bebe Gelles, one of the Women's Auxiliary, entered the fray. She recalled, the three Ford men "turned on me, knocking me to the ground and kicking me in the stomach, then pushing me to the streetcar." The attack lasted 45 minutes, and dozens of union men were treated for lacerations and multiple bruises. At least two of the unionists "never fully recovered" from the beatings. The "Battle of the Over-pass" received national exposure thanks to *Detroit News* photographer James Kilpatrick, who successfully prevented Bennett's thugs from seizing his camera or film. That attention greatly aided the labor movement and set in motion a campaign that finally led the UAW to organize Ford workers in May 1941.[27]

The rash of sit-down strikes ended by mid-1937 as union leaders focused on consolidating their gains. Two years later, the U.S. Supreme Court ruled sit-down strikes were unconstitutional. Yet, in a few short months, Michigan workers, especially in the Motor City, "had made Detroit the American labor movement's most influential city," according to labor historian Mike Smith.[28]

—— City of Champions

To escape some of the stresses of the Great Depression, Michiganians turned to sports as Detroit's professional teams created a "City of Champions." During the mid-1930s, Tiger greats (all eventually headed to the Baseball Hall of Fame) included Mickey Cochrane (catcher manager), Charlie Gehringer

Some Tigers who made Detroit a "City of Champions" during the 1930s included (1 to r) Tommy Bridges, Charlie Gehringer, Hank Greenberg, and Gee Walker.

(second base), "Hammerin'" Hank Greenberg (first base), and Leon "Goose" Goslin (outfielder). The "G-Men," as they were called, teamed up with pitchers Tommy Bridges and Lynwood "Schoolboy" Rowe to rule the American League. Detroiters so loved their Tigers that they represented 25 percent of professional baseball's customers during the mid-1930s. In 1934, the Tigers (with six batters hitting over .300) won their first pennant since 1909. Though badly beaten in Game Seven of the World Series (11-0 at home to the St. Louis Cardinals), the Tigers roared back the following year winning another American League pennant. Despite a slow start that included losing Goslin to a broken wrist in the second game, the Tigers defeated the Chicago Cubs in the sixth game of the World Series. Detroit "went collectively crazy" as it celebrated the championship.[29]

In that same magical year, the Detroit Lions, in their second year as a franchise, won the team's first National Football League title by defeating the New York Giants. Months later, the Detroit Red Wings won their first Stanley Cup beating the Toronto Maple Leafs. The following year, the Wings repeated as champs, stopping the New York Rangers. Both championship victories came at the heralded Olympia Arena, site of many athletic and entertainment memories.[30]

No Detroit athlete of the mid-1930s rivaled Joe Louis for national attention. Born in Alabama in 1914 and a grandson of slaves, Joe Louis Barrow moved north in 1926 with his family as part of the Great Migration. The Barrows settled in Detroit's Black Bottom and young Joe was introduced to boxing at the local recreation center. On the night the seventeen-year-old fought his first amateur fight, Joe Louis was "born." Joe dropped his last name, probably in hopes of keeping his mother ignorant of his growing passion for the ring. Following an impressive 50-4 amateur record, Louis worked to overcome the racial bias that kept black fighters out of serious title contention. He never gloated over a beaten opponent and avoided anything flamboyant, especially in relations with white women. Louis even refused to be seen eating watermelon (a favorite food), fearing it fed racial stereotypes. As a professional, Louis enjoyed victory after victory, while earning the nickname "Brown Bomber." The number one heavyweight contender and recipient of the 1935 Associated Press Athlete of the Year award, Louis inspired the nation's black community. As one Harlem Renaissance writer observed, "No one else in the United States has ever had such an effect on Negro emotions."[31]

Despite all his triumphs, Louis stumbled badly in June 1936 when European champion Max Schmeling of Germany knocked him out in the 12th round. A 10-to-1 favorite, Louis took his opponent too lightly and trained poorly, while Schmeling took advantage of Louis's subtle tendency to drop his left after a jab. One of Louis's friends noted, "Usually after Joe Louis got through fighting, everybody would be out in the streets, driving, honking their horns. . . . Not that night, no . . . . it was a sad night. . . . it was like a funeral."

Louis won the heavyweight title in June 1937, but the Schmeling loss haunted him. "I don't want to be called champ until I whip Max Schmeling," he said. The defeat hurt even more as Nazi Germany exploited the victory as proof of its claim to Aryan superiority. When the rematch was announced, Louis trained incessantly, even accepting an invitation from the White House where President Roosevelt told the fighter, "We need muscles like yours to beat Germany." Louis later claimed he had to win because "the whole damned country was depending on me." On June 22, 1938, in front of a sellout crowd at Yankee Stadium and with millions more around the world listening on radio, Louis destroyed Schmeling in one of the century's most heralded sporting events. In two minutes and four seconds, the Brown Bomber battered the German, knocking him down three times before the referee stopped the fight.

After an unexpected loss to Max Schmeling in 1936, Joe Louis demolished the German boxer in a rematch two years later.

With the coming of World War II, Louis joined the U.S. Army, fighting dozens of morale-building exhibition matches before thousands of soldiers. He also encouraged black enlistment and used his personal contacts to help the cause of black officer school candidates, including a young Jackie Robinson. Louis addressed criticism of his enthusiasm for a segregated army by explaining that there are "lots of things wrong with America, but Hitler ain't going to fix them." Technical Sergeant Joe Louis left the service in late 1945 the recipient of the Legion of Merit (rarely issued to enlisted men) for making an "incalculable contribution to the general morale." When Louis retired from boxing in 1949, he left the ring an undefeated heavyweight champion who held the title longer than anyone before or since. However, after years of success in the ring, Louis experienced a range of personal problems, including owing the Internal Revenue Service tens of thousands of dollars in unpaid back taxes that drove him back into the ring for fights he lost badly. Louis died in 1981 and was buried with military honors in Arlington National Cemetery. A few years later, Detroit honored his legend when *Sports Illustrated* (which ranked him the century's eleventh greatest athlete) commissioned a massive sculpture called "the Fist." The 24-foot, 8,000-pound symbol sits prominently on Jefferson Avenue along the riverfront.[32]

CHAPTER
17

World War II

Michiganians like these women assembling gas masks contributed to the war effort in many ways.

"For many of us, our lives had changed forever."

—Duane T. Brigstock remembering the impact
of Pearl Harbor

On the fateful Sunday morning of December 7, 1941, Fireman First Class Peter Stork of Hamtramack joined a group of fellow sailors who left the USS *Vestal* to attend mass on the mainland. Soon, Japanese planes streaked across the water dropping bombs and torpedoes on the unsuspecting American fleet tied up at Pearl Harbor. As he came under fire, Stock remembered that the Japanese planes "were so close you could almost count the stitches in the pilots' helmets." Quickly dismissing the notion this was a drill, Stock and his comrades began "pulling the sailors out from the harbor who had been blown off or abandoned their ships." Despite continuous strafing by enemy planes, the men set up a temporary aid station. After the attack ended, Stock returned to the *Vestal* to discover his battle station had taken a direct hit and was underwater. Next to Stork's ship lay the USS *Arizona*, where Gunner's Mate First Class Jim Green of Troy was knocked from his bunk by an

297

explosion when a Japanese bomb hit the ill-fated ship. Other bombs followed, including one that hit the ship's ammunition storage bay. Though wounded, Green followed orders to abandon ship; of at least thirty Michiganians aboard the ill-fated ship, he was the sole survivor.[1]

Across the harbor from the *Arizona* lay the USS *Oklahoma.* Among its crew was 22-year-old Ensign Francis Flaherty of Charlotte. When an enemy torpedo hit his boat, Flaherty held a flashlight so the men in his gun turret could get out of the sinking battleship. Flaherty was not so lucky. For his heroism, he was awarded the Medal of Honor—the first Michiganian to receive the medal during World War II. Also aboard the *Oklahoma* was Russell Davenport of Detroit. When the damaged ship rolled over, Davenport and a few others were trapped in a compartment in the bow of the boat. In total darkness, they found a wrench and began banging on the boat's hull until others discovered them. Although it took 30 hours to cut through the hull, the men were rescued. The last man out, Davenport remained in the navy until after the war ended.[2]

When many Michiganians back home heard the news about the attack, most would have agreed with ten-year-old William G. Richards (Marquette) who "wasn't sure where Pearl Harbor was, but I knew what it meant: our country was at war!" There was confusion and plenty of fear. Virginia Weaver (Lansing) remembered, "We thought this awful monstrosity could not be happening. How far will they come? Everyone in the house feared the future. None of us slept well that night." When Elinore Sheel (Midland) awoke from a nap she heard the radio report about the attack and "snapped out of my dreamy haze, literally freezing in place. I had a brother in the army and knew what that would mean for him. I thought of the rest of the young men in my family, including another brother, and my classmate from nursing school." Driving in a car, George Brocklehurst (Davison) remembered, "Everyone in the car fell silent, lost in our own private thoughts." U.S. Army Reserve officer William Falvey (Niles) heard the news while lying on the sofa listening to a professional football game. He got up and checked his uniforms, anticipating the "report for duty" orders that arrived the next day. Celebrating their first wedding anniversary when the radio reported the attack, Christine Stevinson (Royal Oak) remembered the fun stopped and, since "all the men there were of draft age, that sobered us and the party ended early." A freshman at present-day Michigan State University, Margaret Hunter recalled, "We were eating lunch when one of the girls announced that Pearl Harbor had been attacked. We turned on the radio to verify this. There was dead silence as we listened to the news. Then we all stood and sang, "'America.'" Duane T. Brigstock (Battle Creek) succinctly concluded, "For many of us, our lives changed forever."[3]

—— Creating the Arsenal of Democracy

The early months of World War II did not go well for the United States. Yet, Lt. General Brekon B. Somervell spoke confidently that America would win the war against the Germans and Japanese. Responsible for making sure the army had the necessary equipment to fight a war, Somervell reminded Americans that when German leader Adolf Hitler "hitched his chariot to an internal combustion engine, he opened up a new battle front—a front that we know well. It's called Detroit." Somervell was talking about the American automobile industry, "the mecca of mass-production technology." Once American automakers turned their attention away from cars to tanks and bombers, the Allies "would surely put fascism on the run." Hailed as the "linch-pin of the Arsenal of Democracy," Detroit, according to the *New York Times*, became "a city forging thunderbolts."[4]

The "production miracle" that contributed significantly to the Allied victory began slowly. As the world raced toward war during the late 1930s, American automakers were more interested in leading the United States out of the Great Depression than in preparing for war. As economic depression receded and car sales rose, the industry reluctantly responded to the notion of converting to war production. Automakers bitterly recalled their experience during World War I when they had paid to convert their factories to war production. When the Great War ended, the government cancelled the contracts, and the auto companies found themselves producing weapons that had no markets.

Alfred Sloan, the man who helped make General Motors the world's largest manufacturer, remained detached to events in Europe. In a spring of 1939 response to the claim that GM's German operations were too closely tied to the Nazi war machine, he wrote, "such matters should not be considered the business of the management of General Motors." Months later, as German armed forces dominated most of the European continent, Sloan rejected a federal government request to stand ready for a possible war production contract. He rebutted, "It looks as if the war in Europe is rapidly moving toward a conclusion. . . . It seems the Allies are outclassed on mechanical equipment and it is foolhardy to talk about modernizing their Armies in times like these, they ought to have thought of that five years ago." Sloan attributed the failure to modernize their armies earlier to the "stupid, narrow-minded and selfish leadership which the democracies of the world are cursed with."[5]

At the same time, some automakers, most notably Henry Ford, joined with other "isolationists" to limit United States involvement in a world engaged in war. On one side of the debate of America's role in world affairs stood President Franklin D. Roosevelt (FDR) who believed defeating Nazi Germany was essential for the security of the United States. FDR supported arming the British, while improving American preparedness. His critics argued that his "course would end in participation in the same sort of pointless blood-bath—if on a grander scale—as the Great War." Ford endorsed the Neutrality Acts of 1935–1937, which were designed to minimize American involvement in world affairs. The automaker even predicted on August 29, 1939, that Europe would not go to war, declaring, "It's all a big bluff." Three days later, Germany invaded Poland. Besides Ford, some of the nation's leading isolationists included Detroit native Charles Lindbergh and Congressman Clare Hoffman. Lindbergh, who enjoyed worldwide admiration for flying nonstop across the Atlantic Ocean in May 1927, was a member of the America First Committee. On April 23, 1941, the famed flyer told supporters, "We ask you to share our faith in the ability of this nation to defend itself, to develop its own civilization, and to contribute to the progress of mankind in a more constructive and intelligent way than has yet been found by the warring nations of Europe." Among the most ardent isolationists was Congressman Hoffman. The Republican from Allegan not only opposed American aid to Great Britain but did not believe Adolf Hitler posed a threat to America. Instead, Hoffman accused President Roosevelt, whose "aim is a dictatorship," with trying "to confuse and frighten the American people into the belief that they are confronted by a stupendous danger." As early as 1939, Hoffman argued that Roosevelt's foreign policy program was "designed to provoke Hitler and invite retaliation." On numerous opportunities, Hoffman railed against FDR, calling him "a crazy, conceited megalomaniac." The congressman even claimed that the president had "most of the instincts and ambitions" of Adolf Hitler but lacked the German leader's "abilities." When FDR ordered the U.S. Navy to sink German submarines that attacked British merchant vessels off the U.S. Atlantic coast, Hoffman accused him of trying to pick a fight and called for Roosevelt's impeachment.[6]

Despite intense isolationist rhetoric, Michiganians experienced "changes induced by a world at war." In October 1940, Michigan National Guard units, part of the 32nd Division, headed to Louisiana for twelve months of training. At the same time, Congress narrowly approved a peacetime draft. (Most of Michigan's congressional delegation opposed the conscription bill.) By the following summer, 15,000 recruits were training at Camp Custer, which

Enthusiastic Marquette men prepare to join the U.S. Army.

was reactivated and expanded. The army's return to Battle Creek provided money and jobs, but the arrival of thousands of young men also "involved crowding in almost every aspect of life, the noise and expansion of the seedy tavern setting and all those conditions associated with military camps from time immemorial."[7]

—— Tanks from Chrysler in the War

Recognizing the essential role the auto industry would play in winning a war, and seeking to improve relations with automakers, President Roosevelt appointed William S. Knudsen, president of General Motors, as industrial production specialist of the National Defense Advisory Commission (later called the Office of Production Management). Hailed as the "ablest production man in the auto industry," Knudsen had immigrated to the United States from Denmark at the age of twenty. He eventually worked for the Ford Motor Company and, it was said, without Knudsen "the Model T could not have reached its phenomenal position in automotive history." In 1921, Knudsen moved to General Motors where he made the Chevrolet one of the nation's most popular cars. General Motors Chairman Alfred Sloan discouraged Knudsen from leaving GM. Knudsen recalled saying, "I came to this country with nothing. It has been good to me. Rightly or wrongly, I feel I must go."[8]

Less than a week into his new job, Knudsen called K. T. Keller, who headed the Chrysler Corporation. As German tanks raced across Europe overpowering all who stood in their way, the U.S. Army realized its fledgling armored force, which existed basically on paper, needed serious upgrading. Knudsen believed the auto industry could help and asked Keller if Chrysler could build tanks. Keller confidently responded, "Yes." Then he queried, "Where can I see one?" Within weeks, Chrysler and the U.S. government signed a contract. As Chrysler engineers reviewed the army's blueprints for tanks, the government agreed to build a plant in a rural area north of Detroit in Warren where Chrysler could produce tanks. To design the new factory, Chrysler turned to factory architect Albert Kahn. Within months, the massive, 1.1 million-square-foot plant—the world's largest—took shape. Simultaneously, Chrysler engineers developed a tank prototype. According to one ordnance officer:

> Only a man who has taken part in the design, tooling and production of the new model of automobile or other complicated piece of machinery can adequately understand the unforeseen and unforeseeable difficulties of such a task. . . . And this new product was not just a new automobile adapted from last year's model; it was a tank, which was an entirely new and strange product for private industry, and even for the Ordnance Department itself.

On April 24, 1941, Governor Murray Van Wagoner and U.S. Army dignitaries, along with hundreds of workers, watched as Chrysler's first tank, a 30-ton steel monster "performed dramatically, firing its guns, smashing through telephone poles and casually turning a specially built house into matchwood." The day's event marked the beginning of a successful relationship between government and business to modernize the U.S. Army that continues to this day.[9]

Tanks soon began rolling off the Detroit Arsenal assembly line. When the U.S. entered the war in December 1941, additional assembly lines were added (eventually five), and the arsenal ran round the clock, seven days a week. One year after the plant's dedication, the arsenal delivered its two thousandth tank. In July 1942 workers started building Sherman tanks, one of the war's best-known armored vehicles. In December, the arsenal's five thousand workers set an all-time monthly record producing 907 Sherman tanks. Besides these numbers, the plant demonstrated the ability to retool for new models without

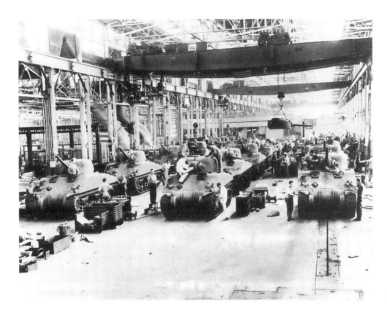

Chrysler's Detroit Arsenal in Warren produced more than 22,000 tanks—
about 25 percent of all American tanks made during the war.

interrupting production. Given these accomplishments, it is not surprising
these workers won the government's first "E" flag for production excellence.
By war's end, Chrysler's Detroit Arsenal had produced 22,234 tanks—about
25 percent of all American tanks in World War II and equal to all German
tank production. General Levin H. Campbell, the army's head of ordnance,
offered no understatement when he declared the success at the Detroit Arsenal was a perfect example of applying Detroit's "industrial might to battle."[10]

—— The Willow Run Bomber Plant

As tanks rolled off the Detroit Arsenal assembly lines, the Ford Motor Company undertook an unprecedented effort to apply assembly-line production techniques to produce one of the war's biggest and most complicated
weapons. The Willow Run Bomber Plant struggled during its early days, but
became Michigan's best-known wartime industrial achievement.

The Willow Run saga began in the spring of 1940 when President Roosevelt announced plans to increase American aircraft production to 50,000

planes a year. Up to that point, Henry Ford had refused to take the war in Europe seriously, even suggesting the United States should give the Allies and Axis nations "the tools to keep on fighting until they both collapse." However, the president's announcement led Ford to mention casually how his company could produce 1,000 planes a day—if left to its own devices and "without meddling by government agencies." Ford's comments flashed all across the world. The French, struggling to resist the German invaders, distributed thousands of leaflets carrying Ford's claim to bolster French morale. (One French official even suggested dropping the leaflets over the Third Reich "to scare the devil" out of the Germans.) Although caught off guard, American authorities, like production guru William Knudsen, conceded, "If Mr. Ford says he can, I guess he can."[11]

While American airplane manufacturers scoffed at Ford's claim as "sheer fantasy," Knudsen asked the Ford Motor Company to fill an immediate British order for 6,000 airplane engines. Company president Edsel Ford and production manager Charles Sorenson agreed. But after the contract was announced, Henry Ford rejected the contract, denouncing President Roosevelt on the grounds that he and his followers "want war." Despite the embarrassment Ford caused the U.S. government (Packard Motors filled the engine order), Knudsen offered the Ford Motor Company a contract to build 4,000 Pratt & Whitney 18-cylinder engines for the U.S Army Air Corps. The elder Ford reluctantly accepted the contract. As workers built these engines at the River Rouge plant, the government approached Ford about building the B-24 Liberator—an enormous plane with a 3,000-mile range, capable of carrying up to four tons of bombs.[12]

In January 1941, Edsel Ford and Sorensen visited San Diego where Consolidated Aircraft built the heavy bomber. After inspecting the plant, an unimpressed Sorensen told Consolidated officials their production methods would never achieve the goal of manufacturing one bomber a day. Urged to suggest a better way, Sorensen "worked all night" in what he later called "the biggest challenge of my production career." As he later recalled, "To compare a Ford V-8 with a four-engine Liberator was like matching a garage with a skyscraper." Despite the many differences, Sorensen applied the same production fundamentals, while keeping in mind a principle that proved successful with the Model T: "The only thing we can't make is something we can't think about." The next morning, Sorensen produced a pencil sketch of a production facility that would deliver one bomber every hour if the federal government provided $200 million for the plant and equipment. Consolidated, which had produced only a few dozen bombers, suggested Ford just build wing sections. Sorensen rebutted, "We'll make the complete plane or nothing." Despite their skepticism, Consolidated gave Ford a license to build B-24s and an enthusiastic Knudsen drew up the contract.[13]

In April 1941, Ford Motor Company broke ground four miles southeast of Ypsilanti near a small stream called Willow Run. Designed by Albert Kahn, the L-shaped main structure, which became the bomber plant, covered 2.5 million square feet and "was not so much beautiful as just plain enormous." As the world's largest assembly plant (until 1943), Willow Run received more attention than any other American industrial operation. Dignitaries from around the world visited Willow Run, while newspapers described it as "one of the wonders of the world," "a promise of revenge for Pearl Harbor," and "like infinity, it stretches everywhere into the distance of man's vision." At the same time, production claims (that Ford did not initiate, but refused to deny) grew to unbelievable levels, peaking at 1,000 bombers every 24 hours. But there were problems, partly caused by the enormity of the undertaking, as well as the need for tens of thousands of workers who had to be trained to build a complex machine—one that had more than 100,000 parts (as opposed to 15,000 parts for an average automobile). Transporting and housing a workforce to rural eastern Washtenaw County further complicated the

Workers at the Ford Willow Run Bomber plant achieved a production miracle of completing one bomber every hour.

matter for Ford. As the months dragged on and no planes were produced, Willow Run lost much of its luster. Critics called it "Willit Run?" while the president of one aviation company added insult to injury by explaining that "you cannot expect blacksmiths to learn how to make watches overnight." Even the delivery of the first Ford-built B-24 in September did not slow down the negative talk.[14]

Finally, in the spring of 1943, *TIME* reported, "Willow Run seems to be really underway . . . [it] may yet achieve the miracle of a bomber an hour." By January 1944, Ford boasted it was the "largest supplier of B-24s." Three months later, Willow Run reached the elusive one bomber-an-hour production goal; in August annual production peaked at 9,000 bombers. Although Ford led all B-24 producers, the War Department shifted to newer bombers made at other factories. On June 24, 1945, Ford's last B-24, named "Henry Ford," rolled off the Willow Run assembly line. The elder automaker had his name removed from the fuselage and asked employees to sign their names.[15]

Despite the headaches, the achievement at the Willow Run bomber plant contributed to the myth that Henry Ford and his company made a greater contribution to the Arsenal of Democracy than other companies. One late war poll even ranked Ford second among all American industrialists. Although Henry Ford "gave more attention to Willow Run than any other of his wartime plants," his age and health left him, according to Charles Sorensen "the glorified leader who had nothing to do with the program." As historian David Lewis concludes:

> Neither the Ford Motor Company, nor any other person or company won the homefront war singlehandedly. A massive team effort was required, and perhaps the greatest heroes of all, at least in the aggregate, were the millions of workers who toiled in defense plants across the nation.[16]

Michigan's Arsenal of Democracy contributions went beyond tanks and bombers. With a halt in passenger car production in early 1942, the auto industry accounted for 20 percent of America's defense production by war's end. The automakers produced many of the complex tools of war containing thousands of precision-made parts, including 4 million engines, 2.6 million trucks, nearly 50,000 tanks, 27,000 complete aircraft, 245 million shells, and nearly 6 million guns. Chrysler redesigned the Swedish Bofors 40mm anti-aircraft gun, reducing production time from 450 hours (hand filing and fitting) to less than 14 hours (assembly line), while producing 120,000 gun barrels during the war. Oldsmobile in Lansing made artillery shells "in prodigious numbers," while assembling a 20mm cannon that required cooperation among 58 different parts' suppliers. Yet, the company steadily reduced the cannon's unit price and beat the promised delivery times by 20 percent. Not only did these automakers hire tens of thousands of new and inexperienced employees (GM hired 750,000 new workers alone), but the products kept changing. By 1944, General Motors reported the War Department was "not using a single weapon in the same form or design as before Pearl Harbor." The state's industrial role also went beyond automakers. DeFoe Boat and Motor Works in Bay City expanded its capacity, eventually employing 4,000 workers and introducing a new construction technique called the "upside-down and roll over" method. The process, which expedited the welding process, allowed the company to produce one 173-foot patrol boat a week. Daisy Manufacturing Company (Plymouth) quit making BB guns to make shell casings and canisters; Round Oak Stoves (Dowagiac) used its foundry to make made powder cans, bomber wheels, and steel landing mats; the Featherbone Company (Three Oaks) stopped making rubberized baby pants to produce jungle netting and machine-gun belts; and the S. E. Overton Company (South Haven), whose craftsmen excelled in producing an assortment of wooden products (steering wheels, venetian blind slates, and baseball bats) turned to M1 carbine stocks. By war's end, Overton had manufactured 2.6 million gunstocks. The list seems endless.[17]

—— Women, Farmers, and POWs

With tens of thousands of men going off to war, American industry turned to women to help fill its wartime contracts. Rosie the Riveter became part of a government-sponsored advertisement campaign that recognized the contributions women made during the war. Thousands of women worked in Lansing-area industrial plants, including among the 8,500 workers at the Nash-Kelvinator plant, the world's largest producer of airplane propellers. By mid-war, 30 percent of General Motor's hourly workers were women; a comparable figure existed at Chrysler, which even hired women in its engineering division, a "historically all-male bastion." In Grand Rapids, the Hayes Body Corporation (a manufacturer of auto bodies) employed more than 1,500 women (30 percent of its work force) to sew parachutes for the U.S. Navy. In Michigan, an estimated 200,000 women—half of whom had never worked outside the home—filled jobs in the state's auto plants during the war.[18]

An estimated 200,000 Michigan women, like these working on a B-24 at Willow Run, filled industrial jobs.

Michiganians contributed more to winning the war than factory-produced materiel. Farmers also played an important role. During the early 1940s, Michigan ranked among the top ten states in an assortment of farm products. The federal government encouraged farmers to produce as much food as possible, reminding them they also could contribute to an Allied victory. Overcoming fears from World War I when farmers responded to similar demands and then witnessed the bottom fall out of agricultural prices after the war, Michigan farmers broke all previous state records for production in the first year of the war. Although subsequent years fell short of the 1942 results, harvests remained considerable. As thousands of men left the fields and their tractors to join the armed forces, labor shortages posed a serious problem. Solutions included agricultural draft deferments, as well as migrant workers (most notably Mexicans and West Indians). In 1944, about 2,000 *braceros* (strong arms) picked much of the state's sugar beets and cherries. Volunteers also helped out; one federal program, called Victory Farm Volunteers, introduced city dwellers, including children, to farm life.[19]

The U.S. government also "hired out" prisoners of war (POWs) to work in the fields. Between October 1943 and early 1946, thousands of German prisoners offset the labor shortage. Carefully following guidelines of the 1929 Geneva Convention, which allowed prisoners to work in non-war-related occupations, this nationwide program housed POWs in central camps before dispersing them to smaller temporary camps. The camps were fenced-in and guarded with a ratio of one guard for every seven prisoners. The POWs

During World War II, German prisoners of war labored on Michigan farms.

lived in tents placed on concrete slabs in a compound that offered showers, a dispensary, dining, and recreational facilities, as well as a post exchange. A contractor hired the POWs, paying the going labor wage. In turn, the POWs earned 80 cents an hour in coupons they could use to purchase soft drinks (no alcohol), snacks, and toiletries at the post exchange. The POWs worked a six-day, 48-hour week and wore blue clothes with the letters PW stenciled in white. In camp, they were allowed to wear their uniforms. After the evening meal, prisoners spent their free time taking classes in English, watching movies, and listening to music.[90]

In Michigan, Fort Custer in Battle Creek served as the central camp, and more than two dozen communities housed branch camps. The first German soldiers arrived at Benton Harbor in October 1943, and the local newspaper reminded readers these men were "prisoners instead of conquerors." In early 1944 the government recruited the Michigan Agricultural College Agricultural Extension Program to help administer the program. Some communities initially opposed having a POW camp nearby, but they overcame those apprehensions when the prisoners "performed credibly in their work." American civilians were not permitted to the visit the POW camps, but there

was some fraternization. One teenager who met Germans working on a veg-
etable farm near Plainwell remembered, the POWs were "nice guys who loved
it here." By war's end, an estimated 6,000 Axis prisoners worked in Michigan, including about 1,000 in the U.P. who lived in former Civilian Conservation Corps camps, cutting down trees for pulpwood, railroad ties, and fence
posts. Escape attempts were rare, because as one German noted, "It's not the
guards or snow fence that keeps us in. It's the Atlantic Ocean." In assessing
the program, Army sources claimed that the POWs prevented crop loss and
increased production, crediting them with an estimated 35 percent of Michigan's agriculture and food processing during 1944. Michigan farmers "not
only fed the American people, the armed forces, and a significant proportion of the Allied population, but, thanks largely to government production
and rationing policy, greater emphasis than ever before was placed upon the
growing of nutritive foods."[21]

—— On the Battle Front

Approximately 670,000 Michiganians served in the U.S. armed forces during the war. Among the earliest Michiganians sent to war was the 32nd Division, which included National Guard units. Mobilized in October 1940, the
division trained in Louisiana before being shipped to California shortly after
Pearl Harbor. One of the division's two Michigan regiments (the 125th) was
reassigned as coastal artillery, while the other Michigan unit, the 126th (with
units from Coldwater, Adrian, Kalamazoo, Muskegon, Big Rapids, Grand
Haven, Ionia, and Grand Rapids), remained part of the 32nd and headed to
Australia. In November 1942, the 32nd engaged the Japanese in a brutal campaign for possession of New Guinea. General Douglas MacArthur's chief engineer called New Guinea the "ultimate nightmare country." More succinctly,
one Michigan soldier noted, "If I owned New Guinea and I owned hell, I
would live in hell and rent out New Guinea." The Midwesterners were neither
trained nor equipped for the conditions they experienced. "Never, perhaps,
have American soldiers been more poorly equipped." *TIME* reported in late
December 1942, "Nowhere in the world today are American soldiers engaged
in fighting so desperate, so merciless, so bitter, or so bloody." Not only enemy
action, but disease—malaria, dysentery, and hookworm among others—took
a toll. The 126th entered New Guinea with 131 officers and 3,040 enlisted
men. When they returned in late January, the regiment was down to 31 officers and 579 enlisted men. The 32nd was the army's first division to go into
combat in World War II, earning the nickname the Ghost Mountain Boys

because of New Guinea's mountainous terrain (over 10,000 feet) and the unit's miserable condition after the campaign ended. The 32nd also saw action in the liberation of the Philippines and ended the war with 654 combat days— more than any other U.S. Army division. Among its heroes was Dirk J. Vlug, a Grand Rapids private who earned the Medal of Honor for single-handedly destroying five Japanese tanks in one day fighting in the Philippines.[22]

For Michiganians on the home front, no campaign played a greater role than the much-anticipated Allied invasion of northern France. Reports, though fragmentary, went over the airwaves about 1:00 AM (EST) where patrons of all-night theatres heard the news first. Most Michiganians awoke to learn of the invasion from newspaper headlines that screamed "INVASION." Governor Harry Kelly designated June 6 as "D-Day in Michigan" and set aside a minute of statewide meditation and prayer to mark the moment that "has arrived to test our hearts." In schools, factories, and homes, Michiganians paused, bowed their heads, and paid tribute to the men fighting on the bloody beaches in distant France. Working alone in his orchard near Montrose, Donald Sanborn stopped his work and said a short prayer, later reflecting, "I hope it helped." Throughout the day, churches kept their doors open for parishioners who sought a moment of prayer. Some also held special invasion prayer sessions, reporting an increase in attendance for a weekday service. In one town, striking workers returned to work after hearing about the landings. The chaplain at the Marquette maximum state prison prepared a special prayer service with skepticism. However, as he later reflected, the 300 inmates who attended showed "great respect and concern for the men giving their lives for the freedom of many throughout the world." According to the director of the Office of Civilian Defense, the statewide observance was "very, very successful," concluding, it was "the first time" in Michigan history "when so great a body of people [had] been brought together for a single moment of prayer."[23]

One little-known, but distinctly Michigan, aspect of the Allied invasion was the photo of General Dwight "Ike" Eisenhower meeting members of the 101st Airborne Division before they dropped behind enemy lines on June 6. In an often-published image, Ike stopped to talk with Lt. Wallace C. Strobel of Saginaw. After the war, Strobel recalled, "Once he learned I was from Michigan, [the general] talked to me about fishing in Michigan."[24]

The enormous Battle of the Bulge in late 1944 proved a serious and unanticipated Allied setback. Howard M. Trowern, Jr., of Grosse Pointe commanded a small patrol in General George Patton's Third Army coming to rescue the beleaguered 101st Airborne Division at Bastogne, Belgium. As he later recalled, his men confronted another small American patrol shortly

Lt. Wallace Strobel of Saginaw receives inspiration from General Dwight D. Eisenhower as the 101ˢᵗ Airborne prepared for the D-Day invasion.

after learning Germans disguised as GIs were infiltrating the lines. A suspicious Trowern asked the officer leading the other group, "What team did Ty Cobb play for?" The response, "Wasn't he a baseball player?" was not a comforting reply. Other questions about the Detroit Tigers followed with no better results. Finally the officer told an increasingly uneasy Trowern, "Look, I don't follow baseball." Just then, one of the officer's soldiers suggested asking Trowern, "Where's the house that Ruth built?" Trowern responded that he was just out of high school and "I don't know anything about house building." The second group of Americans eyed Trowern wondering, "Maybe you guys are the German commandos." Then asked to explain the infield fly rule, Trowern flubbed again. While the officer did not recognize the former Tiger great, Trowern failed to recognize that it was Babe Ruth who had "built" Yankee Stadium. As both groups relaxed, the officer dryly noted, "Not everyone comes from Michigan." The two men shook hands and parted company with a promise to "see you in Berlin."[25]

Another Michigan connection to the Battle of the Bulge dealt with a Detroit native who became the only American soldier executed for desertion since the Civil War. Drafted in 1943, 23-year-old Eddie Slovik had spent much of his adult life in prison for crimes that ranged from breaking and entering to auto theft. Six weeks after the D-Day landings, Slovik joined a front-line infantry unit. After surviving his first German artillery barrage, he deserted, admitting to a friend, he "wasn't cut out for combat." Six weeks later, he returned to his unit, and when his request for reassignment was denied, he deserted once more. He turned himself in, but presented a note promising to desert again if sent to the front. Slovik rejected several opportunities to destroy the self-incriminating piece of paper and be reassigned to a different unit where he could begin with a "clean slate." Instead, he sought a court-martial, confident incarceration was his worst fate. Found guilty in a trial where he refused to testify, Slovik was sentenced to death by a firing squad. Upper-echelon officials approved the sentence because Slovik was either a "habitual criminal" or "to maintain that discipline upon which alone an army can succeed against the enemy." A week after the Battle of the Bulge started, General Eisenhower approved Slovik's execution, which was carried out in a ceremony cloaked in secrecy on January 31, 1945. Slovik's body was buried in a remote part of the U.S. cemetery at Oise-Aisne American Cemetery and Memorial in northern France with a tombstone marked by a number and no name. Only years later did Antoinette Slovik learn of her husband's fate. Her efforts to secure his remains or pension (the latter forfeited by his dishonor-able discharge) proved unsuccessful. After her death Slovik's remains came home, thanks to the efforts of Bernard V. Calka, a former Macomb County Commissioner and World War II veteran. Slovik was buried next to his wife in Detroit's Woodmere Cemetery. Slovik's story became a best-selling book by William B. Huie (*The Execution of Private Slovik*) and a television movie by the same name starring Martin Sheen. Years after the war, one of the officers who sat in judgment of the Detroit private determined that Slovik's execution was "a historic injustice," especially since the 48 other American soldiers who faced the death sentence for desertion escaped the firing squad.[26]

During the war, life changed dramatically on the Michigan home front. "Use it up, wear it out, make it do or go without," the catchy government phrase from the Depression years, served double duty during the war years. Shortages and rationing led to conservation. Meat, sugar, gas, tires, and shoes were among the rationed items, while bananas, candy, and nylon stockings disappeared. One Michiganian remembered "practicing conservation dili-gently," while another recalled having to present an empty tube of toothpaste "to buy a new tube of toothpaste." One new teenage driver recalled scarce items like tires led to two flats one night and the embarrassment of "having your father drive you to your girl's house so you can say good-night." A short-age of young men led a Detroiter to recall, "many girls missed out on dating,

Children in Grand Rapids contribute to the war effort by planting a victory garden in 1944.

losing a big chunk of their youth [since] there were no young men around to date." To cope with food shortages, Michiganians planted victory gardens by the thousands, often under the direction of the Michigan Agricultural College Cooperative Extension Service. Prompted by patriotic slogans like "Food Will Win the War," Michiganians canned an estimated 170 million quarts of food by 1944.[27]

—— Detroit Explodes

Home front stresses, especially in racially divided Detroit, also led to one of the nation's worst wartime civil disturbances. Between 1910 and 1970, an estimated 6.5 million blacks left the South and moved north. The hardships of sharecropping in the rural South and the attraction of a better life in the industrial North explain the population shift called the Great Migration. For blacks who endured political, social, and economic oppression in the South, the North also looked like the Promised Land with higher wages, fewer segregation laws, and no poll taxes or literacy tests preventing blacks from voting. Racial prejudice existed in the North, but blacks did not suffer the constant fears of humiliation, lynching, and degradation they experienced in the South. In the early 1940s an estimated 50,000 blacks moved to Michigan. They quickly realized that equal rights, most notably fair and equal housing, did not exist, especially in Detroit, which was a model of racial segregation. Furthermore, as tens of thousands of southern whites moved into southeastern Michigan, hatemongers stirred up traditional racial fears.[28]

As black Americans fought against oppression on distant shores in the war, at home they campaigned for an end to inequality and discrimination. The Detroit chapter of the National Association for the Advancement of Colored People (NAACP) declared that the issue of civil rights "must be raised now." As blacks served in a segregated U.S. Army and suffered "Jim Crowism" in the industrial plants producing war materiel, President Roosevelt remained silent on civil rights and "ignored the deteriorating domestic situation." In early 1942, more than 1,000 armed white Detroiters rioted to stop blacks from leaving the ghetto and moving into the federally sponsored Sojourner Truth Housing Project, which had been built in a white neighborhood. Federal officials investigating the disturbances advised "strong and quick intervention" to avoid problems. In August 1942, *Life* magazine chronicled the growing racial problems in the Motor City in a disturbing expose entitled, "Detroit is Dynamite." In the months that followed, blacks and whites clashed in schools, factories, and on city streets. In June 1943, 25,000 white workers at the Packard Motor Company staged a wildcat strike protesting the promotion of three black workers. Although black leaders "openly predicted greater violence unless something was done quickly to provide jobs and housing," nothing was done.

The explosion came on July 20, 1943, as thousands of blacks and whites sought relief on Belle Isle on a hot summer day. Brawls throughout the day led to more serious fighting and, by evening, the bridge connecting the popular island to the mainland was a "war zone." Police arrested 28 blacks and 19 whites, halting the disturbance without firing a shot. However, the violence spread across the city. Blacks vented their pent-up rage by destroying white property, while whites attacked blacks "caught outside of the ghetto." Blacks riding streetcars or leaving all-night movies were beaten, and whites targeted black drivers, forcing them from their cars, which they then set on fire. As state and local officials fumbled to regain control, "rumors kept refueling the frenzy, and the rioting grew." Police forces could not contain the rioters, transportation lines and schools shut down, firemen could no longer control the growing number of fires, and injured Detroiters entered the Receiving Hospital at a rate of one every minute. After a delay of hours, federal troops (eventually 6,000 strong) arrived and quickly restored order. The riot left 34 people dead, 700 injured, 1,800 arrested, and more than $2 million in property damage, as well as the loss of untold hours of industrial production time. The Nazis claimed the riot proved "the internal disorganization of a country torn by social injustice, race hatreds, regional disputes, the violence of an irritated proletariat, and the gangsterism of a capitalistic police."

As troops patrolled Detroit's streets in the days after the violence "the search for answers and scapegoats" began. Some blamed German agents who hoped to disrupt war production. Congressman Martin Dies (D-Texas), who chaired the House Un-American Activities Committee, blamed Japanese Americans released from internment camps, while another southern congressman attributed the discord to "attempting to mix races in all kinds of employment." A Mississippi newspaper blamed Eleanor Roosevelt, claiming her support for "social equality" led Detroit's impudent and insolent blacks "to put [her] preachments into practice." Closer to home, the city's police commissioner blamed blacks for "starting the riot and Army authorities for prolonging it." According to Detroit Police chief John H. Witherspoon, whites only retaliated, never explaining why police shot 17 of the 25 blacks killed in the riot. Mayor Jeffries agreed with the police, maintaining black leaders needed to do a better job "educating their own people of their responsibilities as citizens." The Common Council "heartily approved" the official reports, with one member concluding nothing needed to be done since "the racial conflict has been going on in this country since our ancestors made the first mistake of bringing the Negro to the country." Governor Kelly also exonerated whites, blaming black agitators who "constantly beat the drums of 'racial prejudice.'" The governor also mocked the "presumed grievances" and "alleged Jim Crowism" of the city's black citizens.

Conversely, Thurgood Marshall, working for the NAACP, spent more than two weeks two in Detroit before authoring an expose that explained "the attitude and efficiency of the police" led to the riot. Recounting numerous attacks by whites on blacks—often as the police stood by and watched—the future U.S. Supreme Court justice likened the actions of the Detroit police force "to the story of the Nazi Gestapo." He concluded:

> This record by the Detroit police department demonstrates once more what all Negroes know only too well; that nearly all police departments limit their conception of checking racial disorders to surrounding, arresting, maltreating and shooting Negroes. Little attempt is made to check the activities of whites. The certainty of Negroes that they will not be protected by police, but instead attacked by them is a contributing factor to racial tensions leading to overt acts. The first item on the agenda of any group seeking to prevent rioting would seem to be a critical study of the police department of the community, its record in handling Negroes, something of the background of its personnel, and the plans of its chief officers for possibly meeting racial disorders.[29]

Despite these accusations, federal, state, and city leaders accepted the official conclusions, and Detroit resumed business as usual. A congressional investigation was rejected, while Senators Homer Ferguson and Arthur Vandenberg were accused of blocking efforts to improve black housing in the city's white suburbs. Governor Kelly appropriated one million dollars to train riot troops to quell future problems, while Mayor Jeffries enjoyed reelection as a defender of white supremacy.

—— Rejecting Isolationism

As the war neared its end, one unlikely Michiganian became a central figure in an effort to prevent future wars. An outspoken critic of President Roosevelt's New Deal, Senator Vandenberg turned down his party's vice presidential nomination in 1936. A firm isolationist who opposed U.S. cooperation with the League of Nations and supported stronger neutrality laws, Vandenberg believed the United States could not "hope to control the destiny of power politics in the Old World." However, the senator experienced something of an epiphany after surviving a German air raid in London and returned home "fully supporting the war effort." During the summer of 1943, he admitted that he was "hunting for the middle ground between those extremists at one end of the line who would cheerfully give America away and those extremists at the other end of the line who would attempt a total isolation which has become an impossibility." A few weeks later, Vandenberg invited Republican leaders to Mackinac Island's Grand Hotel to discuss supporting plans for a postwar international peace organization. The *Detroit News* described this gathering as "the most important political party meeting to be held in Michigan" since the birth of the Republican party in Jackson in 1854. Despite polls showing most Americans supported the formation of the United Nations, some Republicans opposed American involvement in a postwar international organization. Vandenberg firmly declared that his party "will not retire to its foxhole when the last shot in this war has been fired and will blindly let the world rot in its own anarchy." Under the senator's leadership, the Republicans adopted the Mackinac Charter, endorsing the United Nations "to prevent military aggression and to attain permanent peace with organized justice in a free world."[30]

In February 1945, President Roosevelt chose Vandenberg to serve as one of the American delegates working to design the United Nations. The senator's efforts helped the U.S. win a crucial victory in negotiations with the

Russians, prompting Vandenberg to declare his "deep conviction" for the United Nations Charter, which he characterized as a "new emancipation proclamation for the world." The Senate overwhelmingly ratified the charter with strong bipartisan support. In the following years, Vandenberg—in his capacity as chairman of the Senate Foreign Relations Committee—also led Republican support for the Marshall Plan, NATO, and the Truman Doctrine. Vandenberg also campaigned for a young challenger named Ford who defeated an isolationist Grand Rapids Republican congressman. Gerald Ford's surprising victory in 1948 began a long and distinguished career that took him to the White House nearly three decades later.[30]

Germany surrendered on May 8, 1945, and Japan quit three months later. All across the state, Michiganians took to the streets and made noise. Five hundred thousand Detroiters spilled into the streets to celebrate the war's end, while in Sault Ste. Marie the boats in the Soo Locks blew their horns without interruption and "there was pandemonium and delirium." In Mackinaw City, the ringing of church bells, ferry-boat whistles, and fire sirens was mixed with "a number of men [who] gathered on the commons behind the village hall to fire off valuable hunting ammunition." In Saginaw, Marie Hillman explained to her son (then serving with the 15th U.S. Air Force in Italy) how all the neighbors gathered at the Hillman house bringing with them prized bottles of liquor that had been saved to be opened only at war's end. She added, "The streets were crowded and the noise was really something to hear, it was a grand sight to see those happy people, and one we shall never forget."[31]

18

Postwar Michigan and the Turbulent 1960s

Opened in 1957, the Mackinac Bridge remains an icon.

"You can take the girl out of Michigan, but you can't take Michigan out of the girl."

—Madonna at the 2008 Traverse City Music Festival

Michiganians experienced a period of instability as World War II came to an end. Money was plentiful, but products, especially new automobiles, were scarce. The federal government allowed auto manufacturers to resume civilian car production following the surrender of Germany in May 1945. This advance planning helped speed conversion from tanks and Jeeps to cars and trucks, but automakers struggled to meet demand. By the end of 1945, they had furnished only two new cars to each of the nation's 33,000 dealers. Full capacity did not return to the auto industry until 1949.

During the 1950s the American auto industry dominated the world as the Big Three (General Motors, Ford Motor Company, and Chrysler Corporation) sold nine million vehicles in 1955—two-thirds of the world's output for that year. An enthusiasm to take advantage of a temporary auto vacuum also led two new automakers to enter the highly competitive business.[1]

319

Henry J. Kaiser, a Californian whose success at building ships during the war earned him the nickname "Miracle Worker," and Joseph Frazer, who rose from manual laborer to president of Detroit's Graham-Paige Motor Company, formed the Kaiser-Frazer Corporation in 1945. In 1947, the company produced 144,000 cars (the higher-priced "Frazer" and the lower-priced "Kaiser") in the former Ford Willow Run bomber plant near Ypsilanti. Developing a nationwide dealer network and producing "gracefully designed" cars that had market appeal, Kaiser-Frazer enjoyed early success and became the nation's fourth leading automaker. However, as the Big Three returned to car production, Kaiser-Frazer faced "a handful of hope-inspiring incidents and a long list of numbing, depressing setbacks." Market share dropped to less than two percent as raw materials became increasingly difficult to obtain. Production ended in 1955 after manufacturing 750,000 cars.[2]

At about the same time, Preston Tucker stole industry headlines as one of the industry's more intriguing personalities. Born in Capac, Tucker devoted his life to automobiles, everything from working on the assembly line at Ford to building Indy 500 racecars. The armored combat car he invented in his Ypsilanti machine shop proved unattractive because it went too fast (115 mph), but the U.S. military liked the gun turret of the Tucker Tiger and used it on PT boats and bombers. After the war, the futuristic "Tucker Torpedo" excited an auto-starved market. The Torpedo's new design placed the engine in the rear and offered an assortment of safety features including a padded dashboard, a center "Cyclops" headlight that turned with the car, and a windshield that popped up during an accident. Company literature boasted that the Torpedo was "the most talked about car in the world." After setting up an extensive dealer network, Tucker acquired a Chicago manufacturing plant before running into problems with the Securities Exchange Commission. During a lengthy trial, the government accused Tucker of never intending to manufacture an automobile. Although Tucker was acquitted on all counts of fraud, his dream of manufacturing the Torpedo had ended. Today, the 50 Torpedoes Tucker finished are mostly in private hands, although The Henry Ford and the Smithsonian Institution each have one in their collections.[3]

—— Soapy Reinvigorates the Democrats

The postwar period also saw the emergence of "one of the most formidable and effective political campaigners in Michigan history." G. Mennen "Soapy" Williams—a native Detroiter, heir to the Mennen toiletries fortune, graduate of Princeton University and the University of Michigan Law School, and World War II veteran—challenged enormous odds to run for governor in 1948. An indefatigable campaigner who could say "Hello" in 17 languages and give up to 50 speeches a day, Williams ignored all polls that guaranteed the re-election of incumbent Kim Sigler (R-Hastings). Two years earlier, the Democrats had received a drubbing, and few gave Williams much chance, especially when 60 of the state's 61 daily newspapers endorsed Sigler. Although Michigan voters supported Republican Thomas Dewey (an Owosso native and University of Michigan graduate) in that year's presidential race, Williams beat Sigler by a comfortable margin. Williams narrowly won re-election in 1950 and 1952 (surviving recounts in both cases) on his way to an unprecedented six consecutive terms—the most of any Michigan governor.[4]

Williams' 1948 victory, dubbed by the press as "the Michigan miracle," also marked the beginning of a distinct change in Michigan politics, especially among Democratics. Liberals Hicks Griffiths and Neil Staebler and union leaders Walter Reuther, August Scholle, Adelaide Hart, and Mildred Jeffrey "built one of the most effective political organizations in American history." Union leaders sought "to influence the development of wide-ranging programs of social and other humanitarian reforms," while liberals sought to continue progressive programs of the New Deal. Coupling these goals with Williams' ability to espouse the "causes of the little people," the Democratic party grew stronger with each election. By the 1954 elections, Williams easily won re-election and the Democrats won statewide offices, controlling both U.S. Senate seats and electing an increasing number of congressional representatives. In Williams they

Serving an unprecedented six terms as governor, G. Mennen "Soapy" Williams was an indefatigable campaigner. He is shown with a polio victim in 1954.

also had a candidate who was memorable for many reasons, including his green-and-white polka-dot bow tie that became his trademark. Years later, Williams' campaign billboards only needed the famed bow tie, not even his name.[5]

Despite the mounting Democratic threat, the Republicans remained formidable opponents. President Dwight Eisenhower named Arthur Summerfield of Flint (the country's largest Chevy dealer) as Postmaster General and Charles E. Wilson, president of General Motors, as Secretary of Defense. (In the closed confirmation hearing, Wilson was quoted as saying, "What is good for General Motors is good for the country." He actually said, "What is good for our country is good for General Motors, and vice versa." The misquote hounded Wilson for years, allegedly confirming the selfish tendencies of American business.)[6]

Throughout the 1950s, Williams and the Republican-dominated legislature tangled over government's role. As biographer Thomas J. Noer explains:

> Mennen Williams assumed that government had an obligation to improve society and meet the needs of the people. . . . "Necessary services" such as expanded educational opportunities, health care, housing, roads, and conservation. In addition, government must use its power to move society toward racial and economic equality. Williams argued that government must *first* look at the needs of the people and *then* find the revenue to pay for programs to help meet them. . . . Those who were financially successful, both individuals and corporations, should pay the costs of expanded state services. . . . Michigan Republicans rejected all of Williams's assumptions. They were dedicated to minimal government and taxation. . . . [Government's] primary obligation was to maintain order and ensure a climate that stimulates private enterprise. . . . They argued that you first judge the amount of revenue the state can expect and then initiate only those programs this income can fund. They strongly opposed increases in taxes.

The major source of funding was the sales tax, and by the 1950s, demand greatly outweighed available revenues. Williams favored increasing corporate taxes, while the Republicans supported increasing the 3 percent sales tax. With each passing year, the state's financial problems worsened.[7]

Despite the Democrats executive and judicial successes, the outdated and unfair apportionment of legislative seats benefitted the Republicans. The 1908 State Constitution called for the state House to be reapportioned every ten years with the federal census, but the constitution seemed unclear about the Senate. Representation had not kept up with Detroit's enormous growth during the early years of the twentieth century, with rural Michigan (generally a Republican bastion) being overrepresented. Over the years, the legislature showed little signs of addressing the issue, ignoring the 1930 census for both the House and the Senate in 1940. Even when pushed to address the matter, the solution remained inadequate. The house did reapportion in 1943, giving heavily populated Wayne County 27 seats, when it should have received 38 seats. Even a 1952 voter-supported "balanced legislature" initiative left widely disproportionate districts. The population extremes between the largest and smallest state house districts was 67,000 and 32,000; the gap in the state senate was worse—364,000 and 61,000.[8]

—— Building the Big Mac

The Mackinac Bridge stands as one of Williams' great accomplishments. He recounted that it began with a haircut while campaigning in St. Ignace in 1948, when he discovered that "people in the Upper Peninsula felt alienated from the Lower Peninsula." Wondering what he should say to mollify this concern, a *Detroit Free Press* reporter suggested, "Tell them you'll build a bridge." Williams agreed and vowed to fulfill this long-held dream if elected. At about the same time, W. Stewart Woodfill, owner of Mackinac Island's Grand Hotel and a Republican, started lobbying for a bridge. It is doubtful that either Williams or Woodfill anticipated the challenges that lay ahead.[9]

As early as the 1880s, Michiganians had discussed the prospects of bridging the Straits of Mackinac. Proposals included a floating tunnel or a series of bridges and causeways linking Cheboygan to St. Ignace. In 1923, the state began running a car ferry between Mackinaw City and St. Ignace. But during the peak periods, most notably deer-hunting season, motorists waited hours to cross the Straits of Mackinac. Formed in 1934 to address the problem, the Mackinac Straits Bridge Authority lost momentum during World War II and the proposed cost of the project seemed overwhelming. In 1947, the legislature dissolved the bridge authority. After Woodfill strong-armed Republicans, the legislature created an agency called the Mackinac Bridge Authority. Woodfill did not seek an appointment to the Authority, submitting that his only goal was the completion of "a great project for the benefit of all Michigan." On June 6, 1950, Williams signed the bill creating the Authority; he chose former U.S. Senator Prentiss M. Brown (D-St. Ignace) as chairman of the six-member, bipartisan commission.[10]

During the next two years, the Authority worked with engineers who determined the bridge could be safely built. In early 1952, the legislature passed a bill allowing the Authority to issue revenue bonds to fund construction. They also insisted that no state agencies be used to build, maintain, or repair the bridge. To make their point, the legislature granted the Authority one dollar of state monies to construct what critics started calling, "Soapy's Folly." According to historian Richard Shaul, "The legislature's not-so-subtle message separating itself from what might be a losing venture, motivated the Authority to pursue its goal with greater persistence and determination." The bridge would cost $99 million to build and the Authority hired Dr. David Steinman, who had designed 400 bridges, as the project's chief designer.

Throughout 1953, the project faced one obstacle after another. After an intense lobbying campaign by Authority members, the legislature allowed state funds that were lost annually by running the state ferry at the straits (approximately $500,000) to operate and maintain the bridge. A December 31, 1953 legislatively mandated deadline for the sale of the revenue bonds, the absence of the state's financial backing of the bonds, and a weak investment market posed problems. As the deadline approached, State Treasurer D. Hale Brake, a member of the State Administrative Board that would approve the bond sale, complicated matters by arguing that the matter should be submitted to the voters for their approval. Finally, at the eleventh hour, bridge critic Senator Haskell L. Nichols (R-Jackson) filed a petition with the State Supreme Court challenging the use of any state monies for the bridge project. According to Shaul:

> Some believed that legislative opponents were protecting the taxpayers from being burdened with the cost of a failed project, while others thought that they were willing to deep-six the bridge to prevent Governor Williams from receiving the credit.

Regardless of Haskell's motives, if the court accepted the petition, the project faced its death-knell. Brown raced to Lansing from St. Ignace and reassured court justices they could review Haskell's petition (which he pointed out could have been submitted months earlier) after the bond sale. The court agreed with Brown's logic. The State Administrative Board approved the bond sale on the last possible day. "Soapy's Folly" would be built.

Dodging numerous pitfalls, Governor Williams got the Mackinac Bridge built—one of his greatest achievements.

Construction began in late 1954, and the Mackinac Bridge opened to traffic on November 1, 1957. The central suspension span extends 3,800 feet between the main towers that rise 552 feet above the water. The total length of the bridge is 26,372 feet and the suspension bridge (including anchorages) is 8,614 feet. The last of the construction bonds were retired in mid-1986. Fare revenues maintain the massive structure, which is the longest suspension bridge in the Western Hemisphere and the third longest suspension bridge in the world. Today, the Mackinac Bridge is one of Michigan's most-admired attractions and the site of an annual Labor Day Bridge Walk, begun by Governor Williams, that draws on average 60,000 participants.[11]

Williams also addressed the many needs in the area of education. In 1950 there were too many school districts and almost half the state's school buildings had been constructed before 1900. With the postwar baby boom, the schools were also overcrowded. Public school enrollment of slightly more than one million students in 1950 had doubled a decade later. The governor recommended a consolidation program that reduced the number of school districts by more than half during the 1950s. Larger districts meant newer buildings and more buses. At the higher education level, enrollments also skyrocketed. During the postwar years, the state provided financial aid to community colleges, while the number of four-year schools increased. Colleges became universities (Michigan State, Western, Eastern, Central, and Northern); other four-year schools joined the state system (Wayne, Ferris, Grand Valley, Saginaw, Lake Superior), and Michigan State and the University of Michigan opened branches (MSU at Oakland and Michigan at Flint and Dearborn). All of this education expansion, coupled with escalating costs of other state services, demanded more revenue and contributed to a looming financial crisis.[12]

—— The Red Menace

America in the early 1950s also meant "McCarthyism," a period when charges of disloyalty, often fueled by rumor and innuendo, destroyed lives, careers, and reputations in the name of patriotism. Michigan was not immune from fears of the "Red menace." As early as 1922, federal agents had raided a national communist gathering in the small rural community of Bridgman. During the early 1930s, communists marched in the streets of Detroit protesting capitalism. Communists also belonged to auto unions. During the postwar period, Congressman Kit Clardy (R-Ionia) enthusiastically used the investigative power of the House Un-American Activities Committee to seek out communists, earning the nickname "Michigan's McCarthy." At the same time, Michigan required civil servants to take a loyalty oath, created a legislative "loyalty commission" to investigate communists, and moved to outlaw the communist Party, which had fewer than 1,000 members. Law enforcement also responded as the Michigan State and Detroit police "Red Squads" kept files on suspected communists. During these uncertain times, the decision of one little-known Michiganian to stand up to the excesses of McCarthyism had national implications.[13]

In mid-October 1953, readers of *The Detroit News* learned that Lt. Milo Radulovich was being separated from the U.S. Air Force because a "close and continuing association" with his father and sister left him a security risk. According to the Air Force, Milo's father read a Serbian newspaper dubbed by the U.S. attorney general as communist. John Radulovich, who barely spoke English, had migrated to this country years earlier and worked for Ford for years, also read non-communist publications to keep abreast of events in his native Yugoslavia. Milo's sister, Margaret, was an activist who participated in protests, but Milo rarely saw her. In his ten years in the Air Force, Radulovich had earned a spotless record, which included excellence commendations and his selection for a top-secret mission in Greenland. In the fall of 1953, Radulovich attended the University of Michigan to pursue a career in meteorology and lived in nearby Dexter, where he and his wife, Nancy, raised their two young daughters.[14]

The options available to Radulovich included resigning honorably with his service record carrying the stigma of "resignation in lieu of elimination" or seeking a formal hearing. He chose the latter. After his military-appointed defense lawyer explained that he had lost four similar cases, Radulovich hired Charles Lockwood, a semi-retired, former professor from the Detroit College of Law (present-day MSU College of Law). According to historian Michael

Ranville, the hearing, held at Selfridge Air Force Base and closed because of negative publicity, was "nothing more than a disappointing charade." The charges against Radulovich remained in a sealed envelope and not shared with the defense. There were no witnesses, there was no one to cross-examine, and the accusers were never identified. The board of three colonels sustained the separation decision, and its president even accused Lt. Radulovich of embarrassing the Air Force.

In New York City, famed journalist Edward R. Murrow and producer Fred Friendly who collaborated to produce "See it Now," a weekly television program on CBS, saw the *Detroit News* story. As Friendly reflected years later, "Milo Radulovich was the perfect little picture to illustrate the ravages of McCarthyism." Murrow and Friendly quickly sent a reporter and camera crew to Dexter and developed a "See It Now" program within a week. The controversial nature of "The Case Against Milo Radulovich" worried the CBS hierarchy, led the show's commercial sponsor to pull its support, and prompted the Air Force to request that the show not be aired. According to Murrow's biographer, "the Radulovich case reeked of a sickness abroad in the land. A man was being punished without due process of law, without being permitted to know the evidence against him, indeed without having committed a crime. His ordeal was being shared by hundreds of other Americans." The Milo Radulovich story revealed to Americans "the wretched excess of communist witch-hunts," Friendly later reflected. Several weeks after the show appeared, the Air Force reinstated Radulovich. Even more significantly, this show provided the impetus for another "See It Now" show five months later that went directly after Senator Joe McCarthy and started the Wisconsin senator's downfall. According to Friendly, the show against McCarthy never would have appeared without the Radulovich program. Milo Radulovich's story later appeared in *Good Night, and Good Luck*, a well-received 2005 movie directed by George Clooney.

By the mid-1950s, Governor Williams moved forward to seek the 1960 Democratic presidential nomination. However, two issues blocked his success. Williams refused to consider political compromise on matters of racial equality. After the Republicans defeated his 1950 proposal over a fair employment act, he accused them of "a record studded with broken promises, political weasel words, the quick brush off and the double cross." By executive action, he desegregated the Michigan National Guard, pressured the state police to hire black troopers, appointed the state's first black judge (Charles Jones to the Detroit Recorder's Court), and lobbied the all-white Detroit Tigers to sign black players. The governor's "militant liberalism," according to his biographer, had national ramifications since not all Democrats, especially southerners, held similar commitments to civil rights.[15]

A second destabilizing matter was the ongoing problem with the state finances. A decline in defense contracts to automakers (since new weapons systems went to companies that made rockets and missiles, not tanks and trucks) coupled with industrial automation led to a rise in unemployment. Michigan auto plant employment declined from 503,000 in 1953 to 293,000 five years later. At the same time, automakers opened plants outside Michigan. By early 1959, the mounting state deficit created negative publicity for Williams and Michigan. Some conservative Republicans put off dealing with the financial problems, especially tax reform, in hopes of embarrassing the Governor Williams. A telegram from the head of the Michigan Manufacturers Association leaked to the press congratulated the Republicans for having Williams "over the barrel for first time in ten years" and urged them to "keep him there 'til he screams 'uncle.'" In May 1959, state employees suffered a "payless payday." The ensuing negative national publicity damaged the state's reputation and led the legislature to adopt a one percent "use tax," basically a sales tax increase that circumvented the constitutional limit of 3 percent, that the Michigan Supreme Court struck down. The legislature responded with nuisance taxes (liquor, cigarettes, and beer) and, when those failed to raise necessary revenues, "raided" the Veterans Trust Fund. The problem awaited a future resolution, but greatly damaged Williams' bid for higher office.[16]

Williams did not seek a seventh term as governor. He became a strong supporter of John F. Kennedy's bid for the Democratic presidential nomination. After Kennedy's victory, Williams accepted an appointment to be Assistant Secretary of State for African Affairs. As America's main diplomat in Africa, Williams angered some white Africans by announcing that he supported "Africa for the Africans." According to Williams' biographer:

> He defied most of the rule of diplomacy, and that was the source of both his success and his failures. To liberals and Africans, he was a solitary voice for an African first orientation in U.S. policy that demanded the nation live up to its ideals of equality, democracy, and freedom. To critics, Williams was a publicity-seeking politician who did not understand the process and protocol of policy-making and had the unrealistic expectation that Washington should champion Africa regardless of the cost of alienating traditional allies and jeopardizing strategic interests.

Years after his service in Africa, Williams and his wife Nancy met South African Bishop Desmond Tutu in Detroit. When Williams mentioned his previous State Department service, Tutu didn't appear impressed until Nancy Williams mentioned this was "Soapy Williams." "Oh," Tutu beamed. "Soapy Williams!

. . . You're a great man." After an unsuccessful run for the U.S. Senate, Williams was elected to the Michigan Supreme Court, where he served as chief justice until his retirement in 1986.[17]

——JFK and the Peace Corps

One legacy from the 1960 presidential campaign that continues to have a lasting impact occurred during the early hours of October 15 as thousands of enthusiastic supporters greeted Senator John Kennedy in Ann Arbor. Despite running hours behind schedule (which left some co-eds anxious about violating their dorm curfew), Kennedy made brief remarks from the front steps of the University of Michigan Union and easily won over the crowd by noting he was "a graduate of the Michigan of the East, Harvard University." In his brief remarks, Kennedy challenged the students to volunteer to go abroad and assist people living in the developing world. A few weeks later when he formally proposed the Peace Corps, hundreds of enthusiastic students volunteered. Critics, including Kennedy's opponent, Richard Nixon, claimed recent college graduates either lacked the necessary skills and maturity for this task or the Peace Corps would become a haven for draft dodgers. Since its March 1961 founding, the Peace Corps has sent more than 200,000 Ameri-

Senator John F. Kennedy proposes the creation of a program that would become the Peace Corps from the steps of the Michigan Union during the 1960 presidential campaign.

cans to 139 countries—an accomplishment clearly in keeping with Kennedy's inaugural charge to Americans that they "ask not what your country can do for you—ask what you can do for your country."[18]

When G. Mennen Williams left the state political scene, an equally charismatic politician replaced him. Born in Mexico to American parents in 1907, George Romney grew up in Utah. He arrived in Michigan in the 1940s and worked with auto manufacturers before becoming president of the newly organized American Motors Corporation (AMC) in 1954. Romney turned AMC into a profitable company by promoting the Rambler, a small, fuel-efficient vehicle that quickly became America's third best-selling car. Romney criticized other car companies because their cars kept getting bigger and bigger. "Who wants to have a gas-guzzling dinosaur in his garage," he once asked, "Think of the gas bills." Romney also turned his attention to politics. In 1959 he founded Citizens for Michigan, a group that hoped to resolve annoying issues like state finances and legislative representation by calling for a state constitutional convention.[19]

—— The Con-Con

On October 3, 1961, Michigan Secretary of State James Hare gaveled into session one of the state's most significant political events of the century. The elected delegates (99 Republicans and 45 Democrats, one from each house and senate district) gathered in Lansing with a mandate to write a new state constitution. The group was mostly white males, with only a handful of women and blacks among the group. The Con-Con, as it was called, met in numerous sessions from October 1961 through May 1962. They debated, discussed, and argued, considering more than 800 different proposals in a convention where partisan bickering rose to a fever pitch. In May 1962, the delegates adopted a final product by a partisan vote of 99-44. Following a lively campaign debating the merits of the proposed constitution, voters gave their consent on April 1, 1963, by a narrow margin of 7,500 votes out of 810,000 votes cast.[20]

The new constitution went into effect on January 1, 1964. Most notably, it expanded the powers of the governor, who began serving four-year terms in 1966. Consolidating the existing 120 existing state agencies into no more than 20 departments improved government efficiency and also gave the governor more power by (in most cases) appointing department heads. Requiring the governor and lieutenant governor to run as a team made it impossible to choose candidates from different parties, and further strengthened the governor's office. The state senate expanded from 34 to 38 members, and the terms of office increased from two to four years. Population would be used for house reapportionment every ten years, but a compromise in the senate led to the use of a formula of 80 percent population and 20 percent geography. (A 1964 federal court mandate forced Michigan to change senate apportionment and base it exclusively on population.) Some candidates were removed from the ballot, while others were placed on it. In the process, the ballot got longer. A restructuring of the state judiciary abolished the justices of the peace and created the state court of appeals. The document's education provisions won high praise, expanding the powers and the responsibilities of the state board of education, while limiting the board's powers over universities and colleges.

After serving as one of the Con-Con vice presidents, Romney resigned from AMC and ran for governor as a Republican in 1962. He won, ending fourteen years of Democratic control of the governorship. Voters re-elected Romney in 1964 and 1966. A gifted speaker, Romney had a great smile and a friendly handshake. He exercised regularly, and even after turning 80 years old, he either jogged or walked each day. According to legendary political columnist George Weeks, the single word that best described Romney was "intense." Romney's popularity and leadership, which included getting the legislature to adopt a state income tax stabilizing the state budget, led the three-term governor to make a run at the presidency. Then, two events derailed his candidacy.[21]

—— The Civil Rights Movement

In the spring of 1963 Detroiters looked for a way to recognize the anniversary of racial violence that tore through their city twenty years earlier. The Detroit Council for Human Rights called for a "walk to freedom" because many of "the same basic, underlying causes" of the 1943 disturbance still existed. On June 23, 1963, an estimated 125,000 people marched down Detroit's Woodward Avenue carrying placards and singing "We Shall Overcome." National and state leaders who joined the Reverend Martin Luther King, Jr., included UAW president Walter Reuther, former Governor John B. Swainson, and Detroit mayor Jerome Cavanagh. Recalling recent attacks during similar protests in the South, Detroit police commissioner George Edwards reassured King, "You'll find no dogs and fire hoses here." The march ended at Cobo

Hall where thousands cheered the Reverend King when he called for an end to segregation. In his speech, King spoke of having a "dream" where whites and blacks walked together in harmony and equality. The *Michigan Chronicle*, Detroit's weekly black-owned newspaper, called the march "a long-awaited day of triumph." Two months later, King shared these same thoughts with thousands of Americans in Washington, DC, at a Lincoln Memorial rally that became one of the greatest moments in American civil rights history.[22]

During the early 1960s, several Detroiters played prominent roles during the civil rights movement. Among the architects of the Freedom March was the Reverend Clarence L. Franklin, "one of the most charismatic African Americans of twentieth-century Detroit." Mississippi-born, the 31-year-old Franklin settled in Detroit and assumed the pastoral duties of the New Bethel Baptist Church in 1946. "A spellbinder whose traditional African American oratory combined singing and public speaking," Franklin stood out among many black preachers. His daughter Aretha recalled that at the end of the ser-

Civil rights leaders who joined Detroit's Freedom March in June 1963 included (l to r): UAW President Walter Reuther, Benjamin McFall, Reverend Martin Luther King, Jr., and Reverend C.L. Franklin.

vice, "everyone would be on their feet, testifying and praising the Lord. The whole church would be up and shouting 'Go ahead!' and 'Yes, sir!'" When the Reverend Franklin was not touring the country with gospel shows, he preached black pride and co-founded the Detroit Council for Human Rights that sponsored the Freedom March.[23]

Detroit also became the home to Rosa Parks, "Mother of the Freedom Movement." Parks had gained notoriety in late 1955 when she refused to give up her bus seat to a white customer in her hometown of Montgomery, Alabama. "Tired of being pushed around," she later recalled, "I felt a determination cover my body like a quilt on a winter night." Her arrest for violating the city's segregated busing laws sparked a 381-day black boycott of the city's buses that nearly drove the bus company bankrupt. At the same time, the U.S. Supreme Court declared Alabama's bus-segregation laws unconstitutional. Park's protest gave the civil rights movement cohesion, but it also made her *persona non grata* in Montgomery, and she moved to Detroit in 1957. Besides working for Congressman John Conyers (D-Detroit), she and her husband founded an institute to motivate young Detroiters, "emphasizing love of God, self-respect, hard work and an appreciation of history." In 1996, President Bill Clinton awarded Parks the Presidential Medal of Freedom. When she passed away in 2005, Parks became the first woman to lie in state in the U.S. Capitol. She was buried in Detroit, and the bus she made famous is in the collection of The Henry Ford in Dearborn.[24]

One black leader with Michigan roots who rejected the nonviolence strategy of the civil rights movement told a Detroit audience in November 1963, "There's no such thing as a nonviolent revolution. The only kind of revolution that is nonviolent is the Negro revolution. It's the only revolution in which the goal is a desegregated public toilet." Malcolm Little was born in Omaha, Nebraska, in 1929, where his father, a Baptist minister, had been an outspoken member of Marcus Garvey's Pan-African movement. Driven out of Omaha by the Ku Klux Klan, the Littles, as Malcolm recounted in his autobiography, moved to Lansing "for some reason" when he was four years old. Life only got worse for the Little family, which grew to eight children. The Black Legion, a hate group, threatened the elder Little partly because his family settled outside the city's black neighborhood. Arsonists destroyed their home, and the family moved to East Lansing where Malcolm later remembered, "East Lansing harassed us so much that we had to move again." Then the Reverend Little died mysteriously in a streetcar accident that some thought was murder. According to Malcolm, "We began to go downhill."[25]

Outspoken black leader Malcom X (in 1964) spent his childhood near Lansing.

His mother suffered a mental breakdown, and the state placed her in the State Mental Hospital in Kalamazoo. The family was split up, and the children sent to foster homes. Malcolm ended up in Mason. The only black in his class, he was a good student, enjoying English and history (despite a teacher who told racist jokes). However, Malcolm's life "began to change" after what he later labeled the "first major turning point" in his life. As he recounted in his autobiography, his eighth grade teacher, whom he admired, asked about his career aspirations, and Malcolm answered "a lawyer." The teacher told him that was an unrealistic goal. He recommended that he "think about something you can be. You're good with your hands—making things. Everybody admires your carpentry work. Why don't you plan on carpentry?" Malcolm claimed his teacher meant well, but he couldn't forget the demeaning comments. He later wrote, "I was one of his top students, one of the school's top students, but all he could see for me was the kind of future 'in your place' that almost all white people see for black people." Malcolm dropped out of school after eighth grade and moved to Boston where an older sister lived. He later reflected:

> If I had stayed in Michigan, I would probably have married one of those Negro girls I knew and liked in Lansing. I might have become one of those state capitol shoeshine boys, or a Lansing Country Club waiter, or gotten one of the other menial jobs which, in those days, among Lansing Negroes, would have been considered "successful"—or even become a carpenter.

After years of wandering (at times living in Flint and Detroit and marrying a Lansing woman in 1958), Little turned to the Nation of Islam. He dropped his surname, changing it to "X" (a common practice among Nation of Islam members) and declared the X "replaced the white slavemaster name of Little which some blue-eyed devil named Little had imposed on my paternal forefathers." Malcolm X became an outspoken activist for a movement that rejected integration. Labeling the Reverend Martin Luther King, Jr., a "chump" and a "stooge," Malcolm X proposed a separate black country. The white community found his message frightening, especially as his rise in the Islam movement coincided with a growth in its membership. Malcolm X left the Islam movement in 1964, and assassins with ties to the Nation of Islam gunned him down the following year. Malcolm X's autobiography (completed by Alex Haley of *Roots* fame) stands as one of the most influential books of the twentieth century.

—— Riot or Rebellion?

The issue of civil rights received a shocking jolt during the early morning hours of Sunday, July 23, 1967, when Detroit police raided an illegal drinking establishment. They expected to find twenty people there. Instead, they found more than 80 people, celebrating the return of two local soldiers just home from the war in Vietnam. As police arrested everyone, a growing crowd turned violent. When it was over almost a week later, Detroit had witnessed one of the worst urban disturbances in American history. Some Detroiters viewed the disturbance as a "rebellion," others label it a "riot."[26]

The chaos that erupted in Detroit in July 1967 destroyed whole city blocks.

In the years immediately following the 1963 Freedom March, Detroit did not look like a candidate for racial disturbances. In many ways, Detroit during the early 1960s was recognized as a leader in race relations. The *New York Times* noted Detroit has "more going for it than any other major city in the North." Detroit had two black congressmen—half of the nation's black congressmen at the time. Black representatives sat in the state legislature, and white Mayor Cavanagh, who was admired both locally and nationally, reassured Detroiters they did not "need to throw a brick to communicate with city hall." Detroit also had been the beneficiary of millions of federal dollars through President Lyndon Johnson's Great Society programs.

But beneath the surface there were plenty of problems. A post-riot survey of blacks discovered much unhappiness, most notably with relations between blacks and the nearly all-white police force. Black Detroiters reported white officers harassed them or called them "boy." Unemployment, twice as high among blacks as whites, posed a great concern, especially since the auto industry's new plants were in the suburbs. Urban renewal reshaped the city, but housing discrimination still existed. Finally, inner city shoppers paid more (20 percent in one study) for the same groceries purchased by a white suburbanite.

As the disturbances intensified and spread that Sunday in July 1967, Detroit Tiger leftfielder Willie Horton, who grew up in a nearby neighborhood, and Congressman John Conyers pleaded for calm. They were shouted down and fled. Initially, Mayor Cavanagh ordered the police not to make any more arrests, hoping that they could contain the disturbance. It did not work. Soon, city police and state troopers began making arrests in earnest. Firefighters, who faced gunfire, contended with hundreds of fires. Looting worsened, and the arrival of the state's entire National Guard (about 8,000 strong) failed to establish order. Governor Romney's request for federal troops ran into a snag when President Johnson insisted that the governor first declare a state of insurrection. Romney balked, saying he feared such a declaration might allow future insurance companies to avoid at paying post-riot claims. Johnson claimed that an 1807 insurrection law obligated this declaration before he could send federal troops into an American city. (Critics later charged President Johnson with playing politics over the matter.) Twenty-four hours after Romney's request, federal troops arrived, and within two days the violence ended. The toll included 43 dead (33 were blacks). Among the dead were innocent victims like a four-year-old child killed when guardsmen fired into a building in response to alleged sniper fire. Of the 467 injured, half were policemen, firefighters, or soldiers. More than 7,000 people were arrested, and more than 2,000 buildings destroyed with an estimated property cost of $80 million.

The riot left Detroit a badly polarized community. A white group called "Breakthrough" feared if Detroit became all black there would be "guerilla warfare in the suburbs." Breakthrough supporters blamed the disturbances on the failure of the police to protect the white community. They also blamed communists, theorizing that terrorizing blacks would lead them into the "Black Power" movement before moving "in on the whites." Breakthrough leaders urged whites to arm themselves for the next "much more terrifying" riot. "Many whites," according to historian Sidney Fine, "simply fled Detroit in the wake of the riot." Rumors and concerns about the future also permeated the city's black community. According to Fine, "Blacks heard rumors that whites would try to provoke a race war and then would invade the inner city to murder blacks, that the police were training suburban whites to shoot, and that the police were anxious for a [new] riot 'to get even' with blacks." Detroit also experienced an "arms race," as blacks and whites purchased guns in record numbers and vendors could not keep up with the demand for ammunition. A Canadian newspaper noted a year after the riot that Detroit was a "sick city where fear, rumor, race prejudice, and gun-buying have stretched black and white nerves to the verge of snapping."[27]

Detroit Mayor Jerome P. Cavanagh (center with U.S. Senator Philip Hart to his right) inspects damage resulting from the 1967 Detroit riot.

—— Setback

The urban disturbances also impacted the presidential campaign of Governor George Romney. As Detroiters attempted to put their city back together, Romney appeared on Lou Gordon's television talk show. A native Detroiter, Gordon had attended the University of Michigan and worked as a Washington, DC muckraker before returning to Detroit. One Detroit critic labeled Gordon "the most feared man in television, maybe in the history of the local medium." In his Southfield studios one late summer afternoon in 1967, Gordon asked Romney if he had changed his opinion on the increasingly controversial Vietnam War. The governor confessed that during his visit to South Vietnam two years earlier, American officials had "brainwashed" him. According to political historian Theodore White, Romney's comment "was just a toss-away line." But the governor received "quick and devastating" criticism for appearing naïve. An indignant former U.S. ambassador to South Vietnam rejected Romney's assertion, protesting, "I never brainwashed anybody in my life."[28]

In the months after the show's airing, Romney's poll numbers as a potential presidential nominee steadily fell. Detroit's hot summer and the "brainwashing" comment, coupled with a poor performance in the February 1968 Republican New Hampshire primary, led Romney to withdraw from the race. In January 1969, he resigned as governor and accepted newly elected President Richard Nixon's appointment as Secretary of the U.S. Department of Housing and Urban Development. Romney's "toss-away line" haunted him. Even in death, the comment appeared in headlines or the lead of his obituary.

—— The Motown Sound

For all the trauma of the 1960s, Michigan also was home to a wealth of musicians and singers who had a national impact. A Detroit native coming from a large family, Berry Gordy struggled as a youth. He quit high school in the eleventh grade and failed as a boxer. Drafted into the U.S. Army, he served in the Korean War, returning to Detroit where he wrote songs and opened a jazz record store that failed. While Gordy worked on the Ford assembly line, his friend Jackie Wilson gave up a boxing career to record one of Gordy's songs that became a modest hit. (Wilson eventually had two dozen Top Forty hits.) Gordy convinced his family to loan him $800 to start a recording company. Tamala Records evolved into Motown Records. Combining the right writers, producers, singers, and musicians who worked in Gordy's house (renamed "Hitsville") on West Grand Boulevard, Motown enjoyed unprecedented success. From 1960 to 1971, Motown's artists had 110 Top Ten hits. According to Beatle Paul McCartney, "when we came over to the States, [Motown] was one of the first places we wanted to go. We wanted to see these people and meet them and just try to get some kind of bead on this . . . . greatness." Among the many Motown stars were The Temptations, Smokey Robinson and the Miracles, Martha and the Vandellas, Marvin Gaye, Wilson Pickett, and Stevie Wonder (born Stephen Hardaway Judkins in Saginaw). None had more success than The Supremes.[29]

In January 1961, the Primettes, four female Detroit teenagers, earned a chance to record a song if, Gordy insisted, they changed their group's name. He gave group member Florence Ballard a list of names that included Darleens, Sweet Ps, Melodees, Royaltones, and Supremes. She chose The Supremes, a selection group member Diana Ross disliked because it sounded too masculine. Between 1961 and 1963, the Supremes (reduced to the trio

of Ross, Ballard, and Mary Wilson after Barbara Martin left the group) released eight singles. None was a hit, leading the group to be nicknamed "no-hit Supremes" at Hitsville. All three sang the lead until late 1963 when Gordy chose Ross as the group's official lead singer. In the spring of 1964, "Where Did Our Love Go" reached number one, followed by four consecutive number one hits: "Baby Love," "Come See About Me," "Stop! In the Name of Love," and "Baby in My Arms Again." Within a year, The Supremes were international stars with an impressive list of accom-

Governor George Romney with the Supremes at the 1965 Michigan State Fair.

plishments, including seventeen appearances on The Ed Sullivan show. Among the many accolades, a *Detroit News* writer observed, "They don't scream or wail incoherently. An adult can understand nine out of every 10 words they sing. And, most astounding, melody can be clearly detected in every song."[30]

Adapting a factory-like operation used in the nearby auto plants, Hitsville operated round the clock cranking out hits. According to one session musician, "It was like a family atmosphere; everybody talked to each other. Everybody kicked around, everybody joked, everybody laughed." Otis Williams of the Temptations reflected, Hitsville "was such a fun, loving place and with a family orientated kind of feel." The songwriting and production team of Holland-Dozier-Holland was among the largest contributors to the Motown sound. Between 1962 and 1967, Lamont Dozier and Brian Holland composed and produced each Motown song, while Eddie Holland wrote the lyrics and arranged the vocals. According to one observer, Motown producers held true to the KISS principle—"Keep it simple, stupid." Motown songs expressed emotions "known to everybody—love, heartache and joy." But it was not just the sound. Equally important was the look. Fastidiously groomed, the singers rehearsed their choreography, and Gordy hired stylists who prepared the artists for touring. Motown songs also bridged the gap between blacks and whites during the civil rights movement. Martha Reeves, lead singer for the Vandellas, added, "We were as active in the civil rights movement as any other organization. The difference is we didn't picket or march and parade. We got onstage and sang our music, and everybody fell in love." In 1972, Gordy moved Motown to Los Angeles and later sold the corporation. Forty years after Motown's creation, Otis Williams of the Temptations reflected, "I'm very proud that I came along at that point of time and was part of something that will no doubt be going on when we're all dead and gone."[31]

One black Detroit artist who did not record at Motown was Aretha Franklin. Born in Memphis, Tennessee, in 1946, Franklin moved to Detroit with her family four years later. As a child she sang in her father's church and with his gospel shows. Franklin started releasing singles and albums during the early 1960s, and in April 1967, earned her first number one single on the pop charts with "Respect." The song also earned her a Grammy—the first of eighteen she has won. Franklin's lengthy list of accomplishments include being the first woman inducted into the Rock 'n Roll Hall of Fame (1987), ranked the ninth greatest artist of all time by *Rolling Stone,* and recipient of the Presidential Medal of Freedom from President George W. Bush (2005). In 2010, Franklin and Madonna joined each other on *Time* magazine's list of the "25 Most Powerful Women of the Past Century."[32]

—— Rockin' Michigan

Michigan musicians also made major rock 'n roll contributions. In 1953, Bill Haley, a native of Highland Park, and His Comets released "Crazy Man, Crazy," the first hit of the rock 'n roll era. The following year, the band's "Shake, Rattle and Roll" and "Rock Around the Clock" reached number one on both the U.S. and United Kingdom pop charts. Haley became "the most popular rock & roll performer in the world." William Levise, Jr., who picked a name out of the Detroit phone book and resurfaced as Mitch Ryder, led a "white soul" quintet called the Detroit Wheels. Tommy James of Niles piloted the Shondells to a series of hits beginning with "I Think We're Alone Now" (1967). Glenn Frye of Royal Oak collaborated with Bob Seger before heading west to Los Angles and forming the Eagles with Don Henley. Born to Italian immigrants in Detroit in 1935, Salvatore Phillip Bono also moved to California where he teamed up with his wife Cherilyn "Cher" Sarkisian and released "I Got You Babe" (1965). During the early 1970s, Flint's Grand Funk Railroad with leader Mark Farner was the country's "most commercially successful heavy metal band."[33]

Two heavy rockers with Detroit connections include Vincent Damon Furnier and Ted Nugent. Born in Allen Park in 1948, Furnier moved with family to Arizona following middle school. After high school, Furnier's band (The Spiders) played Los Angeles clubs, until a search for a gimmick led him to name the band and himself after a seventeenth-century witch. (One legend claims the inspiration for "Alice Cooper" followed a session with an Ouija board.) The band's theatrics contrasted with the "peace and love" hippie bands of the early 1970s, leading Cooper to boast, "We drove a stake through the heart of the Love Generation." After moving back to Detroit in 1970, Alice Cooper released some of their greatest hits: "I'm Eighteen" (1970), "Under My Wheels" (1972), and "School's Out" (1972). Surviving a bout with alcoholism, Alice Cooper continued his musical career—becoming part of the "Guitar Hero" craze and hosting a syndicated a radio show ("Nights With Alice Cooper"). Cooper is a registered Republican and a born-again Christian, but refuses to mix religion, politics, and music. Rockers who endorse politicians are traitors to the "ethos of rock itself," he claims. In contrast, Ted "Motor City Madman" Nugent began performing professionally in 1958. Nugent's first group, The Amboy Dukes, enjoyed success with "Journey to the Center of the Mind" (1968). Despite having sold millions of records with a mantra, "If it's too loud, you're too old," Nugent is more than music. His reality shows have included "Wanted: Ted or Alive," where contestants killed and cleaned their own food to survive, while his *God, Guns and Rock 'n Roll* made the *New York Times* best-seller list. The Redford-born Nugent is a staunch defender of the right to bear arms and is a national spokesperson for anti-drug and anti-alcohol programs.[34]

Few rockers rival the devoted following of Bob Seger, about whom *Rolling Stone* declared, "In Michigan, he might as well be a Beatle." Born in Dearborn in 1945, Seger moved to Ann Arbor at the age of six and later graduated from Pioneer High School. He loved music and by fifteen was writing songs and performing with an assortment of bands (Decibels, Town Criers, Omens, Last Heard, Teegarden, and Van Winkle). Beginning in the 1970s, Seger and his Silver Bullet Band earned national recognition and a string of fourteen Top Forty singles. None was bigger than "Old Time Rock & Roll," immortalized by Tom Cruise in the movie *Risky Business* (1983). After selling "Like a Rock" to Chevrolet for commercial use, Seger explained his motivation was not money, but admiration for autoworkers. "I'm from Cartown and these are my people," he explained. During the mid-1990s, Seger took a ten-year sabbatical from the music business to spend time with his wife and raise their two children. In a 1986 interview, Seger, who lives in Orchard Lake, pointed out, "You can't put on airs around people in Michigan. They just laugh at you if you drive down the street in a Mercedes, or wear some Italian suit or something. They keep you down to earth."[35]

Finally, few artists have reached the commercial success of Madonna, who has survived repeated criticisms, including condemnation by the Vatican. Born in Bay City in 1958, Madonna Louise Ciccone moved with her family to Rochester Hills as a child. An all-A student and a cheerleader at Rochester Adams High School, Madonna headed to the University of Michigan with a dance scholarship. After a year in Ann Arbor, she struck out for New York City with only $35 in her pocket. She later admitted it was "the bravest thing" she had ever done. Working as a dancer, playing in a band, and choreographing "her own unique shows that combined dance, outrageous dress and singing," Madonna got a break when a dance club disc jockey produced her first single in 1982. Her stage presence and manner of dressing ("black lace, beads, and fishnet stockings topped off with a headful of super-blond hair"), the lyrics of the songs, and the arrival of MTV left her the rage of a generation of girls during the eighties. Madonna sold 300 million records, making her the top-selling female recording artist of the twentieth century and rock's most successful solo artist. In 2012, VH1 named her the "greatest woman in music." Besides music and elaborate tours, Madonna turned to acting, co-starring in *A League of Their Own* (about women's professional baseball in the 1940s) and *Evita*. In the musical about the legendary Argentine ruler Eva Peron, she had 370 costume changes and earned a Golden Globe award for best actress. Despite all Madonna's accomplishments, one critic claimed her greatest success was reinventing herself. As the "Queen of Reinvention," Madonna "started a revolution among women in music. . . . Her attitudes and opinions on sex, nudity, style and sexuality forced the public to sit up and take notice." Madonna also earned accolades as a role model for the successful businesswoman and "America's smartest businesswoman." The London Business School called her a "dynamic entrepreneur" worth copying. In July 2008, she attended Michael Moore's Traverse City Film Festival, where she admitted, "You can take the girl out of Michigan, but you can't take Michigan out of the girl."[36]

CHAPTER

19

1970s and Beyond

As Betty Ford looks on, Chief Justice Warren Burger swears in Gerald R. Ford as the 38th President of the United States on August 9, 1974.

"God has been good to America, especially during difficult times. At the time of the Civil War, he gave us Abraham Lincoln. And at the time of Watergate, he gave us Gerald Ford—the right man at the right time who was able to put our nation back together again."

Congressman Thomas Phillip "Tip" O'Neill,
Speaker of the House of Representatives,
on President Gerald R. Ford

Moments after taking the oath of office as President of the United States on August 9, 1974, Gerald R. Ford told Americans, "Our long national nightmare is over." He conceded, "I assume the Presidency under extraordinary circumstances . . . . This is an hour of history that troubles our minds and hurts our hearts." Although he had "not sought this enormous responsibility," Ford promised not to "shirk from it." Instead, the former Grand Rapids congressman reassured a troubled nation that his administration would be guided by "openness and candor" since he had "full confidence that honesty is always the best policy." It was an unusual time. Never in American history had a president resigned.[1]

Gerald Ford's life began "in the shadow of domestic violence." He was born in Nebraska on July 14, 1913, and named after his father Leslie Lynch King. Two weeks after his birth, his mother Dorothy took her young son and escaped an abusive husband who beat and threatened her and his son with a butcher knife. She settled in Grand Rapids with her parents. Her son later reflected, "She had the guts to get out of that situation." In 1916, Dorothy married Gerald R. Ford, a Grand Rapids businessman. Taking his stepfather's name, Gerald R. Ford, Jr., described his youth as "a superb family upbringing." Earning an Eagle Scout status (the only president to achieve that honor), Ford became an All-State high school football player. At the University of Michigan, Ford contributed to two national championship teams and captained the football team his senior year. After the players chose Ford their most valuable player, his fraternity house kiddingly added in its 1935 yearbook:

> The football team chose him as their most valuable player, because he was a good student and got better grades than anyone else on the squad; because he put the [fraternity] house back on a paying basis; because he never smokes, drinks, swears or tells dirty jokes—qualities quite novel among the rest of his fraternity brothers . . . and because he's not a bit fraudulent and we can't really find anything nasty to say about him.

Ford turned down an offer to play professional football and sought a law degree. He graduated from Yale University Law School in mid-1941, achieving his highest grades in legal ethics. Six months after he opened a law practice in Grand Rapids, the Japanese attacked Pearl Harbor. Ford joined the U.S. Navy, serving as a gunnery officer aboard an aircraft carrier in the Pacific "that saw almost continuous action." After the war, Ford practiced law until entering politics and winning a surprising upset victory over an incumbent congressman in the 1948 Republican primary. Ford won the general election and was re-elected thirteen times in the solidly Republican district. Between 1965 and 1973, he served as the House Minority Leader, earning respect from members of both political parties.

When Spiro Agnew resigned the vice presidency in October 1973 following accusations of tax evasion and bribery, President Richard Nixon asked senior congressional leaders who might fill the vacancy under provisions of the Twenty-Fifth Amendment. Democratic House Speaker Carl Albert recalled, "We gave Nixon no choice but Ford." Ford's biographer later added, "His peers in Congress put him in the White House because he told the truth and kept his word." Congress overwhelmingly approved Nixon's choice of Ford, believing they were "selecting the next president."

During Ford's eight months as Vice President, President Nixon struggled to survive a scandal that became known simply as Watergate. During the summer of 1972, members of Nixon's re-election committee had been arrested after a botched attempt to "bug" the headquarters of the Democratic party in the Watergate Hotel and Office Building. Although Nixon apparently knew nothing about the break-in, he played an active role in the cover-up, even taping discussions of how to obstruct the criminal investigation. By the summer of 1974, extensive congressional investigations revealed the existence of the White House tapes. Nixon refused demands to release the tapes until the U.S. Supreme Court unanimously voted they must be surrendered. At that point, even Nixon's staunchest congressional allies abandoned him, including ranking House Judiciary Committee member Representative Edward Hutchinson (R-Fennville). Facing certain impeachment and probable conviction, a desperate Nixon sent Chief of Staff Alexander Haig to the Vice President proposing a deal—Nixon would resign if Ford agreed to pardon him. According to Ford's biographer, he pondered for twenty-four hours, seeking counsel from his closest advisors, including his wife, Betty. They all advised him to reject the deal. Ford agreed and told Haig, "No deal." On August 9, 1974, President Nixon resigned. After being sworn in as the 38th president by Chief Justice Warren Burger, Ford added, in an "inaugural speech" ranked as among the greatest presidential speeches, "Our Constitution works; our great Republic is a government of laws and not of men."[1]

One month after entering the White House, Ford granted Nixon "a full and unconditional pardon for any crimes he may have committed as president." In a nationally televised address, the new president explained that his decision was in the nation's best interests. He reasoned that the Watergate tragedy "could go on and on and on, or someone must write the end to it. I have concluded that only I can do that, and if I can, I must." The fervor of the public outrage shocked Ford. He understood the pardon would be unpopular, but "he thought the American people would be forgiving, that they would accept Nixon's resignation as punishment enough." The *New York Times* viewed the pardon as "a profoundly unwise, divisive and unjust act" that in a stroke had destroyed the new president's "credibility as a man of judgment, candor and competence." To counter Capitol Hill criticism, Ford took the unusual step of testifying before Congress—the first sitting president to do this since

Abraham Lincoln. He reassured the House Judiciary Committee, "There was no deal." Peter Secchia, a family friend who was with the president the night before he issued the pardon, remembered that Ford believed his decision later cost him the 1976 presidential election. Historians agree, but Ford never doubted "he acted in the national interest." Others later agreed. In 2001, Ford received the John F. Kennedy Profile in Courage Award for the Nixon pardon. Senator Edward Kennedy, who made the presentation, admitted that he had opposed the pardon, but later came to understand Ford's decision.

As President, Ford tackled a wealth of problems, including runaway inflation, a depressed economy (the worst since the Great Depression), skyrocketing oil prices, and energy shortages. He continued shuttle-diplomacy in the Middle East, worked toward détente with the Soviet Union, and visited China and Japan. The seemingly intractable Vietnam War ended during his presidency when the communists captured Saigon in April 1975. In an effort to put America's most divisive war behind the country, Ford also introduced a controversial program to pardon draft dodgers and deserters. During the 1974 midterm elections, voter outrage with the Republicans gave the Democrats a commanding majority of 291 seats—one more than was necessary to override presidential vetoes—which further compromised Ford's executive power.

Although Ford had intended to retire from politics before his vice presidential appointment, he actively sought the 1976 Republican presidential nomination. He survived a stiff challenge from former California Governor Ronald Reagan. During the general election, Ford started 33 points behind Democratic challenger, Georgia Governor Jimmy Carter. Despite this seemingly insurmountable deficit, Ford closed the gap thanks to his performance in the first televised presidential debates since 1960. Despite an embarrassing misstatement in the second debate when Ford declared, "There is no Soviet domination in Eastern Europe," the election was too close to call when voters went to the polls. Carter won with 50.1 percent of the popular vote and 297 electoral votes; Ford received 48 percent and 240 votes. A slight shift of voters in Ohio and Wisconsin (where Ford's numbers froze after Carter announced a plan for a full pardon of draft evaders—unlike Ford's earlier conditional plan) would have won Ford the election.

After leaving the White House, the Fords enjoyed considerable wealth and retired to homes in southern California and Colorado. The President remained an active Republican, although he occasionally disagreed with his party. In 2001, in stark contrast to the opinion voiced by many Republicans, Ford declared that gays and lesbians "should be treated equally" with heterosexuals. The former president also took exception with President George W. Bush's decision to attack Iraq, which he labeled "a big mistake." In 2005, he told *Washington Post* writer Bob Woodward, "I felt very strongly it was an error in how they should justify what they were going to do. I just don't think we should go hellfire damnation round the globe freeing people, unless it is directly related to our own national security."

During the post-presidency, Betty Ford continued to garner publicity. Her decision to deal openly with breast cancer, alcohol dependency, and addiction to painkillers—coupled with her unswerving commitment to equal rights for women—earned her enormous respect and popularity. In 1982, she co-founded the Betty Ford Center, a chemical dependency recovery hospital in Rancho Mirage, California.

In 1999, President Bill Clinton recognized Ford's service as chief executive by awarding him the Presidential Medal of Freedom. (Betty Ford already had received the medal from President George H. W. Bush.) Thanking Ford for his "steady, trustworthy" service as President, Clinton concluded that when Ford left the presidency, "America was stronger, calmer and more self-confident. America was, in other words, more like President Ford himself."

Ninety-three-year-old Gerald Ford died on December 26, 2006, earning the distinction of having lived longer than any previous U.S. president. A state funeral in Washington, DC, was followed by internment in Grand Rapids near the Gerald R. Ford Museum, which opened in 1981. Other important ways Michigan's only U.S. president are remembered include the Gerald R. Ford Library and the Gerald R. Ford School of Public Policy (renamed in 1999) on the University of Michigan Ann Arbor campus, as well as the Gerald R. Ford Institute of Public Policy at Albion College in Albion, Michigan. On May 3, 2011, a statue of Ford's likeness joined former U.S. Senator Lewis Cass in the U.S. Capitol's Statuary Hall. An inscription from former House Speaker "Tip" O'Neill reads:

> God has been good to America, especially during difficult times. At the time of the Civil War, he gave us Abraham Lincoln. And at the time of Watergate, he gave us Gerald Ford—the right man at the right time who was able to put our nation back together again.

—— William Milliken

While Gerald Ford enjoyed much of the limelight of the 1970s, in Michigan the decade belonged to William B. Milliken. Born in Traverse City in 1922, Milliken left Yale University, joining the U.S. Army Air Corps, where he flew

Governor William Milliken (left) championed Ford's 1976 election bid. Milliken is the state's longest-serving governor.

50 missions and survived two crash landings as a B-24 bomber waist gunner. After the war, he finished his studies at Yale. In 1960, voters sent Milliken to the state Senate, and four years later, he won the Republican party's nomination for Lieutenant Governor. When Governor George Romney resigned to join the Nixon administration in January 1969, Milliken became governor. He won the election in 1970 and re-elections in 1974 and 1978. (With Michigan's adoption of term limits in 1992, Milliken's record as Michigan's longest-serving governor will probably never be surpassed.)[2]

In a 2004 interview with biographer Dave Dempsey, Milliken reflected on his political heritage and politics today. Among his greatest political influences was Governor Chase Salmon Osborn, who he says "taught me, among many other things, about the responsibility of a politician to his or her party—that even if you don't always agree with the direction of your party, you should work to change it from within." Important lessons learned in his political career included that "honorable compromise is essential in a democratic society," as is openness to both the press and public. Responding to being labeled a "liberal," Milliken noted:

> The term "liberal" has come to be used by some, and certainly by many Republicans, as a term of opprobrium. It's spoken with scorn and derision. But I find it to be an honorable word. The dictionary definition of "liberal" includes terms like tolerant, broad-minded, progressive, tending toward democracy and personal freedom for the individual and so on. If that's the meaning of "liberal," I plead guilty to being one.

A strong supporter of consumer protection and the environment, Milliken helped Michigan become the first industrial state to enact a beverage container deposit law. During the postwar years, America's love affair with "throwaways" left Michigan's beaches and roadsides littered with tons of no-deposit, no-return cans and bottles. During the mid-1970s, Governor Milliken announced his support for a bill banning throwaways introduced by Representative Lynn Jondahl (D-East Lansing). Despite overwhelming popular support for the bill, the lobbying efforts of the beverage industry stalled the bill. The Michigan United Conservation Clubs responded with a petition drive placing the measure (soon known as "the bottle bill") on the November 1976 ballot. The first person to sign the petition was Governor Milliken who hoped to make Michigan a leader in the fight against pollution. In one of the most successful petition drives in Michigan history, the MUCC collected 400,000 signatures—nearly double the required number—in six weeks. Despite strong industrial opposition, the measure overwhelmingly passed by nearly one million votes. (In 1989 the deposit was raised to 10 cents.) The bottle bill greatly reduced roadside litter, and according to the Center for Marine Conservation's annual international coastal cleanup, Michigan consistently has the nation's lowest percentage of bottle and can litter on its beaches.

Nicknamed the "ghetto governor" because of his support for the state's urban areas, Milliken also established a close working relationship with Detroit Mayor Coleman Young. Milliken "understood the importance of Detroit to the rest of Michigan and carried out policies which recognized the interdependence of the city and the state," Young explained. According to Milliken aide and *Detroit News* political writer George Weeks:

> Young and Milliken were the odd couple of Michigan politics. Democrat Young grew up in the streets of Detroit, and Republican Milliken grew up in the wealth along the placid shores of Grand Traverse Bay. The white governor and the black mayor used to battle, and on occasion, swear at each other (Young was better at this), but they became friends.

Milliken later added that his relationship with Young was "one of the most meaningful and important friendships and alliances" of his entire governorship. "We were able to work together constructively to solve critical problems," he continued, "and I think that's what the state needed."

When Milliken left office in 1982 observers complimented his skills at maintaining an effective coalition of moderates from both political parties that could seek solutions to problems. According to longtime newspaperman

William Kulsea, "Skeptics smirked when Milliken took over as governor. Many suggested he was too nice, in manner and speech, to last. . . . No threats to punch noses, no desk-pounding, just a firm approach by a man who was learning that good politics was good government." Since leaving the governorship, Milliken struggled with the direction of the Republican party and some of its elected officers, most notably President George W. Bush. More recently he has been a supporter of Governor Rick Snyder, and according to Milliken's biographer, "He's had more impact post-governorship than any previous governor in Michigan history."

——Young, Griffiths, and Hart

Other prominent Michigan political leaders during this period included Coleman Young, Martha Griffiths, and Philip Hart.

Described by one writer a "shoot-from-the-lip politician who at times seemed out of sync during a time when elective office seems increasingly held by cautious policy wonks," Coleman Young served twenty years as Detroit's mayor. In 1923, the five-year-old Young arrived in Detroit with his family from their native Alabama. His membership in the fledgling UAW while working on the line at Ford Motor Company in the mid-1930s led the FBI to investigate Young—the first battle in a "poisonous relationship" that dogged him for the rest of his life. During World War II, Young served with the Tuskegee Airmen, the all-black fighter pilot group that achieved a distinguished combat record. Although Young never saw combat, his years in the nation's segregated armed forces began his long struggle for civil rights. After the war, Young entered politics and became the first black to serve on the Wayne County Council. "Young's radicalism," especially as he protested segregation in Detroit, "hurt him badly," according to writer Bill McGraw. However, when the 33-year old Young challenged the House Un-American Activities Committee, he earned recognition and respect, especially from the city's black community. Young reminded the panel that he had fought for the country, and "I am now in the process of fighting . . . against un-American activities such as lynchings and denial of the vote." After serving as a delegate to the 1961–62 Constitutional Convention, Young was elected to the state senate before becoming the city's first black mayor in 1974. In four terms, Young dealt with a city that suffered from economic setbacks and white flight. Young's influence in Washington grew considerably, leading President Jimmy Carter to admit, "There is no other mayor closer to me than Coleman Young. He could have had a cabinet position had he wanted one." Using federal monies, Young rebuilt

Detroit—expanding Cobo Hall and adding Joe Louis Arena, the People Mover, and the controversial Poletown auto plant. According to Detroit historian Arthur M. Woodford:

> While much had been accomplished during his twenty years as mayor, Young was criticized by many as being anti-business, antagonistic toward the suburbs, and caring little about neighborhood development versus downtown development and big-ticket projects. Yet many of his supporters viewed him as a fighter who brought Detroit through tough, changing times; when many businesses and residents were fleeing to the suburbs, he brought key projects into town that kept the city afloat.[3]

As Congress debated President Lyndon B. Johnson's 1964 Civil Rights Act, which prohibited discrimination based on race, ethnicity, or religion, Congresswoman Martha Griffiths (D-Detroit) advocated that the word *sex* be added to the words *race, ethnicity, or religion.* Her proposal enjoyed little support from the mostly male Congress. Even President Johnson "was skeptical about specifically identifying women in the measure." Undeterred, Griffiths told her colleagues, "If you don't add 'sex' to this bill, you are going to have white men in one bracket, you are going to try to take colored men and colored women and give them equal employment rights, and down at the bottom of the list is going to be a white woman with no rights at all." Congress added the word *sex* to the bill.[4]

A native Missourian, Martha Wright married Hicks Griffiths, who she had met at the University of Missouri. They both attended the University of Michigan Law School and were the first married couple to graduate from the school. The couple settled in Detroit and opened a law office with G. Mennen Williams in 1946. Motivated to broaden the base of the Democratic party and encouraged by her husband and the memory of her suffragette grandmother, Martha entered politics. In 1948 (after an earlier election defeat), she won and became one of only two women in the Michigan House. Six years later, Griffiths defeated an incumbent and headed to Congress. During her eighteen years in the House, she earned recognition and numerous accolades, including being the first woman appointed to the prestigious House Ways and Means Committee. Griffiths, according to biographer Sheryl James, "was fearless, independent, intelligent and hard working." Fellow Congressman Gerald R. Ford (R-Grand Rapids) who worked with her to get the Equal Rights Amendment (ERA) sent to the states, acknowledged that "she was smart, she knew the rules and she had deep convictions." Her most notable achievements included securing enough House votes (from both sides of the aisle) to get the ERA released to the states for ratification after 47 years in committee. The ERA earned ratification from a majority of states, including Michigan, before progress slowed. Nicknamed the "Mother of the ERA," Griffiths left Congress in 1975 but then served two terms as Michigan's Lieutenant Governor (1983–91).

Congresswoman Martha Griffiths devoted her career to getting the Equal Rights Amendment ratified.

Years after leaving active public life, Griffiths remained outspoken. In one of her last public speeches, she rejected the notion that Philadelphia was America's birthplace: "It was born on the prairies, in the covered wagons, in the log huts and wigwams of this nation. America was born out of the anguish and pain of women. Many died in childbirth. No man has ever paid tribute." There are war memorials and tributes "for men who died killing other men," she continued, "but nothing for the women who died bringing forth the nation."

In September 1934, 22-year-old Philip A. Hart arrived in Michigan from his hometown near Philadelphia ready to enter the University of Michigan Law School. A graduate of Georgetown University, Hart prospered in Ann Arbor. He accepted an invitation to work on the *Michigan Law Review* and met fellow student G. Mennen Williams. According to Hart biographer Michael O'Brien, "The pair became kindred spirits in Democratic politics." Following graduation, Hart took a job with a Detroit firm but as a former ROTC cadet, he was called to active duty in July 1941. Eventually transferring to the Fourth Infantry Division, Hart landed on Utah Beach on the fateful morning of June 6, 1944. As he crossed the beach he was struck by shrapnel, suffering a serious arm wound that led to his evacuation. As he later observed, "I was just one of many who landed early and didn't stay long." After a lengthy hospital stay (five months) and several surgeries, Hart returned to the Fourth and survived the Battle of the Bulge, dysentery, and the horrors of liberating a Nazi concentration camp.[5]

After hospitalization at the Percy Jones Hospital in Battle Creek for bouts of depression, Hart resumed his legal career. But as his wife Janey, daughter of successful Detroit industrialist Walter O. Briggs Sr., observed, her husband's enthusiasm for law "was down to zilch." At first politics seemed a long shot since Hart proved to be an ineffective campaigner. But he improved, and in 1954 voters elected him lieutenant governor. (At the time the governor and lieutenant governor were elected separately.) Re-election in 1956 led him to challenge incumbent U.S. Senator Charles Potter (R-Lapeer) in 1958. Endorsed by the traditionally Republican *Detroit News*, Hart won with 53 percent of the vote. The morning after his election, he returned to the plant gates where he had earlier campaigned. When asked why by one curious worker, Hart simply responded, "To thank you." Hart would be easily re-elected in 1964 and 1970.

In his eighteen years in the U.S. Senate, Hart cited the 1965 Voting Rights Act and the creation of the Sleeping Bear Dunes National Lakeshore as his most important accomplishments. After serving as one of four floor managers for the 1964 Civil Rights Act, Hart became the chief strategist for the Voting Rights bill. According to biographer Michael O'Brien, Hart "memorized the bill, line by line, so he could answer every question thrown at him and every amendment proposed by opponents who intended to kill it." The bill was directed largely at southern states where literary tests and other "legal" obstacles prevented blacks from registering to vote. The success of the measure was remarkable. In Mississippi, for example, the number of black voters rose from 29,000 in 1964 to 325,000 fifteen years later. During the late 1950s, the National Park Service identified the northwest coast of the Lower Peninsula as

Senator Philip Hart, with a sample of polluted water from the lower Detroit River, advocated environmental causes like protecting Sleeping Bear Dunes.

an area of remarkable beauty and natural diversity that warranted national protection. Having witnessed how private overdevelopment had "ruined the natural beauty of the idyllic area" of New Jersey he loved as a youth, Hart moved to save the Sleeping Bear Dunes. It would not be easy and he endured "withering criticism," even being burned in effigy by outraged area residents. Hart persevered, and in 1970 the Sleeping Bear National Lakeshore became a reality.

Hart's greatest contribution may have been his demeanor. By the end of his third term in office political columnists "singled him out for special praise." In 1974, Jerald terHorst, *Detroit News* Washington Bureau chief (and later President Ford's press secretary), summed up the commonly held opinion of Michigan's senior senator: "Hart is one of those rare men in public life whose ego is smaller than his talent; whose directness and sense of conscience have led others to regard him as the moral compass of the Senate." Hart died of cancer on December 26, 1976. Eleven years later, the Philip A. Hart Senate Office Building was dedicated in Washington, DC. According to Massachusetts Senator Edward Kennedy, "The last thing Phil Hart ever wanted was a building in his name, but we went ahead and named it for him anyway because we loved him." Hart's widow hoped that "every young person who was thinking of entering politics would read the inscription and say, 'That is the way I can be.'" It reads:

> This building is dedicated by his colleagues to the memory of Philip A. Hart with affection, respect and esteem. A man of incorruptible integrity and personal courage strengthened by inner grace and outer gentleness, he elevated politics to a level of purity that will forever be an example to every elected official. He advanced the cause for human justice, promoted the welfare of the common man and improved the quality of life. His humanity and ethics earned him his place as the conscience of the Senate.

—— The New Left Emerges

As the 1950s ended, students on several college campuses expressed growing concern with issues like McCarthyism, the possibility of nuclear holocaust, Jim Crowism in the South and *in loco parentis* rules that restricted student activities. These movements could be found at the University of California–Berkeley, Harvard, Brandeis, and the University of Michigan. Leading the fledgling Ann Arbor faction was Robert Alan Haber, a graduate student whose professor father had been involved in the Democratic Party. In early 1960, the younger Haber held a leadership position in the Student League for Industrial Democracy (SLID), a labor-supported organization founded in the 1930s and committed to involving students in solving "present-day problems." Frustrated by what he perceived as a "lack of vision" in the SLID and inspired by the writings of a Columbia University sociologist who maintained that the young intelligentsia—not the working class as Karl Marx argued— would be the agents of meaningful social change, Haber became the driving force behind a new group called the Students for a Democratic Society (SDS). The SDS soon served as "the chief organizational expression" of the New Left, "a profoundly American movement, inspired by the civil rights movement, and fashioning its early political beliefs from a combination of American radical traditions."[6]

As the first SDS president, Haber organized a May 1960 meeting in Ann Arbor that brought together white radicals and black students protesting segregation in North Carolina. As Haber worked to use the SDS to coordinate the activities of student groups around a single issue, optimism abounded. Following an early SDS meeting, one young radical recalled, "We talked about a new life, a new world—no one had ever put down on paper what it would look like, though we all had a notion about it." Haber hoped to spotlight civil rights. When this goal appeared too difficult to achieve, he pursued a "fundamental statement of the values and ideas that gave [SDS] members a shared sense of commitment."[7]

To prepare this declaration, Haber turned to Tom Hayden, a University of Michigan undergraduate from Royal Oak who once edited the *Michigan Daily*. At a June 1962 meeting near Port Huron, Hayden delivered his Port Huron Statement, which opened with the declaration: "We are people of this generation, bred in at least modest comfort, housed now in universities, looking uncomfortably to the world we inherit." Hayden called for "participatory democracy," defined as average people making decisions in matters that affected their lives. The 25,000-word discourse emphasized the importance of the university as an essential vehicle to generate social change. According to historian Mark Hamilton Lytle, "In light of the history, The Port Huron Statement seems both brash and naïve." Condemning their parents' generation, the student radicals intended "to harness the energy and idealism of a new generation of students to save the world from its corruptions." Hamilton continues, questioning how this handful of "well-intended radicals could imagine achieving such grandiose ends defies reasonable expectations." Despite this later-day reflection, the Port Huron Statement was widely distributed on college campuses all across the country and became "a manifesto that created a blueprint for the New Left."[8]

As for Tom Hayden, he served as SDS president (1962–63) before moving on to Newark, New Jersey, where he spent several years working among impoverished inner-city residents. As the war in Vietnam raged, Hayden and his new wife, actress Jane Fonda, undertook controversial journeys to North Vietnam. After the war, Hayden served in the California legislature, earning a reputation as "the conscience of the Senate" and "the liberal rebel." He also continued writing, authoring 19 books. Years after Hayden left the SDS, the national correspondent for *The Atlantic* claimed, "Tom Hayden changed America." Former presidential speechwriter Richard Goodwin added, Hayden "inspired" President Lyndon Johnson's Great Society "without even knowing it." Not all observers are as sympathetic. According to historian Klaus Fischer, Hayden was "a dedicated leader but an inefficient and undisciplined organizer. Like most radical students he possessed a surfeit of rhetoric and a lack of consistent action. During his tenure, SDS had little to show but lofty rhetoric."[9]

By the spring of 1965, the war in Vietnam proved to be the turning point for the SDS and the New Left. The worsening conflict, coupled with the draft and the introduction of other protest movements, such as environmentalism and feminism, left the New Left splintered. In the case of the SDS, it also led to a radicalization as new leaders called for a strategy of "disruption, dislocation and destruction."[10]

As Hayden pointed out many years later, "During the Vietnam years, SDS abandoned the Port Huron vision as 'too reformist' and turned instead to more radical ideologies of resistance and revolution." However, on the statement's 50th anniversary, Hayden credited "participatory democratic activism" with many achievements, including: "the ending of the Vietnam War and the draft, the enfranchisement of Southern blacks and young people, the rise of the feminist movement, the Roe vs. Wade decision, the growth and strengthening of public employee unions and California farmworkers, Richard Nixon's unsurpassed environmental laws . . . the Americans with Disabilities Act and much more."[11]

In March 1965, frustrated faculty members at the University of Michigan proposed a one-day strike or "moratorium" in response to the president's actions. When Governor Romney and several state legislators demanded that participating faculty members be punished, the professors suggested a "teach-in," which proved less controversial and encouraged greater faculty involvement. The teach-in also appealed to the university administrators, who permitted the organizers to use school facilities and even suspended the curfew for women living in resident halls who wished to attend. On Friday evening, March 24, 1965, more than 200 faculty members and more than 3,000 students "packed" the Angell Hall auditoriums—three times the anticipated number of participants. One of the featured speakers was Professor John Donahue, a Michigan State University professor of anthropology, who "charged that the United States was merely the latest in a line of aggressors [toward South Vietnam] and not a benevolent savior." Despite several bomb scares and a handful of hecklers, the Ann Arbor teach-in provided a model for subsequent anti-war teach-ins held all across the country. Several months later, anti-war events escalated on homecoming football weekend in Ann Arbor. On Friday afternoon, several hundred anti-war protestors marched from the Diag to the local draft board office. As supporters and opponents outside the office exchanged angry insults, about 40 who had occupied the office were arrested and threatened with the loss of their draft deferments. The next day, an anti-war float, depicting an American soldier guarding a barbed-wire enclosure, appeared at the end of the homecoming parade and attracted the wrath of some onlookers who booed and pelted it with eggs.[12]

The year after these early protests in Ann Arbor, revelations that Michigan State University (MSU) had taken an active role in creating the ruthless regime of South Vietnamese dictator Ngo Dinh Deim fueled the fledgling anti-war movement. The MSU story began in 1952, when Diem, a Vietnamese exile living in New Jersey, met Dr. Wesley R. Fishel, a former World War II language specialist and an assistant professor of political science at MSU. Fishel helped Diem generate American support, even appointing him the Southeast Asian consultant for the university's Governmental Research Bureau in 1953. In that capacity, Diem outlined three areas in South Vietnam that needed attention: public administration, public finance, and police administration. With the French defeat in Indochina in 1954, Diem was elevated to president of South Vietnam. During these chaotic early months, Diem trusted Fishel "as an adviser, while the U.S. State Department used him as an informer." Diem's request for MSU to provide technical assistance evolved into the Michigan State University Vietnam Advisory Group (better known as MSUG). Fishel served as project head (until 1958) and even moved his family to Saigon. An enthusiastic MSU President John Hannah supported MSUG, viewing the program as a way to adapt the school's land-grant philosophy of public service to an international audience.[13]

Anti–Vietnam War protests often led to street demonstrations like this one in Detroit.

MSU professors arrived in Saigon in May 1955. Over the next several years, MSUG assisted in resettling tens of thousands of Vietnamese refugees, designed a civil servant training school (called the National Institute of Administration and considered by MSU as its "greatest achievement" in Vietnam), and improved South Vietnam law enforcement needs. The MSU School of Police Administration and Public Safety was "internationally recognized," but MSUG's success led to staffing shortages that were filled with men connected to the Central Intelligence Agency—a fact that came back to haunt MSUG in the mid-1960s.

The MSUG contract was renewed in 1957 and again in 1959, but articles in the *New Republic* written by disillusioned MSUG professors in 1961 described the South Vietnamese government as "an absolute dictatorship." An incensed Diem demanded the professors be censured. Walking a thin line between academic freedom and not wanting to lose the lucrative federal contract, university officials promised greater future review. These guarantees failed to mollify Diem, and the contract was canceled. MSUG left Vietnam in June 1962. Seventeen months later, South Vietnamese generals—with the tacit approval of the U.S. government—staged a coup and assassinated Diem. In 1966, a biased exposé in *Ramparts* magazine accused MSUG of having acted as a CIA front that permitted Diem to gain dictatorial control over South Vietnam. Critics also questioned the role of institutions of higher education in "nation building." In East Lansing, Fishel became a target for anti-war protestors. He endured on-campus harassment, even leading the university to use plain-clothed policemen to maintain order in his classrooms. At the same time, MSU Professor Walter Adams, who succeeded John Hannah as university president in 1969, characterized MSUG as "a totally corrupting influence" on academicians.

As for the war, despite casualty lists that grew longer, the increasingly unpopular war dragged on until the communists won in April 1975. Dedicated in 2001, the Michigan Vietnam Memorial in Lansing carries the names of 2,654 Michiganians who died in one of America's most controversial wars.

—— Oil Prices Rise and Car Sales Drop

With the Vietnam War winding down, Michigan's economy suffered a severe hit from another war. The Yom Kippur War of October 1973 led to a Middle East oil embargo the following year as the Organization of Petroleum Exporting Countries limited oil production, which raised oil prices for oil-dependent countries like the United States. For Michigan, the subsequent economic depression had a telling impact. Auto sales plummeted from a record 11.5 million units in 1973 to 8.6 million in 1975. At same time, consumers turned to more fuel-efficient imported vehicles, especially cars from Germany and Japan. Then, the Iranian Revolution in the spring of 1979 led to a worldwide recession with gas prices soaring from 42 cents a gallon to $1.35 a gallon. Subsequently, car sales, recovering slightly from the earlier setback, plunged again to just over 5 million units, making 1979 the American automobile industry's worst year in two decades. Japanese imports to the United States increased, and in 1980 the Japanese automakers became the world's number one auto producer—a position held by Americans manufacturers since 1904. As the American industry cutback production, Michigan's unemployment reached 17 percent—nearly twice the national average. At the same time, inflation reached 18 percent in 1979.[14]

These years proved understandably traumatic for the Big Three automakers. The Ford Motor Company suffered with inferior quality vehicles and internal management problems. However, under the direction of Chairman Philip Caldwell (ending 73 years of Ford family control of the company), Ford recovered by cutting costs by several billions of dollars, reducing its workforce by 60,000 employees, placing "a new emphasis on quality control," and spending more money on research.

Things were worse at Chrysler. On the verge of bankruptcy, the corporation hired Lee Iacocca, recently fired from the Ford Motor Company. In 1980, prior to Iacocca's arrival, Chrysler introduced the small, front-wheel-drive, fuel efficient K-cars (Dodge Aries and Plymouth Reliant) "that provided the industry's first real competition with the imports in terms of engineering, gas mileage, and price." Chrysler also closed plants, sold its overseas operations, cut its white-collar work force in half, and obtained wage concessions from the UAW for its blue-collar workers. Iacocca also negotiated a $1.5 billion loan from the federal government as well as financial aid from states with Chrysler plants. Finally, Chrysler rocked the auto world with the introduction of the minivan. By 1984, Chrysler returned to profitability.

At General Motors, chairman Roger Smith's decision to acquire Hughes Aircraft and Electronic Data Systems proved a financial setback, especially when the federal government made cutbacks in defense spending that also affected GM. General Motors slipped in market share from 50 to 36 percent. At the same time, Ford moved up from 15 to 25 percent. By the mid-1990s, the Big Three were once again earning record profits. However, the decline in auto manufacturing jobs proved significant—from 480,000 in 1979 to 300,000 by 1991.

—— The Gales of November

During the mid-1970s, Michiganians were reminded of the ferocity of storms on the Great Lakes when the infamous "Gales of November" sank one of the largest vessels on the lakes and left a mystery that may never be completely solved. As writer Mary Dempsey chronicles, "No one really knows what happened that raging night in November. There were no distress signals, no witnesses, no survivors, no bodies recovered. It is a story without a final chapter."[15]

On November 9, 1975, the *Edmund Fitzgerald* (commonly known as the *Fitz*) left Superior, Wisconsin, for Detroit with a cargo of 26,000 tons of iron ore pellets. Along the way, the 13,632-ton veteran iron ore carrier met with the *Arthur M. Anderson*, which was carrying iron ore pellets to Gary, Indiana. The two boats traveled together with the *Fitz* in the lead. The calm weather soon turned bad, with conditions worsening throughout the night. The two boats sailed in a northeasterly direction—a longer route, but less dangerous and away from the worsening storm.

By late afternoon on November 10, hurricane-like rains and 75-mile-per-hour winds with 30-foot waves pounded the two boats. At about the same time, the *Anderson* saw the *Fitz* near a hard, rocky shallow called Six Fathom Shoal. Captain Gerald McSorley of the *Fitz* radioed Captain Jesse Cooper of the *Anderson* that his boat was listing, but the pumps were working. After the storm ripped away the *Fitz*'s two radar antennas, McSorley turned his radio direction finder to the beacon from the Whitefish Point Lighthouse. Suddenly, the radio beacon went dead, leaving the *Fitz* running blind. At 7:10 PM the *Anderson* radioed the *Fitz*, "How are you making out with your problems?" McSorley replied, "We're holding our own." Minutes later, the *Fitz* disappeared from the *Anderson's* radar screen.

As soon as the *Fitz* disappeared, the *Anderson* radioed the Coast Guard, which launched a search. Air and water rescue teams found flotsam, including a lifeboat from the *Fitz*. Four days after the boat disappeared, a specially equipped airplane located the boat's remains on the lake bottom. The following spring, the Coast Guard made twelve dives on the *Fitz* and spent many hours filming the mangled wreck. The *Fitz*, one of the largest boats on the Great Lakes, had slammed to the bottom of Lake Superior and settled more than 500 feet below the surface. The ore carrier lay in two parts with the bow upright and the stern upside down.

Both the Coast Guard and the National Transportation Safety Board (NTSB) determined that the *Fitz* sank after massive flooding of the cargo hold caused by "ineffective hatch closures." According to this theory, as the waves crashed over the deck, more and more water entered the hold through these open hatches. Finally, the "bow pitched down and dove into a wall of water and the vessel was unable to recover." The quickness of this sinking explains the failure to issue a distress call. The two reports differed slightly. The Coast Guard said the hatches fit poorly, while the NTSB claimed they had collapsed. The Lake Carrier's Association and captains of other ships "vehemently dismissed those explanations." Basing their analysis on McSorley's skills as a veteran captain, they theorized the boat was hit "by a quick succession of gargantuan waves—until the bow was pushed more toward the lake bottom, the stern was left out of the water and the vessel snapped in half." Captain Cooper of the *Anderson* added his opinion that the *Fitz* had been taking on water several hours before it disappeared, and then "an unexpectedly furious wave could have forced the ship's bow toward the bottom, splitting the *Fitz*."

In the years since the sinking, fascination with the shipwreck led to a series of dives to explore the wreck, videotape it, and retrieve the boat's 200-pound ship's bell. (A replica was placed on the boat in a solemn ceremony, and no effort has ever been made to retrieve the crewmen's bodies.)

The *Edmund Fitzgerald* sank in eastern Lake Superior in November 1975.

The *Fitzgerald* was the largest boat sunk by the Gales of November, which have claimed about half of the 6,000 boats sunk in the Great Lakes. Among the worst losses occurred in 1913 when a November storm sank twenty ships (including one of the largest ore carriers on the lakes), damaged dozens more, and claimed more than 250 lives. As the sinking of the *Fitzgerald* showed, boat size mattered little. In November 1958, the 640-foot *Carl D. Bradley* sank in a Lake Michigan storm. Although two crewmen survived, the wreck shocked Rogers City, home to most of the *Bradley*'s crew.

During the 1980s, Michigan, which owns about 40 percent of the Great Lakes, took the lead to protect its endangered shipwrecks from scavengers. Today, the Michigan Bottomlands Preserves, a collection of shipwreck-rich areas, have preserved Michigan's maritime heritage for researchers and divers. Notable maritime museums are also located in Alpena, South Haven, Whitefish Point, and Detroit. Finally, Michigan's extensive maritime heritage can also be explored at some of the many lighthouses that have guided thousands of ships since the first Michigan lighthouse was erected at Fort Gratiot near Port Huron in 1825.

—— Stage and Screen

Michigan also has been the home to some of the nation's leading performers of both stage and screen.

Michael Moore was born into a blue-collar, autoworker family in Flint and has earned considerable fame as a documentary director. His first film, *Roger & Me* (1989), chronicled the devastating impact of General Motor's decision to move auto manufacturing from Flint to Mexico where labor costs were cheaper. Throughout the movie, Moore seeks out GMC chairman Roger Smith to explain why the company abandoned its birthplace. Other documentaries have criticized guns and violence in America (*Bowling for Columbine*), the Second Iraq War (*Fahrenheit 9/11*), the American health care system (*Sicko*), and the most recent financial crisis (*Capitalism: A Love Story*). His work has enjoyed commercial success and earned the nickname as the "new Tom Paine." Moore also started the Traverse City Film Festival in 2005. In that same year, *TIME* magazine hailed him one of the world's 100 most influential people.[16]

Tim Allen is one of the country's most successful comedians, but on the road to fame he experienced several monumental pitfalls. Allen moved to Michigan with his mother and his five siblings (following the death of his father at the hands of a drunk driver). After graduating from Birmingham Seaholm High School and then Western Michigan University, he accepted a dare from a friend to make a stand-up appearance at a Detroit comedy club. But an arrest for trafficking in cocaine and 28 months in prison halted temporarily a budding career in comedy. After prison, Allen moved to Los Angeles, where he earned an opportunity to star in a new television sitcom. "Home Improvement" first appeared in the fall of 1991 and put Allen on the road to enormous success. In 1994, Allen's book, *Don't Stand Too Close to a Naked Man*, which offered men advice on how to deal with women, topped the *New York Times* best-seller list. Having the nation's top-selling book, a number one television program ("Home Improvement"), and a smash movie (*The Santa Clause*) led him to admit in an understatement, such success was "difficult to achieve [and] when I'm gone, maybe it'll be a Jeopardy question." More recently, Allen has been the voice of the state's Pure Michigan commercials, as well as the official voice of Chevrolet commercials.[17]

Although his voice is quickly recognized, James Earl Jones spent much of his adolescence "functionally mute." Born in Mississippi, five-year-old Jones moved to Michigan with his grandparents, settling in Brethren (near Manistee). In high school, an English teacher asked his students to write and read their poems aloud. According to one biographer, "Jones found he could speak without stuttering." Jones competed in high school debates and earned a scholarship to the University of Michigan. At Michigan, Jones excelled in both drama and as an ROTC cadet. He completed his bachelor's degree in 1955. After being commissioned an officer, Jones attended Ranger School but left the army to pursue an acting career. Following early stage performances at Manistee's Ramsdell Theatre, Jones made his Broadway debut in 1957. His performance as a black boxer (based on world champion Jack Johnson) in *The Great White Hope* earned him a Tony Award for Best Leading Actor in 1969, an Academy Award in 1970 for Best Actor (only the second black to receive such recognition), and a Golden Globe for New Star of the Year-Actor in 1971. He is well known as the voice of Darth Vader (*Stars Wars*), Mufasa (*The Lion King*), and the "This is CNN" tagline.[18]

According to one reviewer, Jeff Daniels "ranks as one of Hollywood's most versatile leading men and over his career he has played everything from villains and cads to heroes and romantic leads to tragic figures and lovably goofy idiots, in movies of almost every genre." Born in Georgia in 1955, Daniels grew up in Chelsea, Michigan, attended Central Michigan University, and majored in theatre. During the summer of 1976, Daniels headed to New York City and Broadway. In 1991 he founded the regionally acclaimed Purple Rose Theatre Company in Chelsea. His most-noteworthy movies include *Terms of Endearment, Purple Rose of Cairo, The Squid and the Whale, Gettysburg, Dumb and Dumber,* and *Good Night, and Good Luck.* A decade ago, Daniels picked up his guitar and started performing songs he wrote about his experiences. When asked why he and his wife chose Michigan to raise their family, he explained,

> We wanted to raise our kids in a place we understood. And that made me get on that airplane and take red-eyes back and forth every two weeks or so. It made me spread the career around to supporting roles and get off the Oscar trail of trying to become the biggest star in the history of stars. Family just became more important. The career was second—it was a close second, but it was second.[19]

—— Engler Turns Things Around

The 20th century closed with considerable optimism in Michigan. In 1990, State Senator John Engler (R-Mt. Pleasant) won a surprising victory over Governor James Blanchard (D-Beverly Hills), denying the once-popular incumbent a third term. (Blanchard's missteps included dropping 78-year-old Lieutenant Governor Martha Griffiths from the ticket, an action that led to voter outrage.) Through spending cuts and government reorganization, Engler erased a substantial state budget deficit—improving the state's economy and lowering the unemployment rate to 7 percent. One of the most successful efforts was a school-funding initiative proposed by State Senator Debbie Stabenow (D-Lansing) and endorsed by Engler. The measure considerably reduced property taxes (then used primarily to fund schools), lowered the income tax rate from 4.6 to 4.4 percent, and replaced the lost revenue by increasing the sales tax from 4 percent to 6 percent. Under the measure, the state assumed "nearly all" public school funding, allotting $5,000 for each student. In March 1994, voters approved the measure, "ending the decades-old search for a new way of handling K–12 financing." By 1998, the state's unemployment rate dropped to a remarkable 3.5 percent. A myriad of tax cuts, coupled with a reduction in welfare roles, successful changes in school funding, and $6 billion allotted to improve the state's bridges and roads earned Engler "national praise as a conservative politician who had turned around Michigan's fortunes." Engler understandably boasted "Michigan is moving forward, not backward" and voters rewarded him with a third term in 1998.[20]

Postscript

Michigan flag: Si Queris Peninsulam Ancenam.

"Detroit once served as the engine that powered
Michigan and a large chunk of the national
economy. It may never regain its lost stature, but
it does not have to be a symbol of failure."

New York Times, July 22, 2013

Michigan in the twenty-first century continues to experience its ups and downs.

Politically, especially in presidential elections, Michigan remained largely
a "blue state"; the last time a Republican presidential candidate (George H.
W. Bush) won Michigan was in 1988. In 2002, voters elected Jennifer Granholm the state's first female governor. A Canadian raised in California and a
Harvard Law School graduate, Granholm first served as Michigan's attorney
general (1998–2002), succeeding Frank Kelley, whose 37 years in office made
him the longest-serving state attorney general in American history. Governor of the state with the nation's toughest economy, Democrat Granholm
focused much of her attention on education and sought to make Michigan
less dependent on the auto industry. Her efforts are credited with increasing the number of the state's college graduates, while her "No Worker Left

Behind" initiative, which trained unemployed workers for new jobs, received national recognition. Granholm, who also reduced the size of state government, received a record-setting number of votes in her 2006 re-election. Term limits restricted her to two terms in office, so she returned to California.[1]

Michigan's congressional delegation has several notable members. A native Detroiter first elected to the U.S. Senate in 1978 when he defeated incumbent Robert P. Griffin (R-Traverse City), Carl Levin (D-Detroit) has earned mostly high marks as chair of the Senate Armed Services Committee, including President Barack Obama's accolade, "Senator Levin is a true champion for all those who serve." Among a minority of senators who opposed sending American forces to war against Iraq in 2003, Levin rejected arguments presented by President George W. Bush's administration that Saddam Hussein had weapons of mass destruction or that Iraq had participated in the 9/11 attacks on the United States. Easily re-elected five times and Michigan's longest-serving senator, Levin is not seeking re-election in 2014.[2]

Levin's retirement elevates Debbie Stabenow to Michigan's senior senator. Born in Gladwin and raised in Clare, Stabenow served in the Michigan House of Representatives and the State Senate before defeating incumbent Congressman Dick Chrysler (R-Brighton). Four years later, she narrowly defeated another Republican incumbent (Spencer Abraham) to enter the U.S. Senate. Easily re-elected in 2006 and 2012, Stabenow serves as chairwoman of the Senate Agriculture Committee, has supported the Affordable Care Act ("ObamaCare"), and has railed against the continued discrimination experienced by women, pointing out that the pay gap between men and women in Michigan is among the nation's highest. (A recent study placed Michigan 44th among the states.) As Stabenow explained in 2013, "In Michigan, women are still paid only 74 cents for every dollar a man makes. Over a lifetime, that's more than $500,000 less money than their male counterparts for a typical middle-class woman. . . . This isn't just a women's issue. This is a family issue." Wage discrimination led both Stabenow and Levin to support the Lilly Ledbetter Act of 2009, which amends the Civil Rights Act of 1964 and allows women to bring claims against employers for wage discrimination.[3]

In the House of Representatives as of 2013, two of the nation's most senior congressmen are John Dingell, Jr., and John Conyers, both Detroit Democrats. Dingell was first elected to Congress in 1955, succeeding his father who had entered Congress in 1933. A World War II veteran, Dingell served in Congress longer than any other member. A strong supporter of progressive policies, Dingell also earned recognition for his service on the House Energy and Commerce Committee, especially in uncovering waste and corruption in the federal government. Conyers served in the U.S. Army, seeing action in the Korean War as an officer. An active worker in the Civil Rights movement (registering voters in Selma, Alabama, in late 1963), Conyers entered Congress in 1965. He is a founding member and dean of the Congressional Black Caucus, as well as a longstanding member of the House Judiciary Committee. Conyers has been a thorn in the sides of two Republican presidents. Criticism of Richard Nixon during the Watergate Affair gained Conyers a place on Nixon's "enemies list." In 2006, Conyers' report, *The Constitution in Crisis*, asserted that the George W. Bush administration altered intelligence evidence to justify the 2003 invasion of Iraq.[4]

Three other long-serving congressmen include Sander Levin (D-Southfield, the senator's older brother, first elected in 1982), Fred Upton (R-St. Joseph, first elected in 1986), and Dave Camp (R-Midland, first elected in 1990). As a result of the 2000 and 2010 national censuses, Michigan lost two congressional seats. In both cases, redistricting pitted incumbent Democrats against each other. As of 2013, Michigan's House members stand at nine Republicans and five Democrats.

A highly controversial issue that promises to influence future elections arose in late 2012 when the Republican-controlled state legislature and Governor Rick Snyder (R-Ann Arbor) made Michigan a "right-to-work" state. The state's outraged unions vowed to fight this law that challenges their power and Michigan's reputation as a labor-friendly state.

During the early years of the new century, Michigan's century-old dependence on the auto industry once again spelled disaster for the state's economy. During the mid-1990s, domestic automakers enjoyed high profit margins on gas-guzzling pick-up trucks and SUVs. (One study indicated that American automakers needed to sell ten small cars to enjoy the same profit for one larger vehicle.) However, periodic economic downturns, uncertainty of the stock market that impacted company contributions to worker pension funds, and higher gas prices soon affected corporate profits. At the same time, the involvement of GMAC, General Motor's financial arm, in making home mortgages, especially subprime loans, caused the parent company to suffer heavy losses with the nation's mortgage collapse. As the American automakers confronted the unprecedented 2008–09 economic recession in a weakened financial condition, they also lacked fuel-efficient models to counter competition from foreign automakers. Domestic sales plummeted from an annual capacity of 17 million units to only 10 million vehicles in 2008. The banking crisis meant tens of thousands of customers could not use home equity loans to buy new cars or even obtain auto loans. The worsening situation forced GM and Chrysler into Chapter 11 bankruptcy protection. After a harrowing time—and with the support of President Obama who recognized that, directly or indi-

rectly, one of every ten jobs in the country is tied to the domestic auto industry—federal government loan guarantees put GM and Chrysler back on the
road to recovery and profitability. Several prognosticators in 2013 anticipated
that the American auto industry will hit the 17 million mark by 2016.[5]

The American auto industry begins a new century headquartered in
Michigan—GM completed a renovation of the Renaissance Center in 2004,
while the Ford Motor Company remains in Dearborn, and the Chrysler Corporation in Auburn Hills. However, the situation in Detroit remains bleak.
The 2010 census recorded only 713,777 people living in Michigan's largest
city—a drop of 25 percent since 2000. Detroit is now the nation's eighteenth
largest city, down from the fifth in 1950 with 1.85 million people. Detroit also
earned the dubious distinction of being the only American city of one million people to fall below that figure. Finally, the future of the state's largest
city became even more uncertain when Detroit declared financial bankruptcy
in July 2013. Detroit's decline in population also left Michigan the only state
in the 2010 federal census to show a loss of people (minus 0.6%). By 2014,
Michigan will drop from the eighth most populous state to tenth, passed by
Georgia and North Carolina.[6]

Although the state has lost much of its vaunted manufacturing prowess,
national leaders with Michigan factories include Kellogg's (breakfast cereal),
Steelcase and Herman Miller (office furniture), and Dow Chemical (pharmaceuticals). The state still has a forest products industry, and mining along the
Marquette Range accounts for about one-quarter of the nation's iron ore production. More recently, entrepreneurs are exploring closed iron and copper
mines in the western U.P. In 2011, Michigan's University Research Corridor
(URC), which consists of the University of Michigan, Michigan State University,
and Wayne State University, contributed $15.5 billion in state economic activ-
ity. Reports indicate that "activity attributable to the URC boosted state tax revenues by $375 million in 2011," a 24 percent increase since 2007. In 2011, the
URC research and development growth rate topped six other major university
research clusters in five other states. According to a 2013 report, for every dollar the state invested in the three URC universities, it yielded $17 in economic
benefits. According to University of Michigan president Mary Sue Coleman,
"Our graduates are key to strengthening and expanding Michigan's economy,"
while Michigan State University president Lou Anna K. Simon, added that the
URC is "deeply committed to continuing our efforts to help Michigan's businesses innovate and grow by providing research and talent they need." Michigan ranks third among all states in graduating college engineers, while MSU is
also home to the National Superconducting Cyclotron Laboratory.[7]

The efforts of Michigan's more than 50,000 farmers place the state second only to California in agriculture production. Agricultural leaders include livestock and diary production, fruit (blueberries, cherries, apples, grapes, and peaches) along the eastern shore of Lake Michigan, and navy beans and sugar beets in the Thumb. Founded in 1906, the Michigan Sugar Company, headquartered in Bay City, is nation's third largest sugar refinery and sells products under the Big Chief and Pioneer labels.[8]

Tourism remains an important part of the economy, and the state's "Pure Michigan" website ranks among the nation's busiest. In Detroit, new stadiums for the Tigers (Comerica Park, which opened in April 2000) and the Lions (Ford Field, which opened in 2002) host tens of thousands of fans. The restoration of Detroit's Fox Theatre, a National Historic Landmark and one of many projects undertaken by Little Caesars Pizza founders Mike and Marian Ilitch, offers a distinctive theatre experience rarely found anywhere else in the country. Michigan's forests, lakes, and beaches remain popular destinations for both tourists and residents. The Michigan Department of Natural Resources manages the largest dedicated state forest system in the nation, while the federal government operates three national forests as well as Isle Royale National Park, Pictured Rocks National Lakeshore, Seney National Wildlife Refugee, and Sleeping Bear National Lakeshore. The state also has the nation's highest number of golf courses, registered snowmobiles, and licensed hunters (more than one million).[9]

The Great Lakes play an essential role in Michigan's past, present, and future. The 1972 Clean Water Act introduced efforts to address decades of neglect and abuse. But with each new effort to reduce pollution another challenge poses a problem. Recent threats to the Great Lakes ecosystem include proposed oil drilling beneath the lakes, lowering lake levels (caused by climate change, and selling Great Lakes water to quench thirsts elsewhere in the country and the world), and Asian carp, an invasive species that poses an assortment of risks to native fish and the commercial and recreational fishing industries. The Great Lakes represent one-fifth of the world's fresh water, and they are "not limitless." Beyond these problems are the numerous decision makers in two countries, two provinces, eight states, and numerous localities that border the lakes. In *On the Brink: The Great Lakes in the 21*st *Century*, Dave Dempsey chronicles how the lakes have been neglected and mistreated for the past 150 years. He concludes that "the last two centuries of ecosystem instability, caused by greed and folly as much as understandable human ignorance, have penalized the people with periodic economic hardship and a fouled home." As the citizens of the Great Lake State, Michiganians must not lose sight of their responsibility to keep this precious and irreplaceable resource safe for future generations.[10]

In the final paragraphs of his 1995 edition of *Michigan: A History of the Wolverine State*, historian George May recounted the transitional changes Michigan experienced at the beginning of recent centuries. The 17th century brought the Europeans; the 18th century led to the founding of Detroit; the 19th century marked Michigan's "entry" into the United States; and, the 20th century introduced the "automobile age." Professor May pondered what stimulus ("if any") might impact the state's future development. Today, the recently resurgent American automobile industry still calls Michigan home, while tourism and agriculture continue to play key roles in the state's economy. At the same time, the state's mid-2013 unemployment figures are among the nation's worst. There is the uncertain future of Detroit—the country's largest city to declare financial bankruptcy. However, as the *New York Times* editorialized, "Detroit once served as the engine that powered Michigan and a large chunk of the national economy. It may never regain its lost stature, but it does not have to be a symbol of failure." Senators Levin and Stabenow optimistically added that, while Detroit's government is bankrupt, "Detroit and the spirit of our people are not."[11]

Michiganians may find inspiration about the future from one of its often-overlooked entrepreneurs. In 1909, as an impatient Billy Durant raced from Flint to Detroit, he veered his car into and out of a ditch to pass a slow-moving vehicle. A shaken passenger heard something snap (a spring) and asked, "What was that?" Without slowing down, the unfazed founder of General Motors responded, "Never mind, we're still running." So is Michigan.[12]

Endnotes

Chapter 1 Notes

1. May, George & Willis Dunbar, *Michigan: A History of the Wolverine State*, 3rd ed. (hereafter, May, *Michigan*) (William B. Eerdmans Publishing Company, 1995), p. 10. .
2. John R. Halsey, "Native Copper," *MHM*, November/December 2001, pp. 20–25.
3. May, *Michigan*, pp. 12–14.
4. Ibid., p. 14.
5. Ibid., p. 15; "The Huron Indians," *The Mitten, Michigan History Magazine*; Charles E. Cleland, *A Brief History of Michigan Indians* (Lansing: Michigan History Division, 1975), p. 11; Michael G. Johnson, *North American Indian Tribes of the Great Lakes* (Oxford, United Kingdom: Osprey Publishing, 2011), pp. 6–8; Cleland, *Brief History*, p. 11.
6. Stuart A. Kallen, *Native Americans of the Great Lakes* (San Diego, Lucent Books, 2000), p. 22.
7. Ibid., pp. 6–7; James A. Clifton, George L. Cornell & James M. McClurken, *People of the Three Fires* (Grand Rapids: The Grand Rapids Inter-Tribal Council, 1986), 75–107.
8. Cleland, *Brief History*, pp. 9–10; James M. McClurken, *Three Fires: Ottawa*, pp. 1–38.
9. Cleland, *Brief History*, p. 17–20, James M. McClurken, *Gah-Baeh-Jhagwah-Buk: The Way It Happened* (East Lansing: Michigan State University Museum, 1991), pp. 77–79.
10. Cleland, *Brief History*, pp. 8–9; James A. Clifton, *Three Fires: Potawatomi*, pp. 39–74.
11. http://www.ipl.org/div/natam/bin/browse.pl/A85; see James A. Clifton, *The Pokagons, 1683–1983, Catholic Potawatomi Indians of the St. Joseph River Valley* (Lanham, MD: University Press of America, 1984).
12. Johnson, *North American Indians*, p. 11–12.
13. Ibid., pp. 14–15.
14. Kallen, *Native Americans*, p. 25.
15. www.nps.gov/slbe/historyculture/stories.htm; see Kathy-Jo Wargin, *The Legend of Sleeping Bear*.
16. Cleland, *Brief History*, p. 12.
17. Ibid., pp. 25–26.
18. www.census.gov/prod/cen2010/briefs/c2010br-10.pdf; http://aisp.msu.edu

Chapter 2 Notes

1. W. J. Eccles, *The Canadian Frontier* (New York: Holt, Rinehart & Winston, 1969). pp. 23–34; George W. Brown, ed. *Dictionary of Canadian Biography,* (hereafter *DCB*) (Toronto: University of Toronto Press, 1966), 1:186–99; "Samuel de Champlain," www.collectionscanada.ca/explorers/h24-1410-e.html.

2. *DCB,* 1:130–33; Allen Johnson, ed., *Dictionary of American Biography* (hereafter *DAB*), (New York: Charles Scribner's Sons, 1929), 3: 183.

3. *DAB,* 13:512; *DCB,* 1:516–18; Ted Morgan, *Wilderness at Dawn: The Settling of the North American Continent,* (New York: Touchstone, 1993), p. 100.

4. Eccles, *Canadian Frontier,* pp. 19–20.

5. "The Environment and the Fur Trade Experience in Voyageurs National Park, 1730–1870," www.nps.gov/voya/futr/intro.htm.

6. Bald, *Four Centuries,* pp. 26–27.

7. Grace Lee Nute, *The Voyageurs* (St. Paul: Minnesota Historical Society, 1955), pp. 13–74, 103–55; Grace Lee Nute, "The French Voyageur," in *A Michigan Reader: 11,000 B.C. to A.D. 1865,* edited by George May and Herbert Brinks (Grand Rapids: William B. Eerdmans Publishing Company, 1974), pp. 64–71; "The Beaver," www.beaversww.org/beaver/html; Ellen Hardsog, "Nature's Master Builders," *Cobblestone,* June 1982, pp. 32–35; Jack Rudolph, "The Beaver Trade," *Cobblestone,* June 1982, pp. 9–13; Otis E. Hays, Jr., "Fur for Fashion's Sake," *Cobblestone,* June 1982, pp. 18–19; Ida Amanda Johnson, *The Michigan Fur Trade* (Lansing: Michigan Historical Commission, 1919) pp. 1–30.

8. Larry Massie, "Greasy, Grimy, But Good," *MHM,* March/April 1993, pp. 30–33.

9. Nute, *The Voyageurs,* p. 100.

10. *DCB,* 1:248–49.

11. *DCB,* 1:57–58; Harry B. Ebersole, "Early French Exploration in the Lake Superior Region," *MHM,* 1934, pp. 132–34; "The Pageant of 1671," in May & Brinks, *Michigan Reader,* pp. 56–59.

12. Eccles, *Canadian Frontier,* p. 38; Ebersole, "Early French," pp. 126–29; Schultz, James, ed., *Father Marquette Journal: Exploring the Mississippi River for New France, 1673–75* (Lansing: Bureau of History, 1990), p. 8; George Pare, *The Catholic Church in Detroit, 1701–1888* (Detroit: The Gabriel Richard Press, 1951), pp. 22–58.

13. Joseph P. Donnelly, *Jacques Marquette, 1637–1675* (Chicago: Loyola University Press, 1968), pp. 15–183; *DAB,* 1:490–91.

14. *DCB,* 1:393–94, 490–93; Donnelly, *Marquette,* pp. 190–203.

15. Donnelly, *Marquette,* pp. 204–214; Schultz, *Marquette Journal,* pp. 8–13, 15–19.

16. *DCB,* 1:395; Donnelly, *Marquette,* pp. 214–29; Schultz, *Marquette Journal,* p. 51.

17. *DCB,* 1:392–98; Catherine L. Stebbins, "The Marquette Death Site," *MHM,* 1964, pp. 333–68; Donnelly, *Marquette,* pp. 300–23; "The Death of Marquette," in May & Brinks, *Michigan Reader,* pp. 59–63.

18. *DCB,* 1:490–93; Donnelly, *Marquette,* pp. 230–66.

19. *DCB*, 1:172–73; Tony Coulter, *La Salle and the Explorers of the Mississippi* (New York: Chelsea House, 1991), pp. 21–27; Anka Muhlstein, *La Salle: Explorer of the North American Frontier* (New York: Arcade Publishing, 1994), pp. 1–33.
20. *DCB*, 1:173; Coulter, *La Salle*, pp. 34–64.
21. *DCB*, 1:175; Coulter, *La Salle*, pp. 25–37; Muhlstein, *La Salle*, pp. 92–107.
22. *DCB*, 1:176; George I. Quimby, "The Voyage of the Griffin, 1679," *MHM*, 1965, pp. 97–107; Coulter, *La Salle*, pp. 57–59; Peter Roop, "LaSalle's Floating Trading Post," *Cobblestone*, June 1982, pp. 28–31.
23. James C. Woodruff, "LaSalle's Walk on the Wild Side," *MHM*, March/April 1999, pp. 9–14.
24. Coulter, *La Salle*, pp. 67–105; *DCB*, 1:183.
25. Robert C. Myers, & Joseph L. Peyser, "Four Flags over Fort St. Joseph," *MHM* September/October 1991, pp. 11–13; Rosaline K. Burgess and Harry T. Burgess, *Fort St. Joseph in Port Huron, 1686–1688* (Port Huron: Museum of Arts and History, 1985); May, *Michigan*, pp. 47–53; F. Clever Bald, *Michigan in Four Centuries* (New York: Harper & Brothers, 1961), pp. 41–44.
26. *DCB*, 1:352–53; Henry Brown, et. al. *Cadillac and the Founding of Detroit* (Detroit: Wayne State University Press, 1976); Bald, *Four Centuries*, p. 45.
27. Bald, *Four Centuries*, pp. 47–49; Woodford, *Detroit*, pp. 18–19.
28. Bald, *Four Centuries*, pp. 49–50.
29. Woodford, *Detroit*, p. 19; "Fort Ponchartrain du Detroit" in "History 1701–2001, Detroit" at www.historydetroit.com/places/fort_poncharttrain.asp; Paré, *Catholic Church*, pp. 70, 141–44.
30. Cadillac Papers, *MPHC*, 33:111–12, 104 & 138.
31. Stimson, M. Mansfield. "Cadillac and the Founding of Detroit," *MHM*, 1951, pp. 133–35; MPHC, 33:104; Paré, *Catholic Church*, pp. 144–46; Brown, *Cadillac*, pp. 89–90; Cadillac in May & Brinks, *Michigan Reader*, p. 84.
32. Johnson, *Michigan Fur Trade*, pp. 31–51; Bald, *Four Centuries*, pp. 53–54.
33. Bill McGraw, "Will the Real Monsieur Cadillac Please Stand Up," *MHM*, November/December 2000, p. 35; *DCB*, 1:354–55; Cadillac Papers, *MPHC*, 33:424–53.
34. McGraw, "Monsieur Cadillac," p. 34–35.
35. Myers, "Four Flags," pp. 13–16; Johnson, *Michigan Fur Trade*, pp. 52–63.
36. Fred Anderson, *Crucible of War: The Seven Years' War and the Fate of Empire in British North America, 1754–1766* (New York: Alfred A. Knopf, 2000), pp. 28–29.
37. Ibid., pp. 50–65; "Jumonville Glen," www.nps.gov/fone/jumglen.htm; "Fort Necessity National Battlefield," www.nps.gov/fone/fonehist.htm.
38. Sandra Zipperer, "Sieur Charles Michel de Langlade: Lost Cause, Lost Culture." *Voyageur*, Winter/Spring 1999, pp. 24–32; Paul Trap, "He Who Is Fierce for the Land," (n.p., n.d.).

Chapter 3 Notes

1. Howard H. Peckham, *Pontiac and the Indian Uprising* (1947; Detroit: Wayne State University Press, 1994), pp. 57–58.
2. Ibid., pp. 58–65.

3. Ibid, p. 65.

4. Ibid., pp. 67–69; David Dixon, *Never Come to Peace Again: Pontiac's Uprising and the Fate of the British Empire in North America* (Norman: University of Oklahoma Press, 2005), p. 82.

5. Dixon, *Never Come*, pp. 73–78.

6. Ibid, p. 88; Peckham, *Pontiac*, pp. 71–75.

7. Peckham, *Pontiac*, pp. 79–86; Dixon, *Never Come*, pp. 92–93.

8. Peckham, *Pontiac*, pp. 88–90.

9. Peckham, *Pontiac*, pp. 93–98, 128–29; Dixon, *Never Come*, p. 100.

10. Dixon, *Never Come*, pp. 106–07; Peckham, *Pontiac*, pp. 101, 128–29.

11. Dixon, *Never Come*, p. 104.

12. Ibid., pp. 107–08.

13. Ibid, pp. 107–10.

14. Peckham, *Pontiac*, pp. 121–33; Dixon, *Never Come*, pp. 109–10.

15. Peckham, pp. 133–44; Russell, Nelson Vance, *The British Regime in Michigan and the Old Northwest, 1760–1796*, (Northfield, MN: Carleton College, 1939), p. 38; *MPHC* 33:501.

16. Peckham, *Pontiac*, pp. 159–65; Dixon, *Never Come*, pp. 121–24.

17. Peckham, *Pontiac*, p. 143.

18. Peckham, *Pontiac*, pp. 201–08; Paul D. Mehney, "The Battle of Bloody Run," *MHM*, November/December 2000, p. 40.

19. Ibid., pp. 229–42; Dixon, *Never Come*, pp. 213–14.

20. May, *Michigan*, p. 64; Dixon, *Never Come*, pp. 214–15.

21. May, *Michigan*, pp. xx–xx; Bald, *Four Centuries*, pp. 76–77, 78–79.

22. Russell, *British Regime*, p. 186; Bald, *Four Centuries*, pp. 80–85.

23. Russell, *British Regime*, p. 187

24. Ibid., p. 191; May, *Michigan*, p. 94.

25. Russell, *British Regime*, p. 193.

26. Ibid., pp. 194–200.

27. Ibid., p. 202.

28. Ibid., pp. 113–14; May, *Michigan* , p. 97.

29. Russell, *British Regime*, pp. 202–03; Clark to Lernoult, March 16, 1779, *MPHC* 10:308–09.

30. Bald, *Four Centuries*, p. 84; *DCB*, 6:101–03; http://battleofbluelicks.org/html/history.html

31. Lawrence Kinnaird, "The Spanish Expedition Against Fort St. Joseph in 1781: A New Interpretation," in May and Brinks, ed. *A Michigan Reader*, pp. 143–55; Myers, "Four Flags," p. 21.

32. Russell, *British Regime*, pp. 219–29, 223; May, *Michigan*, pp. 87–88; Starbuck, James C. "Benjamin Franklin and Isle Royale" *MHM*, 1962, pp. 157–66.

33. May, *Michigan*, pp. 88–89.

34. Ibid., pp. 90–97.

35. Wiley Sword, *President Washington's Indian War: The Struggle for the Old Northwest, 1790–1795*, (Norman: University of Oklahoma Press, 1985), pp. 11–143.

36. Sword, *Indian War*, pp. 159–191.

37. Ibid., p. 201, 207; Roger L. Rosentreter, "Fallen Timbers: The Last Battle of the American Revolution," *MHM*, July/August 2003, pp. 18–27.
38. Paul David Nelson, *Anthony Wayne: Soldier of the Early Republic.* (Bloomington: Indiana University Press, 1985), pp. 228–48; Sword, *Indian War*, pp. 208–98.
39. Nelson, *Wayne*, pp. 249–68; Sword, *Indian Wars*, pp. 299–307; Alan D. Gaff, *Bayonets in the Wilderness: Anthony Wayne's Legion in the Old Northwest* (Norman: University of Oklahoma Press, 2004), pp. 254–313.
40. Nelson, *Wayne*, pp. 267–68; Sword, *Indian War*, pp. 307–11; Russell, *British Regime*, pp. 264–66; Anthony Wayne & William Campbell correspondence, *MPHC*, 25:16–19; Gaff, *Bayonets*, pp. 314–27.
41. John Sugden, *Blue Jacket: Warrior of the Shawnees* (Lincoln: University of Nebraska Press, 2000), pp. 179–80; Sword, *Indian Wars*, pp. 324–31.
41. May, *Michigan*, pp. 120–21.
42. Sword, *Indian War*, p. 332; Bald, *First Decade*, p. 18–19.

Chapter 4 Notes

1. Clever F. Bald, *Detroit's First American Decade* (Ann Arbor: University of Michigan Press, 1948), pp. 19–20, 42–44, 95–96, 209.
2. Ibid., pp. 71–72, 98–101.
3. Ibid., pp. 49–50.
4. Ibid., pp. 27–39.
5. Ibid., pp. 39–41.
6. Ibid., pp. 56–57; Warren J. Wolfe, "The First American Citizens of Detroit: Pierre AuDrain, 1725–1820," *Detroit in Perspective*, Volume 5, Number 2, Winter 1981, pp. 45–58.
7. Bald, *First Decade*, pp. 139–41.
8. Ibid., p. 132.
9. Ibid., pp. 142–47.
10. Charles Moore, "The Beginnings of Territorial Government in Michigan," *MPHC*, 31:510–35; Clarence Edwin Carter, ed., the *Territorial Papers of the United States, The Territory of Michigan*, 10:5–10; Alec R. Gilpin, *The Territory of Michigan, 1805–1837* (East Lansing: Michigan State University Press, 1970), pp. 6–9; Silas Farmer, *History of Detroit and Wayne County and Early Michigan* (Detroit: Silas Farmer & Co., 1890), p. 87.
11. Bald, *First Decade*, pp. 239–41; Farmer, *Detroit*, pp. 489–91; Gilpin, *Territory*, p.1; Frank B. Woodford, *Gabriel Richard: Frontier Ambassador* (Detroit: Wayne State University Press, 1958), pp. 42–43.
12. Bald, *First Decade*, pp. 131–32; Woodford, *Gabriel Richard*, pp. 3–48.
13. Gilpin, *Territory*, pp. 7–8; Moore, "Beginnings," *MPHC*, 31:514.
14. Moore, "Beginnings," *MPHC*, 31:511, 531–35.
15. Frank B. Woodford, *Mr. Jefferson's Discipline: A Life of Justice Woodward* (East Lansing: Michigan State College Press, 1953), pp. 17–25; Gilpin, *Territory*, pp. 32–37.

16. Woodford, *Woodward*, pp. 36–52.
17. Ibid., pp. 84–91; Gilpin, *Territory*, pp. 29, 43–44; Tim Sherer, "Governor Hull and the Michigan Indians," *Detroit in Perspective*, Volume 7, Number 1, Spring 1983, pp. 33–45.
18. Alan S. Brown, "An Ultimate Symbol: Tecumseh: A Life," *MHM*, September/October 1998, pp. 48–54; David R. Edmunds, *The Shawnee Prophet* (Lincoln: University of Nebraska Press, 1983), pp. 94–116; Bald, *Four Centuries*, pp. 116–18; see *The Gods of Prophetstown*, by Adam Jortner (Oxford University Press, 2012).
19. Farmer, *Detroit*, pp. 274–80; Fred C. Hamil, "Michigan in the War of 1812," *MHM*, 1960, pp. 257–67; "William Hull" in John K. Mahon, *The War of 1812* (Gainesville: University of Florida Press, 1972), pp. 43–53; Le Roy Barnett and Roger L. Rosentreter, "War of 1812" in *Michigan's Early Military Forces* (Detroit: Wayne State University Press, 2003), pp. 71–86; Alfred B. Vorderstrasse, *Detroit in the War of 1812* (Detroit: Wayne State University Press, 1951); Donald R. Hickey, *War of 1812* (Urbana: University of Illinois, 1995), pp. 5–22.
20. Hamil, "1812," pp. 257–62.
21. Ibid., pp. 262–69; Farmer, *Detroit*, p. 275; Harry L. Coles, *The War of 1812* (Chicago: The University of Chicago Press, 1965), pp. 47–48.
22. Brian Leigh Dunnigan, *The British Army at Mackinac: 1812–1815* (Mackinac Island: Mackinac Island State Park Commission, 1980), pp. 10–11.
23. Ibid., pp. 12; Keith R. Widder, *Reveille Till Taps: Soldier Life at Fort Mackinac, 1780–1895* (Mackinac Island: Mackinac Island State Park, 1975), pp. 28–32; Hamil, "1812," p. 267–72.
24. Hamil, "1812," pp. 267–72.
25. Ibid., pp. 273–74; Farmer, *Detroit*, pp. 275–80.
26. Farmer, *Detroit*, pp. 277–80; Sandy, Antal, *A Wampum Denied: Proctor's War of 1812* (Ottawa: Carleton University Press, 1997), pp. 91–103.
27. Woodford, *Woodward*. p. 109; Willard Carl Klunder, *Lewis Cass and the Politics of Moderation* (Kent, Ohio: Kent State University Press, 1996), pp. 12–15; Frank B. Woodford, *Lewis Cass: The Last Jeffersonian* (New Brunswick: Rutgers University Press, 1950), pp. 67–71.
28. Willard Carl Klunder, *Lewis Cass and the Politics of Moderation* (Kent, Ohio: Kent State University Press, 1996), pp. 13–15; Woodford, *Cass*, pp. 71–74; "Documents Relating to Detroit and Vicinity," 1805–1813," *MPHC*, 40:477–85.
29. "Documents," *MPHC*, 40:477–85; Farmer, *Detroit*, pp. 289–98.
30. Antal, *Proctor's War*. p. 100.
31. Rosentreter, Roger L. "Remember the River Raisin," *MHM*, November/December 1998, pp. 40–45; Glenn Clift, *Remember the Raisin!* (Frankfort: Kentucky Historical Society, 1961), pp. 23–79.
32. Rosentreter, "Remember," pp. 45–48; Clift, *Remember*, pp. 80–106.
33. Woodford, *Woodward*, pp. 100–23.
34. *The War*, New York City, New York in Antal, *Proctor's War*, p. 292; Farmer, *Detroit*, p. 283; Hamil, pp. 278–82; Gerry T. Altoff, "Oliver Hazard Perry and the Battle of Lake Erie," *Michigan Historical Review*, Fall 1988, pp. 25–57; Hickey, *War of 1812*, pp. 38–39; see David Cursit Skaggs & Gerald T. Altoff, *A Signal Victory: The Lake Erie Campaign of 1812–1813* (Annapolis, MD: Naval Institute Press, 1997).

35. Hamil, "1812," pp. 282–84; Brown, "Ultimate Symbol," p. 54; Antal, *Proctor's War*, pp. 331–49; Skaggs and Altoff, *Signal Victory*, pp. 159–63; Hickey, *War of 1812*, p. 41.
36. Hamil, "1812," pp. 285–91.
37. Brian Leigh Dunnigan, *The British Army at Mackinac: 1812–1815* (Mackinac Island: Mackinac Island State Park Commission, 1980), pp. 17–19.
38. Ibid., pp. 20–34; Brian Leigh Dunnigan, "The Battle of Mackinac Island," *MHM*, Winter 1975, pp. 240–54; Widder, *Reveille*, pp. 32–35.
39. Woodford, *This is Detroit*, p. 45.
40. Klunder, *Cass*, p. 19; Farmer, *Detroit*, pp. 287–88.
41. Klunder, *Cass*, p. 15; Woodford, *Cass*, pp. 90–96.

Chapter 5 Notes

1. John M. Gordon, "A Speculator's Diary," in *Making of Michigan: 1820–1860*, edited by Justin L. Kestenbaum (Detroit Wayne State University Press, 1990), pp. 115–56.
2. Madison Kuhn, "Tiffin, Morse, and the Reluctant Pioneer," *MHM*, June 1966, p. 111.
3. May, *Michigan*, pp. 167–74; Catton, *Michigan*, pp. 65–70; John Humin, "Furs, Astor and Indians: The American Fur Company in the Old Northwest," *MHM*, March/April 1985, pp. 24–31; *DAB*, 1:397–99.
4. Alan S. Brown, "Mr. Tiffin's Surveyors Come to Michigan," *MHM*, September/October 1990, pp. 35–36.
5. Kuhn, "Tiffin," pp. 130–33.
6. Clarence E. Carter, ed., *Territorial Papers of the United States: Michigan Territory, 1805–1820*. Volume 10:642–45, 677–82.
7. Kuhn, "Tiffin," p. 118; May, *Michigan*, p. 155.
8. Brown, "Mr. Tiffin's," p. 34; May, *Michigan*, pp. 154–55; John S. Burt, "Boys, Look Around and See What You Can Find," *MHM*, November/December 1994, pp. 10–15; Austin Burt, "Burt's Solar Compass," *MPHC*, 38:114–16; Le Roy Barnett, "U.P. Surveyors," *MHM*, September/October 1982, pp. 24–31.
9. Woodford, *Yesterdays*, pp. 119–20; Kuhn, "Tiffin," pp. 130–33; T. J. Suilot, "Hail to the Chief," *MHM*, May/June 1991, pp. 36–38.
10. Klunder, *Cass*, pp. 35–36; Bald, *Four Centuries*, pp. 147–48; Le Roy Barnett, "For Family and Friends: The Saginaw Treaty of 1819," *MHM*, September/October 2003, pp. 28–35.
11. Bald, *Four Centuries*, pp. 147–48; *Dictionary of American Biography*, 16:456–57.
12. Klunder, *Cass*, pp. 50–56; May, *Michigan*, pp. 146–54; James Clifton in *Pioneering Michigan*, by Eric Freedman (Franklin: Altwerger and Mandel Publishing Company, 1992), p. 190; James A. Clifton, *The Pokugons, 1683–1983, Catholic Potawatomi Indians of the St. Joseph River Valley* (Lanham, NY: University Press of America, 1984), pp. 43–90; www.pokagonband-nsn.gov

13. Gilpin, *Territory*, pp. 136–37; R. Carlyle Buley, *The Old Northwest: Pioneer Period 1815–1840* (Indianapolis: Indiana Historical Society, 1950), 1:54, 456–57, 461; R. C. Crawford, "Reminiscences of Pioneer Life in Michigan," *MPHC*, 4:42; "On the Michigan Stage," by Le Roy Barnett, *MHM*, September/October 2005, pp. 42–50.

14. Fred Van Hartesveldt, "Yankee Lewis: Prince of Innkeepers," *Grand River Valley Review*, v. 3 no. 1, pp. 14–21; *Michigan History for Kids*, Spring 2004, p. 14; Buley, *The Old Northwest*, 2:90; according to Ruth Hoppin in "Personal Recollections of Pioneers Days" (*MPHC*, 10:561) the Buckhorn tavern was the "most important building" in her pioneer settlement.

15. Gilpin, *Territory*, pp. 137–38; Woodward, *This is Detroit*, pp. 49–50; Buley, *The Old Northwest*, 1:420–21.

16. Bald, *Four Centuries*, pp. 183–87; Gilpin, *Territory*, p. 152.

17. Ronald Shaw, "Michigan Influences upon the Formative Years of the Erie Canal," *MHM*, 1953, p. 1; May, *Michigan*, pp. 159–60; Edward W. Barber, "A Zion in the Wilderness," in Kesentbaum, *The Making of Michigan*, pp. 161–62; "The Journal of Thomas S. Woodcock at Traveling the Erie Canal, 1836" in *Eyewitness to History* (2004) at www.eyewitnesstohistory.com/eriecanal.htm; www.archives.nysed.gov/projects/eriecanal/essays/ec_sheriff.shtml; William Nowlin, "The Bark-Covered House, or Pioneer Life in Michigan," *MPHC*, 4:482–83.

18. Shaw, "Erie Canal" pp. 12–18; *Territorial Papers*, 11:321.

19. Shaw, "Erie Canal," pp. 7–8; Bernard C. Peters, ed., "Henry Parker Smith's Reminiscences of a Young Pioneer," *MHM*, 1975, p. 256; Farmer, *Detroit*, pp. 335–36; Mrs. W. G. Doty, "Ann Arbor," *MHM*, 1923, pp. 197–98. The poem has eight verses; verses one and eight are offered here.

20. Gilpin, *Territory*, p. 152.

21. Catton, *Michigan*, p. 79; Farmer, *Detroit*, p. 335.

22. Buley, *The Old Northwest*, 2:96; Gregory S. Rose, "South Central Michigan Yankees," *MHM*, March/April 1986, pp. 32–39; J. Harold Stevens, "The Influence of New England in Michigan," *MHM*. 1935, pp. 321–53; May, *Michigan*, p. 170; Farmer, *Detroit*, p. 335.

23. A. D. Jones, *Illinois and the West* in Buley, *The Old Northwest*, 2:98.

24. Bald, *Four Centuries*, pp. 184–87, May, *Michigan*, pp. 166–69; William L. Jenks, "History and Meaning of the County Names of Michigan," *MPHC*, 38:439–77; Carl Pray, "An Historic Michigan Road," *MHM*, 1927, p. 335.

25. Buley, *Old Northwest*, 2:94; Alexis de Tocqueville, "A Fortnight in the Wilderness," Harriet Martineau, "The Delights of Mackinac," Charles Fenno Hoffman, "The Romantic Wilderness," in Kestenbaum, *The Making of Michigan*, 17–100; Anne Jameson, "Impression of Detroit," *MHM*, 1924, pp. 51–76, 140–69, 349–91, 486–533.

26. Gilpin, *Territory*, pp. 132–36.

27. Joseph M. Griswold, "Some Reminiscences of Early Times in Brooklyn, Jackson County, Michigan," *MHPC*, 26:256; *Detroit Daily Advertiser* 24, 1836, in Buley, *The Old Northwest*, 1:460–61; Barber, "A Zion," in Kestenbaum, *The Making*, pp. 162–64.

28. Henry P. Cherry, "Early History of Johnstown, Barry County" *MPHC*, 26:226–27; A. B. Copley, "Sturdy Pioneers of Van Buren and Cass," *MPHC*, 38:641; Melvin D. Osband, "My Recollections of Pioneers and Pioneer Life in Nankin," *MPHC*, 14:434–36, 238; Bald, *Four Centuries*, pp. 157–58; Barber in Kestenbaum, *Making*, pp. 164–65; A. D. P. Van Buren, "'Raisings' and 'Bees' Among the Early Settlers," *MPHC*, 5:297–98; Nowlin, "Bark-Covered House," *MPHC*, 4:485.

29. Ruth Hoppin, "Personal Recollections of Pioneer Days," *MPHC*, 38:416; Bald, p. 158; Osband, "My Recollections," 14:439; Barber, "A Zion," p. 166; W.J. Beal, "Pioneer Life in Southern Michigan in the Thirties," *MPHC*, 32:239–42, 245; A. D. P. Van Buren, "What Pioneers Ate and How They Fared—Michigan Food and Cookery in the Early Days," *MPHC*, 5:293–94; Nowlin, "Bark Covered House," *MPHC*, 4:504–05.

30. Hoppin, "Recollections," 38:416; Bald, *Four Centuries*, pp. 157–58; Alzina Calkins Felt, "Incidents of Pioneer Life," *MHM* 1922, pp. 291–93; Osband, "My Recollections," *MPHC*, 14:438, 443; Buley, *The Old Northwest*, 1:213–16; Beal, "Pioneer Life," *MPHC*, 32:241–42, 245; Nowlin, "Bark-Covered House," pp. 497–99.

31. Joseph Busby, "Recollections of Pioneer Life in Michigan" *MPHC*, 9:126–27; Osband, "My Recollections," *MPHC*, 14:438, 440–42; Rev. R. C. Crawford, "Reminiscences of Pioneer Life in Michigan," *MPHC*, 4:44; Beal, "Pioneer Life," *MPHC*, 32:236; Barber, "A Zion" in Kestenbaum, *The Making*, pp. 171–72; Nowlin, "Bark-Covered House," pp. 486–87, 490, 492–93, 500.

32. Buley, *Old Northwest*, 1:244; Osband, "My Recollections," *MPHC*, 14:443; Beal, "Pioneer Life," 32:239; Hoppin "Reminiscences," *MHPC*, 38:414; R. B. Nye, "The Lure of the West A Century Ago," *MHM*, 29:204–08; Farmer, *Detroit*, pp. 48–51; Busby, "Recollections," 9:126–27; John W. McMath, "The Willow Run Settlement," *MPHC*, 14:493–94; Andrew McClary, "Don't Go to Michigan, That Land of Ills," *MHM*, January/February 1983, pp. 46–48; J. Harold Stevens, "The Influence of New England in Michigan," *MHM*, 1935, p. 338; A. D. P. Van Buren, "The Fever and Ague—'Michigan Rash'—Mosquitoes—The Old Pioneers' Foes," *MPHC*, 5:300–04; Nowlin, "Bark-Covered House," *MPHC*, 4:486.

33. Bald, *Four Centuries*, 192–93; Hemans, *Mason*, pp. 78–84, 119–121; C. M. Burton, "Detroit in the year 1832," *MHPC*, 28:168–69; Woodford, *Detroit*, pp. 140–41; Gilpin, *Territory*, pp. 145–47; Farmer, *Detroit*, pp. 48–51.

34. Hoppin, "Recollections," *MPHC* 38:414; Buley, *Old Northwest*, 1:240, 268, 271–73; Margaret Lafever, "Story of Early Day Life in Michigan," *MPHC*, 38:675; A. M. Beardsley, Reminiscences and Scenes of Backwoods and Pioneer Life, *MPHC*, 28:139; Keith R. Widder, *Dr. William Beaumont: The Mackinac Years* (Mackinac Island: Mackinac Island State Park Commission, 1975).

35. Robert W. Malcolm, "Scotch Settlers of Oakland County," *MPHC*, 39:368; Rev. W. B. Williams. "Personal Reminiscences," 26:521; Bald, *Four Centuries*, p. 179; Ronald A. Brunger, "Methodist Circuit Riders," *MHM*, Fall 1967, pp. 250–67; Robert Bolt, "Reverend Leonard Slater in the Grand River Valley," *MHM*, Fall 1967, pp. 243–51; R. C. Crawford, "Reminiscences of Pioneer Ministers of Michigan," *MPHC*, 17:226–37; Barber, "A Zion," in Kestenbaum, *The Making*, pp. 176–78; A. D. P. Van Buren, "The First Settlers in the Township of Battle Creek," *MPHC*, 5:279–80.

36. Abraham Edwards, "A Sketch of Pioneer Days," *MPHC*, 3:149; Edwin S. Smith, "Pioneer Days in Kalamazoo and Van Buren," *MHPC*, 14:272–80; Crawford, "Reminiscences," *MPHC* 4:50; Beal, "Pioneer Life," *MPHC*, 32:245.
37. Peters, "Smith's Reminiscences," *MHM*, 1975, pp. 268–74; Barnett & Rosentreter, "Black Hawk War," *Early Michigan Military Forces*, pp. 147–61; Beal, "Pioneer Life," *MPHC*, 32:237.
38. Florence Woolsey Hazzard, "Pioneer Women of Washtenaw County," *MHM*, 32:188; Buley, *Old Northwest*, 1:309; Roger L. Rosentreter, "Lapeer," *MHM*, July/August 1985, pp. 8–9.
39. Buley, *Old Northwest*, 1:322–23, 370, 316; Busby, "Recollections," 9:125; Cherry, "Johnstown," *MPHC*, 26:226–27; Harvey Haynes, "Reminiscences of Early Days in Coldwater and Vicinity," *MPHC*, 17:287; Kenneth N. Metcalf, *Fun and Frolic in Early Detroit* (Detroit: Wayne State Press, 1951); Bernard C. Peters, ed., "Henry Parker Smith's Reminiscences of a Young Pioneer," *MHM*, 1975, pp. 268–74; Van Buren, "Raisings," *MPHC*, pp. 296–300; A. D. P. Van Buren, "The Frolics of Forty-Five Years Ago," *MPHC*, 5:304–09.
40. Louis Leonard Tucker, "The Correspondence of John Fisher," *MHM*, 1961, pp. 219–36.
41. Klunder, *Cass*, pp. 56–57.

Chapter 6 Notes

1. George Fuller, ed., *Messages of the Governors of Michigan*, 4 vols. (Lansing: Michigan Historical Commission, 1926), 1:129–39; Lawton T. Hemans, *The Life and Times of Stevens T. Mason* (Lansing: Michigan Historical Commission, 1930), pp. 136–38; House of Representatives, *Report of Committees, Report 380*, 24th Congress, 1st Session, pp. 25–27 (hereafter, *House Report 380*).
2. Hemans, *Mason*, pp. 13–37, 47.
3. Ibid., pp. 47–59.
4. Ibid., pp. 59–64.
5. Ibid., pp. 65–66.
6. Ibid., pp. 119–22.
7. Fuller, *Messages*, 1:125; May, *Michigan*, pp. 204–05.
8. Hemans, *Mason*, pp. 138–40; Claude S. Larzelere, "The Boundaries of Michigan," *MPHC*, 30:1–20; Anna May Soule, "The Southern and Western Boundaries of Michigan," *MPHC*, 27:346–60; *House Report 380*, pp. 1–19, 61–62, 73–76.
9. Hemans, *Mason*, pp. 138–140; *House Report 380*, pp. 84–90.
10. *U.S. Senate Documents, Document 6*, 24th Congress, 1st Session, pp. 22–24, 30–37 (hereafter *Senate Document 6*).
11. *Senate Document 6*.
12. Hemans, *Mason*, pp. 143–44.
13. *Senate Document 6*, pp. 61–65.
14. U.S. House of Representatives, *Executive Documents*, Document 7 24th Congress, 1st Session, 59–61, 212–13, 220–21 (hereafter *Executive Document 7*); "The Battle of Phillips Corners," *MPHC*, 12:409–14; *Senate Document 6*, pp. 57–61, 145–46; *House Report 380*, pp. 90–91.

15. William D. Hoyt, Jr., ed., "Benjamin C. Howard and the 'Toledo War': Some Letters of a Federal Commissioner," *Ohio State Archaeological and Historical Quarterly*, 60 (1951), p. 304; *House Report 380*, pp. 103–04.
16. Hemans, *Mason*, pp. 156–57.
17. Ibid., pp. 158–60.
18. Ibid., pp. 160–64.
19. Willard Way, *The Facts and Historical Events of the Toledo War of 1835* (Toledo: Commercial Steam Book and Job Printing, 1869), pp. 26–28; Sister Mary Karl George, *The Rise and Fall of Toledo, Michigan . . . The Toledo War!* (Lansing: Michigan Historical Commission, 1971), pp. 49–50, 106–09; *Executive Document 7*, pp. 166–72, 281–85.
20. *Senate Document 6*, pp. 69–74; George, *The Rise and Fall of Toledo*, p. 53.
21. *House Report 380*, pp. 112–17.
22. J. Wilkie Moore, "How They Fought: Personal Recollections of the Contest with Ohio Fifty Years Ago," *MPHC*, 7:70.
23. Hemans, *Mason*, pp. 170–72.
24. Way, *The Facts*, pp. 42–45.
25. Hemans, *Mason*, pp. 183–89, Fuller, *Messages*, 1:253–56.
26. Clarence Edwin Carter, comp., *The Territorial Papers of the United States: Territory of Michigan, 1827–37* (Washington, DC: Government Printing Office, 1945), 12:984–86; *House Report 380*, pp. 98, 102–03, 124–27; Hemans, *Mason*, pp. 178–89.
27. *Register of Debates in Congress* (Washington, DC: Gales and Seaton, 1836), 12:1019–20, 4253–58.
28. *Register of Debates*, 12:1017–18; Roger L. Rosentreter, "Michigan's Quest for Statehood," *MHM*, May/June 1986, p. 34.
29. Roger L. Rosentreter, "Michigan's Quest for Statehood," *MHM*, September/October 1986, pp. 32–34.
30. Carter, *Territorial Papers*, 12:1149–67, 1177–79; *Detroit Democratic Free Press*, March 23, 1836.
31. George W. Thayer, ed., "Letters of Lucius Lyon," *MPHC*, 27:478–80.
32. Fuller, *Messages*, 1:177–78.
33. Gilpin, *Territory*, p. 189; Hemans, *Mason*, p. 231.
34. *Detroit Democratic Free Press*, August 10, 1836; *Constantine Republican*, August 24, 1836; *Monroe Sentinel*, July 9 & August 24, 1836; *Niles Gazette*, September 7, 1836.
35. Dorr, *Conventions*, pp. 421–41, 540–67, 591–92; see also Roger L. Rosentreter, "The Quest for Statehood," *MHM*, September/October 1986, pp. 30–32.
36. *Detroit Democratic Free Press*, November 2 & 16, 1836 and December 3, 1836; Hemans, *Mason*, pp. 243–44, George, *The Rise and Fall of Toledo*, p. 72.
37. *Detroit Democratic Free Press*, November 2 & 16, 1836; Hemans, *Mason*, p. 244; Dorr, *Conventions*, pp. 568–72; Roger L. Rosentreter, "The Quest for Statehood," *MHM*, November/December 1986, pp. 17–19 & January/February 1987, pp. 20–22.
38. Dorr, *Conventions*, pp. 572–74; *Detroit Democratic Free Press*, November 16, 1836.
39. Dorr, *Conventions*, pp. 442–58, 575–78.

40. Hemans, *Mason*, pp. 249–50; *Congressional Globe*, 24th Congress, 2nd Session, 1836–37, 4:54; *Register of Debates*, 13:204–325; *Detroit Democratic Free Press*, February 8, 1837; Rosentreter, "Quest," *MHM*, November/December 1987, pp. 20–22.

41. *Detroit Democratic Free Press*, February 15, 1837; Hemans, *Mason*, p. 250.

Chapter 7 Notes

1. May, *Michigan*, pp. 225–31.

2. Ibid., pp. 232–37; Hemans, *Mason*, pp. 276–83.

3. Joseph E. and Estelle L. Bayliss, *River of Destiny: The Saint Marys* (Detroit: Wayne State University Press, 1955), pp. 101–10; Richard D. Shaul, "Northern Passages at the Soo: The Locks at 150," *MHM*, July/August 2005, pp. 28–38; Carolyn Damstra, "The Locks that Followed," *MHM*, July/August 2005, pp. 42–43.

4. Floyd Dain, "The Birth of the Michigan School System," in Alan S. Brown, John T. Houdek and John H. Yzenbaard, *Michigan Perspectives* (Dubuque, IA: Kendall/Hunt Publishing Company, 1974), pp. 69–90; Alan S. Brown, "The Northwest Ordinance and Michigan's Quest for Excellence in Education," *MHM*, November/December 1987, pp. 24–31; Floyd R. Dain, *Education in the Wilderness*, (Lansing: Michigan Historical Commission, 1968), pp. 71–84, 171, 203.

5. Dain, *Education*, pp. 202–13; Harold C. Brooks, "Founding of the Michigan Public School System," *MHM*, 1949 pp. 291–306.

6. Dain, *Education*, pp. 215–39.

7. Ibid., pp. 241–91.

8. Willis F. Dunbar, *The Michigan Record in Higher Education* (Detroit: Wayne State University Press, 1963), pp. 47–81.

9. Ibid., pp. 64–67.

10. Ibid., pp. 83–89.

11. Ibid,. pp. 89–97; see Keith R. Widder, *Michigan Agricultural College: The Evolution of a Land-Grant Philosophy, 1855–1925* (East Lansing: Michigan State University Press, 2005).

12. William W. Upton, "Locating the Capital of the State of Michigan," *MHM*, 1939, pp. 275–90; Justin L. Kestenbaum, "A Choice in the Wilderness," *MHM*, November/December 1986, pp. 45–51; Craig A. Whitford and David L. Mackey, *Postmarked: Michigan, Mich. 1847–1848* (Lansing: n.p., 1987).

13. Roger L. Rosentreter, "The Island Kingdom of James Strang," *MHM*, November/December 2003, pp. 80–82; Jean Huges Raber, "Beaver Island King, Prophet and Editor: James Jesse Strang and the Northern Islander," *MHM*, September/October 1991, pp. 24–30; see Roger Van Noord, *Assassination of a Michigan King: The Life of James Jesse Strang* (Ann Arbor: University of Michigan Press, 1988, 1977).

14. Van Noord, *Michigan King*, p. 274.

15. Roger L. Rosentreter "To Free Upper Canada: Michigan and the Patriot War, 1837–1839" (Michigan State University, PhD, 1983).

Chapter 8 Notes

1. Roy E. Finkenbine, "A Beacon of Liberty on the Great Lakes, Slavery, and the Law in Antebellum Michigan," in *The History of Michigan Law*, edited by Paul Finkelman and Martin J. Hershock (Athens: Ohio University Press, 2006), p. 83; John E. Kephart, "A Pioneer Michigan Abolitionist," *MHM*, 1961, pp. 34–42; Carol L. Mull, *The Underground Railroad in Michigan* (Jefferson, NC: McFarland & Company, Inc., 2010), pp. 20–21, 70–75.
2. Russell E. Bidlack, *John Allen and The Founding of Ann Arbor* (Ann Arbor: The University of Michigan, 1962), p. 6; Finkenbine, "Beacon," pp. 83–85.
3. Mull, *Underground Railroad*, pp. 41–45; Arthur Raymond Kooker, "The Antislavery Movement in Michigan, 1796–1840" (PhD Dissertation, University of Michigan, 1941), pp. 130–60.
4. Kooker, "Antislavery Movement," pp. 63–77; Farmer, *Michigan*, pp. 345–46.
5. John C. Sherwood, "One Flame in the Inferno: Revising the Legend of the 'Crosswhite Affair,'" *Heritage Battle Creek*, Winter 1999, pp. 69–77; Frank Woodford, *Father Abraham's Children* (Detroit: Wayne State University Press, 1961), pp. 7–14; Debian Marty, "In the Words of a Slavecatcher," *MHM*, January/February 2008, pp. 20–29; John H. Yzenbaard, "The Crosswhite Case," *MHM*, 1969, pp. 131–43; John C. Patterson, "Marshall Men and Marshall Measures," *MPHC*, 38:244–279; Benjamin C. Wilson, "Kentucky Kidnappers, Fugitives, and Abolitionists in Antebellum Cass County, Michigan," *MHM*, 1976, pp. 339–58; Mull, *Underground Railroad*, pp. 105–15.
6. "Elizabeth Chandler and the Spread of Antislavery Sentiment in Michigan," *MHM*, 1955, pp. 481–94.
7. Mildred A. Danforth, *A Quaker Pioneer: Laura Smith Haviland, Superintendent of the Underground* (New York: 1961); Tom Calarco, *People of the Underground Railroad: A Biographical Dictionary* (Westport, CT: Greenwood Press, 2008), pp. 144–52.
8. Diana Paiz Engle, "A Never-Ending Sojourn," *MHM*, January/February 2000, pp. 28–39.
9. Janice Martz Kimmel, "Break Your Chains and Fly for Freedom," *MHM*, January/February 1996, pp. 20–27; Henry Bibb, *The Life and Adventures of Henry Bibb*. (1849, Madison: University of Wisconsin Press, 2001), introduction by Charles Heglar; Roger W. Hite, "Voice of A Fugitive: Henry Bibb and Ante-Bellum Black Separatism," *Journal of Black Studies*, March 1974, pp. 269–84.
10. Mull, *Underground Railroad*, pp. 56–68; Hussey, "A History of the Underground Railroad," *Heritage Battle Creek*, pp. 55–59; Farmer, *Detroit*, p. 347; Elizabeth Neumeyer, "'Be Ye Therefore Perfect,'" *Heritage Battle Creek*, Winter 1999, pp. 4–10; C. Peter Ripley, *The Underground Railroad* (Washington, DC: Department of the Interior, 1998); Blanche C. Coggan, "Searching for the Underground Railroad," *Heritage Battle Creek*, Winter 1999, pp. 11–18; Perry Sanford, "Out of Bondage," *Heritage Battle Creek*, Winter 1999, pp. 78–81; Elizabeth Comstock, "Friendly Resistance," *Heritage Battle Creek*, Winter 1999, p. 37; Pamela Thomas,

"Memories of a Conductor," *Heritage Battle Creek*, Winter 1999, pp. 19–22; Dave Person, "Risking Everything for Freedom, *Kalamazoo Gazette*, October 31, 2010; Charles E. Barnes, "Battle Creek Stations on the Underground Railroad," *MPHC*, 38:279–88; Harold B. Fields, "Free Negroes in Cass County Before the Civil War," *MHM* 1960, pp. 375–83; Charles Lindquist, *The Antislavery-Underground Railroad Movement in Lenawee County, Michigan, 1830–1860* (Adrian, Lenawee County Historical Society, 1999); see Stanley W. Campbell, *The Slave Catchers: Enforcement of the Fugitive Slave Law, 1850–1860* (New York: Norton, 1968).

11. Yvonne Tuchalski, "Erastus Hussey, Battle Creek Antislavery Activist," *MHM*, 1972, pp. 1–18; Mary G. Butler, "'Onward and Upward' For the Cause," *Heritage Battle Creek*, Winter 1999, pp. 47–54; Hussey, "Underground Railroad," *Heritage Battle Creek*, pp. 55–58; Mull, *Underground Railroad*, pp. 94–95.

12. Calarco, *People*, pp. 91–94, 187–90; Mull, *Underground Railroad*, pp. 30–31.

13. Thomas, "Numbers," pp. 19–22; Pamela Thomas, "A Station on the Underground Railroad," edited by Alexis A. Praus, *MHM*, 1953, pp. 177–82; 14. Finkenbine, "Beacon," pp. 92–100.

14. Butler, "Onward," p. 50; Hussey, "Underground Railroad," pp. 55, 57; Mull, *Underground Railroad*, pp. 100-103; Finkenbine, "Beacon," pp. 92–100.

15. Betty Fladeland, *James Gillespie Birney: Slaveholder to Abolitionist* (Ithaca: NY: Cornell University Press, 1955); Calarco, *People*, pp. 22–26.

16. "Mexican War" in Barnett and Rosentreter, *Michigan's Early Wars*, pp. 333–42.

17. Jeff Charnley, "'Sword into Plowshares,' A Hope Unfilled: Michigan Opposition to the Mexican War, 1846–1848," *The Old Northwest*, Fall 1982, pp. 199–222.

18. Floyd Benjamin Street, *Political Parties in Michigan, 1837–1860* (Lansing: Michigan Historical Commission, 1918), pp. 84–96; Klunder, *Cass*, pp. 162–80; Woodford, *Cass*, pp. 250–54.

19. Klunder, *Cass*, pp. 180–89; Woodford, *Cass*, pp. 254–59; Streeter, *Political Parties*, pp. 99–103.

20. Klunder, *Cass*, pp. 190–94; Woodford, *Cass*, pp. 259–63.

21. Klunder, *Cass*, pp. 195–234; Woodford, *Cass*, pp. 264–68.

22. Klunder, *Cass*, pp. 228–33; Woodford, *Cass*, pp. 269–71.

23. Streeter, *Political Parties*, pp. 184–201; Klunder, *Cass*, pp. 264–71.

24. Streeter, *Political Parties*, pp. 182–89; Bald, *Four Centuries*, pp. 257–59; Ronald E. Seavoy, "The Organization of he Republican Party in Michigan, 1846–854," *The Old Northwest*, Winter 1980–81, pp. 343–76.

25. Butler, "'Onward,'" p. 51; Streeter, *Political Parties*, pp. 190–92; Woodford, *Cass*, pp. 302–03; Robert Charles Harris, "Austin Blair of Michigan: A Political Biography" (PhD, Michigan State University, 1969), pp. 55–66; Sister Mary Karl George, *Zachariah Chandler: A Political Biography* (East Lansing: Michigan State University Press, 1969), pp. 8–10; Robert E. Seavoy, "The Organization of the Republican Party in Michigan, 1846–1854," *The Old Northwest*, Winter 1980–1981, pp. 343–76.

26. Streeter, *Political Parties*, pp. 197–203.

27. Tom George, "Lincoln Visits Kalamazoo," *MHM,* July/August 2006, pp. 40–49.
28. Streeter, *Political Parties,* pp. 203–06, 254–56; George, *Chandler,* pp. 14–15.
29. Harris, "Blair," pp. 84–87; George, *Chandler,* pp. 26–27.
30. Harris, "Blair," pp. 87–89; Streeter, *Political Parties,* pp. 283–92; George, *Chandler,* pp. 28–32.
31. *Lansing Republican,* November 21, 1860.

Chapter 9 Notes

1. Roger L. Rosentreter, "For the Glory of the Peninsula State," in *Michigan and the Civil War: An Anthology* (Lansing: *Michigan History Magazine,* 1999), p. 9; *Detroit Free Press,* April 13, 1861.
2. Robert Charles Harris, "Austin Blair of Michigan: A Political Biography" (Michigan State University, PhD, 1969), pp. 91–92, 107; *DAB,* 9:278.
3. *Detroit Advertiser* in Frank B. Woodford, *Father Abraham's Children: Michigan Episodes in the Civil War* (Detroit: Wayne State University Press, 1961), p. 17; Klunder, *Cass,* p. 309.
4. Rosentreter, "For the Glory," p. 9.
5. Ibid., p. 9.
6. Woodford, *Father Abraham's Children,* pp. 25–35; Jonathan Robertson, *Michigan in the War* (Lansing: W. S. George & Co., 1882), pp. 17–24; Harris, "Blair," pp. 108–11.
7. Robert W. Hodge, ed., *The Civil War Letters of Perry Mayo* (East Lansing: Michigan State University Museum, 1967), pp. 167–68.
8. Rosentreter, "For the Glory," p. 10.
9. Ibid., pp. 10–11.
10. Philo Gallup, "The Second Michigan Joins the Army of the Potomac," edited by Chester McArthur Destler, in *Michigan and the Civil War: An Anthology,* p. 46.
11. Fred D. Williams, *Michigan Soldiers in the Civil War* (Lansing: *Michigan History Magazine,* 2002), pp. 12, 15–16, 18–21, 68–69; "Rendering Invaluable Service," by Steven Dunker, in *Michigan in the Civil War,* pp. 72–75; Roger L. Rosentreter, "Three Generals and an Unlucky Regiment," *MHM,* September/October 2008, pp. 25–26; Roger L. Rosentreter, "Surviving that 'Dismal Hole' in Georgia," *MHM,* May/June 2009, pp. 48–55; see George May, *Michigan and the Civil War Years, 1860–1866, A Wartime Chronicle* (Lansing: Michigan Civil War Centennial Observance Commission, 1964).
12. Roger L. Rosentreter, "Michigan at Gettysburg," *MHM,* July/August 1998, pp. 114–20; Roger L. Rosentreter, "Those Damned Black Hats," in *Michigan and the Civil War,* p. 85–91; Paul Mehney, "Cowardice or Confusion: Norman Welch and the Sixteenth Michigan at Little Round Top," *MHM,* July/August 1998, pp. 60–65; Edward G. Longacre, *Custer and His Wolverines* (Conshocken, Combined Publishing, 1997), pp. 121–65; O. B. Curtis, *History of the Twenty-Fourth Michigan* (reprint; Gaithersburg: Olde Soldier Books, 1988), pp. 137–96; Alan T. Nolan, *The Iron Brigade* (Madison: Historical Society of Wisconsin, 1975),

pp. 224–59; Woodford, *Father Abraham's Children*, pp. 91–126; Michael Phipps, *Come On, You Wolverines*, (Gettysburg: Fransworth House Impressions, 1995); Gregory J. W. Urwin, *Custer Victorious: The Civil War Battles of General George Armstrong Custer* (Rutherford: Farleigh Dickinson University Press, 1983), pp. 256–60.

13. www.tebbsbend.com; Terry VandeWater, *A Bend in the River*, (Bloomington: Author House, 2005); Robertson, *Michigan in the War*, pp. 451–54.

14. Robert Garth Scott, ed., *Forgotten Valor: The Memoirs, Journals, & Civil War Letters of Orlando B. Willcox* (Kent: Kent State University Press, 1999); Roger L. Rosentreter, "A Michigan Warrior: Orlando Bolivar Willcox," unpublished; Albert Castel, "Old Pap: Michigan's Top Civil War General," *MHM*, July/August 1998, pp. 18–27; Milo M. Quaife, ed. *From the Cannon's Mouth: The Civil War Letters of General Alpheus S. Williams* (1959, Lincoln: University of Nebraska Press, 1995); Jack Mason, *Until Antietam: The Life and Letters of Major General Israel B. Richardson, U.S. Army* (Carbondale: Southern Illinois University Press, 2009); Rosentreter, "Three Generals," pp. 20–29.

15. Minnie Dubbs Millbrook, *Michigan Medal of Honor Winners in the Civil War* (Lansing: Michigan Civil War Centennial Observance Commission, 1966); Rose Sydlowski, "Beyond the Call of Duty," *MHM*, July/August 1998, pp. 101–03.

16. Robertson, *Michigan*, pp. 68, 751.

17. Roger L. Rosentreter, "Fighting is Not Very Funny Business," in *Michigan and the Civil War*, pp. 76–79; Rosentreter, "For the Glory," p. 12.

18. Stephen W. Sears, ed., *For Country, Cause & Leaders: The Civil War Journal of Charles Haydon* (New York: Ticknor & Fields, 1993), pp. 106, 138; Gallup, "The Second Michigan," p. 45.

19. Haydon, *For Country*, p. 52; Rosentreter, "Those Damned Black Hats," p. 86; Rosentreter, "For the Glory," p. 11.

20. George M. Blackbun, ed., "A Michigan Soldier Views Slavery" in *Michigan and the Civil War*, pp. 58–62; John C. Schneider, "Detroit and the Problems of Disorder: The Riot of 1863," *MHM* 1974, pp. 4–24; Woodford, *Father Abraham's Children*, pp. 63–70.

21. McRae, Norman, *Negroes in Michigan During the Civil War* (Lansing: Michigan Civil War Centennial Observance Commission, 1966); Hondon Hargrove, "Their Greatest Battle Was Getting into the Fight," in *Michigan and the Civil War*, pp. 80–84.

22. Robertson, *Michigan in the War*, pp. 122–34; Willis F. Dunbar, *Kalamazoo* (Kalamazoo: Western Michigan University, 1969), p. 83; see also *Michigan Women in the Civil War* (Lansing: Michigan Civil War Centennial Observance Commission, 1963) and Robert Spiro, "History of the Michigan Soldiers' Aid Society, 1861–1865," (University of Michigan, PhD, 1959).

23. Weldon Petz, "Michigan's Florence Nightingale," *MHM*, July/August 1998, pp. 66–74; Julia Susan Wheelock Freeman, *The Boys in White: The Experience of a Hospital Agent in and Around Washington*, (New York: Lange & Hillman, 1870).

24. Lois Bryan Adams, *Letters From Washington, 1863–1865*, edited by Evelyn Leasher. (Detroit: Wayne State University Press, 1999); "Letter from Washington," *MHM*, May/June 1999, pp. 6–27.

25. Woodford, *Father Abraham's Children*, pp. 283–84; Elizabeth D. Leonard, *All the Daring of the Soldier*, (New York: Penguin, 1999), pp. 106–13; E. F. Conkin, *Women at Gettysburg, 1863*, (Gettysburg: Thomas Publications, 1993), pp. 93–104.

26. S. Emma Edmonds, *Nurse and Spy in the Union Army*. (Hartford: W. S. Williams & Company, 1865); Betty Fladeland, "Alias Franklin Thompson," in *Michigan in the Civil War*, pp. 53–56; Webb Garrison, *Amazing Women of the Civil War*, (Nashville: Rutledge Hill Press, 1999), pp. 13–20; Leonard, *All the Daring*, pp. 169–85; Woodford, *Father Abraham's Children*, pp. 127–35.

27. "She Followed the Guidon," by Barbara Shafer, *MHM*, November/December 2002, pp.66–75; see Louise Barnett, *Touched by Fire: The Life, Death, and Mythic Afterlife of George Armstrong Custer*, (New York: Henry Holt, 1996).

28. *Detroit Free Press*, September 2 and 4, 1862.

29. Albert Castel, "Dearest Ben," in *Michigan in the Civil War*, pp. 95–99.

30. Lewis Beeson & Victor F. Lemmer, *The Effects of the Civil War on Mining in Michigan.* (Lansing: Michigan Civil War Centennial Observance Commission, 1966); Kenneth N. Metcalf, *Effects of the Civil War on Manufacturing in Michigan.* (Lansing: Michigan Civil War Centennial Observance Commission, 1966), p. 27.

31. Metcalf, *Manufacturing*, p. 6, 13; Joseph J. Marks, ed., *Effects of the Civil War on Farming in Michigan.* (Lansing: Michigan Civil War Centennial Observance Commission, 1966); Albert A. Blum, "Guns, Grains and Iron Ore," in *Michigan in the Civil War*, pp. 68–71; Herbert Brinks, "The Effect of the Civil War in 1861 on Michigan Lumbering and Mining Industries," *MHM*, 1960, pp. 101–07; Richard H. Sewell, "Michigan Farmers and the Civil War," *MHM*, 1960, pp. 353–74.

32. *Statistics of the State of Michigan Collected for the Ninth Census of the United States, June 1, 1870* (Lansing: W.S. George & Co., 1873), pp. xiv, xxxviii, xxxix, xliv, xlvi

33. Harris, "Blair," pp. 171–72, Robertson, *Michigan in the War*, pp. 79–84; p. Jean Joy L. Fennimore, "Austin Blair: Civil War Governor, 1863-1864," *MHM*, 1965, p. 358; Winfred A. Harbison, "Detroit's Role in the Re-election of Abraham Lincoln" in Weldon E. Petz and Roger L. Rosentreter, *Michigan Remember Lincoln* (Lansing: *Michigan History Magazine*, 2009), pp. 53–59.

34. Sister Mary Karl George, *Zachariah Chandler* (East Lansing: Michigan State University Press, 1969); Hans L. Trefousse, "I Have Done My Share," *Civil War Times Illustrated*, May 1970, pp. 22–29; Maria Quinlan Leiby, "Profane, Hard Drinking & Eternally Grim: Zachariah Chandler Defends the Constitution," *MHM*, January/February 1994, pp. 18–23; Wilmer C. Harris, *Public Life of Zachariah Chandler, 1851-1875* (Lansing: Michigan Historical Commission, 1917).

35. Jacob M. Howard in *DAB*, 9:278–79; Allan G. Bogue, *The Earnest Men: Republicans of the Civil War Senate* (Ithaca: Cornell University Press, 1981), p. 39.

36. Woodford, *Father Abraham's Children*, pp. 88; Robertson, *Michigan in the War*, pp. 87–93; Rosentreter, "For the Glory," p. 13.

37. Roger L. Rosentreter, "Our Lincoln is Dead," *MHM*, March/April 2000, pp. 28–39; Knox Mellon Jr., ed., "Letters of James Greenlach," *MHM*, 1960, p. 237; Weldon Petz, "When Lincoln's Funeral March Made Detroit Musical History," in *Michigan Remembers Lincoln*, pp. 97–101; Lloyd Lewis, "The Four Who Hanged," in *Michigan Remembers Lincoln*, pp. 102–07.

38. Adams, "Letters from Washington," *MHM*, May/June 1999, pp. 23–24.
39. Paul D. Mehney, "Capturing a Confederate," *MHM*, May/June 2000, pp. 42–49; Woodford, *Father Abraham's Children*, pp. 229–43.
40. Edward G. Longacre, "Unwilling Frontiersmen," *MHM*, July/August 1998, pp. 76–84; Robertson, *Michigan in the War*, pp. 678–85.
41. Robertson, *Michigan in the War*, pp. 87–93; Alfred J. Freitag, *Detroit in the Civil War*. (Detroit: Wayne State University Press, 1951), p. 19.

Chapter 10 Notes

1. Donald I. Dickman and Larry A. Leefers, *The Forests of Michigan* (Ann Arbor: University of Michigan Press, 2004), p. 120; Rolland H. Maybee, *Michigan's White Pine Era* (Lansing: Bureau of History, 1988), p. 10–11.
2. Maybee, *White Pine*, pp. 13–14.
3. Dickman & Leefers, *Forests*, p. 121; Bald, *Four Centuries*, pp. 282–83; Irene M. Hargreaves & Harold M. Foehl, *The Story of Logging the White Pine in the Saginaw Valley* (Bay City: Red Keg Press, 1964), pp. 9–10; Robert W. Wells, *Daylight in the Swamp* (New York: Doubleday, 1978), pp. 34–35; Rolland H. Maybee, "David Ward: Pioneer Timber King," *MHM*, 1948, pp. 6–14.
4. Hargreaves & Foehl, *Story*, pp. 9–10, Bald, *Four Centuries*, pp. 282–83; Wells, *Daylight*, pp. 71–87; Dickman & Leefers, *Forests*, pp. 121–23.
5. Maybee, *White Pine*, p. 18–23; John J. Heilala, "In An Upper Michigan Lumber Camp," *MHM*, 1952, pp. 55–79.
6. Hargreaves & Foehl, *Story*, pp. 13–31; Wells, *Daylight*, 35–36; Maybee, *White Pine*, pp. 23–24.
7. Wells, *Daylight*, 37; Jacob Dye and Rex Dye, *Lumber Camp Life in Michigan* (New York: Exposition Press, 1975), p. 15; Dorothy Dill, "Lumberjack Stories," *MHM*, 1957, pp. 328–30; Bald, *Four Centuries*, p. 287.
8. Dill, "Stories," pp. 328–30; Bald, *Four Centuries*, p. 287.
9. George B. Engberg, "Who Were the Lumberjacks?," *MHM*, 1948, pp. 238–46; Bald, *Four Centuries*, p. 286.
10. Wells, *Daylight*, p. 38.
11. Lewis C. Reimann, *When Pine Was King* (AuTrain: Avery Studios, 1952, 1981) pp. 116–17; Dickman & Leefers, *Forests*, pp. 135–37.
12. *Michigan Log Marks* (East Lansing: Michigan Agricultural Experiment Station, 1941), pp. 1–81; Bald, *Four Centuries*, p. 286; Robert Garrett, "Bringing Order to Chaos," *MHM*, March/April 2002, pp. 18–25.
13. Wells, *Daylight*, pp. 88–94; Dickman & Leefers, *Forests*, pp. 138–42; Maybee, *White Pine*, pp. 27–34.
14. Wells, *Daylight*, pp. 88–90.
15. Ibid., p. 88.
16. Ibid., pp. 94–98; Arthur S. Mann, "The Vanishing Lumberjack," *MHM*, July/August 2001, pp. 48–49.
17. Ibid, p. 94.

18. Barnett, "Michigan's Buried Treasure," *MHM*, May/June 2009, pp. 8–13; Maybee, *White Pine*, p. 34–35; Garrett, "Order," p. 25; Dickman & Leefers, *Forests*, p. 140.

19. Bald, *Four Centuries*, pp. 281–86; Maybee, *White Pine*, pp. 43–52.

20. Bald, *Four Centuries*, pp. 281–82; Wells, *Daylight*, pp. 38, 193; Maybee, *White Pine*, pp. 43–52; Dickman & Leefers, *Forests*, pp. 143–45.

21. Bald, *Four Centuries*, pp. 286–87; Roy M. Overpack, "The Michigan Logging Wheels" *MHM*, 1951, pp. 222–25.

22. Carl Bajema, "Timber Express," *MHM*, November/December 1993, p. 43.

23. Ibid., pp. 43–46; Maybee, *White Pine*, pp. 37–43.

24. Dickman & Leefers, *Forests*, p. 152.

25. Josephine Sawyer, "Personal Reminiscence of the Big Fire of 1871, *MHM*, 1932, pp. 422–30.

26. Dickman & Leefers, *Forests*, pp. 152–57.

27. Ibid., p. 159-63; Roger L. Rosentreter, "Huron County," *MHM*, July/August 1983, pp. 10–11; James H. Lincoln & James L. Donahue, *Fiery Trial* (Ann Arbor: Historical Society of Michigan, 1984); Janet Kreger, "Fire and Failure," *MHM*, January/February 1998, pp. 15–20; Paul Mehney, "Michigan Engulfed," January/February 1998, *MHM*, P. 21; J. A. Mitchell & D. Robson, *Forest Fires and Forest Fire Control in Michigan* (Michigan Department of Conservation, 1950), pp. 6–20; see Betty Sodders, *Michigan on Fire* (Alpena: Thunder Bay Press, 1997).

28. Dickman & Leefers, Forests, pp. 183–68, 176–78; *The Metz Fire of 1908* (Presque Isle County Historical Society, n.d.); Arthur W. Thurner, *Strangers and Sojourners: A History of Michigan's Keweenaw Peninsula* (Detroit: Wayne State University Press, 1994), p. 161.

29. May, *Michigan*, pp. 346-48.

30. Laura L. Bennett, "Not Just Another Pretty Mansion," *MHM*, November/December 1997, pp. 28–35; John H. McGarry III, "Who Was Charles Hackley?" *MHM*, November/December 1997, pp. 32–33; Richard H. Harms, "Life After Lumber: The Entrepreneurs of Muskegon," *MHM*, January/February 1987, pp. 12–19; Marla Miller, "Sculpture of Charles H. Hackley Unveiled in Downtown Muskegon," *Muskegon Chronicle*, October 8, 2009.

31. Lewis C. Reiman, *Incredible Seney* (AuTrain, Avery Color Studios, 1982, 1953), pp. 1–7; May, *Michigan*, p. 344; Wells, *Daylight*, pp. 152–55.

32. Daniel Hoffman, *Paul Bunyan: Last of the Frontier Demigods* (Lincoln, University of Nebraska Press, 1952, 1983), pp. 3–6; Dickman & Leefers, *Forests*, pp. 130–31; Kay Houston, "The Man Who Could Out-Lumber Paul Bunyan," *The Detroit News*, June 14, 1996; *Paul Bunyan of the Great Lakes*, Stanley D. Newton (1946, AuTrain: Avery Studios, 1985), pp. 67–71.

33. Carl Sandburg, *The People, Yes*, (New York: Harcourt, Brace and Company, 1936), p. 97.

34. Dickman & Leffers, *Forests*, pp. 145–46.

35. Ibid., pp. 169–70; see also pp. 173–237.

36. Ibid., p. 169.

Chapter 11 Notes

1. David J. Krause, *The Making of a Mining District: Keweenaw Native Cooper, 1500–1870* (Detroit: Wayne State University Press, 1992), p. 115.
2. Krause, *Keweenaw,* pp. 18–43; Arthur W. Thurner, *Strangers and Sojourners: A History of Michigan's Keweenaw Peninsula* (Detroit: Wayne State University Press, 1994), pp. 20, 29–30; John R. Halsey, "Native Copper," *MHM,* November/December 2001, pp. 20–25.
3. Krause, *Keweenaw,* pp. 60–68.
4. Krause, *Keweenaw,* pp. 72–77; Klunder, *Cass,* pp. 36–37; Woodford, *Cass,* pp. 134–35; Henry Rowe Schoolcraft, "The Ontonagon Boulder," in Kestenbaum, *Making,* pp. 101–12; Richard G. Bremer, "Henry Rowe Schoolcraft: Explorer in the Mississippi Valley, 1818–1832," *Wisconsin Magazine of History,* Autumn 1982, pp. 40–48.
5. Krause, *Keweenaw,* pp. 78, 85, 91; *MPHC,* 7:193, 195–97.
6. Krause, *Keweenaw,* pp. 97–102.
7. Ibid., pp. 103–08.
8. Ibid., pp. 108–116; Bremer, "Schoolcraft," p. 53.
9. Krause, *Keweenaw,* pp. 132–35.
10. Ibid., 136–38; Bald, *Four Centuries,* pp. 232–34.
11. Bald, *Four Centuries,* p. 234.
12. Ibid., 234; Krause, *Making,* pp. 205–20; Charles K. Hyde and Larry D. Lankton, *Old Reliable* (Hancock: The Quincy Mine Hoist Association, 1982), p. 4; Roger L. Rosentreter, "Keweenaw County," *MHM,* March/April 1985, pp. 8–11.
13. Krause, *Keweenaw,* pp. 143–44; Thurner, *Strangers,* p. 43.
14. Bald, *Four Centuries,* pp. 235–36.
15. Ibid., pp. 235–37; Thurner, *Strangers,* pp. 44–52; William H. Pyne, "Quincy Mine: The Old Reliable," *MHM* 1957, pp. 219–42; Mentor L. Williams, "Horace Greeley and Michigan Copper," *MHM* 1950, pp. 120–32; see Hyde and Lankton, *Old Reliable.*
16. Bald, *Four Centuries,* pp. 276–78.
17. May, *Michigan,* p. 358.
18. Thurner, *Strangers,* pp. 158–91; Jerry Stanley, *Big Annie of Calumet: A True Story of the Industrial Revolution,* (New York: Crown Publishers, 1996), p. 20.
19. Stanley, *Big Annie,* pp. 6–12; Larry D. Lankton, "Died in the Mines," *MHM,* November/December 1983, pp. 33–41.
20. Thurner, *Strangers,* pp. 193–96; Stanley, *Big Annie,* p. 23.
21. Thurner, *Strangers,* p. 197; Stanley, *Big Annie,* pp. 23–27.
22. Thurner, *Strangers,* pp. 197–99; Diana Engle, "Standing Tall with Big Annie," *MHM,* July/August 1999, p. 17.
23. Thurner, *Strangers,* p. 203; Engle, "Annie," pp. 17–18; Stanley, *Big Annie,* pp. 27–31.
24. Thurner, *Strangers,* p. 203; Engle, "Annie," pp. 17–18.
25. Thurner, *Strangers,* pp. 203, 208, 211.

26. Ibid., p. 213; Steve Lehto, *Death's Door: The Truth Behind Michigan's Largest Mass Murder* (Troy: Momentum Books, 2006), pp. 87–97, 121–24, 143–48.

27. Ibid., p. 215.

28. Bald, *Four Centuries*, p. 349; May, *Michigan,* p. 361; Thurner, *Strangers,* p. 227.

29. Thurner, *Strangers,* pp. 217–18.

30. May, *Michigan,* pp. 385, 465, 503–05, 554, 642–43.

31. John S. Burt, "Boys, look around and see what you can find.'" *MHM,* November/December 1994, pp. 11–15; Alan S. Brown, "William Burt and the Upper Peninsula," *MHM,* May/June 1980, pp. 14–17.

32. Burton H. Boyum, *The Saga of Iron Mining in Michigan's Upper Peninsula* (Marquette: John M. Longyear Research Library, 1977), pp. 5–7; Donna Stiffler Bollinger, "The Iron Riches of Michigan's Upper Peninsula," *MHM,* November/December 1978, pp. 9–13.

33. Boyum, *Saga,* pp. 13–14.

34. Boyum, *Saga,* pp. 15–18, 23, 32–33; George Merk, "From Surveyors to Scientists," *MHM,* November/December 1994, pp. 16–23; www.exploringthenorth. com/cornish/pump.html.

35. Boyum, *Saga,* pp. 20–22, 35.

36. Ibid., p. 37; Maria Quinlan Leiby, "Iron Making at Fayette" in *Fayette Historic Townsite* (Lansing: *Michigan History Magazine,* 2007), pp. 7–15.

37. Maria Quinlan Leiby, Thomas G. Friggens, John R. Halsey, Brenda J. Laakso, *Fayette Historic Townsite* (Lansing: *Michigan History Magazine,* 2007); Clint Dunathan, "Fayette," *MHM* 1957, pp. 204–08.

38. Thomas G. Friggens, *No Tears in Heaven: The 1926 Barnes-Hecker Mine Disaster* (Lansing: *Michigan History Magazine,* 1998).

39. Peter J. Kakela, "The Shift to Taconite Pellets," *MHM,* November/December 1994, pp. 70–75.; Jackie Stark, "Empire Mine Winding Down," March 5, 2013; *Marquette Mining Journal;* Johanna Boyle, "Empire Mine Production to be Slashed," *Marquette Mining Journal,* December 5, 2011.

Chapter 12 Notes

1. Richard Bak, "A Fair to Remember," *Hour Detroit,* February 2009.

2. Ibid.

3. Patricia A. Cooper, *Once a Cigar Maker: Men, Women, and Work Culture in American Cigar Factories, 1900–1919* (Urbana: University of Illinois Press, 1987), pp. 189–98; Michael Boettcher, "The Best 5¢ Cigar Town, *MHM,* November/December 2000, pp. 42–51; Thomas L. Jones, "Up in Smoke: Cigar Making in Detroit," *The Detroit News,* February 18, 2000.

4. Peter H. Blum, "Brewed in Detroit," *MHM,* March/April 2000, pp. 18–26; Farmer, *Detroit,* p. 776; May, *Michigan,* p. 410.

5. Hillary Whitcomb Jesse, "The Sizzle and Fizzle of Round Oak Stoves," *MHM,* March/April 2004, pp. 18–26. See also, Leland Haines, *Round Oak: A Good Thing from Doe-Wah-Jack* (Northville: Round Oak Company, 1994); Geoffrey G.

Drutchas, "The Man With A Capital Design," *MHM*, March/April 2004, p. 32; Vivian M. Baulch and Patricia Zacharias, "Detroit's Giant Stove and Tire," *The Detroit News*, February 26, 1997; Woodford, *Detroit*, pp. 75–80; May, *Michigan*, p. 413–14.

6. *Grand Rapids Made: A Brief History of the Grand Rapids Furniture Industry* (Grand Rapids: Grand Rapids Public Museum, 1985), pp. 1–8; James Stanford Bradshaw, "Grand Rapids, 1870–1880: Furniture City Emerges," *MHM*, 1971, pp. 321–42; see Christian G. Carron, *Grand Rapids Furniture: The Story of America's Furniture City* (Grand Rapids: Grand Rapids Public Museum, 1998).

7. Ted O'Neil, "Dow Dynasty," *MHM*, May/June 1997, pp. 28–32; Harry J. Loynd, "Parke, Davis & Company and the Never-Ending Search for Better Medicines," *MHM*, 1958, pp. 367–77; Woodford, *This is Detroit*, p. 81; May, *Michigan*, p. 408; James W. Armstrong, "Dr. Upjohn's Company," *MHM*, May/June 1986, pp. 24–31.

8. Sally Helvenston, "From Feathers to Fashion: How the Turkey Revolutionized Women's Clothing," *MHM*, September/October 1996, pp. 28–35; Michael Landry, "It's a Daisy," *MHM*, January/February 2006, pp. 28–39.

9. Roger L. Rosentreter, "Cereal City," *MHM*, July/August 1999, pp. 6–13.

10. Francis X. Blouin, Jr., "Not Just Automobiles: Contributions of Michigan to the National Economy," in *Michigan: Visions of Our Past*, Richard Hathaway, ed. (East Lansing: Michigan State University Press, 1989), pp. 154–57.

11. C. Warren Vander Hill, *Settling the Great Lakes Frontier: Immigration to Michigan, 1837–1924* (Lansing: Michigan Historical Commission, 1970), pp. 1–4; May, *Michigan*, pp. 244–49, 511–13; Jean Lamarre, *The French Canadians of Michigan* (Detroit: Wayne State University Press, 2003), pp. 75–160.

12. Vander Hill, *Settling*, pp. 14–26; Jeremy W. Kilar, *Germans in Michigan* (East Lansing: Michigan State University Press, 2002), pp. 7–24; Daniel E. Sutherland, "Michigan's Emigrant Agent: Edward H. Thomson," *MHM*, 1975, p. 3–37.

13. Vander Hill, *Settling*, pp. 27–44.

14. Ibid., pp. 45–67.

15. Ibid., pp. 68–81; Cooper, *Cigar*, p. 190.

16. Vander Hill, *Settling*, pp. 82–87; Arthur M. Woodward, *The Michigan Companion* (Detroit: OmniData, Inc., 2012), pp. 28–29.

17. "Letters from the 34th Michigan Volunteer Infantry" at www.spanamwar.com.

18. Paul Mehney, "The War with Spain," *MHM*, May/June 2002, pp. 28–40; John Stronach, "The 34th Michigan Volunteer Infantry," 1946, pp. 289–304; Mary Karshner, "'Nice Fellows and Good Brave Men': The Spanish-American War Experience of Clyde F. Karshner," *MHM*, September/October 1996, pp. 14–156; "The Spanish-American War," Michigan Department of Military & Veterans Affairs at www.michigan.gov/dmva.

19. Victor Clarence Vaughn, "A Doctor's Memories," *MHM*, May/June 2002, p. 37.

20. Jasper B. Reid, Jr., "Russell A. Alger as Secretary of War," *MHM* 1959, pp. 225–39; George P. Merk, "A Profile of Courage," *MHM*, January/February 2003, pp. 28–39; Chase S. Osborn, *The Iron Hunter* (1919, Detroit: Wayne State University Press, 202), pp. 121–25.

21. Paul Carlson, *"Pecos Bill: A Military Biography of William R. Shafter"* (College Station: Texas A& M University Press, 1989), pp. 160–88.

22. A. B. Feuer, "Our Only Option was to Attack," *MHM*, September/October 1996, pp. 8–13.

23. Laura Rose Ashlee, "Ellen May Tower: Guardian Angel of the Michigan Volunteers," *MHM* January/February 1990, pp. 46–47.

24. Roger L. Rosentreter, "Three Oaks Against the World," *MHM*, May/June 1999, pp. 28–32.

25. Jeremy W. Kilar, "I Am Not Sorry," *MHM*, November/December 1995, pp. 10–17; see also Eric Rauchway, *Murdering McKinley: The Making of Theodore Roosevelt's America* (New York: Hill and Wang, 2003).

26. Melvin G. Holli, "Hazen S. Pingree," *MHM*, January/February 1980, pp. 38–39; Charles R. Starring, "Hazen S. Pingree, Another Forgotten Eagle," *MHM*, 1948, pp. 145–46; see Melvin G. Holli, *Reform in Detroit: Hazen S. Pingree and Urban Politics* (New York: Oxford University Press, 1969).

27. Holli, "Pingree," p. 38; H. Roger Grant, "Pingree's Potato Patches: A Study of Self-Help during the Depression of the 1890s." *Detroit in Perspective*, Winter 1980, pp. 61–71.

28. Holli, "Pingree," p. 38; Starring, "Pingree," pp. 132–38.

29. Ibid., Holli, *Reform*, pp. 185–218; Osborn, *Iron Hunter*, p. 132.

30. May, Michigan, pp. 444–446; Bald, *Four Centuries*, pp. 339–40; see also Jean M. Fox, *Fred M. Warner: Progressive Governor* (Farmington Hills, MI: Farmington Hills Historical Commission, 1988).

31. Robert M. Warner, *Chase Salmon Osborn* (Ann Arbor: The University of Michigan, 1960), p. 3.

32. Ibid., pp. 5–12.

33. Ibid., pp. 13–15.

34. Ibid., pp. 16–20, 22–25.

35. Bald, *Four Centuries*, pp. 344–45.

36. John Pepin "Roosevelt, Publish Tangle in Court Case," *20th Century in the Upper Peninsula* (n.p, n.d.) p. 23; Larry Chabot, "Presidents Seeking A Pleasant Peninsula," *MHM*, November/December 2001, p. 72; Warner, *Osborn*, pp. 20–22.

37. Warner, *Osborn*, pp. 26–30.

Chapter 13 Notes

1. George, *A Most Unique Machine: The Michigan Origins of the American Automobile Industry* (Grand Rapids: William B. Eerdmans Publishing Company, 1975), pp. 15–16.

2. Ibid., *Michigan*, p. 485; David L. Lewis, "From Rumble Seats to Rockin' Vans, *MHM*, March/April 1996, pp. 72–79.

3. May, *Unique Machine*, pp. 40–48; William John Armstrong, "What About the Baushkes?," *MHM*, March/April 1996, pp. 24–27.

4. May, *Unique Machine*, pp. 89–94; Brinkley, *Wheels*, 3–23.

5. May, *Unique Machine*, pp. 49–61; George S. May, *R. E. Olds: Auto Industry Pioneer*, (Grand Rapids: William B. Eerdmans, 1977), pp. 9–62.
6. May, *Unique Machine*, pp. 62–72, 109–126; May, *R. E. Olds*, pp. 73–203.
7. May, *Unique Machine*, pp. 127–30.
8. May, *R. E. Olds*, pp. 204–85.
9. May, *R. E. Olds*, pp. 158–61.
10. Lewis, *Image*, pp. 17–19; May, *Unique Machine*, pp. 83–108, 238–44; Brinkley, *Wheels*, pp. 30–48.
11. Brinkley, *Wheels*, pp. 49–73; Harry Barnard, *Independent Man: The Life of Senator James Couzens* (New York: Charles Scribner's Sons, 1958), pp. 22, 46–47.
12. Brinkley, *Wheels*, pp. 99–112, Lewis, *Image*, pp. 40–59.
13. Lewis, *Image*, pp. 41–43.
14. Ibid., p. 42.
15. Brinkley, *Wheels*, pp. 135–38; "Albert Kahn: Architect of Detroit," *MHM*, November/December 2000, pp. 86–93; David Lewis, "Ford and Kahn," *MHM*, September/October 1980, pp. 17–28.
16. Ibid., pp. 138–39; Lewis, *Image*, p. 53.
17. Brinkley, *Wheels*, pp. 151–55.
18. Ibid., pp. 154–44, 162.
19. Ibid., pp. 162, 167.
20. Ibid., pp. 170–71; Lewis, *Image*, pp. 70–73.
21. Brinkley, *Wheels*, pp. 172–73.
22. Ibid., pp. 174–75.
23. Lewis, *Image*, pp. 20–24.
24. Larry Gustin, "Flint, Billy Durant & the Beginning of General Motors," *MHM*, September/October 2008, p. 38.
25. Ibid., pp. 39–40.
26. May, *Unique Machine*, p. 317; May, *Michigan*, pp. 438–39; Hyde, p. 21.
27. Larry Gustin, *Billy Durant: Creator of General Motors* (Grand Rapids: William B. Eerdmans Publishing Company, 1973), pp. 116–22, 135; Gustin, "Flint," p. 41.
28. Gustin, *Billy Durant*, pp. 124, 140–43.
29. Ibid., pp. 145–63.
30. Ibid., pp. 175–78; John B. Rae, *The American Automobile Industry* (Boston: Twayne Publishers, 1985), pp. 47, 50.
31. Gustin, *Billy Durant*, pp. 164–89, 197; Rae, *American*, pp. 50–51.
32. Gustin, "Flint," p. 42; Gustin, *Billy Durant*, pp. 199–201; Rae, *American*, p. 51; David Farber, *Sloan Rules: Alfred P. Sloan and the Triumph of General Motors* (Chicago: University of Chicago, 2004) pp. 28–36.
33. Gustin, *Billy Durant*, p. 222.
34. Rae, *American*, pp. 50–54.
35. Ibid., pp. 52, 62–63; Farber, *Sloan Rules*, pp. 28, 45–105.
36. Rae, *American*, pp. 52–66; Lewis, *Image*, pp. 189–97; Larry B. Massie, "Horseless Humor and Car-Toons," *MHM*, March/April 1996, pp. 54–57.
37. Charles K. Hyde, *Riding the Roller Coaster: A History of the Chrysler Corporation* (Detroit: Wayne State University Press, 2003), pp. 1–13.

38. Ibid., pp. 29–42.
39. Ibid., pp. 45–55, 48–49, 51; Charles Hyde, "Let's Not Forget the Dodge Brothers," *MHM*, March/April 1996, 28–32; see also Charles K. Hyde, *The Dodge Brothers: The Men, The Motor Cars and the Legacy* (Detroit: Wayne State University Press, 2005).
40. Hyde, *Riding the Roller Coaster*, pp. 56–57.
41. Ibid., pp. 45, 61–71.
42. Rae, *American*, pp. 66–69
43. John Rae, "Why Michigan?" in *The Automobile and American Culture* (Ann Arbor: University of Michigan Press, 1983), pp. 1–9; May, *Unique Machine*, pp. 343–48; May, *Michigan*, pp. 513–14.

Chapter 14 Notes

1. May, *Michigan*, p. 460; Lewis, *Image*, p. 78.
2. Lewis, *Image*, pp. 79–92; Steven Watts, *The People's Tycoon: Henry Ford and the American Century* (New York: Alfred A. Knopf, 2005), pp. 226–40; Brinkley, *Wheels*, pp. 194–98; Carl Wittke, "An Echo from the Ford Peace Ship," *MHM*, 1948, pp. 257–69.
3. *Detroit Free Press*, March 22, 1917.
4. Ibid., April 6, 8, 1917; *Michigan Biographies* (Lansing: The Michigan Historical Commission, 1924), p. 37.
5. *Detroit Free Press*, April 4, 1917.
6. Ibid., April 6, 8, 1917.
7. Ibid., April 7–8 & 13, 1917.
8. Ibid., April 3, 6, 1917.
9. Ibid, April 1 & April 9, 1917.
10. Ibid., March 27, April 3, 1917.
11. Phillip D. Schertzing, "'Very Difficult to Let Go Of': The Birth and Development of the Michigan State Police," *MHM*, March/April 1992, pp. 25–33.
12. Douglas Galuszka, "Michigan in the Great War," *MHM*, July/August 1993, p. 31; www.arlingtoncemetery.net/thomaset.htm.
13. Godfrey J. Anderson, *A Michigan Polar Bear Confronts the Bolsheviks: A War Memoir* (Grand Rapids: William B. Eerdmans Publishing Company, 2010), pp. 28, 31, 34.
14. Galuszka, "Michigan," p. 31.
15. Joint War History Commissions of Michigan and Wisconsin, *The 32nd Division in the World War: 1917–1918* (Madison: Wisconsin War History Commission, 1920), pp. 70, 113–15; "Highlights of the 32nd Division in the World War," www.32nd-division.org/history/ww1/32ww1.html; Paul Mehney, "Les Terribles," *MHM*, May/June 2001, pp. 30–36.
16. James Glenn Wilson, "The Sights We Have Seen We Will Never Forget," *MHM*, July/August 1993, pp. 24–30; Paul Meheny, "The Custer Division," *MHM*, May/June 2001, pp. 38–46.

17. Paul Mehney, "To Save Our Necks," *MHM*, January/February 1999, p. 35; Roger Crownover, "Stranded in Russia," *MHM*, January/February 1999, pp. 28–43; Richard M. Doolen, *Michigan's Polar Bears: the American Expedition to North Russia, 1918–1919* (Ann Arbor: University of Michigan, 1965); see Stanley Bozich, *'Detroit's Own' Polar Bears: The American North Russian Expedition Forces, 1918–1919* (Polar Bears Publishing Co., 1985).

18. Crownover, "Stranded," p. 31; *Detroit Free Press*, December 6, 1918.

19. Paul D. Mehney, "A Matter of the Most Complex and Difficult Sort," *MHM*, January/February 1999, p. 31; Mehney, "Save," 31–35; Crownover, "Stranded," p. 37; Neil G. Carey, *Fighting The Bolsheviks* (Presidio, 1997), p. 52.

20. Anderson, *Michigan Polar Bear*, pp. 106–08.

21. Crownover, "Stranded," pp. 33–34, 40.

22. Ibid., pp. 40–42; Patricia Zacharias, "Detroit's Polar Bears and Their Confusing War," *The Detroit News*, July 22, 2000; Rosentreter, *MHM*, January/February 1999, p. 2.

23. www.worldwar1.com/dbc/helmet17.htm; Lewis, *Image*, pp. 93–95; Brinkley, *Wheels*, pp. 208–17; Paul Mehney, "Packards for Pershing," *MHM*, March/April 1999, 28–35; Hyde, *Riding*, pp. 53–54; Richard M. Rupley, "The Model T Goes to War," *MHM*, November/December 2008, p. 27; *New York Times*, August 22, 1918; "Ford Model T Ambulance," www.nationalmuseum.af.mil/factsheets/factsheet; A. B. Feuer, "Built to Preserve Liberty," *MHM*, March/April 1998, pp. 40–43.

24. *Baltimore Sun*, October 6, 1918; *The Detroit News*, September 30, 1918; *Grand Rapids Herald*, December 16, 1918; *Grand Rapids News*, December 16, 1918; *Potential Influenza Effects on Military Populations* (December 2003), John N. Bombardt, Jr., Heidi E. Brown, vaccines.mil/documents/831P3786final.pdf pp. 21–22; May, *Michigan*, pp. 463–65; Woodward, *Yesterdays*, pp. 273–74.

25. *Detroit Free Press*, April 1, October 23 & November 8, 1917.

26. Bald, *Four Centuries*, p. 376; Arthur Lyon Cross, "The University of Michigan and the Training of Her Students for the War," *MHM*, 1920, pp. 115–40.

27. *Detroit Free Press*, October 21, 22, 23, 1917; Bald, *Four Centuries*, p. 377.

28. Fox, *Warner*, pp. 408–09.

29. Emerson Hough, *The WEB: A Revelation of Patriotism* (Chicago: Reilly & Lee, 1919), pp. 286–92.

30. *Detroit Free Press*, April 8, 1917; Woodford, *Yesterdays*, p. 273; Fox, *Warner*, pp. 210–17; Matthew Goode, "'Obey the Law and Keep Your Mouths Shut,' German Americans in Grand Rapids During World War I," *MHM*, March/April 1994, p. 18; May, *Michigan*, p. 536; Kilar, *Germans*, p. 38.

31. Kilar, *Germans*, p. 38; Brinkley, *Wheels*, pp. 224–28.

32. Goode, "Obey," pp. 18–23.

33. Timothy Reese Cain, "'Silence and Cowardice' at the University of Michigan: World War I and the Pursuit of Un-American Faculty," *History of Education Quarterly*, Volume 51, August 2011; James D. Wilkes, "Van Tyne: The Professor and the Hun," *MHM*, 1971 pp. 183–204; http://um2017.org/faculty-history/faculty/william-herbert-hobbs; umhistory.dc.umich.edu/history/Faculty_History/V/Van_Tyne,_Claude_Halstead.html

34. Fox, *Warner,* p. 410; Kilar, *Germans,* p. 39.
35. *Detroit Free Press,* November 12, 1918; Patricia Zacharias, "The First Armistice Day," *The Detroit News,* November 11, 1998; William K. McElhone, "Armistice Day Tragedy," *MHM,* November/December 1999, pp. 40–44; Paul Meheny, "It's Over, Over There," *MHM,* November/December 1999, p. 43.
36. Jenny Nolan, "The Red Arrow Division: Fierce Fighters of World War I," *The Detroit News,* September 17, 1997.

Chapter 15 Notes

1. Larry D. Engelmann, *Intemperance: The Lost War Against Liquor* (London: The Free Press, 1979), pp. 11–15.
2. Ibid., 22; Phillip P. Mason, *Rum Running and the Roaring Twenties: Prohibition on the Michigan-Ontario Waterway,* (Detroit: Wayne State University Press, 1995), p. 14; Larry D. Engelmann, "Billy Sunday: 'God, You've Got a Job on Your Hands in Detroit,'" *MHM,* 1971, pp. 1–21.
3. Engelmann, *Intemperance,* p. 32; Mason, *Rum Running,* pp. 16–17; Phillip P. Mason, "Anyone Who Couldn't Get a Drink Wasn't Trying," *MHM,* September/October 1994, pp. 12–22; Helen Sanecki, "'Whether we wanted entertainment of not, we got it," *MHM,* September/October 1994, pp. 23–24; Paul G. Labadie, "Liquid Gold," *MHM,* September/October 1994, pp. 25–26.
4. Engelmann, *Intemperance,* p. 46.
5. Ibid., pp. 67–68.
6. Ibid., p. 73.
7. Mason, *Rum Running,* p. 39.
8. Engelmann, *Intemperance,* p. 125; *New York Times,* June 25, 1927, in Mason, *Rum Running,* pp. 45–46.
9. Ibid., pp. 126, 137–39.
10. Ibid., pp. 152–53.
11. Mason, *Rum Running,* p. 144.
12. Engelmann, Intemperance, pp. 130, 156, 183–88.
13. Kenneth T. Jackson, "The Ku Klux Klan in Michigan," in Robert Warner & C. Warren Vanderhill, *A Michigan Reader: 1865 to the Present,* (William B. Eerdmans Publishing Company, 1974), pp. 169–71; JoEllen McNergney Vinyard, *Right in Michigan's Grassroots: From the KKK to the Michigan Militia* (Ann Arbor: University of Michigan Press, 2011), pp. 42–46.
14. Vinyard, *Grassroots,* pp. 46, 71–79; Jackson, "KKK," p. 173.
15. Vinyard, *Grassroots,* pp. 72–74.
16. Vinyard, *Grassroots,* pp. 74–75.
17. Ibid., pp. 84–85; Jackson, "KKK," pp. 174–79.
18. Kevin Boyle, *Arc of Justice: A Saga of Race, Civil Rights and Murder in the Jazz Age* (New York: Henry Holt, 2004), p. 26; see also Patricia Zacharias, "'I have to die a man or live a coward: The Saga of Dr. Ossian Sweet," *The Detroit News,* February 12, 2001; Lowell Cauffiel, "Bittersweet Victory," *The Detroit News,* February 15, 1987.

19. Boyle, *Saga*, pp. 109–12.
20. Ibid., pp. 23–25, 145, 150–58; Joseph Turrini, "Sweet Justice," *MHM*, July/ August 1999, p. 24.
21. Boyle, *Saga*, pp. 129–32; Turrini, "Sweet Justice," pp. 24–25.
22. Boyle, *Saga*, pp. 13–43; Turrini, "Sweet Justice," p. 25; Lowell Cauffiel, "Bitter-sweet Justice," *The Detroit News Magazine*, pp. 8, 12.
23. Turrini, "Sweet Justice," pp. 25–26.
24. Turrini, "Sweet Justice," pp. 26–27.
25. Boyle, *Saga*, pp. 299–336; Turrini, "Sweet Justice," p. 27.
26. Turrini, "Sweet Justice," p. 27; Cauffiel, "Bittersweet," p. 22.
27. Thomas E. Brown, "Alexander J. Groesbeck," *MHM*, January/February 1981; pp. 40–41; May, *Michigan*, pp. 550–53.
28. www.bra..deis.edu/centers/wsrc/Ernestine_Rose_website; May, *Michigan*, p. 301.
29. May, *Michigan*, p. 446.
30. Bald, *Four Centuries*, p. 316.
31. Sharon E. McHaney, "Securing the Sacred Right to Vote," *MHM*, March/April 1991, pp. 38–45; see "Neither Delay nor Rest," *MHM*, November/December 2002, pp. 50–57; May, *Michigan*, pp. 471–73.
32. *New York Times*, July 3, 1919; "Anna Howard Shaw" at www.anb.org/articles/ 15/15-00615.html.
33. Englemann, *Intemperance*, pp. 190–91, 193, 204; Mason, *Rum Running*, pp. 143–62.
34. Ibid., p. 202.
35. Ibid., p. 220.
36. Ibid., p. 221.

Chapter 16 Notes

1. Helen Tims, *Detroit Magazine*, October 21, 1979; Sidney Fine, *Frank Murphy: A Michigan Life* (Ann Arbor: Historical Society of Michigan, 1984), p. 8.
2. May, *Michigan*, p. 514; Barnard, *Independent Man*, pp. 193–95.
3. Thurner, *Strangers*, pp. 239, 327; Mike Smith "Sprit of 1937," *MHM*, November/ December 2000, p. 64; May, *Pictorial of Michigan*, p. 171; Polk Laffoon IV, "A Memorable Time," *Detroit Free Press Magazine*, October 21, 1979, p. 10.
4. Richard T. Ortquist, "Unemployment and Relief: Michigan's Response to the Depression During the Hoover Years," *MHM*, 1973, p. 225; William H. Chafe, "Flint and the Great Depression," *MHM*, 1969, pp. 229–30; Richard H. Harms, "Paid in Scrip," *MHM*, January/February 1991, pp. 40; Laffoon, "Memorable," p. 10; David M. Katzman, "Ann Arbor: Depression City," *MHM*, 1966, pp. 306–17.
5. Fine, *Murphy*, pp. 8. See Sidney Fine, *Frank Murphy: The New Deal Years* (Chicago: University of Chicago Press, 1979).
6. Ortquist, "Hoover Years," pp. 226–29; "How the Great Depression Changed Detroit," *The Detroit News*, March 4, 1999.
7. Ibid., pp. 218–24, 230.

8. Donald S. Bowman, "Bound For Glory," *MHM*, March/April 1998, pp. 26–39.

9. T.H. Watkins, *The Great Depression: America in the 1930s* (Boston: Little, Brown & Company, 1993), pp. 91–98; Joyce Shaw Peterson, "Auto Workers Confront the Depression, 1929–1933," *Detroit in Perspective*, Fall 1982, v. 6, no. 2, pp. 57–58.

10. Watkins, *Great Depression*, p. 98.

11. Mary Dempsey, "The Many Faces of Father Coughlin," *MHM*, July/August 1999, pp. 30–39; Alan Brinkley, *Voices of Protest: Huey Long, Father Coughlin & the Great Depression* (New York: Vintage Books, 1982), pp. 82–106.

12. May, *Michigan*, pp. 518–19.

13. May, *Michigan*, pp. 519–21; Susan Estabrook Kennedy, "The Michigan Banking Crisis of 1933," *MHM*, 1973, pp. 237–64; Alex Taylor, "Henry Ford Didn't Care if the Banks Closed," *Detroit Free Press*, October 21, 1979; Woodford, *Detroit*, pp. 123–24.

14. Le Roy Barnett, *A Drive Down Memory Lane*, (Allegan Forest, The Priscilla Press, 2004), pp. 39–40; May, *Michigan*, pp. 521–22; Linda O. Stanford & C. Kurt Dewhurst, *MSU Campus* (East Lansing: Michigan State University Press, 2002), pp. 46, 195, 84, 89, 99; Jennifer Holmes, "Out of Hard Times, An Artistic Legacy," *Detroit Free Press Magazine*, October 21, 1979, pp. 22–25; Christine Nelson Ruby, "Art for Millions," *MHM*, January/February 1982, pp. 17–20; Ilene R. Schechter, "Capturing Resources," *MHM*, November/December 2001, pp. 64–69; Roger L. Rosentreter, "Letter to the Editor," *MHM*, January/February 1982, p. 2.

15. Roger L. Rosentreter, "Roosevelt's Tree Army: The Civilian Conservation Corps in Michigan," *MHM*, May/June 1986, pp. 14–23; Charles A. Symon, *We Can Do It: A History of the CCC in Michigan, 1933–1942* (Escanaba, MI: Richards Printing, 1983), pp. 153, 165–68.

16. Stephen Sears, "Shut Down the Goddam Plant," *American Heritage*, May/June 1982, at www.americanheritage.com/content/"shut-goddam-plant"; Michael Smith, "UAW," *MHM*, March/April 1996, p 49; Watkins, *Great Depression*, p. 277; Sidney Fine, *Sit-Down* (Ann Arbor: University of Michigan Press, 1969).

17. Lewis, *Image*, p. 248; Ford R. Bryan, *Henry's Lieutenants* (Detroit: Wayne State University Press, 1993), pp. 28–34.

18. Carlos A. Schwantes, "'We've Got 'em on the Run, Brothers'": The 1937 Non-Automotive Sit Down Strikes in Detroit," *MHM*, 1972, pp. 180–81; Thomas A. Karman, "The Flint Sit-Down Strike," *MHM*, 1962, pp. 97–125; Smith, "Spirit of 1937," p. 65–66.

19. Watkins, *Great Depression*, pp. 276, 282; Smith, "UAW," pp. 47–50; Thomas Featherstone, "Labor of Love," *MHM*, May/June 2000, pp. 34–41; Sears, "Shut Down."

20. Michael Van Dyke, "Sitting Down to Take A Stand," *MHM*, January/February 2003, pp. 16, 18; Ron Fonger, January 12, 2012, MLive.com, "75 Years Ago, Women's Emergency Brigade Comes to the Aid of Workers in the Sit-Down Strike" at www.mlive.com/auto/index.ssf/2012/01/75_years_ago_womens_emergency.html http://historymatters.gmu.edu/d/136; Fine, *Sit-Down*, pp. 200–01; Watkins, *Great Depression*, pp. 276–84; Sears, "Shut Down."

21. Van Dyke, "Sitting Down," p. 16; Genora Johnson Dollinger/Sherna Gluck, "'I Was Able to Make My Voice Really Ring Out': The Women's Emergency Brigade in the Flint Sit-Down Strike," at http://historymatters.gmu.edu/d/136; Sidney Fine quoted in Sears, "Shut Down."

22. Van Dyke, "Sitting Down," p. 18; Smith, "UAW," pp. 49–50; Sears, "Shut Down."

23. Van Dyke, "Sitting Down," pp. 16, 18; Fine, *Sit-Down,* p. 270; Watkins, *Great Depression,* pp. 284–85; Sears, "Shut Down."

24. Watkins, *Great Depression,* pp. 284–86; Fine, *Sit-Down,* p. 271; Sears, "Shut Down."

25. Schwantes, "We've Got 'em," p. 183; Smith, "1937," pp. 66–69.

26. Schwantes, "We've Got 'em," pp. 183–89.

27. Smith, "UAW," p. 50; Watkins, *Great Depression,* p. 286; Smith, "1937," p. 69; Steve Babson, *Working Detroit* (New York: Adama Books, 1984), pp. 92–93.

28. Smith, "1937," pp. 64, 69.

29. Richard J. Moss, *Tiger Stadium* (Lansing: Michigan Department of State, 1976), p. 13; Patricia, Zacharias, "Detroit: the City of Champions," *The Detroit News,* August 22, 2000; William Anderson, *The Detroit Tigers* (South Bend: Diamond Communications, Inc., 1991), pp. 65–92; Tom Hennessy, "Things Weren't All Bad. You Could Go Watch a Pro Sports Contest; Chances are You'd See a Winner," *Detroit Free Press Magazine,* October 21, 1979, pp. 34–36.

30. Woodford, *Detroit,* pp. 128, 137–38.

31. *American Experience: Joe Louis* at http://www.pbs.org/wgbh/amex/fight/peopleevents/p_louis.html: Joe Louis; Larry Schwartz, "'Brown Bomber' was a Hero to All," at http://espn.go.com/sportscentury/features/00016109.html; Joe Louis, *My Life Story,* (New York: Duell, Sloan and Pearce, 1947); Gerald Astor, . . . *And a Credit to His Race: The Hard Life and Times of Joseph Louis Barrow, a.k.a. Joe Louis* (New York: Saturday Review Press, 1969), p. 169.

32. www.huffingtonpost.com/2012/02/16/monument-to-joe-louis-fist-sculpture-25-years_n_1275709.html; Patricia Zacharias, "The Monuments of Detroit," *The Detroit News,* September 5, 1999.

Chapter 17 Notes

1. "Michigan Goes to War," *MHM,* November/December 1991, pp. 18–27.

2. Ibid.; "A Day Americans Will Never Forget," *MHM,* July/August 2001, pp. 28–37.

3. "Michigan Goes To War," *MHM,* November/December 1991, pp. 33–40.

4. Larry Lankton, "Autos to Armaments: Detroit Becomes the Arsenal of Democracy," *MHM,* November/December 1991, p. 42.

5. Ibid., p. 42; Farber, *Sloan Rules,* pp. 222–25.

6. Ross Gregory, "Living on the Edge: Michiganians Cope With A World at War," *MHM,* November/December 1991, pp. 8–17; Donald Edwin Walker, "The Congressional Career of Clare E. Hoffman, 1935–63" (PhD, Michigan State University, 1982), pp. 75–106; Watts, *People's Tycoon,* pp. 504–08.

7. Gregory, "Living," p. 11.

8. *Encyclopedia of American Business History and Biography: The Automobile Industry, 1920–1980*, pp. 265–83; Farber, *Sloan Rules*, p. 224.

9. Ann M. Bos and Randy R. Talbot, "Enough and On Time: The Story of the Detroit Tank Arsenal," *MHM*, March/April 2001, pp. 26–34; Charles Hyde, *Riding the Roller Coaster: A History of the Chrysler Corporation* (Detroit: Wayne State University Press, 2003), pp. 135–40.

10. Bos & Talbot, "Enough," pp. 35–39.

11. David L. Lewis, "'They May Save Our Honor, Our Hopes—and Our Necks,'" *MHM* September/October 1993, pp. 10–16; Brinkley, *Wheels for the World*, pp. 464–87; Lewis, *Image*, pp. 270–71.

12. Charles E. Sorensen, *My Forty Years With Ford* (Detroit: Wayne State University Press, 2006), pp. 273–78; Lewis, *Image*, pp. 272–73.

13. Sorensen, *My Forty Years*, pp. 279–86.

14. Lewis, "Our Necks," pp. 11–15; Lewis, *Image*, pp. 347–64.

15. Lewis, "Our Necks," p. 15.

16. Ibid., p. 16.

17. Lankton, "Autos to Armaments," pp. 42–49; Helen Jones Early and James R. Walkinshaw, *Setting The Pace: Oldsmobile's First 100 Years* (Lansing: Oldsmobile Division of General Motors Corporation, 1996), pp. 152–203; Hyde, *Chrysler*, p. 132; Alfred P. Sloan Jr., *My Years with General Motors* (Garden City: Doubleday and Company, 1964), pp. 373–89; Landry, "It's a Daisy," pp. 36–37; Grafton H. Cook and Barbara W. Cook, "Good Stock, " *MHM*, March/April 2003, pp. 40–45; Marvin Kusmierz, "DeFoe Boat and Motor Works," *Bay-Journal* at www.bay-journal.com/bay/1he/bus/defoeshiipyard.

18. Nancy Gabin, "The Hand That Rocks the Cradle Can Build Tractors, Too," *MHM*, March/April 1992, pp. 12–21; Richard H. Harms and Robert W. Viol, *Grand Rapids Goes to War: The 1940s Homefront* (Grand Rapids: Grand Rapids Historical Society, 1993), p. 20; Hyde, *Chrysler*, p. 144; Brinkley, *Wheels*, pp. 482–83.

19. Alan Clive, *State of War: Michigan in World War II* (Ann Arbor: University of Michigan Press, 1979), pp. 42–50.

20. Clive, *State of War,* p. 48; Duane Ernest Miller, "Barbed-Wire Farm Laborers," *MHM*, September/October 1989, pp. 12–17.

21. Miller, "Barbed Wire," pp. 12–17; John Eby, "German POWs Kept Farms Going," at http://leaderpub.com/2012/05/02/german-pows-kept-farms-going/. See also "The Enemy in Our Midst: Nazi Prisoner of War Camps in Michigan's Upper Peninsula."

22. May, *Michigan*, p. 532; James Campbell, *The Ghost Mountain Boys* (New York City: Crown Publishers, 2007).

23. Sharon E. McHaney, "Michigan Remembers 'The Longest Day,'" *MHM,* May/June 1994, pp. 28–45.

24. Roger L. Rosentreter, "From The Editor," *MHM,* May/June 1994, p. 2.

25. Howard "Joe" M. Trowern, "What Team did Ty Cobb Play For," *MHM,* January/February 1995, pp. 44–45.

26. Benedict B. Kimmelman, "The Example of Private Slovik," *American Heritage*, September/October 1987, pp. 97–104; Zena Simmons, "The Execution of Pvt. Eddie Slovik," *The Detroit News*, August 25, 1999.

27. Carey L. Draeger, "'Use it all; Wear it out; Make it do; or Go Without,'" *MHM*, September/October 1994, pp. 38–50.

28. Clive, *State of War*, pp. 130–69; Harvard Sitkoff, "The Detroit Race Riot of 1943," *MHM*, 1969, pp. 183–206; Vivian M. Baulch and Patricia Zacharias, "The 1943 Detroit Race Riots," *The Detroit News*, February 11, 1999.

29. Thurgood Marshall, "The Gestapo in Detroit," *The Crisis*, August 1943, pp. 223–34, 246–47, 249.

30. Garry Boulard, "Arthur H. Vandenberg and the Formation of the United Nations," *MHM*, July/August 1987, pp. 38–45; C. David Tompkins, "Senator Arthur Hendrick Vandenberg" Middle Western Isolationist," *MHM*, 1960, pp. 39–58; www.docstoc.com/docs/6464940/Arthur_Vandenberg

31. "Michigan Goes to War," *MHM*, September/October 1995, pp. 46–52.

Chapter 18 Notes

1. May, *Michigan*, p. 539.

2. Ibid., pp. 539–40; Mark S. Foster, "Challenger from the West Coast: Henry J. Kaiser and the Detroit Auto Industry," *MHM*, January/February 1986, pp. 30–39; Richard M. Langworth, *Kaiser- Frazer: The Last Onslaught On Detroit* (Kutztown, PA: *Automobile Quarterly* Publication), 1957.

3. Charles T. Pearson, *The Indomitable Tin Goose: The True Story of Preston Tucker and His Car* (Minneapolis: Motorbooks International, 1960); www.tuckerclub.org; Paul Duchene, "Preston Tucker: The Man Behind the Car," *Chicago Tribune*, February 1, 2011.

4. May, *Michigan*, p. 545; Thomas J. Noer, *Soapy: A Biography of G. Mennen Williams*, (Ann Arbor: University of Michigan Press, 2005), p. 91; Charles E. Harmon, "Soapy Arrives," *MHM*, September/October 2004, pp. 18–25.

5. Noer, *Soapy*, pp. 57, 81; May, *Michigan*, pp. 543, 546.

6. May, *Michigan*, p. 546; E. Bruce Geelhoed, "What was Good for Our Country Was Good for General Motors," *MHM*, September/October 1980, pp. 36–43; Justin Hyde, "GM's 'Engine Charlie' Wilson learned to live with a misquote," *Detroit Free Press*, September 14, 2008.

7. Noer, *Soapy*, p. 87.

8. May, *Michigan*, pp. 548–51.

9. George Weeks, *Stewards of the State: The Governors of Michigan*, (Ann Arbor: The Detroit News & the Historical Society of Michigan, 1991), p. 114; Richard D. Shaul, "Strait Through Adversity," *MHM*, July/August 2007, pp. 22–31.

10. Shaul, "Strait Through Adversity," pp. 22–31.

11. www.mackinacbridge.org; see Linda McMaken, "Building the Mighty Mac," *MHM*, July/August 2007, pp. 36–49.

12. May, *Michigan*, pp. 556–59.

13. *Argus Press*, May 11, 1990; *Detroit News*, March 22, 1996; Babson, *Working Detroit*, pp. 38–40; William John Armstrong, "Red Scare in Bridgman," *MHM*, November/December 1996, 28–39; Noer, *Soapy*, pp. 101–02; Michael Ranville, *To Strike at a King: The Turning Point in the McCarthy Witch-Hunts*, (Troy: Momentum Books, 1997), pp. 39, 191, 224; Woodford, *Detroit*, p. 122; Peterson, "Auto Workers Confront the Depression," pp. 47–71; Donald Woutat, "UAW, Big 3: Forged in the flames of '29," *Detroit Free Press*, October 22, 1979.
14. Michael W. Ranville, "The Case Against Milo Radulovich," *MHM*, January/February 1995, pp. 10–19 and March/April 1995, pp. 10–17; Joseph E. Persico, *Edward R. Murrow: An American Original*, (New York: McGraw, 1988), p. 2.
15. Noer, *Soapy*, pp. 96–97, May, *Michigan*, pp. 546–48.
16. May, *Michigan*, pp. 552–53; Bald, *Four Centuries*, p. 486.
17. Noer, *Soapy*, p. 297; Weeks, *Stewards*, p. 115.
18. "A Passing of the Torch" at //peacecorps.umich.edu/
19. Weeks, *Stewards*, pp. 120–25.
20. Charles E. Harmon, "Out of Chaos, Order: the 1961–62 Michigan Constitutional Convention," *MHM*, November/December 1998, pp. 8–18.
21. Weeks, *Stewards*, pp. 123–25.
22. Tiffany B. Dziurman, "Marching for Freedom," *MHM*, September/October 1993, pp. 40–41.
23. Bill McGraw, "Style to Spare," *MHM*, November/December 2000, pp. 70–77; see also Nick Salvator, *Singing in a Strange Land: C. L. Franklin, the Black Church, and the Transformation of America* (Urbana: University of Illinois, 2006).
24. Grace Lee Boggs, "Rosa Parks," *The Detroit News*, July 19, 2000; Gregory Skwira, "The Rosa Parks Story: A bus ride, a boycott, a beginning of history," *Detroit (Detroit Free Press magazine)*, November 30, 1980; Cassandra Spratling, "Good-Bye, Mrs. Parks," *Detroit Free Press*, October 25, 2005; Marilynn Sambrano, "Keeping Her Seat, Taking a Stand," *MHM*, November/December 1995, pp. 50–52
25. Malcolm X & Alex Haley, *The Autobiography of Malcolm X* (Brattleboro, VT: Parallax, 1965), pp. 1–39; Peter Goldman, *Dictionary of American Negro Biography American Experience Malcolm X* at www.pbs.org/wgbh/amex/malcolmx; www.malcolmx.com/about/bio3.html
26. Sidney Fine, *Violence in the Model City: The Cavanagh Administration, Race Relations, and the Detroit Riot of 1967* (Ann Arbor: University of Michigan Press, 1989), pp. 155–247; Kevin Boyle, "A Dream Gone Awry," *MHM*, September/October 2004, pp. 34–43; Babson, *Working Detroit*, pp. 167–75; Woodford, *Detroit*, pp. 180–83.
27. Fine, *Violence*, pp. 383–85.
28. Michael Ranville, "Forty Years after George Romney's Casual Comment Changed His Life and American history," *MHM*, September/October 2007, pp. 12–17.
29. Richard R. Lingeman, "The Big, Happy, Beating Heart of the Detroit Sound," in Robert Warner & C. Warren Vanderhill, ed., *A Michigan Reader: 1865 to the Present* (Grand Rapids: William B. Eerdman's, 1974), pp. 272–84; Gary Graff, "Speaking of Motown," *MHM*, July/August 1999, p. 31; Woodford, *Detroit*, pp.

197–99; Carolyn Damstra, "The Motown Sound," in *Makin' Music: Michigan's Rock & Roll Legacy* (Lansing: *Michigan History Magazine*, 2002), pp. 52–61; see also Gerald Posner, *Motown: Music, Money, Sex, and Power* (New York: Random House, 2002).

30. http://www.allmusic.com/artist/the-supremes-mn0000477875; See Gerald Posner, *Motown: Music, Money, Sex, and Power* (New York: Random House, 2002).

31. Graff, "Speaking of Motown," pp. 62–65.

32. www.aretha-franklin.com/ and www.arethafranklin.net/us/home; "25 Most Powerful Women of the Past Century," *TIME*, November 18, 2010.

33. LeRoy Barnett, "Makin' Music," *MHM*, May/June 2001, pp. 12–27.

34. http://alicecooper.com; http://www.superseventies.com/ssalicecooper.html; http:// www.nme.com/artists/alice-cooper; "The Preacher's Son Who Became Alice Cooper," *People*, April 1, 1974; http://rockhall.com/inductees/alice-cooper/bio/; http://www.tednugent.com; "Bearing Arms and Cranking Up the Controversy," *New York Times*, Jay Root, May 3, 2012; Amy Bingham, "Ted Nugent: Romney Camp Expressed Support' After Controversial Comments on Obama," May 4, 2012, ABC News.

35. Carolyn Damstra, "Like a Rock," in *Makin' Music: Michigan's Rock & Roll Legacy* (Lansing: *Michigan History Magazine*, 2002), pp. 40–45

36. Carolyn Damstra p. "Lucky Star," in *Makin' Music: Michigan's Rock & Roll Legacy* (Lansing: *Michigan History Magazine*, 2002), pp. 46–51; Stephanie Busari, "Hey Madonna, Don't Give Up Your Day Job," CNN.com, March 24, 2008; Ian Johnston, "Get a Head For Business, Tune into Madonna," *The Scotsman*, September, 23, 2004; Jamie Anderson & Martin Kupp, "Case Study: Madonna," *The Times* (London), January 8, 2007; www.madonna.com

Chapter 19 Notes

1. Sheryl James, "A Workhorse not a Showhorse: The Life and Times of Gerald R. Ford," *MHM*, March/April 2007, pp. 16–31; Sheryl James, "Coming Home," *MHM*, March/April 2007, pp. 32–39; Roger L. Rosentreter, "Let The Campaign Begin," *MHM*, November/December 2004, pp. 54–67; James Cannon at www.pbs.org/newshour/character/essays/ford.html www.fordlibrarymuseum.gov/grf/fordbiop.asp; Charles E. Harmon, "Our National Nightmare: Michigan's Watergate Connections," *MHM*, July/August 1999, pp. 68–77; www.geraldrford foundation.org/medal-public-service/2012-award-recipient

2. Dave Dempsey, "Good Government is Good Politics," *MHM*, September/October 2004, pp. 50–53; Weeks, *Stewards*, pp. 126–31; "Michigan's Bottle Bill," *The Mitten* (Lansing: *Michigan History Magazine*, 2004); Jack Lessenberry, "Michigan's Longest-Serving Governor, William Milliken, Remains Relevant," *HOUR*, February 2011 at www.hourdetroit.com/Hour-Detroit/February-2011/Milliken-Matters/index.php?cparticle=1&siarticle=0#artanc; see Jack Dempsey, *Michigan's Passionate Moderate* (2006).

3. Bill McGraw, "Detroit's Big Daddy: Remembering Coleman Young," *MHM*, January/February 1998, pp. 8–14; Woodford, *Detroit*, p. 234.

4. Sheryl James, "Stealing the Show," *MHM*, November/December 2002, pp. 58–65; www.archives.gov/legislative/features/griffiths/
5. Michael O'Brien, *Philip Hart: The Conscience of the Senate*, (East Lansing: Michigan State University Press, 1995).
6. Maurice Isserman & Michael Kazin, *America Divided: The Civil War of the 1960s*, (New York, Oxford University Press, 2012), pp. 161; Mark Hamilton Lytle, *America's Uncivil Wars: The Sixties Era from Elvis to the Fall of Richard Nixon* (New York: Oxford University Press, 2006), pp. 80-83; http://www.pbs.org/opb/thesixties/topics/politics/newsmakers_1.html
7. Lytle, *America's Uncivil Wars*, p. 84.
8. Isserman & Kazin, *America Divided*, pp. 162; Lytle, *America's Uncivil Wars*, pp. 84–87.
9. Klaus Fischer, *America in White, Black and Gray: A History of the Stormy 1960s*, (New York: Continuum International Publishing Group, 2006), pp. 258; "Tom Hayden" at www.thenation.com/authors/tom-hayden#axzz2bDegKN00
10. Ibid., pp. 265–75; Lytle, *America's Uncivil Wars*, pp. 253–54, 344–45; Isserman & Kazin, *America Divided*, pp. 165, 171–78; http://faculty.txwes.edu/csmeller/human-propect/ProData09/03WW2CulMatrix/Weather/SDS/SDS.tm
11. Sam Roberts, "The Port Huron Statement at 50," *New York Times*, March 3, 2012; Tom Hayden, "The Port Huron Statement: A Manifesto Reconsidered," *Los Angeles Times*, March 6, 2012.
12. bentley.umich.edu/exhibits/dissent/draft.php; www.annarbor.com/news/post-199; modernmajorfilms.com/a2/forum/index.php?topic=122.0; bentley.umich.edu/research/guides/video/stuprotest.php
13. John Ernst, *Forging A Fateful Alliance: Michigan State University and the Vietnam War* (East Lansing: Michigan State University Press, 1998); "The University on the Make," at www.cia-on-campus.org/msu.edu/msu.html
14. May, *Michigan*, pp. 632–36; Woodward, *Detroit*, pp. 222–24.
15. Mary Dempsey, "The Witch of November: The Saga of the Edmund Fitzgerald," *MHM*, November/December 1999, pp. 28–37; Laura Rose Ashlee, "Broken in Two: The Wreck of the Carl D. Bradley," *MHM*, November/December 1990, pp. 32–37; Valerie van Heest, "Rogers City Remembers," *MHM*, January/February 2009, pp. 32–41; John R. Halsey, "A Unique and Undervalued Resource," *MHM*, July/August 1999, pp. 80–85.
16. www.biography.com/people/tim-allen-9542074
17. www.biography.com/people/james-earl-jones-9357354; www.achievement.org/autodoc /page/jon2bio-1; Felica R. Lee, "A Theatrical Patriarch, Onstage and Off," *New York Times*, May 30, 2012.
18. www.michaelmoore.com
19. www.jeffdaniels.com; www.npr.org/2012/06/20/155426877/jeff-daniels-anchoring-the-cast-of-the-newsroom; movies.nytimes.com/person/16881/Jeff-Daniels/biography.
20. May, *Michigan*, pp. 651–59; Rubenstein and Ziewacz, *Michigan: A History of the Great Lakes State* (3rd edition, 2002) (Wheeling, IL: Harlan Davidson), pp. 303–09, 313–16.

Postscript NOTES

1. Governor Jennifer M. Granholm biography at www.michigan.gov.
2. www.levin.senate.gov; bioguide.congress.gov/scripts/biodisplay.pl?index=l000261; www.levin.senate.gov/about; "Will Jennifer Granholm leave CA to run in MI for Carl Levin's seat," SFGate.com blog, April 26, 2013; Jennifer Steinhauer, "Democrat Says He Won't Run for Re-election to the Senate," *New York Times*, March 7, 2013.
3. www.stabenow.senate.gov; http://www.congressmerge.com/onlinedb/cgi-bin/ newmember bio.cgi?lang=en&member=MIJR&site=congressmerge; Kyle Moroney, "Michigan's wage gap between men and women is one of the largest in the country," http://blog.mlive.com, April 9, 2013.
4. http://dingell.house.gov; Perry Bacon, "Dingell is Longest-Serving House Member," *Washington Post*, February 11, 2009; Todd Spangler, "Day 20,977 of Service, Rep. Dingell hits historic mark," *USA Today*, June 8, 2013; http://conyers.house.gov; http://conyers.house.gov/index.cfm/biography; "Congressman John Conyers Talks About Bush Lying America Into War and His Campaign to Hold Bush Accountable: The Downing Street Memo and More" (John Conyers interview), BuzzFlash (June 9, 2005) at http://www.buzzflash.com/interviews/05/06/int05023.html; John Conyers, "The Constitution in Crisis," at http://www.huffingtonpost.com/john-conyers/the-constitution-in-crisi_1_b_26520.html.
5. Jim Harger, "North American car sales headed back to 2000 levels, but in a different world," http://blog.mlive.com, March 7, 2013; Alisa Priddle, "Auto Sales Poised for Recovery," *Lansing State Journal*, August 7, 2013; http://www.mlive.com/auto/index.ssf/2013/07/us_auto_industry_resilient_in.html.
6. Corey Williams and Ed White, "Detroit Declares Bankruptcy," *Lansing State Journal*, July 19, 2013; Katharine Q. Seelye, "Detroit Census Confirms A Desertion Like No Other," *New York Times*, March 22, 2011; "Census Bureau Says Michigan Population Grew in 2012, but Georgia Passes It," Gongwer News Service, December 20, 2012; Paul Krugman, "Detroit: The New Greece," *New York Times*, July 22, 2013; Daniel Okrent, "The Tragedy of Detroit: How a Great City Fell—and How it can Rise Again," *TIME*, October 5, 2009, pp. 26–35; Jack Lessenberry, "For Detroit, it's All About the Unknown," *Traverse City Record-Eagle*, July 28, 2013.
7. "URC responsible for $15.5 billion in statewide economic impact, 74,000 direct and indirect Michigan jobs, $375 million in state tax revenue," http://research.wayne.edu/news.php?id=10869; http://www.urcmich.org; Jeff Mason, "Michigan's Brain Gain: Educating Innovators Benefits Economy," *Lansing State Journal*, July 21, 2013.
8. http://www.nass.usda.gov/Statistics_by_State/Michigan/Publications/ MichiganFactSheets/STHILGTS.pdf; http://www.google.com/search?client= safari&rls=en&q=michigan+sugar+company&ie=UTF-8&oe=UTF-8.

9. http://www.michigan.org; Kathleen Lavey, "Summer Travel Seasons Starts Now," *Lansing State Journal*, May 23, 2013; Elizabeth Browne Losey, *Seney National Wildlife Refuge: Its Story*, (Marquette: Lake Superior Press, 2003); see Arthur M. Woodford, *The Michigan Compendium*.

10. Dave Dempsey, *On the Brink: The Great Lakes in the 21st Century*, (East Lansing: Michigan State University Press, 2004), p. 276.

11. May, *Michigan*, pp. 658–59, http://www.bls.gov/web/laus/laumstrk.htm; "Getting Detroit Back on Its Feet," *New York Times*, July 23, 2013; Kristen M. Daum, "Five Reasons You Should Care about Detroit's Bankruptcy," *Lansing State Journal*, July 20, 2013; Eric Pianin, "Detroit's 60-Year Decline into Bankruptcy Hell," *The Fiscal Times*, July 21, 2013; Fritz Klug, "Detroit's Comeback is Already Underway," at http://www.mlive.com/news/index.ssf/2013/08/detroit_comeback_has_begun_us.html.

12. Gustin, *Billy Durant*, p. 124.

Index

Photo Credits

Architect of the Capitol: *64*

Archives of Michigan: *67, 88, 132, 136, 153, 156, 160, 164, 166, 167, 181*

Bentley Historical Library, University of Michigan

    Elizabeth L. Belen Papers: *270*

    Frank Angelo Papers: *228*

    Frederick Wheeler Papers: *174*

    G. Mennen Williams Papers: *321, 325*

    George W. Romney Papers: *339*

    George Washington Merrill Collection: *241*

    Harry Duink papers: *245*

    Josephine Fellows Gomon Papers: *281*

    Laura S. Haviland Papers: *120*

    Michigan and the Civil War Collection: *134*

    Michigan Historical Collections: *202*

    News and Information Services: *329*

    Philip A. Hart Papers: *337, 354*

    Roy Dikeman Chapin Papers: *216*

    Samuel T. Dana Papers: *162*

Boston Public Library, Leslie Jones Collection: *279, 293*

Burton Historical Collection, Detroit Public Library: *209, 248*

Charles E. Cleland: *3*

Collections of the Henry Ford: *214, 219, 221*

University of Pittsburgh: *58*

Detroit Historical Society: *194*

Gerald R. Ford Presidential Library: *344*

Grand Rapids History and Special Collections, Archives, Grand Rapids Public Library, Grand Rapids, Michigan: *314*

435

Grand Rapids Public Museum: *254*

Harvard University Portrait Collection: *38*

Library of Congress: *11, 20, 28, 118, 121, 138, 140, 184, 187, 196, 205, 233, 238, 275, 290, 295, 308, 312, 334, 353*

Marquette Regional History Center: *301*

Michigan State Capital: *70*

Michigan State University Archives & Historical Collections: *217*

Michigan Tech Archives and Copper County Historical Collections: *185*

Michigan Tech University, Seaman Mineralogical Museum: *178*

Milliken family collection: *349*

MOLLUS/ MASS Photograph Collection, U.S. Army Military History Institute: *147*

Ohio Statehouse Photo Archive: *47*

U.S. Army Center of Military History: *40*

U.S. Army Corps of Engineers Digital Visual Library: *104, 363*

U.S. National Archives and Records Administration: *284*

University of Pittsburgh Library System: *54*

Walter P. Reuther Library, Archives of Labor and Urban Affairs, Wayne State University: *256, 260, 264, 274, 292, 303, 305, 335*
    The Tony Spina Collection: *297, 332, 359*

William L. Clements Library, University of Michigan: *29*

Wisconsin Historical Society: *1*